HANDBOOK OF
GRAPHIC PRESENTATION

A RONALD PRESS PUBLICATION

John Wiley & Sons / New York
Chichester / Brisbane / Toronto

HANDBOOK OF

SECOND EDITION

GRAPHIC PRESENTATION

CALVIN F. SCHMID, Ph.D.

Professor Emeritus
University of Washington
Formerly Director of the Center for
Studies in Demography and Ecology, and
Executive Secretary of the
Washington State Census Board

STANTON E. SCHMID, J.D.

Assistant Vice President for
University Relations and Development
University of Washington

Library of Congress Cataloging in Publication Data:

Schmid, Calvin Fisher, 1901–
   Handbook of graphic presentation.

   "A RONALD PRESS PUBLICATION."
   Includes index.
   1. Statistics—Graphic methods. I. Schmid,
Stanton E., joint author. II. Title.
HA31.S345 1978   001.4′22   78-13689
ISBN 0-471-04724-4

Printed in the United States of America

10 9 8 7 6 5 4 3 2 1

PREFACE

This book has been written as a working manual for all who are concerned with the clear presentation and interpretation of statistical data in graphic form. Large sums of money are often spent by agencies and institutions in gathering statistics, but far too frequently much of this effort is wasted because sufficient attention is not paid to the details of their analysis and presentation. Statistical data must continually be included in reports to business executives, stockholders, and clients; in research papers addressed to professional colleagues; and in advertising matter, publicity releases, magazine articles, and other presentations designed for the general public. This book shows how charts and graphs can translate such data into attractive, succinct, and readily understood diagrammatic forms. Neither columns and rows of statistics in tabular arrangement nor the seemingly endless listings of figures in textual form can possess the clarity, appeal, or meaningfulness of a well-designed chart. By emphasizing important and salient relationships, graphs and charts may also be of immense service in the location and definition of problems and in the discovery of hidden facts.

This book is the outgrowth of many years of experience in directing research projects and teaching graphic presentation to college students. Its aim is to provide all the information likely to be needed by those who construct statistical charts, supervise their construction, and judge the effectiveness of their presentation. Although no attempt has been made to go into the minutiae of every case, the essential theory and practice of graphic techniques are presented in sufficient detail to enable the reader to design appropriate charts and to execute all the basic graphic forms. A separate chapter is devoted to each of the most important types of charts, describing their advantages and disadvantages in presenting data of various kinds, pointing out distortions likely to result from their incorrect use, and discussing any special difficulties that may arise in their construction. For those who are concerned with the details of design and construction there is a step-by-step description of the exact procedure for laying out a chart. A chapter on drafting techniques gives specific information on instruments and equipment, materials, lettering, and special methods peculiar to the delineation of graphs and charts. A discussion of the theory of projection gives help in solving difficult problems involved in the layout of three-dimensional charts. Finally, there is a chapter on the role of electronic computers in the construction of statistical charts.

The book is profusely illustrated with graphs and charts presenting data taken from different fields and designed for different audiences. It is hoped that the reader will find in them helpful suggestions for the solution of his or her own problems. The major considerations in selecting the scores of charts for illustrative purpose were their quality, appropriateness, and relevance. However, it will be found that several charts have been included that do not meet the highest qualitative standards. They were selected for the purpose of illustrating how even minor deficiencies can depreciate or actually spoil an otherwise acceptable chart.

During the years that have elapsed since the first edition of the *Handbook* was published, significant changes and developments have occurred, not only in graphic presentation but in related fields as well. In this regard, among the broader and more general changes that have occurred has been a revitalized interest in statistical graphics, a vastly expanded use of audiovisual presentation, and unprecedented innovations and applications in computer graphics, whereas in a specific sense there have been many new developments in the tools, materials, and techniques used in the preparation of statistical charts. Our aim has been to keep abreast of these changes and developments and to incorporate the more significant and relevant ones in the new edition.

Although the main outline and basic approach of the original edition have been retained, much of the present volume has been rewritten and substantially enlarged. A new chapter on the role of the computer in graphic presentation has been added.

The authors are happy to acknowledge their indebtedness to many persons and organizations: to authors of books and other published sources on the subject of graphic presentation for valuable ideas and suggestions; to many publishers, governmental agencies, and industrial and commercial concerns for permission to reproduce a large proportion of the illustrative material in this book; and to our professional colleagues and our staffs for their generous advice and assistance. More specifically, we wish to reaffirm our indebtedness to those who assisted in various ways in the preparation of the first edition: Gloria M. Austin, Don C. Gibbons, Warren Kalbach, Lloyd Kirry, Vivian Lomax, Earle H. MacCannell, Mildred O. Giblin, and Mary T. Jacobson. Special thanks are due to the following persons for their contributions to this edition: Vincent P. Barabba, Marketing Director of Xerox Corporation, formerly Director of the United States Bureau of the Census; Albert D. Biderman, Bureau of Social Science Research, Washington, D. C.; Robert C. Klove, Richard Schweitzer, Alva L. Finkner, Michael G. Garland, Frederick Broome, John E. Tharaldson, and Peter Ohs of the United States Bureau of the Census; Jerry N. Schneider, Department of Urban Planning and

Civil Engineering, University of Washington; Carl E. Youngman, Department of Geography, University of Washington; Vincent A. Miller, Department of Sociology, University of Washington; and Anna Chiong, Geography Library, University of Washington. Also, we wish to express our gratitude to Beulah E. Reddaway and Karen L. Wayenberg, Department of Sociology, University of Washington for typing the entire manuscript.

Seattle, Washington   CALVIN F. SCHMID
June 1978   STANTON E. SCHMID

CONTENTS

HANDBOOK OF
GRAPHIC PRESENTATION

CHARTS AND GRAPHS CAN REPRESENT AN extremely useful and flexible medium for explaining, interpreting, and analyzing numerical facts largely by means of points, lines, areas, and other geometric forms and symbols. They make possible the presentation of quantitative data in a simple, clear, and effective manner and facilitate comparison of values, trends, and relationships. Moreover, charts and graphs possess certain qualities and values lacking in textual and tabular forms of presentation. These values may be summarized as follows:

1. In comparison with other types of presentation, well-designed charts are more effective in creating interest and in appealing to the attention of the reader.

2. Statistical charts represent a very important form of visual communication. They provide a clear, economical, and precise medium for conveying a message. They are frequently superior to words or figures. Moreover, visual relationships, as portrayed by charts and graphs, are more clearly grasped and more easily remembered.

3. The use of charts and graphs saves time since the essential meaning of large masses of statistical data can be visualized at a glance.

4. Charts and graphs can provide a comprehensive picture of a problem that makes possible a more complete and better-balanced understanding than could be derived from tabular or textual forms of presentation.

5. Charts and graphs can bring out hidden facts and relationships and can stimulate, as well as aid, analytical thinking and investigation.

For anyone who is seriously interested in research, a knowledge of the principles of constructing graphs and charts is indispensable. The average research worker may never actually draw many charts for publication, but most certainly will have to plan them and direct drafters in executing them in their final form.

Although graphic techniques are a powerful and effective medium for presenting statistical data, they are not under all circumstances and for all purposes complete substitutes for tabular and other forms of presentation. The well-trained specialist in this field is one who recognizes not only the advantages but also the limitations of graphic techniques; and knows when to use and when not to use

CHAPTER ONE

BASIC PRINCIPLES AND TECHNIQUES OF CHART DESIGN

graphic methods, is able to select the most appropriate form for every purpose, and is thoroughly conversant with the merits of each specific type and form of statistical chart.

ORIGIN OF MODERN CHARTING TECHNIQUES

The various techniques embodied in this book represent fundamentally a graphic language for presenting statistical data. The origin of statistical charting techniques as we think of them today dates back to 1786, when William Playfair published his famous work entitled *The Commerical and Political Atlas*. Two subsequent editions of this book were published in 1787 and 1801. Playfair's other well-known books were *Lineal Arithmetic* (1798), *Statistical Breviary* (1801), and *An Inquiry into the Permanent Causes of the Decline and Fall of Powerful and Wealthy Nations* (1805 and 1807). Playfair, in referring to his "lineal arithmetic," explains that:

The advantage proposed by this method, is not that of giving a more accurate statement than by figures, but it is to give a more simple and permanent idea of the gradual progress and comparative amounts, at different periods, by presenting to the eye a figure, the proportions of which correspond with the amount of the sums intended to be expressed.[1]

Furthermore, he states:

That I have succeeded in proposing and putting in practice a new and useful mode of stating accounts, has been so generally acknowledged, . . . as much information may be obtained in five minutes as would require whole days to imprint on the memory, in a lasting manner, by a table of figures.[2]

Playfair not only created a new and ingenious technique for analyzing and portraying statistical data, but also delineated the charts themselves in such expert fashion as to compare favorably with the highest standards of modern graphic presentation. Playfair's contributions include various forms of the rectilinear coordinate graph, areal circle graph, pie diagram, and bar chart. It must be recognized, of course, that in studying the history of graphic techniques many basic developments, such as the principle of coordinates and the invention of analytic geometry, antedate the work of Playfair.[3]

CLASSIFICATION OF CHARTS AND GRAPHS

In examining the literature on charts and graphs, many classifications are to be found. Some of the classifications are clear, logical, and useful, whereas others are confused and contradictory. In general, one or more of the following criteria might be utilized as a basis for classifying charts and graphs: (1) purpose, (2) circumstance of use, (3) type of comparison to be made, or (4) form.[4]

With respect to purpose, emphasis may be placed on either: (1) transmission of information, graphic communication, (2) analysis, or (3) computation.

In this book stress is placed on the design and construction of charts for transmitting facts and ideas. Occasionally, the value of certain charts as analytical tools are pointed out, but only in the most incidental and cursory fashion is any reference made to charts for computational purposes.[5]

The second criterion, circumstances under which charts are used, includes: (1) wall charts and charts for exhibits, (2) desk charts, (3) charts for administrative and interoffice purposes, (4) charts for stereopticon slides, (5) charts for moving pictures and television, (6) charts for illustrating lectures, and (7) charts for books, magazines, newspapers, and similar types of reproduction. Emphasis in this volume is on type (7).

On the basis of the third criterion mentioned, type of comparison to be made, charts may be classified as follows: (1) size or magnitude, (2) time,

including both absolute and relative changes, (3) space, (4) component facts, and (5) values in the form of frequency and related distributions.

The fourth criterion for classifying charts is the form of the chart. This classification was considered the most appropriate one for organizing the material in this book. In addition to the chapters on basic principles and techniques of chart design (Chapter 1) and drafting techniques (Chapter 2), there are chapters on rectilinear coordinate charts (Chapter 3), bar and column charts (Chapter 4), semilogarithmic charts (Chapter 5), frequency and related distributions (Chapter 6), miscellaneous graphic forms (Chapter 7), maps, (Chapter 8), pictorial charts (Chapter 9), and charts drawn in projection (Chapter 10). There is also a chapter on computer graphics (Chapter 11).

BASIC DESIGN PRINCIPLES[6]

Survey of Problem

The following discussion attempts to describe in a simple, concrete manner certain basic principles

---

[1] William Playfair, *The Commercial and Political Atlas,* 3rd ed., London: J. Wallis, 1801, pp. ix–x.

[2] Ibid., p. xii.

[3] For more detailed discussions of the history of graphic presentation, see H. G. Funkhouser, "Historical Development of the Graphical Representation of Statistical Data," *Osiris,* 3 (1937), 369–404; Paul J. FitzPatrick, "The Development of Graphic Presentation of Statistical Data in the United States," *Social Science,* 37 (October 1962), 203–214; Herman R. Friis, "Statistical Cartography in the United States Prior to 1870 and the Role of Joseph C. G. Kennedy and the U.S. Census Office," *The American Cartographer,* 1 (1974), 131–157.

[4] Harry Jerome, *Statistical Method,* New York: Harper, 1924, pp. 50–51.

[5] Charts of this kind are commonly referred to as "nomograms." The card catalog of a large library reveals many general as well as specialized treatises on nomography. It is interesting to note that nomograms have been constructed for such specialized fields as physics, general engineering, hydraulic engineering, chemical engineering, medicine, geology, and electronics.

[6] A large portion of this section is based on Committee on Standards for Graphic Presentation, *Time-Series Charts: A Manual of Design and Construction,* New York: American Society of Mechanical Engineers, 1938, pp. 15–22 and *American Standard Time-Series Charts,* ASA Y15.2-1960, New York: American Society of Mechanical Engineers, 1960, pp. 1–16. Brief quotations have been incorporated from these reports.

that should be used in the design and layout of statistical charts. Frequently, the design of a chart may be worked out by a specialist and the more or less routine drawing completed by a draftsman. On the other hand, it is not uncommon practice for one person to be responsible for both the delineation and drafting of a chart.

Before the actual work of designing and laying out a chart is begun, it is necessary to complete certain preliminary steps. First, the designer should become familiar with the data to be presented in graphic form. In successful planning it is assumed that the designer has digested his materials thoroughly and is aware of their major implications. He must be able to select the most salient features of a body of data and translate them into clear, simple, attractive, and meaningful graphic forms. The designer of statistical charts should have a reasonably thorough grasp of statistical methods, as well as an understanding of the basic subject matter in which the data happen to lie. Second, a decision must be made concerning the type of chart most appropriate for the purpose at hand. Usually several factors enter into a decision of this kind, such as: (1) nature of the data, (2) medium of presentation, (3) purpose of the chart, (4) time available for preparation of the chart, and (5) audience for whom the chart is intended.

Nature of the Data

One should recognize that certain types of statistical data do not lend themselves to satisfactory graphic presentation. In such circumstances it is advisable to accept this fact readily and not to attempt to construct a chart that would possess no advantage over the original data, which might be in the form of a table or included as part of the text. Effective graphic presentation presumes familiarity with all the basic chart types, as well as their many variations and adaptations. For example, if the data represent a time series, the expert designer will be able to select one of the following five types of chart: the arithmetic line chart, semilogarithmic chart, column chart, surface or stratum chart, or some adaptation of these different forms. On the other hand, data in which the basic classification is in terms of some geographical or areal category might be presented in one of many types of statistical maps.

Medium of Presentation

Statistical charts may be used for: (1) reproduction in a book, periodical, or a typewritten, mimeographed, Itek or other similar multiple-copy report, (2) exhibit purposes, (3) lectures, (4) slides, (5) administrative purposes in connection with production, distribution, supervision, or other operations, and (6) motion pictures or television. Occasionally, the chart may be designed so that it can be used for more than one purpose. The authors, for example, have been successful in designing charts that have been used both for reproduction in books and for exhibits and slides.

Since most statistical charts will be reproduced in some form, it is essential that, in developing the basic design of a chart, careful consideration be given to the type of reproduction, the amount of reduction, and the purpose and characteristics of the report for which the chart is prepared. This includes the overall size of the chart, thickness of lines, size and style of lettering, and the positioning of the lettering, as well as other features of the chart. For example, if the lines are too thin in the original chart, they may fade out and if the lettering is undersized, it may become unreadable in the reproduction. Conversely, unnecessarily heavy lines and oversized lettering may create an impression of imbalance, disharmony, and poor design. Again, if the style of lettering is ill chosen and idiosyncratic, the chart may look grotesque and grossly incompatible with the basic tenor of the report.

Purpose of the Chart

Charts of all types should fulfill certain basic objectives; they should be: (1) accurate representations of the facts, (2) clear, easily read, and understood, and (3) so designed and constructed as to attract and hold attention. In addition, of course, every chart is designed with one or more specific objectives. If the meaning of a series of figures in textual or tabular form is difficult for the mind to grasp or retain, a statistical chart may clarify the burdensome details and portray the data concisely, logically, and simply. Furthermore, a statistical chart, by emphasizing new and significant relationships, may be of service in discovering new facts and developing hypotheses.

Time Available for Preparation

Time and labor involved in the design and construction of statistical charts are generally of considerable importance. Needless to say, it is shortsighted to emphasize unduly the cost factor. Designing a chart should never be hurried or slipshod. On the other hand, much time can be wasted by indulging in useless details that actually detract from the quality or effectiveness of a chart. If the amount of time needed to do a good job is inadequate because of lack of personnel or funds, or the necessity of meeting a deadline, every effort should be made to simplify and expedite the work, but not at the expense of lowering standards. It would be far more logical, as well as economical in the long run, to construct fewer charts but of the highest quality.

Audience

The educational level and interest of the audience for whom the chart is intended should be given primary consideration. A chart prepared for a popular audience unfamiliar with the more technical type of graphic presentation would be different from one designed for a comparatively small, highly trained group of specialists.

Planning Specifications and Procedures

Without adequate planning it is seldom possible to achieve either proper emphasis of each component element within the chart or a presentation that is pleasing in its entirety. Too often charts are developed around a single detail without sufficient regard for the work as a whole. Good chart design requires consideration of these four major factors: (1) size, (2) proportions, (3) position and margins, and (4) composition.

Size. The dimensions of a chart should be related to (1) ease of construction, (2) visibility and perceptibility, and (3) harmony with the vehicle of presentation. A chart designed for exhibit or lecture purposes normally should be very much larger than one to be used for reproduction in some publication. There are no absolute rules for determining the original size of a chart. If the chart is too small,

it will be difficult to do the drafting work. Moreover, irregularities of execution will be more apparent in the reproduction. As a general rule, the original size of a chart should never be less than twice the size of the reduced chart, and frequently it may be as many as four or six times as large as the reduced size. In general, a relatively simple chart can be made much smaller than one that is more elaborate and detailed. For example, detailed statistical maps would normally be larger than a simple bar chart. The thickness of the lines and the height of the letters are related to the overall size of the chart. Also, if there is stippling or crosshatching on the chart, the spacing between lines or dots on the patterns along with the weight of the inking should be broad and clear when the chart is reduced. In designing a chart for reproduction, extreme care must be taken that the lines and lettering are sufficiently heavy and large not to fade out or become unreadable in the reduction process. Figure 1–1 illustrates a series of letter sizes and line weights in original size and in reduced sizes as indicated.

Proportions. The proportions of a chart either in original or in reduced form should be such that they conform harmoniously with the medium of presentation. Generally, it will be found that a rectangular form is more esthetically pleasing than a square. It is of special importance to consider the proportions of a chart designed for reproduction. In fact, the size and proportions of the particular book for which the chart is made will obviously influence the proportions of the original chart. Suppose that a full-page chart for a book is to be prepared for a space 4.5 in. by 7 in. and it is decided that the width of the original drawing is to be 10 in. Then, according to simple proportion, the height of the original drawing will be

$$4.5:7::10:x \quad \text{or} \quad \frac{4.5}{7} = \frac{10}{x}$$

which, when crossmultiplied, gives $4.5x = 70$, or 15.6 in.

In addition to the simple mathematical formula technique, the size of charts may be reduced or enlarged proportionately in accordance with two other techniques. These techniques are commonly referred to as the "diagonal-line method" and the "proportional-scale method." Figure 1–2 illustrates the diagonal-line method. First, a chart is enclosed by a borderline in accordance with predetermined proportions. Second, a diagonal line is

ABCDEFGHIJKLMNOPQRSTUVWXYZABCDEFGHIJKLN

ABCDEFGHIJKLMNOPQRSTUVWXYZ

ABCDEFGHIJKLMNOPQRS

ABCDEFGHIJKLMN

abcdefghijklmnopqrs

ABCDEFGHIJKLMN

ABCDEFGHIJKLMNOPQ

ABCDEFGHIJKLMNOPQ

ABCDEFGHIJKLM

ABCDEFGH

A

ABCDEFGHIJKLMNOPQRSTUVWXYZABCDEFGHIJKLM

ABCDEFGHIJKLMNOPQRSTUVWXYZABCDEF

ABCDEFGHIJKLMNOPQRSTUVV

ABCDEFGHIJKLMNOPQ

abcdefghijklmnopqrstuvw:

ABCDEFGHIJKLMNOPQ

ABCDEFGHIJKLMNOPQ

ABCDEFGHIJKLMNOPQ

ABCDEFGHIJKLM

ABCDEFGH

B

ABCDEFGHIJKLMNOPQRSTUVWXYZABCDEFGHIJKLM

ABCDEFGHIJKLMNOPQRSTUVV

ABCDEFGHIJKLMNOPC

abcdefghijklmnopqrstuvw

ABCDEFGHIJKLMNOPQ

ABCDEFGHIJKLMNOPC

ABCDEFGHIJKLMNOPQ

ABCDEFGHIJKLMN

ABCDEFGH

Figure 1–1. Reduction of lettering. In the design and layout of a chart for reproduction, allowance should always be made for reduction in size. The largest panel shows original letters as drawn or unreduced. The two other panels represent reductions as follows: A. Area approximately $\frac{1}{4}$ original and B. Area approximately $\frac{1}{16}$ original.

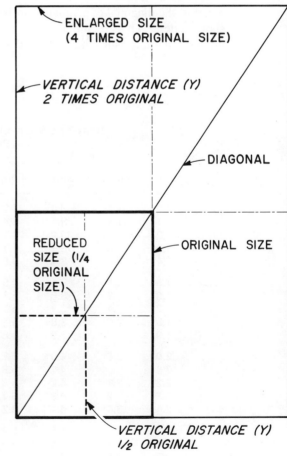

Figure 1–2. Illustration of the Diagonal-Line Technique for enlarging or reducing the size of a chart.

drawn from the lower left corner of the border to the upper right corner. Third, for enlargements it is necessary to project the diagonal line beyond the upper right corner. Fourth, different degrees of enlargement or reduction represented by measurable dimensions can be readily derived by the simple process of interpolation with either vertical or horizontal lines intersecting the diagonal. For example, when a new width is known or specified a perpendicular line is drawn that intersects the diagonal. Next, a horizontal line is drawn at the point of intersection. Thus the new dimensions, either reduced or enlarged as the case may be, are clearly indicated on the sketch.

The proportional-scale method requires a relatively simple and inexpensive commercially prepared instrument in circular shape that consists of an inner and an outer scale, one above the other. Newly determined dimensions will align themselves automatically in proportional relationship on the scale. Also, percentage enlargement or reduction can be derived from the scale.

Root-two dimensions, representing a ratio of 1 (short side) to 1.414 (long side), are particularly appropriate for statistical charts. In a rectangular page, based on root-two dimensions, the long side is equal to the diagonal of a square constructed on the short side. This rectangle also possesses the unique characteristic that when divided in half

widthwise, each resulting rectangle is also of root-two proportions, a characteristic useful in grouping charts on a page. Table 1–1 represents the short and long dimensions computed on the basis of root-two ratio.

Positions and Margins. The placing of a chart on a page should conform to the requirements of good design and ease of reading. To facilitate reading, charts should be so placed on a page so that they can be read from the same position as that from which the other pages are read. Full-page charts set widthwise on the paper should be so placed that the title is always on the left margin. In this way, the chart can be brought to reading position by a clockwise turn of the paper. The margins of a chart designed for reproduction should be consistent with the format of the publication. In the case of full-page charts, the binding margin should be larger than the other three.

Composition. Good composition is a matter of obtaining a harmonious whole through proper interrelation of component elements. Proper interrelation of components is achieved through adjustment of their size, weight, shape, and position. Since the overall structure of a chart is more or less inflexible, the greatest opportunity for adjustment is in variation of size and weight of components. The design of each of the various elements of a chart should be

Table 1–1

Root-Two Short-Side and Long-Side Dimensions for Determining Proportions of Charts in Inches

Short	Long	Short	Long	Short	Long	Short	Long	Short	Long
1.0	1.4	3.0	4.2	5.0	7.1	7.0	9.9	9.0	12.7
1.1	1.6	3.1	4.4	5.1	7.2	7.1	10.0	9.1	12.9
1.2	1.7	3.2	4.5	5.2	7.4	7.2	10.2	9.2	13.0
1.3	1.8	3.3	4.7	5.3	7.5	7.3	10.3	9.3	13.2
1.4	2.0	3.4	4.8	5.4	7.6	7.4	10.5	9.4	13.3
1.5	2.1	3.5	4.9	5.5	7.8	7.5	10.6	9.5	13.4
1.6	2.3	3.6	5.1	5.6	7.9	7.6	10.8	9.6	13.5
1.7	2.4	3.7	5.2	5.7	8.1	7.7	10.9	9.7	13.7
1.8	2.6	3.8	5.4	5.8	8.2	7.8	11.0	9.8	13.9
1.9	2.7	3.9	5.5	5.9	8.3	7.9	11.2	9.9	14.0
2.0	2.8	4.0	5.7	6.0	8.5	8.0	11.3	10.0	14.1
2.1	3.0	4.1	5.8	6.1	8.6	8.1	11.5	10.1	14.3
2.2	3.1	4.2	5.9	6.2	8.8	8.2	11.6	10.2	14.4
2.3	3.2	4.3	6.1	6.3	8.9	8.3	11.7	10.3	14.6
2.4	3.4	4.4	6.2	6.4	9.1	8.4	11.9	10.4	14.7
2.5	3.5	4.5	6.4	6.5	9.2	8.5	12.0	10.5	14.8
2.6	3.7	4.6	6.5	6.6	9.3	8.6	12.2	10.6	15.0
2.7	3.8	4.7	6.7	6.7	9.5	8.7	12.3	10.7	15.1
2.8	4.0	4.8	6.8	6.8	9.6	8.8	12.4	10.8	15.3
2.9	4.1	4.9	6.9	6.9	9.8	8.9	12.6	10.9	15.4

determined as it relates to all other elements. This does not mean that an attempt should be made to weight all the elements equally. Sometimes the most important element may dominate the presentation, with other elements emphasized in accordance with their relative importance. Statistical charts should conform as far as possible to the basic principles of artistic design but at the same time be consistent with clear and accurate portrayal of the data.

In planning a chart, careful consideration must also be given to many other essential features, such as title, subtitle, scales, scale lines, scale figures, scale legends, curves, curve legends, crosshatching, and explanatory notes. Since details of this kind vary with each graphic form, they are discussed at some length in succeeding chapters.

To Chart or Not to Chart

As previously indicated, statistical data may be presented in textual, tabular, and graphic form, either singly or in combination. All three methods possess certain advantages and disadvantages. A text can explain, interpret, and evaluate; a table can provide exact comparisons and supporting evidence; and a chart can demonstrate, communicate at a glance with force, conviction, and appeal, and possibly disclose relationships that might otherwise pass unnoticed.[7] Before a decision is made to present data in graphic form there should be good and sufficient reasons for such a choice. The advantages should unmistakably outweigh any disadvantages in comparison to textual or tabular presentation. Charts are not merely cosmetic appendages; they must serve a useful purpose based on careful insight and judgment.

Choosing the Most Appropriate Type of Chart

For any given set of data there are no absolute standards or criteria for selecting a particular type of chart, nor can it be said that there is a "best" type

---

[7] K. W. Haemer, *Making the Most of Charts*, New York: American Telephone and Telegraph Company, 1960, pp. 2–4.

[8] Table 1–2 and Figure 1–3, as well as most of the related interpretive text, were extracted from U.S. Department of the Army, *Standards of Statistical Presentation*, Washington, D.C.: Government Printing Office, 1966, pp. 67–69.

of chart for a given set of data. The selection of a specific graphic form should be based on a careful evaluation of a number of factors and objectives, most of which have been mentioned in previous sections: (1) nature and characteristics of the data, (2) purpose and emphasis of the message to be conveyed, (3) audience for whom the chart is intended, (4) medium of presentation, and (5) time available for the preparation of the chart. In addition to these factors and objectives, there is an implicit assumption that cannot be overlooked: actually, the ability to make a meaningful decision concerning the appropriateness or suitability of a chart for a given set of data is dependent on a thorough knowledge of all the many graphic forms and their advantages and disadvantages. No one can be considered genuinely proficient in graphic presentation without this knowledge.

Perhaps with few if any exceptions, the simplest set of statistical data can be depicted by more than one graphic form. More elaborate and complex data can be portrayed by as many as 15 or 20 different graphic forms. To illustrate several ways in which a set of data can be shown graphically, let us examine Table 1–2 and Figure 1–3.[8] As is indicated in more detail later, the eight charts in Figure 1–3 by no means exhaust the number of graphic forms that could be developed from the data in Table 1–2.

It will be observed that no two of the charts are identical since each focuses attention on a different aspect of the data or places a different emphasis on a given aspect. This fact is very important since the message that a chart conveys is influenced to a marked degree by the graphic form selected as well as its basic design and execution. For example, the first four charts in Figure 1–3 relate to time series for "all services" totals. If detailed comparisons for each of the seven services seemed appropriate, many additional charts of similar design could be made. The main emphasis in panel A is placed on the total number of vehicles on which repair was delayed 4 days or more. Also, it shows the composition of the total number of disabled vehicles by cause. Panel B portrays the same information as in panel A, but the comparison of the two components is direct. Although perhaps not as arresting as the subdivided-column chart in panel A, the arithmetic line chart in panel B provides a better picture of the interrelationships of the data.

Panel C emphasizes the relative importance of lack of spare parts as cause of delay. The scale figures are expressed in percentages. Instead of a

Table 1–2

General-Purpose Vehicles Disabled 4 Days or More

Service	May		June		July		August		September		October	
	Total	Due to Lack of Parts	Total	Due to Lack of Parts	Total	Due to Lack of Parts	Total	Due to Lack of Parts	Total	Due to Lack of Parts	Total	Due to Lack of Parts
All services	922	625	1271	774	856	533	981	675	1247	679	1486	682
Chemical	98	48	78	43	78	23	39	17	91	51	95	51
Engineers	136	116	136	97	29	29	19	18	29	29	21	17
Medical	41	25	81	44	4	2	6	5	5	2	9	6
Ordnance	252	174	368	221	265	193	353	268	606	218	654	164
Quartermaster	116	63	76	41	61	21	61	23	59	31	58	28
Signal	69	44	80	34	28	15	31	23	39	34	46	30
Transportation	210	155	452	294	391	250	472	321	418	314	603	386

simple arithmetic line chart, this chart could be readily converted into a 100% "surface" chart by stippling and/or crosshatching the two strata and labeling the lower one "lack of spare parts" and the upper one "other." Panel D shows the same data as in panel C, plus the range between the highest and lowest for the seven services along with the average of all of the services combined for each month. This graphic form is referred to as a *range chart*.

The remaining four panels, E through H, emphasize relationships between components of the total for a specified period. Two of the charts examine the causes of disability; two focus on the proportion of vehicles disabled due to lack of spare parts. All of these charts are bar charts. Panel E portrays for each of the technical services the total number of vehicles disabled 4 days or more and also shows how many were delayed in repair by lack of spare parts and by other causes. To obviate confusion it should be explained that the small chart with the two bars in panel E is a "blowup" insert representing in enlarged detail comparative data for the two smallest categories, engineers and medical services.

The subdivided 100% bar chart in panel F shows the proportions of delays resulting from needed repairs that were attributable to lack of spare parts and to other causes. The bar-and-symbol chart in panel G emphasizes "lack of parts" percentages for the several services. Comparisons are shown for the months of September and October and, indirectly, the changes occurring between these 2 months. The sliding bar chart in panel H carries the story presented in panel G a step further. It shows an overall picture for the entire 6-month period rather than just 2 months. The respective lengths of the seven bars represent the minimal and maximal monthly percentages and the short vertical line the 6-month average.

Role of Freehand Sketching in Graphic Presentation

In the process of making a decision concerning the basic design and other features of a chart, it may be found helpful to develop one or more freehand sketches embodying alternate graphic forms. Each sketch can be carefully studied and its advantages and shortcomings evaluated in light of the problem at hand. As part of this procedure, the sketches may be submitted to office mates, colleagues, prospective readers, and others for criticism and suggestions.

In addition to their value in determining the suitability of a particular graphic form and other design features, freehand sketches possess other uses. Frequently, they provide additional insights and meaning to the data by revealing important characteristics and relationships that otherwise may not be readily apparent in tabular form. Also,

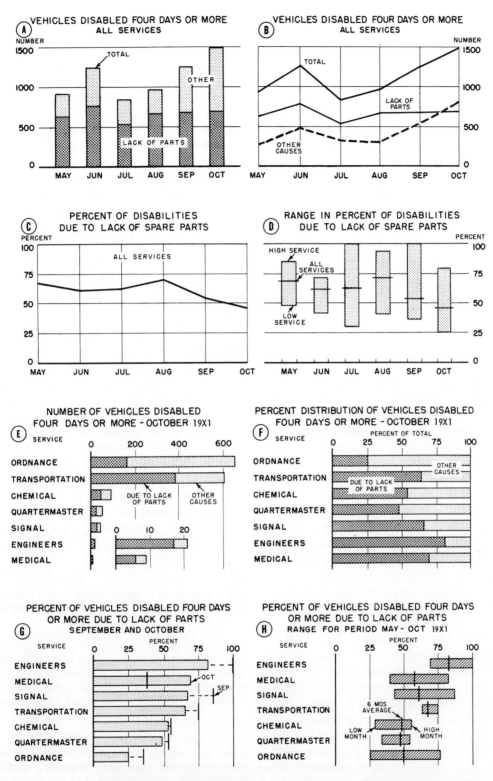

Figure 1–3. Charts illustrate how a relatively simple series of statistical data can be presented in several different ways. Of course, these charts do not exhaust all of the possible alternatives. See Table 1–2 and text for additional details.

freehand sketches are very practicable, if not indispensable, in conveying instructions to drafters concerning design details of a chart.[9]

In sketching charts it is recommended that single, letterhead-size, cross-ruled paper, preferably 10 divisions to the inch, be used. Sometimes a form of printed graph paper, particularly semilogarithmic, may be found helpful. If an organization customarily prepares a fairly large number of charts, it would be expedient to design special types of sketch worksheets that can be reproduced by printing or by some relatively inexpensive process such as diazo. In this connection, for example, the U.S. Department of Agriculture has designed and printed 17 different kinds of sketch worksheets for its staff.[10]

Standards of Graphic Presentation

In every well-established artistic, literary, scientific, and engineering field or specialty there has evolved among experienced, knowledgeable, and proficient practitioners a genuine consensus of values and standards that serve as guideposts in judging what is "good" and "bad" or "acceptable" and "unacceptable." Standards and values are very real and meaningful and are an integral part of a discipline; they give direction to such basic elements as design criteria, practices, and techniques. Frequently, standards develop without conscious direction through such processes as common practice, imitation, and precedent. Also, standards may be formalized and systematized through consensus by special committees or groups created for such purpose.

The first formalized and generally accepted standards in graphic presentation were published in 1915 by a joint committee representing 17 American associations and agencies. Willard C. Brinton was the moving spirit in this endeavor, and the sponsoring organization was the American Society of Mechanical Engineers. The 1915 report was relatively brief, consisting of 17 simply stated basic rules, each illustrated with one to three diagrams.[11]

Since the publication in 1915 of the report by the original Joint Committee, other committees prepared greatly expanded reports on standards of graphic presentation in 1936, 1938, and 1960. Although these publications have been valuable, they are limited in application since they are devoted almost exclusively to time-series charts.[12]

Although standards for all the manifold graphic forms not classified as time-series charts have not been explicitly organized and sanctioned through collective action by a special committee or organization, they nevertheless do exist and are a very real, meaningful, and integral part of the discipline. They simply have not been formally organized and codified through discussion, evaluation, and consensus by a committee or group. For the most part these standards are commonly embodied in textbooks and manuals, and in addition are reflected in the work produced by knowledgeable and proficient specialists. The value and utility of the standards thus presented depend on the fidelity with which the standards conform to the best state of knowledge relating to the theory and practice of graphic presentation. In the present treatise the authors have made every effort to include the most authoritative, up-to-date, and relevant standards pertaining to all types of graphic forms.

As standards become more explicit and formalized through rational evaluation and consensus, graphic presentation can rid itself more easily of uncertainties and inconsistencies. Standards should never be treated as ultimates. Sound standards embody the best current usage and define knowledge at a given point in time, usually by stating what is "best" when judged by some set of criteria. When knowledge increases or criteria change, standards must and do change. As experience in the field of graphic presentation broadens and deepens and as new problems occur, changing practices are inevitable. New standards are

[9] United States Department of the Army (op. cit.), p. 70; U.S. Department of Agriculture, *Tips on Preparing Chart Roughs,* Washington, D.C.: Office of Management Services, 1973, pp. 2–4.

[10] United States Department of Agriculture (op. cit.).

[11] Joint Committee on Standards for Graphic Presentation, "Preliminary Report Published for the Purpose of Inviting Suggestions for the Benefit of the Committee," *Publications of the American Statistical Association,* **14** (1914–1915), 790–797. This report was also published as a separate pamphlet by the American Society of Mechanical Engineers.

[12] Committee on Standards of Graphic Presentation, *Time-Series Charts: A Manual of Design and Construction,* New York: The American Society of Mechanical Engineers, 1938; Subcommittee Y15.2 of the Committee on Preferred Practice for the Preparation of Graphs, Charts and Other Technical Illustrations, *American Standard Time-Series Charts,* New York: American Society of Mechanical Engineers, 1960.

created while other standards may become outmoded.[13]

Some Theoretical Principles of Graphic Communication

Statistical charts occupy a very important niche in graphic communication. Graphic communication encompasses a wide variety of disciplines and specialties ranging from highly specialized technical illustration to visual education.[14] No matter what field or specialty, graphic communication is based on two fundamental principles. The first and primary principle is *graphic thinking*. The second principle is *graphic design*. Graphic design is the vehicle that conveys graphic thought that represents clear and meaningful ideas in visual form. Our main concern is in graphic design. Accordingly, as specialists in communicating statistical facts and ideas visually, our major objective is to design and execute functional, appropriate, interesting, articulate, and readily understood statistical charts. The preparation of statistical charts is not a perfunctory, mechanical procedure; rather, it involves conceptual logic and other basic principles that might in some way enhance and facilitate graphic communication. An effectively designed chart is tantamount to a visual statement, not infrequently equivalent to many paragraphs or even many pages of written words.

Expertise in designing statistical charts involves not only practical experience, but also an understanding of the basic principles of graphic design as well as a thorough knowledge of the best standards and techniques of statistical charting. An important principle of graphic design is the concept of *form*, which consists of five basic elements: point, line, shape, color value (shading), and texture. To be articulate and functional, the various elements are structured conceptually and logically in such a way that the resultant graphic figure represents a clear and reliable visualization of ideas.

Unfortunately, and all too frequently, statistical charts fall considerably short of meeting the principles and standards discussed in this chapter. Although statistical charts are often a more powerful and significant vehicle of communication than words, there is a strange tolerance for poorly constructed charts. Paradoxically, the reader who is outraged by an ungrammatical sentence, an ambiguous statement, or even misplaced punctuation marks may be quite tolerant or indifferent to crudely designed, idiosyncratic, inappropriate, or confusing charts. This situation is essentially reflective of the graphic illiteracy not only of the reader but also of those responsible for the preparation of poorly designed and executed charts.

The basic quality of a statistical chart is judged by its effectiveness in communicating ideas. Is the basic design thoroughly understood by the audience to whom the chart is addressed? Is it clear, simple, meaningful, appropriate, reliable, forceful, or relevant? Does it possess aesthetic appeal? Does it conform to the highest standards of graphic presentation?

What Are the Basic Requirements for Proficiency in Graphic Presentation?

At this point in our discussion one might appropriately ask what the basic requirements are for proficiency in graphic presentation. Since proficiency in graphic presentation involves a combination of skills, all of which are essential, it would be illogical to attempt to rank them specifically in terms of priority or importance. First, it is, of course, advantageous for the specialist in graphic presentation to acquire at least rudimentary drafting skills. Drafting skills should be thought of merely as an essential tool, not an end in itself. Drafting skills and manual dexterity per se are not identical with the creativity and expertise in designing statistical charts. To be sure, some specialists in graphic presentation are excellent draftsmen (drafters), but that is not always the case, whereas even outstanding draftsmen as a group know virtually nothing about graphic presentation. Second, another important prerequisite is a basic knowledge of statistical techniques. At least one, preferably two or more, college-level courses in applied statistics are minimal. Again, statistical training alone is no guarantee for success in graphic presentation. In fact,

---

[13] For a detailed discussion of standards as they pertain to the design and construction of statistical charts, see Calvin F. Schmid, "The Role of Standards in Graphic Presentation," *American Statistical Association, Proceedings of the Social Statistics Section, 1976,* Washington, D. C.: American Statistical Association, 1976, pp. 74–81.

[14] Most of the theoretical principles included in this discussion were derived from William J. Bowman, *Graphic Communication,* New York: Wiley, 1968, passim.

many distinguished statisticians possess very meager understanding of graphic techniques.

Third, closely related to a knowledge of basic statistics is the acquisition of a substantial understanding of electronic computing techniques. We are now entering a revolutionary period wherein computer technology is assuming an increasingly important role in the construction of statistical charts. However, no amount of sophistication in computer technology alone is a substitute for genuine understanding and expertise in the theory and practice of graphic presentation.

Fourth, a sound knowledge of one or more substantive fields or specialities in the social, physical, biological, or applied sciences or arts is essential. Obviously, there is a close and necessary relationship between the ability to design effective and meaningful charts and a knowledge of the subject matter of a particular area.

Fifth, a final basic prerequisite is the acquisition of knowledge and skills pertaining to the theory, principles, and practice of preparing statistical charts. This is the special stage or routine where the various skills and prerequisites of drafting, statistics, computer technology, and knowledge of one or more substantive fields are brought into appropriate focus for the development of expertise in the design and execution of statistical charts. Normally, this calls for special training and guidance; unfortunately, there are very few formal

college and university courses offered in graphic presentation where one might obtain specialized training of this kind. Even in courses in statistics, the subject of graphic techniques is generally ignored or treated in a most cursory and superficial manner. Sometimes where there is special demand, such as in Washington, D. C., where hundreds of persons both in governmental and private agencies are involved in various kinds of graphic communication, occasional seminars or special extension courses may be offered in graphic presentation.[15] In the larger colleges and universities, departments of geography frequently offer one or more courses in cartography. Some of these courses may be found helpful, but characteristically they fail in both content and emphasis to provide a comprehensive and well-balanced approach to the subject of graphic presentation. Under the circumstances, on-the-job training combined with a considerable amount of self-education are frequently the only means of acquiring the necessary knowledge and technique for designing and executing statistical charts. In this connection, it is hoped that the present book will provide an indispensable guide and source of information concerning the theory, standards, practices, and procedures of graphic presentation, not only for the beginner but also for the experienced practitioner.

LAYOUT TECHNIQUES AND PROCEDURES

To demonstrate the actual procedure in laying out a statistical chart, a series of relatively simple data is taken for illustrative purposes (Table 1–3). The most appropriate type of chart for these data is the frequency polygon on a rectilinear coordinate grid. It will be assumed that the chart is to be used for reproduction in a book of more or less standard format, will be of full-page size, and will conform to root-two dimensions. If the original chart is made about three times as large as the reduction, it will be 14 in. by 20 in. The procedure will then be as follows:

1. Procure a sheet of drawing paper, plastic drafting film, tracing cloth, or other suitable ma-

---

Table 1–3

Monthly Salaries of General and Senior Stenographers in the United States (excluding Alaska and Hawaii)—March, 1975

Monthly Salary (Dollars)	Stenographers	
	General	Senior
Total	37,980	41,171
300 and under 400	303	–
400 and under 500	4,515	1,192
500 and under 600	11,725	6,540
600 and under 700	9,145	11,353
700 and under 800	5,767	9,749
800 and under 900	3,756	6,375
900 and under 1000	2,769	3,989
1000 and under 1100	–	1,480
1100 and under 1200	–	493

Based on data from U.S. Bureau of Labor Statistics, *National Survey of Professional, Administrative, Technical and Clerical Pay, March 1975,* Washington: Government Printing Office, 1975, p. 25. The data tabulated here represent samples.

---

[15] Approximately 1800 persons are listed in the 1974 *Directory of U.S. Government Audiovisual Personnel.* Of course, only a relatively small proportion of this number are involved directly with statistical graphics.

terial slightly larger than the overall dimensions of the chart and mount it on a drawing board (see Figures 1–4 and 1–5).[16]

2. Frame in the working area in which the chart is to be laid out with the widest dimension at the

top. Accordingly, a distance of 20 in. is scaled off across the sheet and 14 in. from top to bottom. The plotting points are connected by light pencil lines with a T-square and triangle to form a rectangle 14 in. by 20 in. When the chart is completed, these lines, if desired, may be incorporated into a border design. All elements of the chart will be included within the limits of the penciled border lines.

[16] At this stage a knowledge of basic drafting skills will be extremely helpful. For a brief, simple discussion of drafting techniques, see Chapter 2.

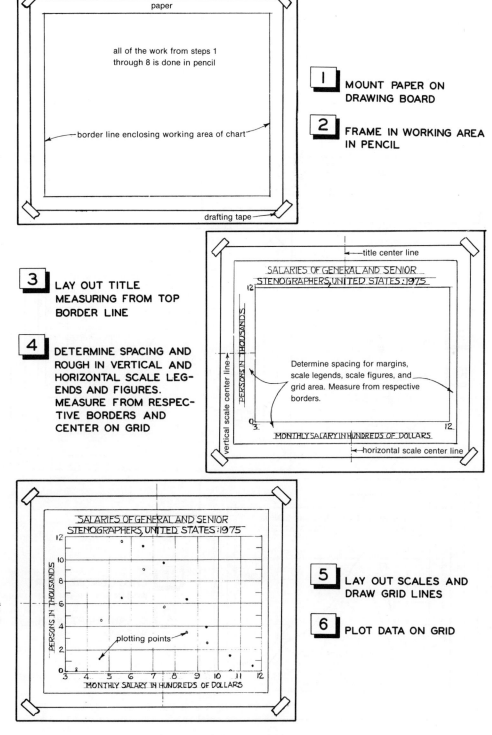

Figure 1–4. Steps in laying out a chart. Illustration based on data in Table 1–3.

3. The title of the chart is sketched in pencil at the top of the working area to determine the exact amount of space required for this purpose. The size of the chart, as well as the amount of reduction, will dictate the size and spacing of the lettering for the title. Without exception, the lettering for the title is larger than any other lettering on the chart. However, to achieve well-balanced composition, neither the title nor, in fact, any other element should be made too large or conspicuous. In measuring the height of the letters and spacing of lines for the title, measurements are made from the top border line. The arrangement of the title across the chart should be centered between the side borders.

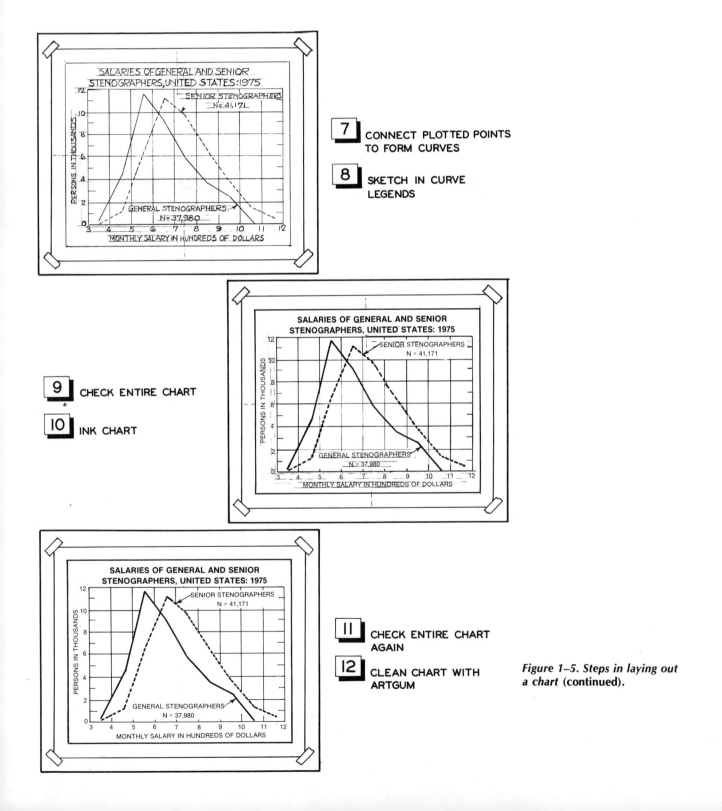

7 CONNECT PLOTTED POINTS TO FORM CURVES

8 SKETCH IN CURVE LEGENDS

9 CHECK ENTIRE CHART

10 INK CHART

11 CHECK ENTIRE CHART AGAIN

12 CLEAN CHART WITH ARTGUM

Figure 1–5. Steps in laying out a chart (continued).

4. The spacing and lettering for the vertical and horizontal scale legends and figures are roughed in. Measurements are made from the respective vertical and horizontal borders but centered with reference to the grid. Generally, all lettering on the chart, except for the title, is of uniform size. The area remaining after the title, scale figures, scale legends, and necessary spacing have been determined will represent the main body of the chart. The various steps described thus far are applicable to such widely used graphic forms as the rectilinear coordinate charts, bar and column charts, and the semilogarithmic chart.

5. If the chart is a rectilinear line graph, the horizontal and vertical scales are completed, including grid lines and scale points. The lettering for scale figures and scale legends is completed next.

6. The data are plotted on the grid. The plotting points are usually dots or small crosses.

---

[17] For a detailed presentation of the characteristics, types, and uses of rectilinear coordinate charts, see Chapter 3.
[18] See Chapter 2.

7. The successive plotting points are then connected by straight lines, which are referred to in statistical terminology as "curves." If there are two or more curves, they are differentiated by distinctive line patterns.[17]

8. Curve legends and any necessary explanatory statements are lettered on the chart.

9. The chart, which has been drawn entirely in pencil, is carefully checked for completeness, clarity, and accuracy. Particular consideration should be given to the scales, plotting of the data, wording of the title, spelling, and punctuation.

10. The chart is inked in. This should be done with meticulous care with proper materials and equipment.[18]

11. The entire chart is checked again for errors and omissions.

12. The chart is cleaned with Artgum or other suitable material.

CHAPTER TWO

DRAFTING TECHNIQUES

THE MASTERY OF AT LEAST THE BASIC techniques of drafting is essential if one is to attain a high degree of proficiency in the field of graphic presentation. Manual skill in drafting should be considered as a means to an end—an indispensable tool in the design and construction of statistical charts. As such, the student should attempt to develop sufficient skill so that the mechanics of drafting become as automatic as writing. When this level of proficiency is attained, the mind will be free to consider the more important problems of planning and design.

In addition, it should be pointed out that it is a real advantage for the young statistician just beginning his professional career to possess drafting ability, since this skill can be put to immediate and practical use. In fact, because of the paucity of capable and well-trained specialists in the field of graphic presentation, drafting skill in combination with an understanding of graphic techniques may mean a higher rate of pay or the difference between obtaining or not obtaining a particular position. Later on, even after advancement to some higher administrative post, the statistician with successful experience in delineating and drawing charts will be in a much better position to judge the appropriateness and quality of a chart and to supervise intelligently and efficiently the work of others.

There are at least three general criteria in drafting that should be observed carefully by the beginning student: accuracy, neatness, and speed. Emphasis must be placed on accuracy and neatness from the very start, since speed can be developed only through practice and experience. One cannot afford to deviate from the highest standards of accuracy and neatness if real proficiency is to be attained in graphic presentation. Careless, slipshod work can only result in lowering the quality, authoritativeness, and effectiveness of a chart.

PREPRINTED GRAPHIC MATERIALS AND MECHANICAL AIDS

In recent years an impressive array of drafting materials and mechanical aids has been developed that are especially useful in graphic presentation. These developments have been a boon not only to the novice, but also to the experienced technician. In general, most are simple to use, save time and labor, eliminate a certain amount of repetition and routine work, and enhance the attractiveness and overall quality of the chart.

The greatest proliferation of these materials has been in the form of preprinted "stick-ons," "paste-ups," or "stick-ups" and "transfers." They include preprinted lettering sheets with hundreds of type styles and sizes; an extraordinary number and variety of hatching and screen patterns; a wide assortment of patterns, colors, and sizes of tapes for curves on rectilinear coordinate and semilogarithmic charts; tapes of varying width, color, and hatching patterns for bar and column charts; pictorial symbols; a wide variety of preprinted statistical and mathematical symbols, Greek letters, arrows, and border materials; and symbols for dot maps and other types of charts. Mechanical aids include phototypesetting machines and special electric typewriters for lettering; projectors for enlarging and reducing the size of charts; improved reservoir pens and other drafting instruments; templates for a wide variety of letters, figures, and symbols; printed aids and mechanical devices for three-dimensional charts; plastic drafting films; machines for quick and inexpensive reproduction of charts; and electronic computers and auxiliary equipment for actually producing completed charts. The various kinds of preprinted graphic aids and mechanical and electronic instruments and equipment are considered in more detail in subsequent sections where they have direct application and relevance to the subject being discussed.

DRAFTING INSTRUMENTS AND MATERIALS

For first-class drafting work it is necessary to have good instruments. Inferior instruments pose a handicap. With reasonable care a good set of drawing instruments will last a lifetime. In purchasing drawing instruments, one can be guided by the recommendations of an experienced friend or place reliance on the trademark of a reputable company. The instruments do not have to be ornate, but should be of high quality in both material and workmanship. In general, the beginner should be advised to purchase the best instruments that he can afford.

Drawing instruments may be purchased separately or in sets. If one can afford it, it is recommended that a complete set of drawing instruments be purchased, including not only the ruling pen but compasses and dividers as well.

It is possible to construct many types of charts with relatively few instruments, but eventually the lack of adequate equipment may prove a serious handicap. A minimal list of instruments and equipment for the construction of charts should include the following items: (1) drawing board, (2) T-square, (3) ruling pen, (4) civil engineer's scale, (5) triangle, 45°, (6) drawing pencil, (7) eraser, (8) Artgum, (9) black waterproof ink, (10) penholder, (11) at least two pens such as a Gillott 404 or 303 and a Crowquill, (12) masking tape, (13) can of tracing-cloth powder and can of inking powder for drafting film, and (14) penwiper. A more complete listing of materials and equipment would include: (1) 30° by 60° triangle, (2) one French curve and two or three ship curves, (3) drafting-table brush, (4) percentage protractor, (5) pencil pointer, (6) erasing shield, (7) 6-in. compass with extension bar, (8) 6-in. divider, (9) $3\frac{1}{2}$-in. bow pencil, bow pen, and bow divider, (10) a minimum of six reservoir pens for ruling lines and for lettering, and (11) scriber or templates to be used with reservoir pens for lettering.

Drawing Board

The drawing board should be constructed of well-seasoned, straight-grained wood with perfectly straight edges so that an accurate and smooth working surface will be provided for the T-square head. Drawing boards are usually made from softwood strips, such as white pine, glued together and reinforced by cleats on the left and right sides. Drawing boards vary in size from 12 in. by 17 in. to 60 in. by 120 in. In addition, there are drawing tables as large as 42 in. by 90 in. For ordinary work the smaller drawing boards are adequate, although if display charts or maps are contemplated, it would be advisable to procure a larger board at the start. To ensure a smooth, clean surface, it is advisable to cover the drawing board with buff or a pastel-green detail paper or special vinyl material especially manufactured for this purpose. The detail paper or vinyl covering can be readily mounted on the drawing board either with rubber cement or with thin wire staples.

Paper, Tracing Cloth, and Plastic Drafting Film

Paper, art board, tracing cloth, plastic drafting film, or other materials used for statistical charts should have a smooth finish, take ink readily, stand some erasing, possess a high degree of dimensional stability by not expanding or contracting with temperature and humidity, be free of loose fibers that might clog the ruling or lettering pen, be relatively durable, and, for most finished drawings, be translucent. In practice it will be found that no single material can fulfill all requirements in the preparation of statistical charts. In preparing preliminary work drawings, detail paper, vellum paper or some other kind of paper may be used. For final finished drawings a high-quality art board, tracing cloth or matte finish translucent polyester plastic may be used. Because of their translucence as well as other qualities, tracing cloth and plastic film have certain advantages over drawing papers. Charts drawn on tracing cloth or plastic film can be reproduced by such relatively inexpensive processes as blueprinting, and ozalid printing. Also, because of their translucence, it is possible to trace in ink directly onto tracing cloth or plastic film a chart from a penciled work drawing.

In mounting drawing paper, tracing cloth, or plastic film on a board, it is suggested that the sheet be placed well up on the board and close to the left-hand edge (Figure 2–1). The top edge of the drawing material should be aligned along the working edge of a T-square and fastened down securely to the board with masking tape.

Drawing Pencils

Drawing pencils are similar to writing pencils in that they are composed of finely ground emulsified

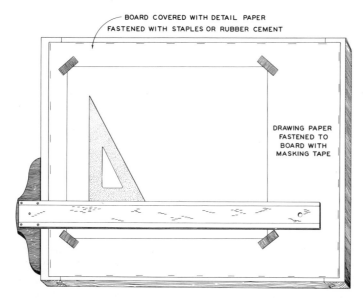

Figure 2–1. Technique in mounting paper, plastic drafting film, or other material on drawing board.

graphite mixed with clay and binding materials in varying proportions, which determine the degrees of hardness. It is recommended that drawing pencils be used for graphic presentation since they are superior in quality to the average writing pencil. The relative hardness of drawing pencils is indicated by symbols ranging from 7B to 9H. The 7B is extremely soft and black. The next gradations are as follows: 6B, 5B, 4B, 3B, 2B, B, HB (medium), F, H, 2H, and on up to 9H, which is relatively hard. In selecting a pencil, consideration should be given to the type of paper to be used. For general, all-around purposes in graphic presentation the pencil should range between HB and H. Occasionally a 2H might be found especially satisfactory for preparation of work drawings on detail paper. Some specialists in the field prefer artists' automatic mechanical pencils to the wood-cased pencils because they are always of uniform length and the length of lead can be adjusted without cutting away the wood. Leads of any degree of hardness can be purchased for this type of pencil. Special nongraphite pencils may be found more satisfactory for drafting film.

To make firm, accurate, and clear-cut lines, it is necessary to have drawing pencils well sharpened at all times. For convenience and to save time it is suggested that a supply of four or five well-sharpened pencils be readily at hand. The pencils

can be sharpened either with a knife or with a draftsman's mechanical sharpener and then pointed properly with fine sandpaper or a metal lead pointer. The conical point will be found especially useful for plotting measurements and for lettering. The chisel point and wedge point are customarily used for drawing lines with a straightedge. Figure 2–2 illustrates the three types of pencil points as well as their preparation. Figure 2–3 indicates the sharpening of the lead with a pencil pointer.

Scales

The purpose of scales is to make measurements on the drawing. The scale should never under any circumstances be used as a straightedge for drawing lines. There are two main types of scales used for laying out statistical charts—the civil engineer's scale and the statistician's scale. The faces of the civil engineer's scale are subdivided into 10, 20, 30, 40, 50, and 60 parts to an inch.

Scales are manufactured usually in 6-in. and 12-in. lengths, either flat with two or four bevels or in triangular form. All types will be found very satisfactory. The triangular scale has the advantage of being less expensive and includes six different faces (Figure 2–4). Although the statistician's

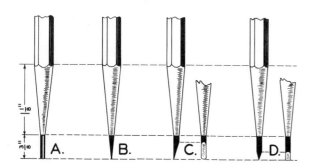

Figure 2–2. Preparing pencil for drawing charts. A. A sharp knife or draftsman's pencil sharpener is used to remove wood. The point is shaped with sandpaper. B. A conical point. C. A wedge point. D. A chisel point.

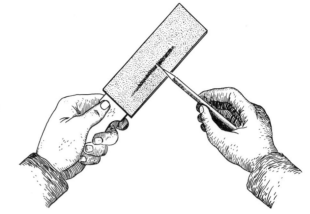

Figure 2–3. Shaping pencil point with sandpaper.

scale has been designed for statistical work, the civil engineer's scale will be found much more flexible for the preparation of statistical charts. The statistician's scale contains logarithmic divisions as well as some decimal divisions similar to the civil engineer's scale.

Figure 2–5 illustrates one of the most important and frequent uses of the scale. The distance between any two parallel lines can be divided into any size units desired by first setting the scale on a par-

ticular point on one line and merely moving it at different angles.

Protractor

The protractor is used for laying out angles that cannot be made with triangles. It is used most often in the construction of pie charts. Protractors may be calibrated either in degrees or in percent-

Figure 2–4. Illustration of scales used in the preparation of statistical charts.

A CIVIL ENGINEER'S SCALE – TRIANGULAR FORM

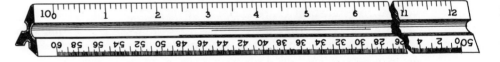

B CIVIL ENGINEER'S SCALE – BEVELED FORM

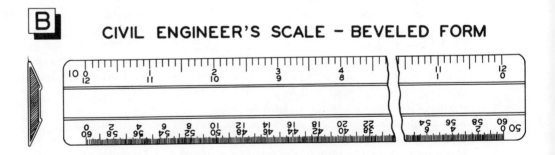

C STATISTICIAN'S SCALE – DOUBLE-BEVELED FORM

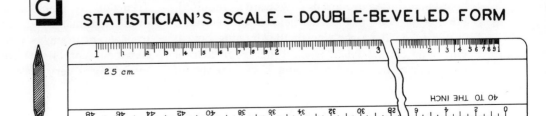

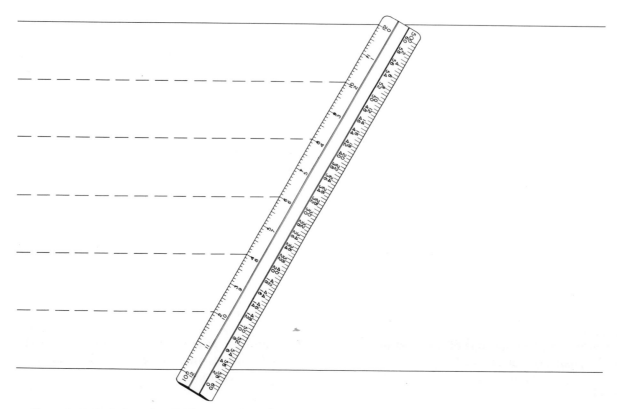

Figure 2–5. Technique for dividing any given distance into equal units.

ages. The percentage protractor is much more convenient for statistical charts since it obviates the necessity of converting percentages to degrees. Most protractors are calibrated, semicircular disks made of brass, steel, nickel silver, or a plastic material. The more elaborate protractors frequently have a movable straightedge adjustment.

T-Square

The T-square is used primarily as a straightedge in drawing horizontal lines and as a base for guiding triangles in drawing vertical or inclined lines. It is also used for "squaring" paper on the drawing board. It is essential that the upper edge of the blade and the inside edge of the head be perfectly straight. For right-handed persons, the head of the T-square is held against the left edge of the drawing board and shifted upward or downward as required. For left-handed persons, the head of the T-square is placed on the right side of the drawing board. Under no circumstances should the lower edge of the T-square be used for drawing lines, nor should

its head ever be placed on the upper or lower edges of the drawing board.

Perhaps the most suitable and inexpensive type of T-square is made with an ebonized hardwood head and a straight-grained maple blade with transparent edges. Some T-squares are made of steel. These are more expensive but have the advantage of lying flatter on the drawing board. There are elaborate and expensive drafting machines available that serve the purpose of a T-square and other straightedges, but such equipment is not necessary for work in graphic presentation.

Triangles

Triangles most commonly used in all types of drafting work are those having angles of 30°, 60°, and 90° and those with two 45° angles and a 90° angle. Triangles are manufactured in different sizes and of different materials. The 8-in., 45° and 30° by 60° transparent triangles will be found most useful for statistical charts. Occasionally a much smaller triangle or a very large one will be found conven-

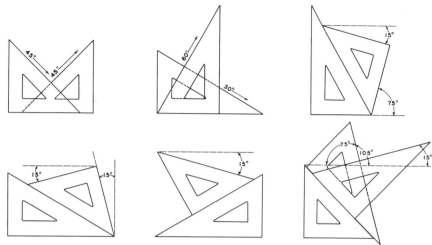

Figure 2–6. Drawing lines at various degrees with triangles.

ient. The triangles are used to guide the pencil and the ruling pen, especially in making vertical lines or angular lines. In drawing vertical lines, the face of the lower leg of the triangle is held firmly against the T-square. Figure 2–6 illustrates techniques in constructing different-sized angles by means of the 45° and 30° by 60° triangles. By use of the 45° and 30° by 60° triangles, together with the T-square, any angle that is a multiple of 15° can be constructed.

Irregular Curves

Irregular curves such as French curves and ship curves in particular will be found useful in drawing lines that are not part of true circles. In addition to the French curves and ship curves, there are many other types that can be used, particularly railroad curves, mechanical engineer's curves, spline and spline weights, and flexible curves that can be formed into different shapes. Figure 2–7 shows an assortment of different types of curves that will be found particularly useful for drawing almost any

type of curve that might be required for a statistical chart.

In laying out a curve, the first step is to sketch freehand the general contour of the curve from the plotting points. The sweep of the curve can be readily determined visually. After the preliminary sketch has been completed, certain curves are selected to fit the segments of the sketch so that the final drawing will be firm, smooth, and without kinks. To draw a smooth curve, the adjoining segments must be tangent to each other where they connect. This relationship is shown in Figure 2–8. Any other manner of joining segments of curves will result in jogs or kinks.

Erasers

Erasing both pencil and ink lines is a necessary part of drafting procedure. Accordingly, it is important to use the best type of erasers and the proper technique so that the paper or other material will not be

Figure 2–7. Samples of French curves, ship curves, and other irregular curves. The French curves, sometimes referred to merely as irregular curves, are represented by the more elaborately scrolled curves in the illustration. The ship curves are characteristically much simpler in form. The relatively straight and long curves at the top and bottom of the illustration are examples of ship curves.

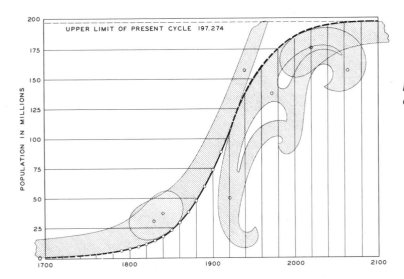

Figure 2–8. Use of French curve and ship curve in drawing a statistical chart.

injured and the erasures will not be detected. For pencil lines a soft eraser, such as Pink Pearl, Ellco Pink, Parapink, and Carnation should be used. If the pencil line is found especially difficult to erase, then a harder-textured eraser, such as Ruby or Electric Red, might be used. The Ruby and the Electric Red will be found very effective for ink lines. Harsh erasers containing abrasive materials should never be used for drafting work. Special erasers such as Magic Rub, Mars, Plastic, and Film Rub are recommended for drafting film. Electric erasers are available at all the larger drafting-supply companies and are very valuable and efficient time-saving equipment.

One should be extremely cautious in using a steel knife or razor blade for removing ink lines because of the danger of removing the surface of the drawing paper, plastic film, or tracing cloth. In fact, it is recommended that the beginner avoid knives and other sharp instruments for erasing until absolutely certain of handling such critical instruments properly. The erasing shield should always be used for making erasures of ink lines. The best erasing shield is made of very thin, tempered spring steel. Shields made of celluloid, German silver, and soft steel are inferior. For cleaning drawings, Artgum or some other similar cleaner can be used. To avoid dimming the lines of the drawing, care should be taken to rub the surface of the paper or film very gently and not too often. Solvents should never be used for cleaning drawings because of the risk of fire and also as solvents tend to dim the ink lines.

Basic Pens for Inking Charts

When the preliminary pencil draft of a chart is ready for inking, one of two basic types of pens may be used: (1) the traditional ruling pen invented some 300 years ago or (2) the cylindrical reservoir pen developed originally in connection with lettering equipment. The ruling pen is an effective and versatile instrument in that the width of lines can vary markedly in size by adjusting the spacing of the nibs. Characteristically, the reservoir pen has a tubular drawing point of fixed size. Accordingly, it is necessary to have an assortment of reservoir pens with points of different sizes for drawing lines varying in width from relatively light to relatively heavy. Normally, six to eight pens should suffice. Actually, some of the reservoir pens are available in as many as 18 line widths. Of course, six to eight reservoir pens are considerably more expensive than a single ruling pen.

An overall practical evaluation of the two types of pens will reveal that the reservoir type is superior. Nevertheless, the traditional ruling pen can be very useful in conjunction with the reservoir pen. On the other hand, some drafters prefer the traditional ruling pen. Frequently the preference is based on habit and inertia. The ruling pen requires more skill to use, since the width of the lines is determined by the spacing of the nibs. It should be pointed out that there are available on the market ruling pens with graduated regulator screws for setting the thickness of lines. This particular feature may be found helpful, especially for the beginner.

Generally, the maximal width of a line made by a ruling pen is approximately $\frac{1}{16}$ in. If a wider line is desired, it is best to draw two thin lines for the outer edges and fill in the space between with the ruling pen.

In the case of the reservoir type of pen no adjustment is necessary since the gauge of each point is of fixed dimension. Accordingly, it is relatively simple to maintain a line of uniform width by using a point of particular size. Again, with the reservoir type of pen it is not necessary to refill with ink nearly as often as with a ruling pen. Also, with the reservoir type of pen it is very easy to make sharp, irregular lines of uniform width. The most common reservoir pens readily available in the United States are the Rapidograph, Leroy, Wrico, and Graphos.

If a ruling pen is selected it is important that it be of the highest quality. The nibs should be of the same length and slightly rounded or parabolic at the ends. They should always be properly sharpened. The inner blade of a well-constructed ruling pen is straight, and the outer blade is slightly curved. The handle should be made of hard, ebonized wood or metal so that it will not break easily.

In drawing straight or curved lines both the ruling pen and the reservoir pen are guided by a T-square, triangle, or irregular curve. It is most important that the pens be absolutely clean. A lint-free penwiper should be readily available for this purpose. The pen should be wiped occasionally during use and always immediately afterward, since India ink dries relatively quickly. To maintain a high level of operational efficiency, it is especially important that the reservoir pen be kept clean at all times. In case ink becomes encrusted either on the outside or inside of the pen, it can be removed by the application of a little water and rubbing with a penwiper. Ammonia solution or some commercially prepared cleaner may also be used for this purpose. In addition, there is special pen-cleaning ultrasonic equipment that is particularly appropriate for large drafting offices. The pen should never be dipped into the ink bottle. The pen—either the ruling pen or the reservoir pen—is filled by means of a quill or pipette, the upper part of which serves as a stopper for the ink bottle. Ink

also may be procured in a plastic squeeze bottle and in cartridges.

The stopper should never be removed from the bottle except for inking the pen, because the bottle may be accidentally tipped over, or the ink, if exposed to the air for any length of time, will thicken and eventually dry up. As another precaution, the ink bottle should not be placed on or very close to the drawing. The purchase of an ink bottle stand will be found to be a good investment, since it will not readily tip over. Or a satisfactory ink-bottle stand can be quickly and cheaply made from a small piece of flexible cardboard, such as a manila file folder or some similar material. The first step is to cut out a circular piece of cardboard about 4 in. in diameter. The ink bottle is then placed in the center of the cardboard, and a circle is drawn by tracing around the bottom of the bottle. Four or five cuts are made across the bottle-sized circle, and the triangular tabs resulting from these cuts are folded upward. The bottle can then be placed in the hole and the tabs fastened to its sides with masking tape or a rubber band.

In drawing straight or curved lines either with a ruling pen or reservoir type of pen, the pen should be held between thumb and forefinger against the straightedge while the other hand is used to hold the straightedge in a firm position.[1]

In using a ruling pen, the pen is inclined slightly in the direction the line is to be drawn. In using a reservoir type of pen, the pen is "pulled" along the straightedge, with the third and fourth fingers used for stabilizing the hand (Figure 2-9).

Figure 2-10 illustrates correct and incorrect positions of the ruling pen in relation to the straightedge. If the pen slopes away from the straightedge at too sharp an angle, the resulting line will be irregular in width. Similarly, if the pen is squeezed too tightly against the straightedge, the resulting line will be of irregular width. When the pen slopes inward at too sharp an angle, there is always the danger of ink running underneath the straightedge. Figure 2-10 shows what might happen if ink collects on the outside of the pen, if there is an insufficient amount in the pen or if the straightedge slips into a wet line.

Similar problems can occur in using the reservoir type of pen, but the danger of smudging and irregularities is not nearly as great. A good, clean reservoir type of pen has a longer, more continuous, and more consistent ink flow than the ruling pen.

---

[1] In mechanical drawing parlance "straightedge" refers not only to T-square and triangles, but also to French, ship, and other types of curves.

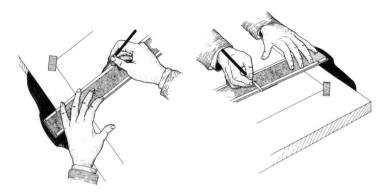

Figure 2–9. Technique in holding the ruling pen and T-square.

Drawing Ink

Drawing ink is different from writing ink in that it does not readily penetrate the paper but rather lies more on the surface. It is more opaque and has certain waterproof qualities so that it will not readily redissolve in water or be affected by moisture as much as writing ink. It is recommended that special drawing ink be used on drafting film. "Pelikan T" drawing ink can be used on drafting film as well as on tracing cloth and detail paper. A blotter should never be used on drawing ink since the carbon particles of the ink are absorbed by the blotter, leaving a dull, grayish line on the paper. Of course, when a mistake is made, the line may be blotted

immediately and can be erased after it has dried thoroughly.

The beginner may become impatient, especially on humid days, when the ink dries slowly. Therefore, it is essential to follow some systematic order in inking the lines to obviate the necessity of waiting each time for a line to dry. For example, one should begin at the top of a drawing and move downward in successive stages or begin at one side and move toward the other side.

Before drawing ink is applied to any surface—tracing cloth, drafting film, or paper—it is essential that the surface be rubbed with powder especially prepared for this purpose. Only a small amount of powder is required, and after it is applied, the sur-

CORRECT

PEN SLOPED AWAY FROM
STRAIGHTEDGE

PEN PRESSED TOO HARD AGAINST
STRAIGHTEDGE

PEN SLOPED TOWARDS
STRAIGHTEDGE

INK ON OUTSIDE OF NIBS

INSUFFICIENT INK IN PEN TO
FINISH LINE

STRAIGHTEDGE SLIPPED INTO
WET LINE

Figure 2–10. Illustration of correct and faulty ink line work.

face should be thoroughly brushed. There are two kinds of powder, one for tracing cloth and paper and one for drafting film.

Compass

In all standard drawing sets there are two types of compasses. The larger one is approximately 6 in. in length, with a free-moving headpiece, a needle point, a pencil leg, a pen leg, and an extension bar. The two smaller ones are known as a "bow pen" and "bow pencil." Each has a spring head and adjusting screws. In using the pencil compass or bow pencil it is important that the lead be sharpened to form a wedge point. In adjusting the lead in the compass, the flat side of the wedge should be placed perpendicular to the radius of the circle. The pen leg of the compass and the bow pen are, of course, similar to the drafting pen and should be operated in much the same manner. Both the small and large compasses are used for drawing circles and arcs. If the arc or circle is less than approximately an inch in radius, the bow pencil and bow pen should be employed. In constructing circles or arcs with relatively large radii the extension bar can be readily inserted into the leg of the compass. Beam compasses with bars of as much as 24 in. or more in length can be used for drawing large display charts.

OPTICAL ILLUSIONS

The beginning student should be aware of the dangers that inhere in the various types of lines, shades,

<hr>

[2] For a brief, up-to-date, theoretical discussion of spatial illusions, including additional examples and approximately 50 references, see R. H. Day, "Visual Spatial Illusions: A General Explanation," *Science,* **175,** (4028) (March 1972), 1335–1340.

and shapes. For example, Figure 2–11 illustrates many of the more common forms of optical illusions in mechanical drawing. The implications of these illustrations are clearly explained in the accompanying annotations.[2]

LETTERING

The importance of good lettering in the construction of statistical charts cannot be overemphasized. Lettering on a chart may spell the difference between an expert and an amateur production and between a favorable or unfavorable impact. Poor lettering can seriously reduce the effectiveness of an otherwise well-designed and well-executed chart and even cast reflection on the ability of the designer. In graphic presentation, there are three basic types of lettering techniques: (1) freehand, (2) "stick-on," "stick-up," or "transfer," and (3) mechanical.

Lettering for statistical charts, regardless of the technique used, should be considered primarily in terms of: (1) legibility, (2) appropriateness, and (3) esthetic appeal. From a secondary point of view, the following factors should be taken into account: (1) time available, (2) ease of execution, and (3) cost.

More specifically, in planning the lettering for a statistical chart, there are several elements that must be considered: (1) style, (2) form, (3) size, (4) method, (5) positioning on chart, and (6) relation of lettering to reproduction. "Style" refers to the design character of the type including thickness of lines. "Form" relates to such characteristics as capitals, lower case, vertical, or slanting letters. "Method" indicates whether mechanical equipment or some form of stick-on lettering is to be used. "Positioning on the chart" is concerned with

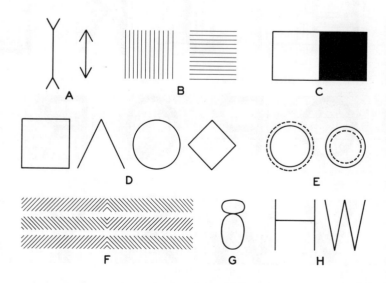

Figure 2–11. Optical illusions. A. The two vertical lines are of the same length, although the one at the left seems to be longer. B. Both shaded sections are identical in height and width. C. The white portion of the rectangle appears larger than the black portion, yet actually the two are identical in size. D. At their widest point the four geometric forms are exactly equal. E. The diameters of the two circles represented by full lines are identical. F. The three crosshatched bars are parallel and of identical width from end to end. The bending impression is an optical illusion resulting from this particular type of hatching. G. The upper and lower parts of this symbol are of the same width. H. The distances between the vertical lines of the letter "H" and the two upper points of the "W" are equal.

the actual placement of the lettering on the chart. Relation of lettering to reproduction indicates that the lettering should be accommodated to the type and process of reproduction.[3]

Freehand Lettering

Although freehand lettering is seldom, if ever, used any more in the final draft of a professionally delineated statistical chart, it is nevertheless a useful skill to learn. At the present time freehand lettering is a dying art. Freehand lettering, however, is still used in graphic presentation, but normally it is done in pencil on the preliminary draft. As indicated in Chapter 1, a statistical chart is first laid out in pencil. It is important that the size, form, and positioning of the lettering be done with great care, since a well-planned and well-executed preliminary draft will save time and trouble as well as provide essential insight and guidance in completing the final draft. For this reason it is important to know the essential characteristics of each letter and figure, understand the order and direction of each stroke in forming the letters, and develop a sense of composition and balance. A simple vertical, capital commercial Gothic alphabet and a series of figures are presented in Figures 2–12, 2–13, and 2–14. It will be observed that the relative widths of letters and figures show characteristic variations. The W, for example, is approximately seven spaces wide, as compared to approximately four spaces for many of the other letters. Also, the letter M is appreciably larger than most of the other letters. It will be observed further that as a general rule, the vertical lines are made first, the horizontal lines second, and the curved lines last. It is essential not only to form the letters and figures carefully, but also to space them properly. To attain proper balance, the individual letters in a word are not spaced at equal distances; rather, they must appear to be spaced at equal distances. This is true not only for freehand lettering, but also for lettering by mechanical means as well as by other techniques. For example, the actual space between A and L and T is much less than, say, that between B and H and I.

As indicated in Chapter 1, freehand lettering should always be done by first drawing guidelines. With some practice and experience lettering in pencil can become almost as automatic and speedy as writing.

---

[3] Arthur H. Robinson and Randall D. Sale, *Elements of Cartography,* 3rd ed., New York: Wiley, 1969, p. 277.

Figure 2–12. Freehand vertical capital letters.

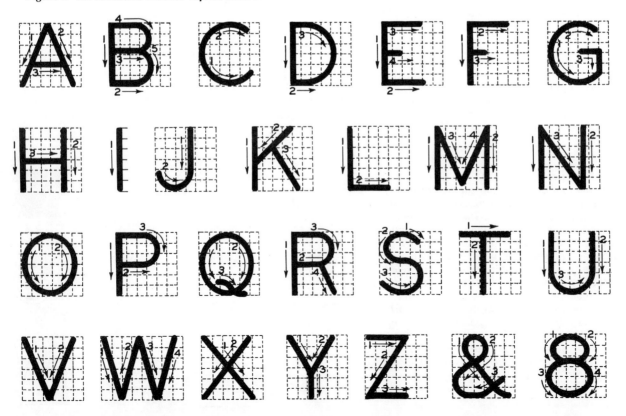

Figure 2–13. Freehand vertical figures.

Stick-on, Stick-up, or Transfer Lettering

Since there are several different types of stick-on, stick-up, or transfer lettering, it would be difficult to state categorically what the advantages and disadvantages of stick-on lettering are over mechanical lettering. It can be said, however, that stick-on lettering requires no special drafting skill and that the variety of styles and forms of available type are incomparably greater for stick-on lettering. On the other hand, certain kinds of stick-on lettering possess serious limitations.

---

[4] High-quality pre-printed letters and other graphic aids are available from art and drafting supply houses. To understand more fully the products available as well as to gain additional insight into their application, it is strongly recommended that one or more sales catalogs of these materials be procured. Catalogs may be obtained from retail outlets or by writing to any of the following companies: (1) Para-tone Incorporated, 512 W. Burlington Avenue, La Grange, Ill. ("Zip-a-tone" patterns and color sheets, "Zip-a-line" charting tapes, etc.); (2) Graphic Products Corporation, Rolling Meadows, Illinois ("Formatt" graphic art aids); (3) Keuffel and Esser Company, Morristown, N. J. ("Mecanorma" graphic products, "Normatype" transfer letters, "Normatone" patterns, etc.); (4) Times Mirror Company, Leeds, Mass. ("Chartpak" graphic products); (5) Prestype, Inc., Gotham Industrial Park, Carlstadt, N. J. ("Prestype" and related products); (6) Tactype, Inc., 43 West 16th Street, New York, N. Y.; (7) Cello-Tak Mfg., Inc., Island Park, L. I. N. Y.; (8) Applied Graphics Corporation, Glenwood Landing, N. Y. ("AG" products); (9) The Craftint Mfg. Co., 18501 Euclid Ave., Cleveland, Ohio ("Craftint" Graphic Art Materials); (10) C-Thru Graphics, 6 Britton Drive, Bloomfield, Conn. ("Better Letter," Dry Transfer Products, etc.); (11) Letraset, U.S.A. Inc., 33 New Bridge Road, Bergenfield, N. J. ("Letraset" Instant Lettering, "Letratone," "Pantone," etc.); (12) Visitype Graphics, Williams and Heintz Map Corporation, 8119 Central Avenue, Washington, D. C. ("Visitype," "Visitints," etc.); (13) Pressure Graphics, Inc., 1725 Armitage Court, Addison, Ill. ("Press-sure Lettering," "Press-sure Tones," "Press-sure Line Charting Tapes," etc.).

There are two basic types and six subtypes of stick-up lettering in accordance with the following classification:

Type I: *Separate Preprinted Letters and Figures*

1. Separate letters and figures preprinted on acetate with a backing of heat-resistant adhesive. This type of lettering is sometimes referred to as "cutout" lettering.

2. Pads of separate letters and figures printed on card-weight paper (and also on transparent acetate).

3. Separate letters and figures printed on acetate or plastic carrier sheets with a protective backing sheet. The letters and figures are dry-transferred or pressed onto a drawing by a burnishing instrument. This type of lettering is often labeled "pressure-sensitive" lettering.[4]

Type II: *Entire Words and Lines Printed in Accordance with Specifications for a Particular Chart or Series of Charts; Lettering Printed on Either Acetate or Paper, Usually with Self-adhesive*

1. Lettering printed on a proof press or some other kind of press where metal type is used.

2. Lettering printed on strips by a phototypesetting machine.

3. Lettering printed by an IBM Selectric Composer, Varityper, or other electrically operated special-face typewriter, usually with a carbon paper ribbon on acetate or on paper, usually with a self-adhesive.

Let us consider in more detail each of the specific types of stick-on lettering. Type I–1 is exemplified by cutout letters printed on thin acetate with a heat-resistant adhesive. Each letter is cut out with a knife, razor blade, or scalpel and placed in proper position on a chart and carefully burnished. A plastic "headline-setter" and/or

Figure 2–14. Freehand vertical fractions.

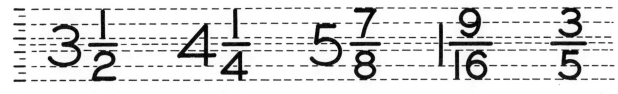

guidelines under each letter are helpful in aligning and spacing the letters.

The best known pre-printed stick-on lettering represented by Type I-2 is known commercially as ''Fototype.'' Fototype letters are printed separately on card stock (also acetate) and collated into small pads with perforated edges. Each letter is placed in juxtaposition by means of a ''composing stick.'' After a word or line is set in the composing stick the letters are held together by a strip of transparent or opaque tape and is then removed from the composing stick. After surplus edges are trimmed, the lettering is mounted in the chart with rubber cement or wax adhesive. If double-coated adhesive tape is used to strip the letters together, it is not necessary to use rubber cement or wax adhesive to mount the lettering on the chart.

The third type of separate, stick-on letters and figures (Type I-3) is printed on transparent plastic sheets, similar in certain respects to Type I-1. Instead of cutting out each letter and mounting it on the chart with its self-adhesive, the letter is transferred directly onto the chart by pressure with a burnishing instrument. Frequently a ball-point pen or a pencil is used for this purpose.

To compose the lettering for an entire chart by means of pre-printed separate letter stick-ons may turn out to be laborious and time consuming. This is particularly the case with large and complicated charts having a considerable amount of lettering. Moreover, when the lettering is small it may be found more difficult to compose words and lines by cutting out and aligning separate letters. For special titles and labels requiring large letters or where the chart is relatively uncomplicated, cutout or pressure-sensitive separate lettering may be both practicable and economical. Of course, as indicated previously, the type of lettering used for any particular chart or series of charts must be evaluated in terms of such criteria as: (1) legibility, (2) appropriateness, (3) esthetic appeal, (4) time required, (5) ease of execution, and (6) cost.

As indicated in a preceding paragraph, the second major type of stick-on lettering consists of entire words or lines prepared especially for particular charts. The first subtype, Type II-1, represents words and lines printed by metal type either on self-adhesive acetate or paper. Generally, since printing press equipment is not readily accessible it is customary to have the work done by a commercial printer. The usual procedure is to turn over to the printer a typewritten copy of all the words, sentences, and figures required for a chart or series of charts with the precise style, size, and form of type specified. Of course, the price of work of this kind will vary from one printer to another and from one locality to another. Generally, in light of the quality of the work as well as the time and labor that might be saved, this type of lettering under certain circumstances could turn out to be most economical.

The other types of stick-on lettering in this category (Type II-2 and Type II-3) are similar in some respects to the first type, except that different printing processes are utilized. In the case of Type II-2 the lettering is formed by a phototypographical process. Machines of this kind are usually equipped with keyboard control for composing the words and sentences to be reproduced. Within the machine a negative image is projected onto a photosensitive strip that after chemical development comes out of the machine as a continuous photographic print of the desired words and figures. The photographic strip then can be cut and mounted on the chart. Rubber cement or wax adhesive are most suitable for mounting strips of this kind. There is a large number of phototypographical machines on the market which range in price from a few hundred dollars to several thousand dollars.[5]

In the third type of lettering (Type II-3) the imprinting process is done by an electrically operated typewriter or similar machine equipped preferably with a carbon-paper ribbon. The IBM Selectric Composer or Varityper with special type faces and sizes is frequently used. For example, the size of the type of an IBM Selectric Composer ranges from 6 points to 12 points. The words and figures typed on self-adhesive paper or acetate are cut out and placed in position on the chart. Since the typewriter lacks the versatility as well as the variety of letters with respect to style, form, and size of a well-equipped printing press or phototypographical machine, its use is restricted in graphic presentation.

In terms of time, labor, and convenience as well as perhaps quality, the type of stick-on lettering

---

[5] At the present time there are over two dozen photounit or phototypesetter machines on the market. The following are a few examples: (1) Compugraphic CG 7200 (Compugraphic Corp.); (2) Diatype and Ministar (Berthold Fototype); (3) Filmotype (Alphatype Sales Corp.); (4) Vari Typer Headliner (Division of Addressograph-Multigraph Corp.); (5) Strip Printer (Strip Printer, Inc.); and (6) Visutek (Visutek Graphic Products Division).

representing entire words and lines is superior to that of the preprinted separate stick-on letter. However, this is not to say that the separate stick-on letter does not have its special values and applications. The cost factor seems to be the most apparent disadvantage of the stick-on lettering in which entire words and lines are printed according to specifications. The individual graphic specialist, to say nothing of many offices and agencies, simply cannot afford to invest in a high-quality, versatile machines for producing stick-up lettering of this kind. Of course, in organizations where large numbers of charts are constructed, phototypesetting machines are virtually indispensable. Accordingly, where only a relatively small number of charts are produced, it may be more expedient and economical to have some outside establishment prepare the lettering. This can be done by a commercial printer with metal type and a proof press or on a phototypographical machine. Many printing plants as well as other establishments are equipped with phototypesetter machines. Work done by phototypographic process should be less expensive than work set in metal type.

The other alternatives would be to use preprinted separate stick-on letters or mechanical lettering equipment such as the Rapidograph, Wrico, Leroy, or Letterguide. In any case, this is an individual decision based on one's needs, objectives, preferences, and resources.

Lettering and Typographical Terminology

Since the hundreds of styles and sizes in various preprinted forms are described and identified in typographical terminology, it would be helpful to clarify a few of the more commonly used concepts.

Type face is descriptive of the style of letter. For simplicity, type faces may be subsumed under seven general categories:[6]

1. Oldstyle. This type style group is patterned after letter forms used on classical Roman inscriptions. Examples are Garamond and Caslon.

[6] International Paper Company, *Pocket Pal: A Graphic Arts Production Handbook,* New York: International Paper Company, 1974, pp. 40–41.

2. Modern. The term "modern" refers not to a time period, but to a style of type designed almost 200 years ago. This group possesses some similarity to *oldstyle* but has a much greater degree of mechanical perfection. Examples are Times Roman and Caledonia.

3. Square Serif. This is a contemporary-type style. The letters have square or blocked serifs. Clarendon and Cairo are examples. A "serif" is one of the relatively fine lines of a letter, especially one of the horizontal lines at the top or bottom, as of the letter I.

4. Sans Serif. Simplicity of design characterizes this group. The letters have no serifs, and the face is generally even in overall weight. Helvetica and Futura are examples.

5. Script. Designed to simulate handwriting, "script" type is used mostly for special affects, formal invitations, and announcements. Examples are Commercial script and Bank script.

6. Text Letters. This group resembles the hand-drawn letters of the early scribes. It is usually selected for religious documents, certificates, diplomas, and invitations. Old English and Engravers Text are examples.

7. Decorative Types. These are novelty styles or faces and are used primarily to command attention. They are designed to express different moods, and may be eccentric in appearance.

In preparing statistical charts some form of sans serif are found most appropriate. Helvetica and Futura light or medium vertical capitals are found especially satisfactory in graphic presentation. The lettering style in most of the charts in this book belongs to one or the other of these classifications. For special cases such as large charts for exhibit purposes, some form of modern style or square serif might be used. Although these styles are attractive and artistic, they are too elaborate and too formal for statistical charts. Script, text letters, and decorative types, because of their ornate and idiosyncratic features should seldom, if ever, be used for statistical charts. It is strongly recommended that the reader examine most carefully the many lettering styles and sizes found in one or more of the commercial catalogs listed in this chapter.

Each style of lettering includes both capital letters called "uppercase" and small letters, referred to as "lowercase." Usually the lettering in statistical charts is all *capital* or *uppercase,* although it is not uncommon to use both *uppercase* and *lowercase* letters.

The various letter styles also may be "vertical" (or "roman") or "slanted" (or "italic"). Generally, *vertical* lettering is preferable to the slanted form for statistical charts as it is simpler, more readable, and more compatible with the printing in most books and periodicals. However, for special legends and explanatory notes, slanted lettering may be found effective. It is extremely important that the style, size, and form of lettering for statistical charts be selected with the utmost discretion.

A complete alphabet of one size and style of uppercase and lowercase characters, with figures, punctuation marks, and whatever else is necessary for printing with that variety of type is called a "font."

When all the type sizes and type styles of a particular *type* are grouped together they are called a "family" of type. For example, in referring to the Helvetica type family it is essential to specify the several variations, such as: (1) Helvetica light, (2) Helvetica light italic, (3) Helvetica regular, (4) Helvetica regular italic, (5) Helvetica medium, and (6) Helvetica medium italic.

In typography there are two basic units of measurement, *points* and *picas*. There are 12 points in a pica and approximately 6 picas in an inch. A point is approximately $\frac{1}{72}$ in., which, of course, indicates 72 points to the inch. The size of type is measured in points. Usually type is available in sizes ranging from 6 to 72 points. The overall length of lines is measured in picas.

Lettering Made with Manually Operated Mechanical Devices

Various mechanical lettering devices may be found to be both efficient and economical in the construction of statistical charts. In fact, this technique is the preferred type of lettering among many spe-

cialists in the field. This procedure is relatively convenient, inexpensive, simple, and flexible.

The best-known mechanical lettering instruments include the Wrico, Leroy, Rapidograph, Varigraph, and Letterguide. Wrico is manufactured in two different types, the standard and the scriber. The standard Wrico lettering equipment consists of guides made of transparent plastic with a series of openings so shaped that when the point of a Wrico pen is moved in contact with their sides, the letters of the alphabet, numerals, and various designs are formed. In the standard Wrico lettering device the pen is not part of a machine but is held in the hand and moved in various directions according to the patterns on the plastic guide. The guide is placed directly over the portion of the layout on which the lettering is to be done. The guides are grooved on the undersides so that the ink will not be smeared when they are moved from one character to another. There are several different sizes of the standard pen, in addition to several sizes of the brush pen. The particular pen that is used is determined by the size and style of letters. Many different styles of lettering can be made, including Gothic, architectural, and Roman.

The scriber type of mechanical lettering devices include the Leroy, Rapidograph, Wrico, Varigraph, and Letterguide. The basic structural and mechanical features of the various scriber type of lettering devices are similar. Each possesses certain advantages with respect to cost, type, and variety of letters and ease and speed of operation. In the scriber type of lettering device the scriber follows the outline of a letter in a template. The pen, which is attached to a separate arm, reproduces the letter on the drawing. There are many sizes and styles of letters with corresponding pens of varying widths.

Every specialist in the field should become sufficiently acquainted with one or more of the mechanical lettering devices so as to judge its application and relative efficiency in the construction of statistical charts.

CHAPTER THREE

RECTILINEAR COORDINATE CHARTS

PERHAPS ONE OF THE BEST KNOWN AND certainly one of the most frequently used type of chart is the simple arithmetic line chart. The arithmetic line chart is one of several types of rectilinear coordinate charts. In addition to the simple arithmetic line chart, there are such variations as the multiple-amount-scale chart, multiple-time-scale chart, charts with special referent lines, charts with adaptations for portraying projections and other kinds of estimates, various kinds of surface charts, such as simple-surface or silhouette chart, net-difference surface chart, and multiple-strata surface chart. All these forms of rectilinear coordinate charts pertain to time series. In addition, however, the rectilinear coordinate chart is used to portray frequency distributions and many other types of charts in which there are two variables. For the most part discussions of non-time-series rectilinear coordinate charts are found in Chapters 6 and 7.

The rectilinear coordinate chart is also referred to as a "rectangular" or "Cartesian coordinate" graph. The basic form of this type of graph is derived by plotting one or more series of figures on a coordinate surface in which the successive plotting points are joined together in the form of a continuous line, customarily referred to as a "curve."

A curve on a graph of this kind is not necessarily smooth and regular, but rather may be straight and angular. The system of coordinates used in the rectilinear chart is laid out in reference to a pair of intersecting lines, called "axes," which are drawn at right angles. The horizontal line is referred to as the "X-axis," or "axis of abscissas," and the vertical, the "Y-axis," or "axis of ordinates." These axes divide the region of the plane into four compartments, called "quadrants," which are numbered counterclockwise, beginning with the upper right quadrant. Figure 3–1 indicates the basic structural characteristics of a rectangular coordinate system. It will be observed further that the point where the two axes intersect is referred to as the "origin of coordinates." Measurements to the right and above the origin are "positive" (plus), whereas measurements to the left and below the origin are negative (minus). In quadrant I the values on both the X- and Y-axes are positive, in quadrant II the values are negative on the X-axis and positive on the Y-axis, in quadrant III the values are negative on both axes, and in quadrant IV the values are positive on the X-axis and negative on the Y-axis. The X- and Y-axes, respectively, can be divided into any desired units of measurements, beginning with the point of origin as zero. Any point plotted in the field of coordinates is determined by distances on both the X- and Y-axes. In Figure 3–1, for example, point P has been located in relation to the following values: $Y = +6.0$ and $X = +4.7$. In descriptive graphic presentation, quadrant I is used almost exclusively. Occasionally quadrant IV may be used along with quadrant I to portray both positive and negative values. Quadrant II is used occasionally and quadrant III rarely, because two negative scales are involved.

In portraying time series, when should the rectilinear coordinate chart be used? Although the rectilinear coordinate chart is particularly effective in portraying time series such as movements or trends over a period of years or variations covering shorter periods—hours, days, weeks, or months—there are, of course, other techniques for charting time series, such as the semilogarithmic graph and the column chart. Under such circumstances the beginner frequently raises the simplistic question as to which technique is best for presenting time series. However, it would be difficult, if not impossible, to present a simple generalized categorical prescription concerning when to use and when not to use the rectilinear coordinate chart, or, in fact, any other graphic form. In selecting a particular graphic form for portraying time series or other kinds of statistics, consideration should be given to the meaning of the data, the problem at hand, the purpose of the chart, and the audience to whom the chart is directed.

Genuine expertise in graphic presentation assumes a thorough knowledge of the characteristics

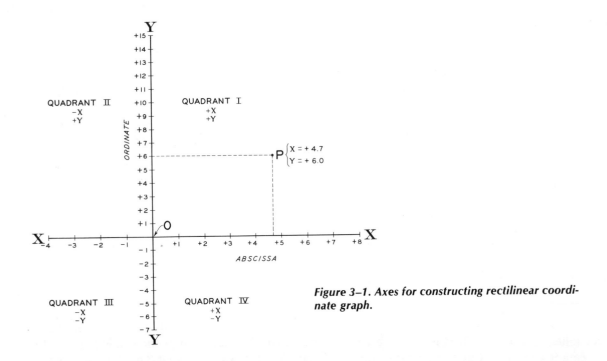

Figure 3-1. *Axes for constructing rectilinear coordinate graph.*

of all the basic graphic forms, including their specific advantages and shortcomings. It is illogical and unrealistic to think of a "best" graphic form in the abstract for presenting time-series data or any other special type of data. The discussion in this chapter covers not only the essential features, techniques, and standards of rectilinear coordinate charts, but also their many applications including their special strengths and weaknesses.

ESSENTIAL COMPONENTS OF ARITHMETIC LINE CHART

Figure 3-2 indicates the characteristic components of the arithmetic line chart. Many of the elements and standards required for the arithmetic line chart also are generally applicable to other graphic forms. These facts are brought out more clearly in succeeding chapters.

Title

The title of a chart is customarily placed at the top, outside of the grid. This is true not only of the rectilinear coordinate chart but of other types as well. Occasionally, the title may be located underneath the chart usually in combination with one or more lines of explanation. In such case the title is set in regular bold type similar to a substantial proportion of the charts in this book. When the title is located at the top the size of the lettering for the title should be larger than any other. As a working principle, the title of a chart should answer clearly and simply the following three basic questions: What? Where? When? Care should be taken to eliminate all superfluous words. A title that is too long may take valuable space that should be used for the main part of the chart. Moreover, a title that is too long, poorly worded, or needlessly technical can detract from the quality and impact of an otherwise good chart. A succinct catchy title, free of journalistic or sensational coloring, will be found especially appropriate for most charts. Normally, a title should not be longer than two lines. Subtitles are sometimes used to explain or qualify the main title, but they should never be used unless they are absolutely necessary. Frequently, explanatory notes may serve as a substitute for subtitles. If at all possible, abbreviations should never be used in a title unless they are standard or generally familiar. The title, as well as the basic design of the chart itself, should be compatible with the audience it is designed to serve. Accordingly, titles, as well as the charts themselves, for the popular lecture group would differ from those prepared for technical and scholarly journals.

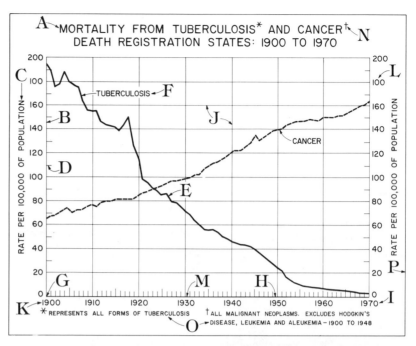

Figure 3-2. Illustration of essential characteristics and rules for an arithmetic coordinate chart. A. Title at top. B. Axis of ordinates or Y axis. C. Scale legend for Y axis. D. Scale points. E. Curves differentiated—solid and dashed. F. Contiguous legend for curves. G. Origin. H. Zero line heavier than other coordinate lines. I. Lettering arranged horizontally whenever possible. J. Grid or coordinate lines—no more should be indicated than is necessary. K. Scale figures for X axis. L. Scale figures for Y axis. M. Axis of abscissae or X axis. N. Reference symbol. O. Explanatory note. P. Border—optional.

Scales

In a rectilinear coordinate chart the horizontal scale represents the so-called independent variable, and the vertical scale, the dependent variable. The usual practice, for example, is to consider time as the independent variable, and amount as the dependent variable. Usually the divisions on the horizontal scale are determined by the time units in the original data. The unit of time may be represented by hours, days, weeks, months, quarters, years, or decades. The divisions on the X-scale are indicated by both scale lines and scale points, or ticks. Normally, the scale begins with the earliest plotting period and ends with the latest. However, it may be found expedient to allow for future plottings by extending the horizontal scale by one or more major time units. Such an arrangement permits the updating of a chart from time to time.

The planning of the horizontal scale may not always turn out to be simple and straightforward be-

cause of incomplete or incomparable data or because of shifting and ambiguous time units. For example, sometimes data are based on either calendar or fiscal years. Moreover, the term "fiscal year" may be defined differently by different organizations and agencies. A day may mean a "work day," a "store day," or a "24-hour day." Sometimes the basic time-unit may change from years to quarters, from quarters to months, or vice versa. Under such circumstances in designing the scale as well as plotting the data proper adjustment should be made to maintain comparability and continuity. It will be observed from the charts in this chapter that the major and minor time units include months, quarters, calendar years, fiscal years, quinquennia, and decennia.

Figure 3-3 illustrates a few problems relating to the plotting of data as a consequence of irregular time intervals, period and point data, omission of data, and shifting time intervals. Panel 1 exemplifies standard plotting for point data. Panel

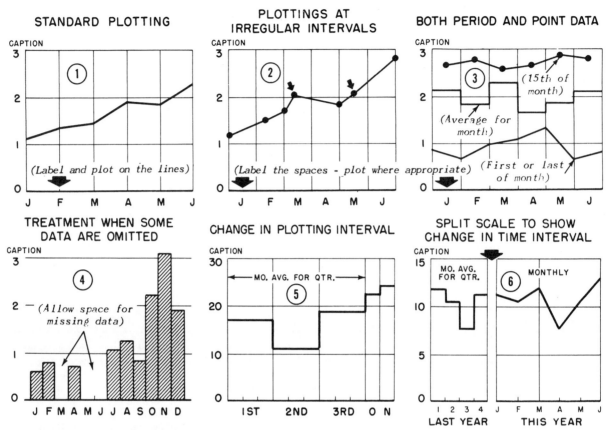

Figure 3–3. Illustration of time–scale plotting techniques. Note standard plotting along with special plottings resulting from irregular intervals, omission of data, and other problems. (From Department of the Army, Standards of Statistical Presentation, *Washington: Government Printing Office, 1966, p. 82.)*

2 shows how data are plotted as a result of unequal time intervals.[1] Panel 3 portrays the plotting of both point data and period data. Panel 4 shows acceptable plotting procedure when there are omissions in the data. Panel 5 demonstrates how data are plotted when there are changes in the major time unit. Panel 6 indicates how data represented by two different time units (quarters and months) can be compared by plotting data on separate grids placed in juxtaposition.

In a rectilinear coordinate chart the amount scale is always represented by the vertical axis, the axis of ordinates or *Y*-axis. The zero baseline should be shown on all rectilinear coordinate charts, except when the data represent index numbers where the reference value is 100 or some other special number. When index numbers are plotted there are usually values both above and below the referent line. As a matter of emphasis, the zero baseline or other referent line is made a little bolder than other grid lines.

The intervals or units selected for the vertical scale should be easy to read and, of course, cover the entire range of values. The basic units of measurement may extend upward into thousands, millions, or even billions. Units or major scale divisions that are easy to read such as 2, 4, 5, 10, 20, 25, 50, and a 100 should be chosen. Awkward divisions such as 7, 11, 13, 17, 19, 21, and 23, for example, should be avoided. If the values of the vertical scale run into the thousands, millions, or larger numbers the zeros are commonly dropped and the scale designation should read ''in thousands of . . .'' or ''in millions of. . . .'' The major scale divisions should be kept to a minimum, if possible less than 10 or 12. The size of the numbers as well

---

[1] When data represent specific points of time, they are known as ''point data,'' and when they refer to periods of time they are described as ''period data.'' These concepts are discussed more fully in a subsequent section in this chapter.

as the range of values to be plotted, of course, will influence the number of scale divisions.

In determining the divisions for the vertical scale, it is essential that the entire range of the data be included. For example, if the range of a series to be plotted varies from 8 to 237 the major scale divisions might be 20, with 12 units extending to 240; 25, with 10 units extending to 250; and 50, with 5 units extending to 250. The coordinate lines may then be drawn at intervals of 20, 25, or 50, and the scale points also can represent even units of, say, 5 or 10 for major divisions of 20 or 50, or 5 for a major division of 25.

Where the values of a series are such that a large part of the grid would be superfluous, it is common practice to break the grid, thus eliminating the unused portion of the scale. Failure to indicate a break in the scale is a frequent omission that distorts the data and gives an erroneous visual impression. Figures 3–4, 3–5, and 3–6 are illustrations of rectilinear coordinate charts in which the vertical scales are broken. Figure 3–4 illustrates why a large portion of a grid is sometimes superfluous.

All the values for the series of fertility rates (total number of births per 1000 women in the childbearing ages—15 to 44 years) in the United States from 1915 to 1970 range between 75.8 in 1936 to 125 in 1915. The vertical scale between zero and 75 is not required and as indicated by B, may properly be omitted by means of a broken scale. Figure 3–5 is another illustration of an arithmetic line chart in which the vertical scale is broken. The break is shown by a wavy line and a zero baseline is entirely omitted. This technique for showing a break in the ordinal scale is more informal than that indicated in Figure 3–4. In Figure 3–6 there are three series of data depicting comparative trends in employment, unemployment, and total civilian labor force. The figures range in value from a few million to close to 100 million. The number of unemployed persons are encompassed in the first major scale division from 0 to 10 million. On the other hand, the number of employed persons and the number of persons in the civilian labor force occupy the upper portion of the scale ranging in value from around 75 million to almost 100 million. The portion of the

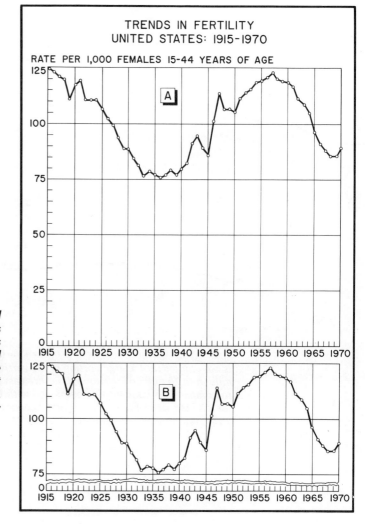

Figure 3–4. Arithmetic line chart with unbroken and broken ordinal scales. In A, the vertical scale is complete, but only the upper portion of the grid is actually used. In B, the vertical scale is broken, and the part of the grid covering slightly more than the range of the values on the curve is portrayed. (Chart drawn from original data published by the U.S. Bureau of the Census and the U.S. National Center for Health Statistics.)

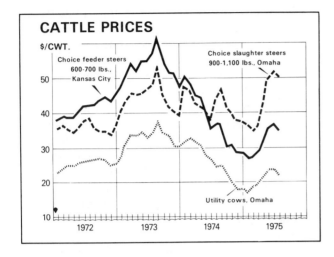

Figure 3–5. Rectilinear coordinate line graph with zero base line omitted. Note the wavy line that symbolizes a break in the scale. [From United States Department of Agriculture, 1975 Handbook of Agricultural Charts, Agricultural Handbook, (491), October 1975, p. 86.]

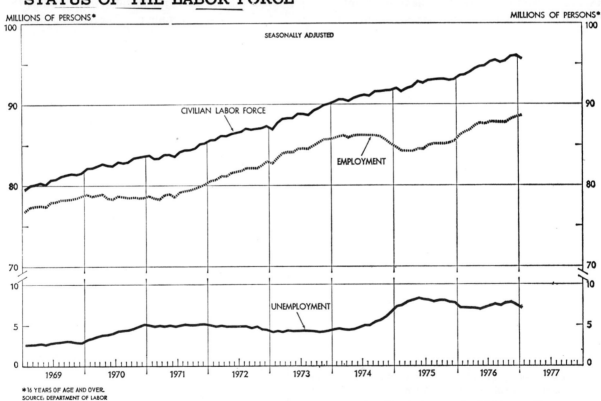

Figure 3–6. Another example of a broken vertical scale. In this illustration the zero base line is not omitted, but a large portion of the vertical scale is. Although the vertical scale from 10 million to 70 million is omitted, it is very easy to maintain continuity in the presentation and to compare the number of unemployed with the number employed and with the number in the civilian labor force. (From Joint Economic Committee, Economic Indicators, February 1977, Washington, Government Printing Office, 1977, p. 11.)

scale from 10 million to 70 million is superfluous and accordingly, a break in the vertical scale covering this range of values has been made.

Scale Figures and Legends[2]

Both horizontal and vertical scales should carry proper explanatory figures and legends. In Figure 3–2, for example, the horizontal-scale lines are drawn at 5-year intervals with specific designations, whereas between the respective scale lines intervening values are indicated by scale points or ticks. Where the meaning of the scale legend is obvious, as in the case of the horizontal axis in Figure 3–2, it may be omitted. However, where there are split years, fiscal years, quarters, or other special time units, horizontal scale designations may be essential. Because of space restrictions, it is frequently necessary to abbreviate or apostrophize scale figures and scale designations. For days of the week, three-letter or single one-letter abbreviations may be used, depending on available space. Similarly, three-letter abbreviations may be used for months, or even single-letter designations if necessary. Again, yearly designations may be apostrophized such as 1930, '40, '50, '60, '70, and '80. Of course, if there is sufficient space, abbreviations and apostrophizations should not be used. An examination of the horizontal-scale figures and legends of the charts in this chapter will provide further insight and suggestions.

Scale figures and legends for the vertical axes should be placed at the left side of the grid, except when the chart is very wide or when the horizontal grid lines are very close together. In such instances it may be found expedient, in order to avoid confusion, to place scale figures and legends on both sides of the grid.[3]

---

[2] The terms "scale designations," "scale headings," "scale captions," and "scale legends" are synonymous and may be used interchangeably.
[3] Since 1915 special committees sponsored by the American Society of Mechanical Engineers have published four reports on standards pertaining to time-series charts. The reader will find that these reports embody many useful principles and excellent suggestions; see *American Standard Time-Series Charts, A Manual of Design and Construction* (1938) and *American Standard Time-Series Charts,* ASA Y15.2-1960, New York: American Society of Mechanical Engineers, 1960.

There are three recommendations in the most recent report (1960) to which we take firm exception. The first,

The scale legend for the vertical axis, when possible, should be placed horizontally directly above the scale. Frequently, however, it will be found that the scale legend in this position greatly interferes with the title of the chart, and hence it may be necessary to run the legend either parallel to the scale or place it partially or completely in a horizontal position within the grid. Another alternative is to add the legend as a subtitle or as an explanatory phrase beneath the title. The vertical-scale legends

---

and most serious, is the recommendation that when there is only one amount scale (Y-axis or axis of ordinates) it should be placed on the right side.

> When interest is focused at the right (as in most time series that are brought up to date currently) the standard procedure is to show the scale at the right. [p. 38]

This recommendation strikes us as unrealistic, confusing, idiosyncratic, and contrary to almost universal usage. Happily, this recommendation is generally ignored by experienced practitioners of graphic presentation. Significantly, immediately following the preceding recommendation the following statements will be found:

> When interest is focused at the left (as in a series of data that has not progressed beyond the left side of the grid) there may be a special virtue in showing the scale at the left instead of the right. . . . Note: Engineers generally feel that the left is the *standard* location, because it shows that the chart is drawn in the right half (or the positive side of the Y-axis) of the Cartesian coordinate system. Therefore the customary location of the amount scale designations is at the left when the charts are to be drawn in engineering publications or to engineering audiences. [p. 38]

The second recommendation to which we take exception is concerned with curve patterns. On page 49 the following recommendation is found:

> A continuous line or "solid" pattern is best for general use, even when there are two or three curves on the chart. Unless the curves crisscross or run together, other patterns are seldom necessary.

We recommend that where there is more than one curve on a chart, each curve should be represented by a distinctive pattern.

The third recommendation, which we consider erroneous, pertains to the use of color on a multiple-curve chart.

> Colored curves are useful for contrast . . . However, the use of several colors may be more harm than good unless the designer knows how to use color properly. A safe procedure is to use only one color in addition to black. . . . [p. 50]

We do not believe that only one color in addition to black be used in a multiple-curve chart. If there are several curves, each curve should be differentiated by a well-chosen, distinctive color. As indicated in the text, there is a wide assortment of self-adhesive tapes with respect to pattern, colors, and width that are available commercially.

of the various charts in this chapter represent all four alternatives. When possible, it is the preferred practice to arrange all lettering in a chart horizontally.

To save space as well as make the scale figures and legends concise and simple, it is common practice to use symbols and abbreviations and to eliminate superfluous numbers. For example, if a scale represents millions of dollars, all zeros in the scale figures can be eliminated and the legend may read "millions of dollars," or "million dollars," or "million" with a dollar sign placed in front of the highest figure on the scale.

Grid Proportions

In laying out a grid for a rectangular coordinate chart, care should be taken to keep the scales in proper balance. More specifically, one of the first considerations is to determine what proportions will best suit the data at hand, since the slope or proportions of the grid have a very significant affect on the appearance of the curve (curves). A chart may be "correct" in every detail but badly proportioned. This fact holds true not only for

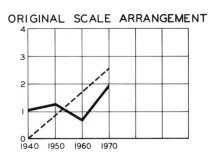

ORIGINAL SCALE ARRANGEMENT

Figure 3–7. Effect of scale alteration on shape and slope of curve. The solid curve represents movement, the dashed curve, trends.

CONTRACTING AMOUNT SCALE

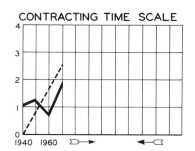

CONTRACTING TIME SCALE

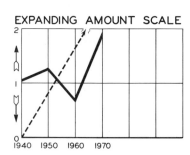

EXPANDING AMOUNT SCALE

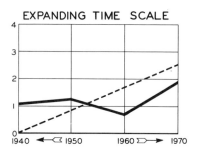

EXPANDING TIME SCALE

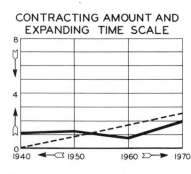

CONTRACTING AMOUNT AND EXPANDING TIME SCALE

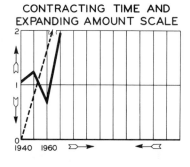

CONTRACTING TIME AND EXPANDING AMOUNT SCALE

rectilinear coordinate charts but also for bar, column, and other kinds of charts. It is extremely difficult, if not impossible, to specify hard and fast rules concerning the technique for determining the most appropriate proportions for any given chart. Trial-and-error experimentation by means of preliminary sketches may be found helpful. The grid should be made to fit the data, not vice versa. Space and other restrictions of the publication in which the chart is to appear may create additional problems. Sometimes a grid that is wider than high will be found most satisfactory, and at other times a grid higher than wide will be most appropriate. Generally a square grid possesses no advantage for a chart of this kind. Figure 3–7 illustrates how contracting or expanding either or both the vertical and horizontal scales can radically alter the configuration of the curves and consequently convey entirely different visual impressions.

Grid Lines

The number of grid lines should be kept to a minimum. This means that there should be just enough coordinate lines in the field so that the eye can readily interpret the values at any point on the curve. No definite rule can be specified as to the optimum number of lines in a grid. This must be left to the discretion of the chart maker and can come only from experience. The size of the chart, the type and range of the data, the number of curves, the length and detail of the period covered, as well as other factors, will help to determine the number of grid lines.

Figure 3–8 illustrates three different coordinate patterns. Illustration A shows a grid with a relatively large number of coordinate lines. Some spe-

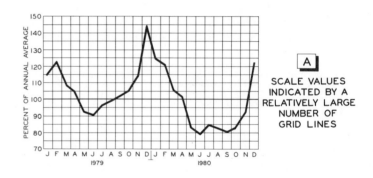

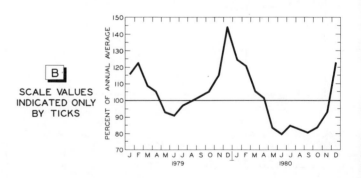

Figure 3–8. The frequency of rulings for both the horizontal and the vertical axes should be sufficient to guide the eye to an approximate reading of the values. See text for further discussion.

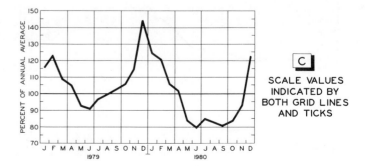

cialists in the field of graphic presentation might consider some of the rulings superfluous. On the commercially printed graph paper coordinate lines are actually spaced much closer together. This is one reason why printed chart paper is not recommended. One is forced to adapt the design of the graph to an arbitrary and rigid system of coordinates without regard to the type of data to be presented. It will be observed further that illustration B contains no grid lines, except the 100% baseline, with all other values on both axes indicated by scale points or ticks. Some chart makers prefer this design, although to others it would seem that there are not sufficient grid lines to measure even approximately the values on the respective scales. Illustration C represents a more balanced pattern in which both grid lines and ticks are used.

Plotting Points

In plotting data on the X-axis of a rectangular coordinate chart, the points may be located either on scale lines or on the spaces between the scale lines,

depending on the design of the chart, which is usually determined by the type of data to be portrayed. When data represent specific points of time, they are known as "point data," and when they refer to periods of time they are described as "period data." Point data should be plotted on specific lines, and period data, midway between specific point-of-time rulings. The distinction between point data and period data is not always followed in actual practice. It is more common to plot both kinds of data on specific lines rather than in spaces between grid lines. Figure 3–9 illustrates the plotting of data according to points of time and periods of time. An examination of the other charts in this chapter will reveal both types of plotting.

Differentiating Curves

Curves for any kind of line chart, such as rectilinear coordinate and semilogarithmic charts, should stand out prominently and be clearly differentiated from one another. The problem of differentiation may be especially difficult when there are several

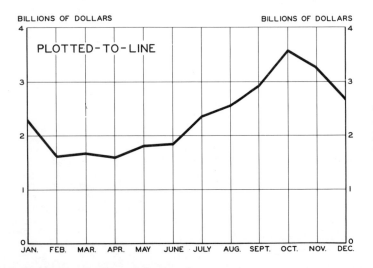

Figure 3–9. In practice, data of this kind are plotted either to space or to line. Theoretically, "point data (values as of specific points of time)" should be plotted on point–of–time rulings, and "period data (values for periods of time)" should be plotted midway between point–of–time ruling.

curves that are close together and cross one another. The use of colors to differentiate curves may be found satisfactory, especially if the chart is to be used for exhibit purposes and not for reproduction. The cost of reproduction in color is considerably more expensive than in black. Moreover, colored lines cannot be effectively reproduced in such inexpensive processes as diazo, blueprint, xerox, and photostat.[4] Colored lines reproduced in this way show such slight difference in shading tones that they are virtually indistinguishable.

Generally, a more practical technique in differentiating curves is by means of single-pattern designs. For example, curves may be represented by a full line, dashed line, dot-and-dash line, or some other pattern such as that illustrated in Figure 3–10. These curve patterns have been drawn with pen and ink.

An excellent selection of preprinted tapes in varying widths with clear and consistent patterns as well as with wide range of colors will be found

useful and economical in time and money for curves in rectilinear coordinate and semilogarithmic charts. The tapes come in rolls and are coated with a heat-resistant self-adhesive. Plastic and metallic dispensers, though not necessary for applying the tapes to charts, may be found convenient. The tapes are printed in matte and glossy finish on both transparent and opaque material. Tapes printed on an opaque base material are recommended for photographic reproduction, and those printed on transparent material are suitable for diazo and other forms of contact reproduction. The tapes as indicated above are available in several widths such as $\frac{1}{64}$ in., $\frac{1}{32}$ in., $\frac{1}{16}$ in., $\frac{3}{32}$ in., $\frac{1}{8}$ in., $\frac{3}{16}$ in., $\frac{1}{4}$ in., $\frac{1}{2}$ in., $\frac{3}{4}$ in., 1 in. and 2 in. There are more than a dozen different patterns and many shades and colors, including black, white, red, orange, blue, green, brown, purple, and yellow along with metallic and fluorescent hues. To obtain additional information concerning preprinted tapes that are available commercially, it is suggested that at least four or five of the catalogs listed in footnote 4 in Chapter 2 be examined.

In differentiating a series of curves on a line

---

[4] Xerox copies can now be reproduced in color, but the cost is substantially higher than in black and white.

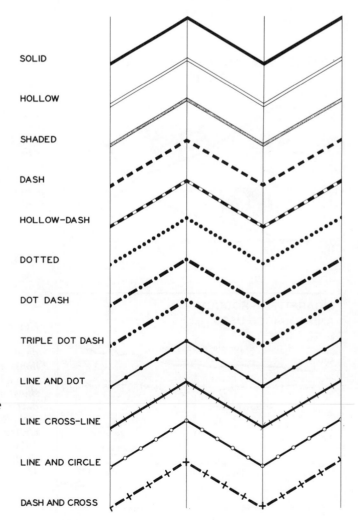

Figure 3–10. Curve patterns for various kinds of line charts.

SOLID

HOLLOW

SHADED

DASH

HOLLOW-DASH

DOTTED

DOT DASH

TRIPLE DOT DASH

LINE AND DOT

LINE CROSS-LINE

LINE AND CIRCLE

DASH AND CROSS

chart, consideration also must be given to the number of curves as well as their distribution on the grid. At times it may be found extremely difficult to differentiate these curves properly, especially if there is a tendency for several of them to be distributed on a relatively narrow portion of the grid with frequent crossing or overlapping. When this situation occurs, one of three alternatives may be selected: (1) enlarge the overcrowded portion of the grid, (2) use some other form of graphic presentation, or (3) abandon altogether any attempt to chart such data. Charts at all times should be unambiguous and easily interpreted.

Curve Labels

To facilitate interpretation, each curve in a rectilinear coordinate or semilogarithmic chart should be clearly and unmistakably labeled. Labels can either be located contiguous to the curves, usually with arrows, lines, or slightly tapered wedges pointing to them, or listed along with the curve patterns in a special key or legend. Most commonly the key legend is located in the grid so that it will not interfere with the interpretation of the chart. Contiguous curve labels are more

straightforward and more easily read since they require less movement of the eye and less remembering. Contiguous labels should be: (1) simple and succinct, (2) easily read, (3) reasonably close to the curve, but never directly on the curve, (4) arranged so as to effect a balanced composition of the chart, and (5) in a horizontal position.

ARITHMETIC LINE CHARTS WITH SPECIAL FEATURES

Multiple-amount Scales

Although as a general principle it is inadvisable to include more than one amount scale on an arithmetic chart, occasionally a multiple-amount-scale arrangement possesses certain advantages. It is important, however, for the beginner to be aware of the pitfalls inherent in this arrangement. Figure 3–11 illustrates an arithmetic line chart with two scales, the one on the left representing horses and mules and the one on the right, tractors. The trends of the two curves are clear, but unless extreme caution is taken in examining and interpreting the chart, an entirely false message may be conveyed to the mind of the unwary reader. This fact

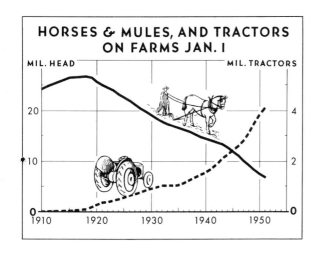

Figure 3–11. A Multiple–amount–scale arithmetic line chart. Scale on left indicates millions of head of horses and mules, and the scale on the right, millions of tractors. Extreme caution must be used in interpreting charts of this kind. (From United States Department of Agriculture, 1952 Agricultural Outlook Charts, p. 28.)

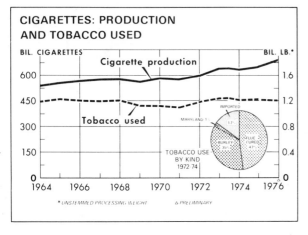

Figure 3–12. A Multiple–amount–scale rectilinear coordinate chart. The left scale indicates cigarette production expressed in billions, and the right scale, tobacco used expressed in billions of pounds. A pie chart showing the proportions of the kinds of tobacco used during the 1972–1974 period is included in the body of the chart. [From United States Department of Agriculture, 1976 Handbook of Agricultural Charts, Agricultural Handbook, (504), October 1976, p. 166.]

was convincingly illustrated when several university students were asked to indicate what the chart showed. Visually, the chart may seem to indicate that after 1944 there were more tractors than horses, but when the values for the respective scales are examined more carefully, this actually is not the case. The lowest value represented by the curve for horses and mules, for example, shows that there are approximately six million horses and mules as compared to approximately four million tractors.

When multiple-amount scales are used they normally should be limited to two scales. More are likely to cause confusion. The zero or other baseline for multiple-amount scales should never be omitted. The curves should start from a common baseline, and the divisions of both scales should be spaced in the same manner.

Figure 3–12 is another example of a multiple-amount-scale chart, but without the interpretive pitfalls of Figure 3–11. The two curves represent complementary measures of cigarette production. The volume of production is indicated by two indexes—the number of cigarettes manufactured and the amount of tobacco used, expressed in pounds. The comparison of the two curves is simple and straightforward. It will be observed that the spacing of the units on each of the scales is similar. Apparently there is a tendency for the number of cigarettes produced to increase at a slightly higher rate than the amount of tobacco used. The small insert in the form of a pie chart portrays additional relevant information concerning the kinds of tobacco used in cigarette production.

Repeated Time Scale

Two or more curves showing monthly, quarterly, or daily figures for different periods of time may be superimposed on the same grid. The most common application of this type of chart is the portrayal of monthly data on a 12-month time scale. This technique makes it possible to compare different series of data by bringing them into close juxtaposition. Figure 3–13 clearly reveals the monthly patterns of the total death rate and the infant mortality rate in the United States. In general, it shows the highest mortality during the colder months and lowest mortality during the warmer months. Also, there is a progressive decline in both the total death rate and the infant mortality rate from 1973 to 1975. If the data had been plotted on a grid as a single continuous curve, with the years arranged in chronological succession, it would have been extremely difficult to make the same clear and accurate comparisons concerning seasonal mortality differentials.

Another illustration of the repeated time scale is shown by Figure 3–14, which portrays the monthly distribution of visits to the National Park System Areas for 1973, 1974, and 1975. The basic configuration of the curves for all three years is characterized by a pronounced midsummer peak that is largely attributable to weather variations and traditional vacation patterns. The chart also reveals substantial increases in the number of visits in 1975 in comparison to 1973 and 1974. The total number of visits in millions was 215.58 for 1973, 217.44 for 1974, and 238.85 for 1975.

A technique similar to the repeated time scale by means of which comparisons can be made between two or more temporal series covering different periods of time is the "multiple time scale." For example, to compare trends and variations of some social, economic, or other phenomenon during World Wars I and II, the horizontal axis would carry double scale figures, placed one above the other beginning with 1918 and 1941, and followed chronologically with 1919 and 1942, 1920 and 1943,

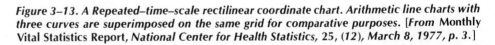

Figure 3–13. A Repeated–time–scale rectilinear coordinate chart. Arithmetic line charts with three curves are superimposed on the same grid for comparative purposes. [From Monthly Vital Statistics Report, *National Center for Health Statistics, 25, (12), March 8, 1977, p. 3.]*

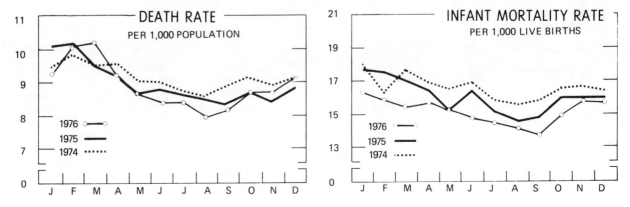

and so on. Of course, there would be only one series of figures for the vertical axis. By means of this technique the respective curves for the two war periods would be brought into close juxtaposition for ready comparison.

Arithmetic Charts with Special Referent Lines

In portraying positive and/or negative values from an established referent line covering a period of time, the arithmetic line chart is used most frequently. Normally, the referent line is designated zero or 100 and represents the so-called base period. The base period may be the average for a designated period of time or not infrequently the value for a particular year. The grid is laid out with reference to the base period expressed in terms of positive and/or negative numbers. One of the most widely used applications of this type of chart is the portrayal of "index numbers" by the economist. The familiar consumer price index is an example. In a period of inflation such as we have been experiencing for many years, all of the values have been positive.

Figure 3–15 shows trends and comparisons of three variables pertaining to milk production, expressed as percentages from a base period. In this instance the base period chosen was 1967. The chart clearly shows that the percentage decline of milk cows from 1958 to 1975 was very pronounced with a value of 140% in 1958 to an estimated figure of approximately 82% in 1975. During the same period the milk production per cow increased. However, as a consequence of the decrease in the number of milk cows, there was a slight decline in total milk production.

Another application of the arithmetic line chart for portraying positive and/or negative values from a special referent line is illustrated by Figure 3–16. The referent line represents the yearly average and

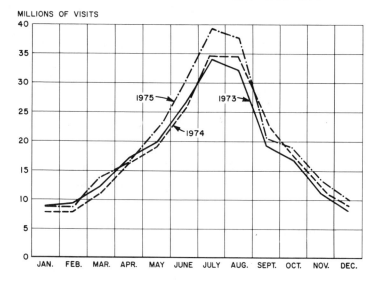

Figure 3–14. Another illustration of a repeated time scale. (Redrawn from chart in United States Bureau of the Census, Status, September 1976, p. 76.)

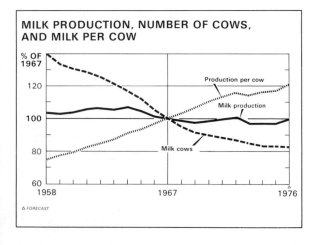

Figure 3–15. Another illustration of a rectilinear coordinate chart with a special referent line or base. In this chart various trends and comparisons relating to milk production are presented with reference to data for 1967, which is represented by a base line of 100%. [From United States Department of Agriculture, 1976 Handbook of Agricultural Charts, Agricultural Handbook, (504), October 1976, p. 95.]

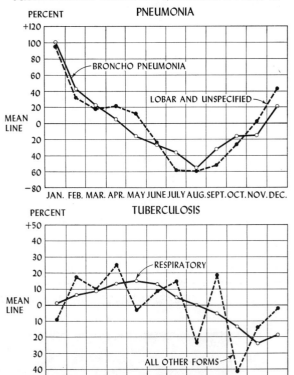

SEASONAL DISTRIBUTION, PNEUMONIA AND
TUBERCULOSIS MORTALITY, MINNESOTA: 1929-31

Figure 3–16. Another technique for showing seasonal variations by means of an arithmetic line chart. Ordinal values represent percentage deviations from annual average. (From Calvin F. Schmid, Mortality Trends in the State of Minnesota, Minneapolis: University of Minnesota Press, 1937, p. 170.)

is designated zero. The extraordinary seasonal pattern of pneumonia mortality is clearly indicated by this chart. In contrast, the incidence of mortality from respiratory and other forms of tuberculosis shows different as well as less distinctive seasonal patterns.

Figure 3–17 was designed to show the percentage increase in forcible rape in the United States from 1968 to 1973. The year 1968 was chosen as the base year and was designated zero. The percentage increases for each year from 1969 to 1973 are based on the actual number of offenses and on the rate per 100,000 of population.

Charts with Special Annotations, Symbols, or Other Similar Features

Frequently an arithmetic line chart can be made more effective by additional explanatory or de-

scriptive data in the form of annotations or pictorial symbols.[5]

Figure 3–18 is an excellent example of this type of chart. It portrays the basic history of inventions in telecommunications including the expanding capacity of communications technologies. The chart also shows that during the next two or three decades through computers and communications technologies additional extraordinary developments will take place. This is not "futurism" or science fiction, but technologies already under development. Some of the more significant of these changes are clearly indicated.

Portraying Trend Lines

It is frequent practice in analyzing and presenting temporal series to derive trend lines. A procedure of this kind is generally referred to as "curve fitting." Curve fitting requires not only a thorough understanding of necessary analytical techniques, but also good judgment. Under appropriate condi-

---

[5] A further discussion, including additional illustrations of charts with these features, particularly pictorial symbols and photographs, is presented in Chapter 9.

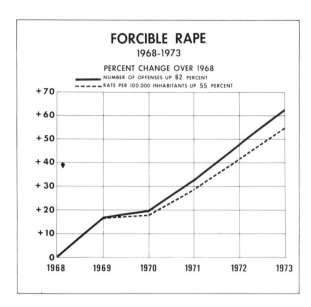

Figure 3–17. A rectilinear coordinate chart showing percentage year–by–year change from a selected base year. Two indices are portrayed: (1) the absolute number of offenses of rape that were reported, and (2) the incidence of rape per 100,000 persons. (From Federal Bureau of Investigation, Crime in the United States: 1973, Washington: Government Printing Office, 1974, p. 14.)

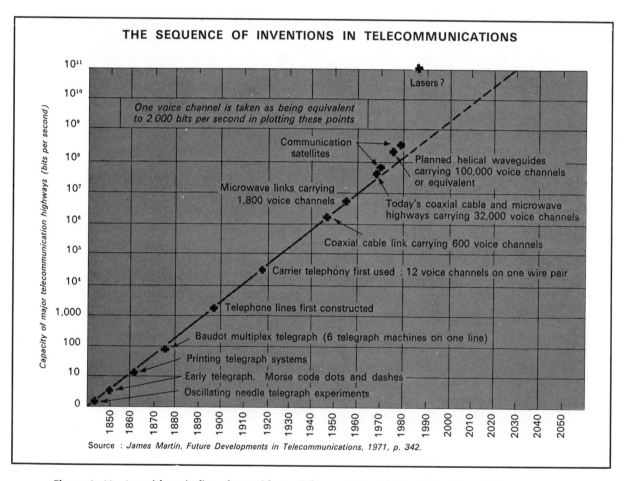

Figure 3–18. An arithmetic line chart with special annotations. [From "The Use of Computers and Telecommunications," OECD Observer, (62), February 1973, pp. 17–22, used by permission. The original source for this chart is James Martin, Future Developments in Telecommunications, 1971, p. 342.)

tions there are two good reasons to describe the trend of a series by some kind of curve:

First, it may be desired to measure the deviations from the trend. These deviations consist of cyclical, seasonal, and irregular movements. Frequently, obtaining these deviations is but one step in attempting to isolate cycles in order to study them. Second, it may be desired to study the trend itself, in order to note the effect of factors bearing on the trend, to compare one trend with another, to discover what effect trend movements have on cyclical fluctuations, or to attempt to forecast the future behavior of the trend.[6]

Trend lines may be developed by freehand estimation or by mathematical techniques such as a simple moving average, a weighted moving average, a semiaverage, the least-squares method, a second or higher degree equation, an asymptotic growth curve, or a Gompertz curve. After the values for the various points of a trend have been determined, they are connected either freehand or by means of a straightedge. A finished "smooth" trend line that manifests some degree of curvature is customarily drawn with a French curve or ship curve.

Figure 3–19 illustrates the superimposition of a trend line on an arithmetic chart. The plotted data are monthly seasonally adjusted fertility rates, and the trend line is a moving average. A 3- or 5-month moving average is appropriate for a series of this kind. The moving average in this illustration provides a simple technique for smoothing the data and revealing basic trends by dampening monthly fluctuations that may be considered fortuitous or even random.

---

[6] Frederick E. Croxton, Dudley J. Cowden, and Sidney Klein, *Applied General Statistics*, Englewood Cliffs, N. J.: Prentice-Hall, 1967, p. 229.

Arithmetic Line Charts Portraying Projections or Other Kinds of Estimates

When time series representing projections and other kinds of estimates are plotted on rectilinear coordinate grids it is common practice to identify the curves by distinctive patterns or other techniques. Figure 3–20 is an example of a chart that portrays past recorded trends of the population 65 years of age and over covering a period of over 70 years along with projections or forecasts covering a period of over 60 years. The projected curves show three series that can be described as low (series I), medium (series II), and high (series III) as determined by certain assumptions. The portions of the curves based on recorded data are shown by full lines and the portions representing projections, by dashed lines. The variations between the lowest and highest projections are emphasized by shading. It is apparent that the farther the projections extend into the future, the wider the variations. The trends and fluctuations in forecast figures portrayed in Figure 3–20 principally reflect increases in the number of births 65–84 years or so before the particular reference date. Improvements in mortality as measured by increases in life expectation after age 65 has had little impact. Average years of life lived below age 65, which can have a peak value of 65, increased from 44 years in 1900–1902 to 60 years in 1974 (i.e., by 16 years), whereas average years of life remaining at age 65 has moved ahead more slowly, from 11.9 years in 1900–1902 to 15.6 years in 1974 (i.e., by 3.7 years). For example, with respect to the number of births, the rapid drop during the 1920s and 1930s in all probability will result in a sharp decline in the amount and rate of increase of the population aged 65 years and over about 1990. Again, the births of the post-World War II "baby

Figure 3–19. A common technique for portraying actual data, as well as a more generalized trend. The trend line represents a simple moving average. [From Monthly Vital Statistics Report, National Center for Health Statistics, 26, (3), June 9, 1977, p. 2.]

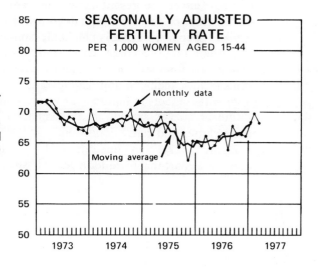

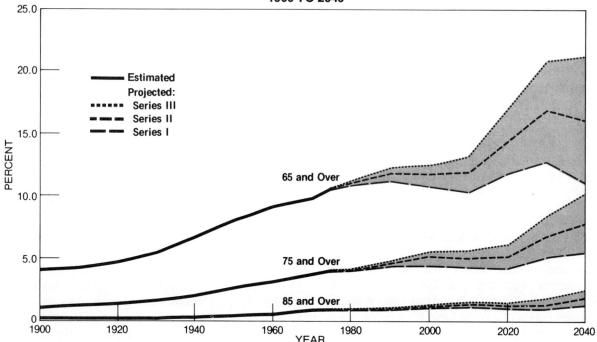

PERCENT OF THE TOTAL POPULATION IN THE OLDER AGES:
1900 TO 2040

Note: Estimates and projections as of July 1, except for 85 and over, 1900-1930, which relate to April 1. Points are plotted for years ending in zero except for 1975.

Figure 3–20. An illustration of a rectilinear coordinate chart portraying demographic projections. (From United States Bureau of the Census, Demographic Aspects of Aging and the Older Population in the United States, Special Studies, Current Population Reports, Series P-23, No. 59, 1976, p. 4.)

boom'' will have a very noticeable impact on the population aged 65 and over around 2010 to 2020.[7]

This chart could be improved in quality and effectiveness by (1) making the curve patterns in the legend consistent with those in the body of the chart, (2) increasing proportionally the vertical dimension of the chart, and (3) including scale lines instead of only ticks.

Figure 3–21 is another example of a series of forecasts drawn on a rectilinear coordinate grid. The five curves represent actual and anticipated enrollments to 1984 for four categories of elementary and secondary schools plus their combined total. Like the preceding chart, enrollment projections or forecasts are frequently presented in terms of low, medium, and high levels. However, to show these facts in Figure 3–21 would require 10 additional curves, which in all likelihood would create clutter and cause confusion.

Figure 3–22 is an illustration of a rectilinear coordinate chart that includes a curve based on cur-

rent and historical estimates that are very different from conventional forecasts or projections. The primary curve represents budgetary estimates expressed in constant dollars for the Soviet military establishment from 1964 to 1975. An effort is made in this chart to assess the adequacy of the United States defense budget against trends in military balance with the Soviet Union. Under the circumstances it is obvious that estimates of this kind are difficult to derive, and in recognition of this fact the curve is drawn as a band rather than as a single line. Presumably, the band indicated by light lines encompasses deviations inherent in estimates of this kind, and the heavy line in between represents the most probable trend. The other two curves are fiscal year budgetary figures (total obligational au-

---

[7] United States Bureau of the Census, *Demographic Aspects of Aging and the Older Population in the United States,* Special Studies, Current Population Reports, Series P-23, No. 59, 1976, pp. 4–26.

ENROLLMENT IN GRADES K-12 OF REGULAR DAY SCHOOLS, BY INSTITUTIONAL CONTROL AND ORGANIZATIONAL LEVEL UNITED STATES, FALL 1963 TO 1983

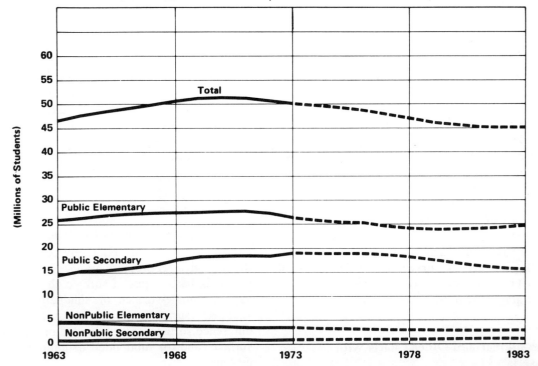

Figure 3–21. A series of curves on a rectilinear coordinate grid showing enrollment trends and forecasts. The forecasts are differentiated from reported data by dashed lines. Because of the wide span of values represented by the five curves, it would have been much more effective to have used a semilogarithmic rather than an arithmetic grid. Incidentally, the three grid lines above 55 million are superfluous. (From Kenneth A. Simon and Martin M. Frankel, Projections of Education Statistics to 1983–84, *HEW, National Center for Education Statistics, Washington: Government Printing Office, 1975, p. 3.)*

Figure 3–22. An arithmetic line chart with a curve portraying a series of current and historical estimates. Note that the curve representing the budgetary estimates for the Soviet military establishment is enclosed by a band, which is indicative of the probable deviations in estimates. (From Secretary of Defense, Annual Report FY 1977, *p. 261.)*

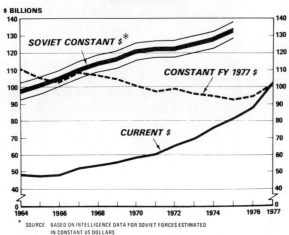

DEPARTMENT OF DEFENSE BASELINE FORCES BUDGET TRENDS
(TOA - $ BILLIONS)

thority) of the U.S. Department of Defense expressed in constant and current dollars, respectively.

Figure 3–23 is another illustration of utilizing the arithmetic line chart in presenting graphically a series of estimates. These estimates, which pertain to net migration in the state of Washington during a 50-year span, are based on the following types of data: births, deaths, population censuses, population estimates, and a limited amount of migration data. Because of the extreme paucity of reliable data on migration, the demographer is forced to derive estimates such as those presented in Figure 3–23. The annual means of net migration for four decennial and two quinquennial periods are shown as distinctive plotting points on the larger grid that in turn are connected by a smoothed curve based on simple interpolation, whereas the insert portrays the pattern of annual net migration for the 1940–1950 intercensal period. In view of the fact that both the larger and smaller curves are based on approximations and the curves have been smoothed, the chart may be considered schematic rather than a precise graphic record.

Rectilinear and Other Charts with Inserts

For purposes of clarification, elaboration, or emphasis, it is often practicable to add an insert to a larger chart. Because of the very nature of its design, a chart may seem incomplete or inadequate; to clarify, round out, or up-date the message that it is supposed to convey, an insert may prove to be a valuable supplement.

For example, the reader again is referred to Figure 3–12, which includes an insert in the form of a pie chart. The primary message concerning cigarette production is clearly conveyed by the two curves. However, the insert provides additional information about the different kinds and proportions of tobacco used in cigarette production.

Also, it will be recalled from the preceding section that there is an insert in Figure 3–23. The main portion of this chart shows migration trends from 1910 to 1960. The insert depicts in detail the yearly patterns of net migration during the 1940–1950 intercensal period when the volume of migration reached an unprecedented peak.

Figure 3–24 shows four more illustrations of charts with inserts. In panel A the primary chart portrays the actual number of deliveries per month for a 2-year period. The insert indicates the monthly proportion of deliveries recorded in terms of preplanned delivery schedule. The insert in panel B is a simple bar chart showing the numerical composition of the primary variable at the latest date. The three bars representing the insert in Panel C are a "blowup" of the last three bars in the primary chart. The insert indicates very clearly the comparative size and composition of these three bars. The insert in panel D is designed to show the total of all the items in a bar chart. It will be observed that this insert has been drawn in a reduced scale, whereas the insert in panel C has been drawn in a expanded scale.

SURFACE CHARTS

Surface charts, sometimes called "band" or "stratum" charts, are relatively common forms of the rectilinear coordinate graph. Figure 3–25 illustrates six basic types of surface charts: (1) simple-surface, single-surface or silhouette, (2) step or staircase surface, (3) band surface, (4) net-difference surface, (5) subdivided or multiple-strata surface, and (6) subdivided or multiple-strata step or staircase.[8]

Simple-surface, Single-surface, or Silhouette Chart

It will be observed from Figures 3–25 and 3–26 that the single-surface or silhouette chart is designed to portray point data. It is merely a line graph in which the area between the curve and the baseline has been stippled, crosshatched, blacked in, or colored, thus giving a silhouette effect. In Figure 3–26 the basic data are in the form of index numbers that show monthly fluctuations in the business cycle. This chart represents a section of an original chart covering a period of 185 years from 1790 to 1975. The portion selected portrays especially the extraordinary fluctuations in the business cycle during the 1930s and during World War II. The single block curve indicates changes in wholesale commodity prices.

[8] *American Standard Time-Series Charts*, ASA Y15.2, New York: American Society of Mechanical Engineers, 1960, p. 73–74.

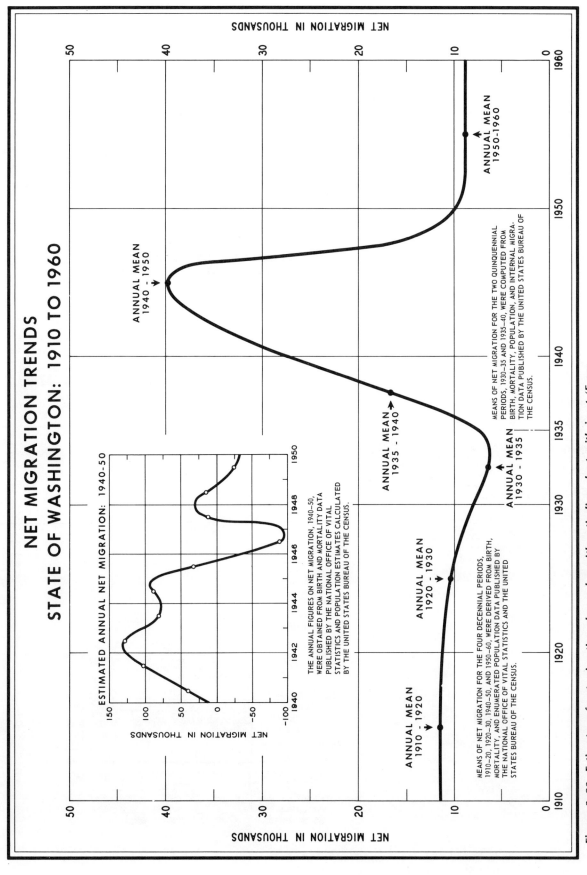

NET MIGRATION TRENDS
STATE OF WASHINGTON: 1910 TO 1960

ANNUAL MEAN 1950-1960

ANNUAL MEAN 1940 - 1950

ANNUAL MEAN 1935 - 1940

ANNUAL MEAN 1930 - 1935

ANNUAL MEAN 1920 - 1930

ANNUAL MEAN 1910 - 1920

NET MIGRATION IN THOUSANDS

ESTIMATED ANNUAL NET MIGRATION: 1940-50

NET MIGRATION IN THOUSANDS

THE ANNUAL FIGURES ON NET MIGRATION, 1940–50, WERE OBTAINED FROM BIRTH AND MORTALITY DATA PUBLISHED BY THE NATIONAL OFFICE OF VITAL STATISTICS AND POPULATION ESTIMATES CALCULATED BY THE UNITED STATES BUREAU OF THE CENSUS.

MEANS OF NET MIGRATION FOR THE FOUR DECENNIAL PERIODS, 1910–20, 1920–30, 1940–50, AND 1950–60, WERE DERIVED FROM BIRTH, MORTALITY, AND ENUMERATED POPULATION DATA PUBLISHED BY THE NATIONAL OFFICE OF VITAL STATISTICS AND THE UNITED STATES BUREAU OF THE CENSUS.

MEANS OF NET MIGRATION FOR THE TWO QUINQUENNIAL PERIODS, 1930–35 AND 1935–40, WERE COMPUTED FROM BIRTH, MORTALITY, POPULATION, AND INTERNAL MIGRATION DATA PUBLISHED BY THE UNITED STATES BUREAU OF THE CENSUS.

Figure 3–23. Estimates of net migration shown by arithmetic line chart with inset (From Calvin F. Schmid, et al., Population Forecasts, State of Washington: 1965 to 1985, Olympia: Washington State Department of Commerce and Economic Development, 1966, p. 58.)

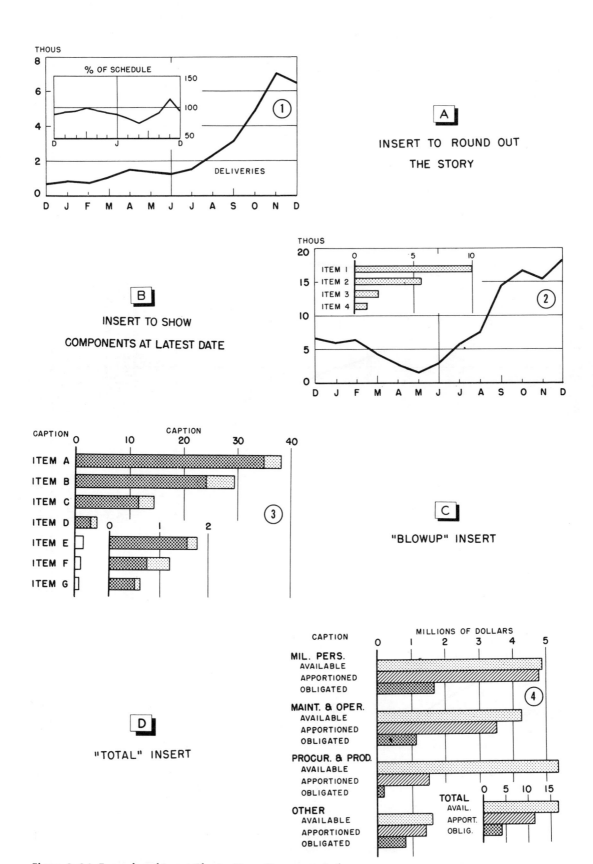

Figure 3–24. Examples of Insert Charts. (From Department of the Army, Standards of Statistical Presentation, *Washington: Government Printing Office, 1966, p. 72.)*

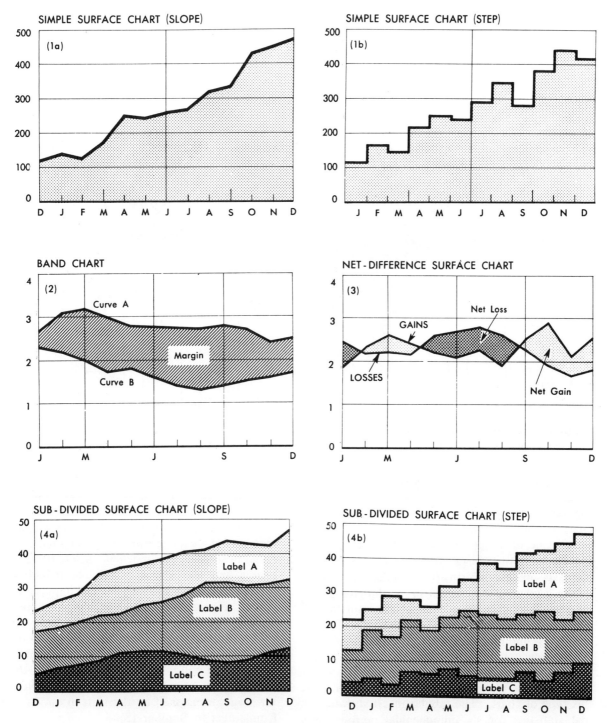

Figure 3–25. Illustrations of basic types of surface charts (extracted from Standard Time-Series Charts, A5AY15.2 —1960, *with the permission of the publisher, The American Society of Mechanical Engineers, 345 E. 47th Street, New York, N.Y. 10017.)*

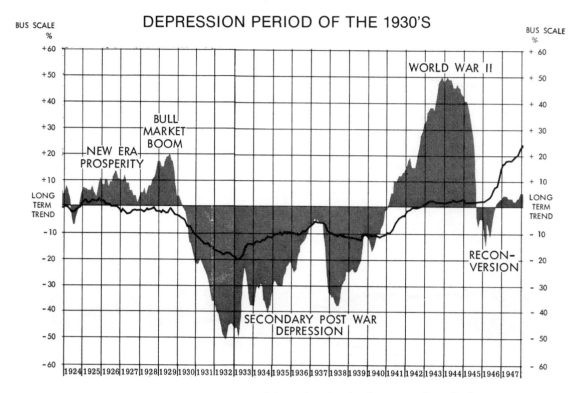

Figure 3–26. Silhouette chart. (Chart prepared from data in circular, "American Business Activity from 1790 to Today," Cleveland Trust, 46 Ed., April 1975.)

Band Type of Surface Chart

Figures 3–25 and 3–27 show the band-type surface chart to emphasize the difference between two time series, one of which is always at a higher level. Figure 3–27 was designed to depict the natural increase—excess of births over deaths—as a factor in the growth of population in Washington State. Population change in an area of constant boundaries, such as a state results from two sets of differentials: (1) difference between births and deaths and (2) difference between inmigration and outmigration. The significance of the "baby boom" during and following World War II is clearly revealed by this type of chart. The tabular insert showing actual statistics for six quinquennial periods summarizes the more salient facts portrayed by this chart.

Net-difference Surface Chart

Figure 3–28 is another illustration of the net-difference surface chart. As this chart clearly shows, it is designed to portray differential changes between two series of data. These differentials may be either positive or negative, increases or decreases. In fiscal matters, differential changes for receipts and expenditures may, of course, result either in surpluses or in deficits; again, there may be profits and losses and assets and liabilities. In foreign trade, exports may exceed imports, or vice versa. Figure 3–28 shows actual and anticipated U.S. government budgetary trends from 1974 to 1980 with respect to differential changes in receipts and outlays and the resultant deficits and budget margins. It will be observed that most of the data on this chart are projections. The "transition quarter" was occasioned by the shift in the fiscal year from July 1 to October 1.

Multiple-strata Surface Chart

The multiple-strata surface or subdivided surface chart is illustrated by Figures 3–25 and 3–29. This type of surface chart portrays the component parts of a total that may be expressed either in absolute

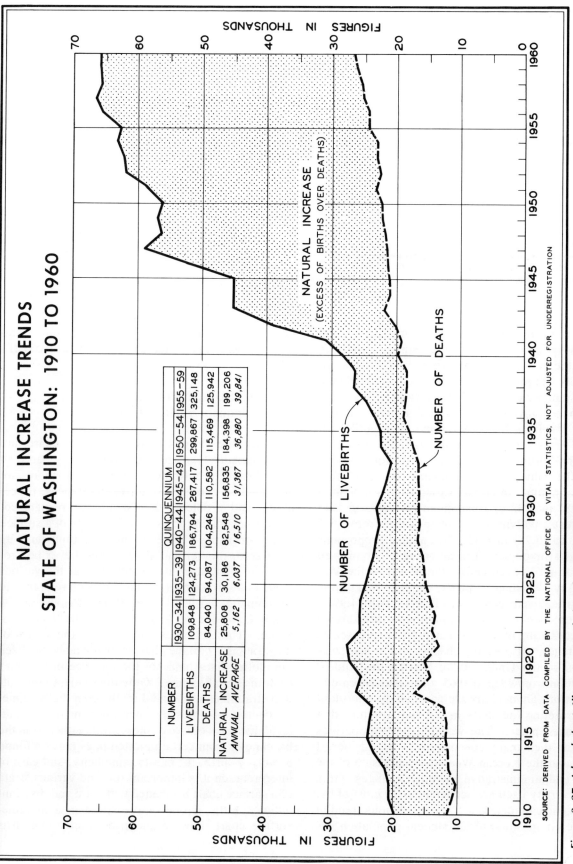

NATURAL INCREASE TRENDS
STATE OF WASHINGTON: 1910 TO 1960

FIGURES IN THOUSANDS

NUMBER	QUINQUENNIUM						
	1930-34	1935-39	1940-44	1945-49	1950-54	1955-59
LIVEBIRTHS	109,848	124,273	186,794	267,417	299,867	325,148
DEATHS	84,040	94,087	104,246	110,582	115,469	125,942
NATURAL INCREASE	25,808	30,186	82,548	156,835	184,398	199,206
ANNUAL AVERAGE	5,162	6,037	16,510	31,367	36,880	39,841

NATURAL INCREASE
(EXCESS OF BIRTHS OVER DEATHS)

NUMBER OF DEATHS

NUMBER OF LIVEBIRTHS

SOURCE: DERIVED FROM DATA COMPILED BY THE NATIONAL OFFICE OF VITAL STATISTICS, NOT ADJUSTED FOR UNDERREGISTRATION

Figure 3–27. A band chart. Illustrates a technique for portraying net change in two series of temporal data by stippling or crosshatching. The World War II and postwar "baby boom" is reflected by the unusually large natural increase of population. (From Calvin F. Schmid et al., Population Forecasts, State of Washington: 1965 to 1985, Olympia: Washington State Department of Commerce and Economic Development, 1966, p. 33.)

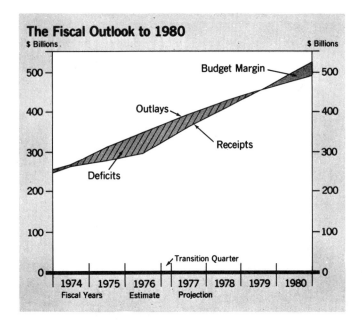

Figure 3–28. Net–difference surface chart (*From The Budget of the United States for Fiscal Year 1976, Office of Management and Budget, Washington: Government Printing Office, 1976, p. 43.*)

numbers or in percentages. Figure 3–29 is an example of the multiple-strata surface chart in which the two components are indicated both numerically and proportionally. The data indicate the annual number of arrests in the city of Seattle from 1931 to 1970 divided into two major categories: (1) arrests involving intoxication and (2) all other arrests. Arrests involving intoxication comprised arrests for "drunkenness" and arrests for "driving under the influence." The upper panel shows that the total number of arrests varied from a minimum of 13,483 in 1932 to a maximum of 43,893 in 1945 and arrests involving intoxication ranged from 5,633 in 1932 to 30,781 in 1943. The annual proportions of arrests involving intoxication never comprised less than 40%, even before the repeal of the Volstead Act. The highest proportion recorded during the entire 39-year period was in 1943 with 74.9%.

Figure 3–30 represents a multiple-strata surface chart consisting of five age categories expressed as percentages. It portrays changes in the age composition of the University of Washington student population from 1920 to 1965. The two-dozen-odd explanatory annotations are particularly important in interpreting the shifts in the age structure that have taken place. The war and postwar periods including their many concomitants—World Wars I and II and the Korean War—the depression of the 1930s, and administrative and other changes within the university itself are accountable for most of the more significant changes. A very obvious trend in the age composition of the student population has

been the marked increase in the proportion of students 22 years of age and over since World War II.

Special Design Procedures and Problems of Surface Charts

Although the various kinds of surface charts are characteristically rectilinear coordinate charts, in comparison to arithmetic line charts there are nevertheless certain distinctive differences, procedures, and problems that should be recognized. First, to maintain the essential features of a surface chart consisting of one or more stratum built up from zero, the vertical scale should never be broken. Second, since it is essential that the various strata of a surface chart be laid out with reference to a complete vertical scale, it is obvious that a multiple-amount scale would be entirely inappropriate. Third, the basis for reading the values of the strata in a surface chart is the distance between the plotted lines, and not the distance of the lines from the zero baseline. Only the total and the bottom stratum can be read directly from the baseline. Of course, at times the measurement of accumulated distances of two or more strata either from the baseline or from certain plotted lines may be found useful. Fourth, for clarity, simplicity, and ease of interpretation it is important that the various strata of a surface chart be shaded with care and discrimination. Fifth, if one of the strata in a multiple-surface chart shows pronounced fluctuations, it is

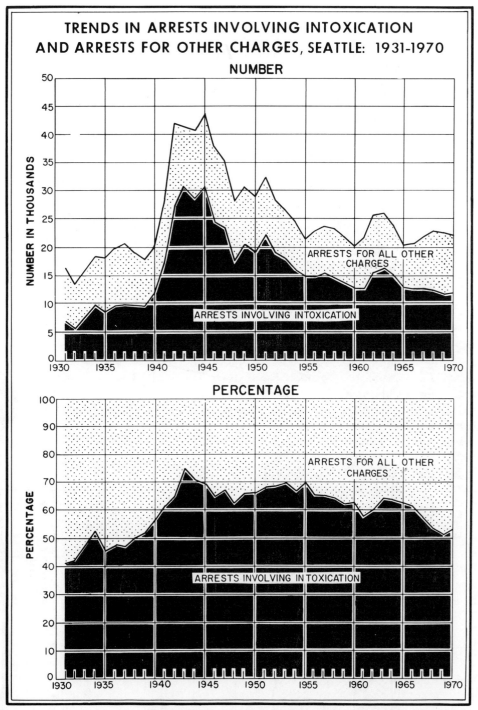

Figure 3–29. Band or stratum chart. This chart indicates trends in the volume of arrests involving intoxication in comparison with arrests for all other charges. The upper portion represents actual number of cases; the lower portion, percentages. (From Calvin F. Schmid and Stanton E. Schmid, Crime in the State of Washington, *Olympia: Law and Justice Planning Office, Planning and Community Affairs Agency, 1972, p. 265.)*

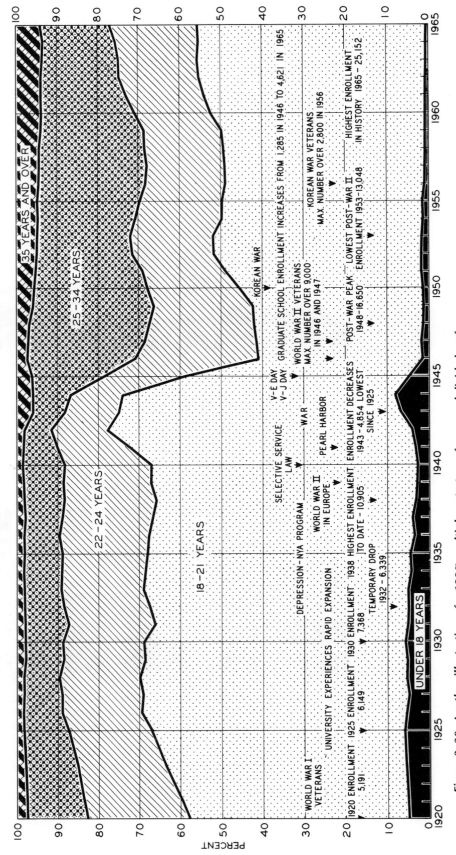

ENROLLMENT TRENDS BY AGE

UNIVERSITY OF WASHINGTON: 1920-1965

Figure 3-30. Another illustration of a 100% multiple—strata surface or subdivided surface chart. Note explanatory annotations that indicate factors influencing the age composition of student population. (From Calvin F. Schmid, Vincent A. Miller, and William S. Packard, Enrollment Statistics, Colleges and Universities, State of Washington: Fall Term 1965, Seattle: Washington State Census Board, 1966, p. 71.)

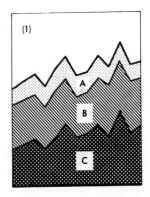 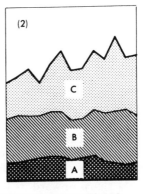

AN IRREGULAR LAYER DISTORTS LAYERS
ABOVE IT. NOTE DIFFERENCE IN APPEARANCE OF
A AND B WHEN LAYER C IS MOVED TO THE TOP.

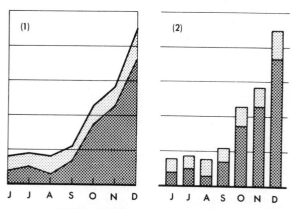

SHARP CHANGES IN LEVEL CAN CAUSE OPTI-
CAL ILLUSIONS IN SURFACE CHARTS (TOP LAYER LOOKS
SMALLER IN DECEMBER THAN IT REALLY IS).

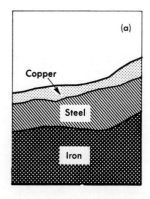 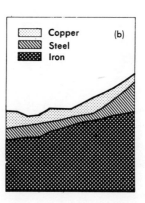

METHODS OF LABELING LAYERS TOO SMALL
TO LABEL DIRECTLY.

*Figure 3–31. Illustration of design problems of surface charts.
(extracted from* Standard Time-Series Charts, A5A Y15.2 —
1960, *with the permission of the publisher, The American
Society of Mechanical Engineers, 345 E. 47th Street, New
York N.Y. 10017.)*

possible that distortions could occur if the respective strata are not properly positioned. Generally, the stratum exhibiting marked irregularities should be placed, if at all possible, at or near the top. Figure 3–31 illustrates how a poorly positioned stratum with marked irregularities may create distortions. It will be observed that when stratum C, which shows considerable fluctuation, is shifted from the bottom to the top position, the obvious distortions in strata A and B are eliminated. Sixth, if a series of strata in a surface chart reflect a sharp upward trend, an optical illusion may be created in the top stratum which may seem to indicate a diminution in its width toward the end of the series. This particu-lar problem is illustrated by Figure 3–31. The optical illusion in a sharply rising stratum of this kind results from a tendency of the eye to interpret the width of the stratum horizontally rather than verti-cally. A suggested solution for a problem of this kind is to abandon the surface chart in favor of the column chart. Normally, the strata designations should be located directly within the strata themselves. In cases where there is insufficient space the designations may be placed outside and "arrowed in." However, arrows should not cross a stratum to reach one that is unlabeled. In such instances, as illustrated by stratum C in Figure 3–31, a key would be an appropriate solution.

THE BAR CHART IS ONE OF THE MOST useful, simple, adaptable, and popular techniques in graphic presentation. The simple bar chart, with its many variations, is particularly appropriate for comparing the magnitude, or size, of coordinate items or of parts of a total. The basis of comparison in the bar chart is linear, or one-dimensional. The length of each bar or of its components is proportional to the quantity or amount of each category represented. In comparing size or in comparing component parts, three basic geometrical forms can be utilized. In addition to one-dimensional or linear forms, there are two-dimensional or areal comparisons and three-dimensional or cubic comparisons.[1]

Figure 4–1 illustrates the three basic geometrical forms. In each instance the larger figure is four times that of the smaller one. The eye can readily appraise this basic difference in the case of the column chart, but it is much more difficult and uncertain for the areal and cubic forms. Also, it should be pointed out that when two- and three-dimensional forms are irregular in shape the problems of comparison become more complicated. Although the bars necessarily possess width, it is the respective length of each bar that determines the magnitude or value of a series of categories.

For comparisons of magnitudes, the geometric form that provides the simplest, most graphic, and most accurate impressions should be used. On the basis of these criteria, one-dimensional or linear forms are usually superior. Sometimes, of course, it may be advisable or even necessary to use areal or cubic forms, especially where there are space or other restrictions, or where areal or cubic symbols seem to be more appropriate. In graphic presentation the two most common one-dimensional forms are the bar chart and the column chart. Basically they are identical. In the bar chart, the bars are arranged horizontally, whereas in the column chart the bars are arranged vertically. As is indicated in this chapter, there are many variations and combinations of both the bar and column charts.

BAR CHARTS

Types of Bar Charts

Eight different types of bar charts are portrayed in Figures 4–2 and 4–3. The most common designations and brief descriptions of each type are as follows:

CHAPTER FOUR

BAR AND COLUMN CHARTS

Simple Bar Chart. This is one of the most useful and most widely used forms of graphic presentation. The simple bar chart is used to compare two or more coordinate items. Comparison is based on direct linear values; the length of the bars is determined by the value or amount of each category. The bars are usually arranged according to relative magnitude of items.

Bar-and-symbol Chart. This is merely a simple bar chart with supplementary information indicated by a cross-line, circle, diamond, or some other symbol.

Subdivided-bar Chart. This type of bar chart, like the 100% bar chart described in the following statement, is also referred to as a "segmented-bar" or "component-bar" chart. The scale values of the subdivided-bar chart are shown in absolute numbers. To portray percentage distribution of components, the 100% bar chart should be used.

Subdivided 100% Bar Chart. This type of chart consists of one or more segmented bars where each bar totals 100%. The various divisions of the bars represent percentages of the whole.

Grouped-bar Chart. This type of chart is also referred to as a "multiple" or "multiple-unit" bar chart. Comparison of items in two, and sometimes three, respects can be made by this type of chart.

Paired-bar Chart. This chart, along with the deviation bar chart and the sliding bar chart (next items), is a special type of "bilateral," "two-way," or "two-directional" chart. Different units and scales can be used for each set of bars.

Deviation-bar Chart. Note that bars extend either to left or to the right of the same baseline. This type of bar chart is especially valuable for

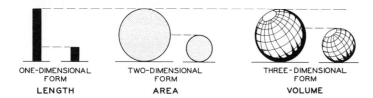

Figure 4–1. Three basic types of geometric forms for comparing sizes. It will be noted that in each form the smaller figure is one–fourth the larger.

presentation of positive–negative and profit–loss data.

Sliding-Bar Chart. This is a bilateral chart in which each bar represents the total of two main components. One part of the bar is left and the other part is right of a baseline. The scale may represent either percentages or absolute numbers.

STANDARDS OF DESIGN FOR SIMPLE BAR CHART

Detailed consideration is given first to the simple bar chart since it is the most widely used, as well as basic to all other forms. The characteristics and standards suggested for the simple bar chart are

generally applicable to the several adaptations and variations already discussed.

Arrangement of Bars

The arrangement of the bars should be adapted to the objectives of the study. Usually the bars are arranged in order of size, starting with the largest. Sometimes, of course, an alphabetical, geo-

---

[1] In addition to one-, two-, and three-dimensional forms, angles are sometimes used for comparing component parts. The various sectors, for example, of a pie chart represent parts of a total. The number of degrees of each sector is drawn in proportion to the size of each component category.

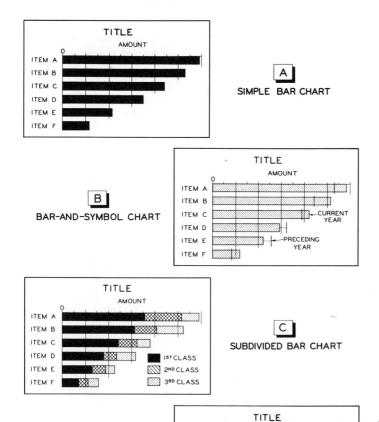

Figure 4–2. Illustrations of different types of bar charts.

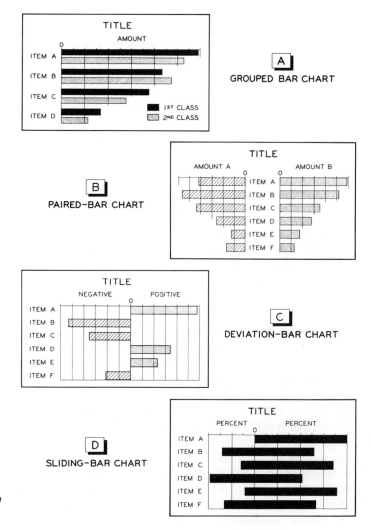

Figure 4–3. Illustrations of different types of bar charts.

graphical, or other systematic ordering of data may be more appropriate to the purposes at hand.

Width of Bars and Spacing

The width of the bars and the intervening spaces has no special significance. The width of the bars should be uniform. The number of bars and the size and proportions of the chart are the determining factors in the width of the bars, as well as the spacing between them. A good general working rule is that the spacing between the bars should be one-half the width of the bars. Sometimes, however, it may be more appropriate to lay out the spaces as little as one-fourth the width of the bars, or as much as their entire width. In any case, the bars should be of uniform width and evenly spaced.

Also in a well-designed chart of this kind, the bars should be neither disproportionately long and narrow nor short and wide.

Characteristics of Bars

It is customary practice to blacken in the bars in a simple bar chart. Various colors, of course, can be used in the preparation of charts for exhibit purposes and certain types of popular publications, where an additional expenditure of funds may be warranted, since color reproduction is more expensive. Stippling and crosshatching also may be used instead of full black bars. Mere outline bars are not generally recommended. If crosshatching is used, care should be taken not to create optical illusions.

Scale

As a general practice, it is recommended that a carefully planned scale be included on every bar chart.[2] The scale enables one to gauge the length of bars with a reasonable degree of accuracy. The scale can be arranged to coincide with the top of the first bar or drawn as an independent line just above the top bar. If the latter type of scale is used, the spacing between the top bar and the line should be equivalent to about one-half the width of the bar. The scale for the simple bar chart should always begin with zero. The zero line usually is the main referent point and should be emphasized by making it slightly heavier than the other scale lines. The scale for a horizontal bar chart should never be broken except under the most unusual circumstances. No doubt the reader has seen bar charts in which this has been done, especially when one category is disproportionately larger than the others on the graph. If one is compelled to resort to this practice, extreme care should be taken to indicate the break in the scale as well as in the bar.

The number of intervals on the scale should be adequate for measuring distances but not so numerous as to cause confusion. The intervals should be indicated in round numbers, preferably in such units as 5s, 10s, 25s, 50s, 100s, and 1000s. Odd-number units such as 3s, 7s, and 13s should be avoided. The intervals on the scales are marked off by lines and ticks. The scale lines and ticks are similar to those described in connection with the rectilinear coordinate chart. They should be drawn relatively light but of sufficient weight to remain sharp and clear in case the chart is reduced in size. Scale figures and a scale legend are also essential parts of a bar chart.

Data

Sometimes it is desirable that data on which the chart is based be included directly on the chart. Optical illusions and confusion may result if the accompanying data are not placed in the proper position. Normally, it is not good usage to place the figures inside the bars or at the right end of the bars. When data are placed inside the bars there is a tendency to compare only the parts of the bars in which there are no figures, rather than the entire length of the bars, and if the data are placed at the end of the bars, the resulting tendency is to add the figures to the bars with respect to comparative lengths. If for some reason it seems necessary to letter within the bar, the lettering should be small enough to leave a strip of shading on all sides. If lettering is placed at the end of the bar, it should be relatively small in size and separated from the bar. Generally, basic data should be placed at the left of the zero line outside the grid.

EXAMPLES OF BAR CHARTS

Simple Bar Chart

A careful examination of Figures 4–4, 4–5, and 4–6 will assist the reader to understand more fully the essential principles and characteristics of the simple bar chart.

Figure 4–4 includes 29 bars arranged in numerical rank order ranging in value from 11 to 264. The data represent doctoral degrees by fields or specialties granted by the University of Washington during a 15-year period. To design a chart within practicable proportions, a more or less arbitrary cutoff minimum of 11 degrees was established. The 13 fields with less than 11 degrees are listed along with the explanatory notes on the chart. It will be observed that nine of these 13 fields granted three or fewer degrees. The scale has been placed at the top with 11 divisions of 25, extending from 0 to 275. For sake of clarity and precision, especially in view of the relatively large number of bars, the number of degrees represented by each of the bars is indicated on the chart. However, it should be pointed out that when figures are placed at the end of the bars there may be a tendency for the eye to add the figures to the bars with respect to comparative lengths. The data in Figure 4–5 represent per capita expenditures of local governments for selected functions in various size groups of standard metropolitan statistical areas (SMSAs). In reality there are six separate but related bar charts, each representing a special governmental function—education, highways, public welfare, police protection, sanitation, and fire protection.

---

[2] It has been argued that for committee and conference purposes a bar chart without a scale, but with the essential data clearly indicated, is preferable since it may be difficult or impossible to read the scale; see R. R. Lutz, *Graphic Presentation Simplified,* (New York: Funk & Wagnalls, 1949, pp. 55–58.

The main emphasis and purpose of simple bar charts are focused on comparative magnitudes. The scale, scale lines, and ordering of categories are laid out with these facts in mind. Since the per capita figures for education are considerably larger than the figures for the other five functions, the scale covers a much wider range. Unfortunately, because of the size of the figures for education it was not possible to make the scale divisions identical with those in the smaller charts. If the scale

divisions in the chart for education were the same, the length of the scale would have had to be made approximately 2.5 times larger. Usually the ordering of the bars in a simple bar chart is based on the magnitude of the various categories beginning with the largest. Because of the complexity of this chart with its six comparative groups the rank order was determined by the relative population size of SMSAs. Although the sequence of bars is determined usually on the basis of magnitude, some

Figure 4–4. A simple bar chart. (From Calvin F. Schmid et al., **Studies in Enrollment Trends and Patterns,** *Seattle: University of Washington, Long–Range Planning Studies, Report No. 17, 1966, p. 142.)*

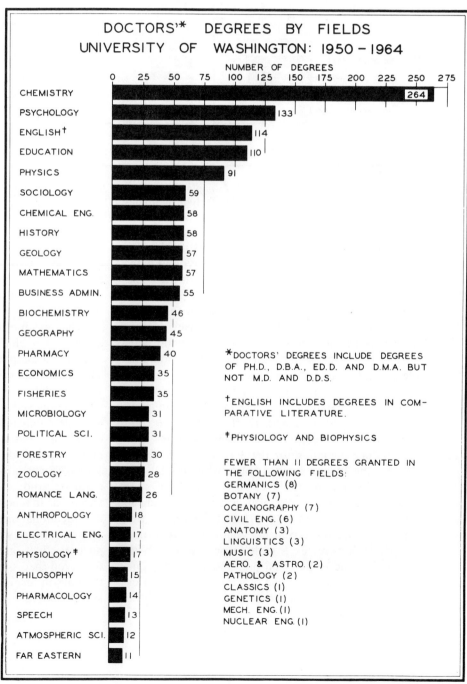

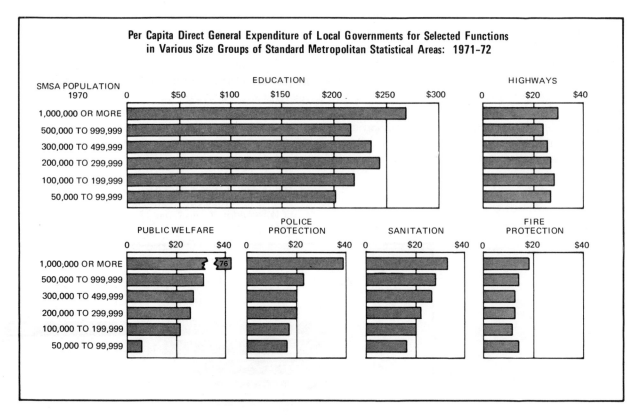

Figure 4–5. Examples of the simple bar chart. [*From U.S. Bureau of the Census, Census of Governments, 6,* Topical Studies, (5), *1972: Graphic Summary of the 1972 Census of Governments, Washington: Government Printing Office, 1975, p. 39.*]

other arrangement may be entirely justifiable, depending on the purpose of the chart or type of data.

It will be observed that the first bar in the chart for public welfare is broken since the per capita figure of $76 is almost twice the range of the scale. In "freak" or extremely "erratic" cases of this kind it is permissible to show a break in the bar. The value represented by the broken bar should be clearly indicated on the chart.

Figure 4–6 exemplifies a bar chart where the ordering of the bars has been determined by the magnitude of the figures, with the largest at the top. The figures represent mean homicide rates per 100,000 of population for the 3-year period, 1968–1970 for the 14 largest cities (cities with populations of 150,000 or more in 1970) on the Pacific Coast. The scale covers a range of 0–20 since the highest rate is a little more than 19. Unlike Figure 4–5, the scale lines are not boxed in. With respect to this particular feature, each style is permissible, with the choice one of personal preference. Since this chart on homicide was one of a comparative series of 10 crime categories, the rank order of any of the

14 cities can be readily determined by the figure on each bar. Also, in view of the fact that the study pertains to the state of Washington, the three Washington cities are readily identifiable by distinctive patterns of stippling and crosshatching.

The design of Figure 4–7, another illustration of a simple bar chart, reflects certain special characteristics or adaptations to the data that it portrays. The data emphasize a consistent positive progression or relationship between education and income. The figures indicate that from age 18 to death an average elementary-school graduate in 1968 could expect an income of approximately $277,000; a high-school graduate, $371,000; a college graduate, $584,000; and a person with one or more years of graduate study, $636,000. Whereas not all these variations in income can be attributed to differences in educational attainment, it would appear that the number of years spent in school does have an important effect on future earning power. It will be observed that, unlike Figure 4–6, the rank order of the bars in terms of magnitude is reversed, that is, in descending value, with the smallest bar at the top

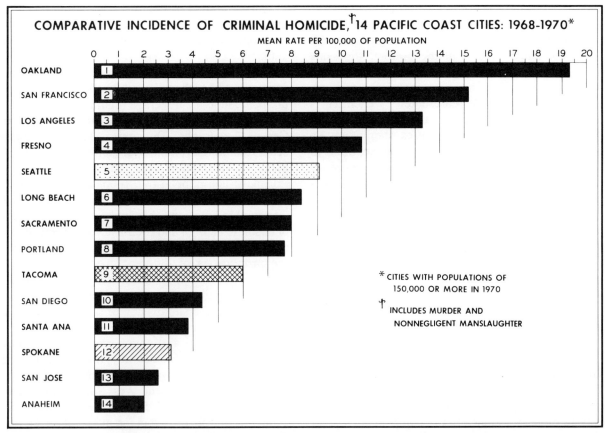

COMPARATIVE INCIDENCE OF CRIMINAL HOMICIDE,[†]14 PACIFIC COAST CITIES: 1968-1970*

MEAN RATE PER 100,000 OF POPULATION

* CITIES WITH POPULATIONS OF
150,000 OR MORE IN 1970

† INCLUDES MURDER AND
NONNEGLIGENT MANSLAUGHTER

Figure 4–6. A simple bar chart. Since this chart is part of an extensive study of crime in Washington, the bars for the three major cities of the state are readily distinguishable by special hatching and stippling. (From Calvin F. Schmid and Stanton E. Schmid, Crime in the State of Washington, *Olympia: Law and Justice Planning Office, Planning and Community Affairs Agency, 1972, p. 317.)*

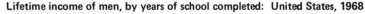

Lifetime income of men, by years of school completed: United States, 1968

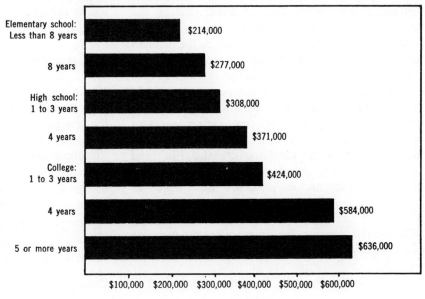

Figure 4–7. Illustration of the simple bar chart, in which the scale is placed at the bottom. Also, note ordering of the bars from smallest to largest. See text for further comments. (From Kenneth A. Simon and W. Vance Grant, Digest of Educational Statistics: 1971 Edition, *HEW, Office of Education, Washington: Government Printing Office, 1972, p. 16.)*

and the largest at the bottom. This arrangement is consistent with the data showing educational progression as indicated by school years completed. Since the longest bar is at the bottom, the scale including scale figures also has been placed at the bottom. Scale lines have been entirely omitted, and the precise amount represented by each bar is indicated by figures placed at the end of each bar. As pointed out previously figures should not be placed either inside the bars or at the right end of the bars unless there is a genuine compensatory reason that can justify such practice. Perhaps it could be argued that the additional information provided by the figures more than compensates for possible misinterpretation resulting from optical illusion. Again, care should be taken not to clutter a chart with too many figures. As a general principle a chart should not be made to do the work of a statistical table.

Subdivided- or Component-bar Chart

The subdivided- or component-bar chart may be developed either from absolute figures or percentages. With this type of chart it is possible not only to present graphically the component parts of several items in a series of data, but also to compare the component parts one with another. When numerical data are involved, the design and procedure in constructing subdivided-bar charts are identical to those of a simple bar chart, except that each of the bars is subdivided into its component categories. In the case of data expressed in percentage, a percentage scale is used; that is, the component parts for each bar are shown as relative proportions of 100%.[3] In each instance the primary purpose is to compare for a single category the individual parts in their relationship to the whole.

The segments of bars in this type of chart should be arranged in accordance with a logical or analytical sequence. The most common arrangement is by order of size. To assist in differentiating the various segments of the bars, crosshatching and stippling are used. Whenever two or more patterns of crosshatching and stippling are used, a key or legend is normally required. The key or legend consists of small blocks of hatching and stippling with short explanatory labels indicating the meaning of each category. Unless there is some special reason, the crosshatching should follow an intensity gradation, beginning with the darkest on the left.

Parts C and D of Figure 4–2 illustrate the essential features of the subdivided-bar chart. Part C represents numerical data and part D, percentage data.

Figure 4–8 is a more detailed illustration of a subdivided-bar chart based on 1972 statistics of tax-paid alcoholic beverage (distilled spirits, wines, and beers) consumption for the nine Bureau of the Census Geographic Divisions. The index represents total annual number of gallons of absolute alcohol consumption per person among the "drinking-age population" (population 15 years of age and over). It will be observed that the Pacific Geographic Division ranks highest, with 3.1 gallons of absolute alcohol and the East South Central Division is lowest with 1.81 gallons. The variation in the proportions of different classes of beverages consumed from one geographic division to another is also significant. These facts are clearly portrayed by the subdivision of the bars. The percentages indicated in each of the segments provide greater specificity and comparability in presenting these differences. Incidentally, the percentages are a special design feature of this chart. At one extreme the residents of the West South Central Division drink mostly beer (55% of their alcohol is consumed in that form), whereas at the other extreme the New England and South Atlantic Division favor distilled spirits (49% of their alcohol is consumed in that form). Only the Pacific Geographical Division obtains a substantial portion of its alcohol (20%) from wine. In the United States as a whole the largest proportion of alcohol consumed is in the form of beer (46% of the total), followed by distilled spirits (42%) and wine (12%).

Grouped-bar Charts

In comparing several magnitudes for each of two or three periods of time or for two or three categories, the grouped-bar chart may be found very appropriate. This type of chart is also referred to as the "multiple-bar" or "compound-bar" chart. It is illustrated by Figure 4–9. The basic data portrayed by this chart pertain to median income of nonwhite races in comparison to the median income of the

---

[3] It should be pointed out that a percentage–component-bar chart may consist of only one bar. This type of subdivided-bar chart is similar in application to the pie chart. For a detailed discussion of this type of chart, see Chapter 7.

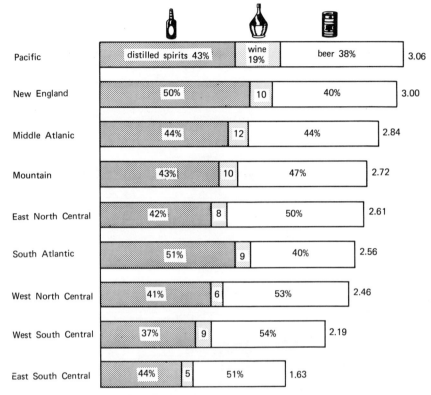

APPARENT CONSUMPTION* OF ABSOLUTE ALCOHOL
FROM ALL ALCOHOLIC BEVERAGES, IN U.S. GALLONS PER PERSON,
IN THE DRINKING–AGE POPULATION,** AND PERCENT OF
EACH MAJOR BEVERAGE CLASS, U.S.A. 1970

Pacific	distilled spirits 43%	wine 19%	beer 38%	3.06
New England	50%	10	40%	3.00
Middle Atlanic	44%	12	44%	2.84
Mountain	43%	10	47%	2.72
East North Central	42%	8	50%	2.61
South Atlantic	51%	9	40%	2.56
West North Central	41%	6	53%	2.46
West South Central	37%	9	54%	2.19
East South Central	44%	5	51%	1.63

The regions are the standard regions of the U.S. Census Bureau.

*For comparative purposes only. Amounts calculated according to tax–paid withdrawals.

**Age 15+

Figure 4–8. A subdivided–bar chart (From U.S. Public Health Service, Alcohol, Drug Abuse, and Mental Health Administration, HEW, First Special Report to the U.S. Congress, Alcohol and Health, Washington: Government Printing Office, 1972, p. 13.)

white race in the state of Washington. Also, income differentials are presented by sex and for two different periods, 1950 and 1960.

The upper portion of Figure 4–9 depicts the median income for the total population of each racial category as well as for each sex. The median annual income for the total population ranged from $1,402 for Indians to $3,115 for whites; for the female sex from $1,000 for Indians to $1,621 for Japanese, and for the male sex from $2,000 for Indians to $4,682 for whites. As will be observed from the legend, the black bars represent the total population, the crosshatched bars the males, and the stippled bars the females. By placing the bars in close juxtaposition the values for each sex and for

each racial category are readily comparable. The rank order of the six different categories was determined by the relative size of the median income for the total population. In this type of chart the bars are sometimes joined laterally, but the more common practice is to leave a small space between them. There is always relatively wide uniform spacing between the groups of bars.

The lower portion of Figure 4–9 is also a grouped-bar chart, but instead of groupings of three bars there are groupings of only two. The two bars represent median-income data for 1950 and 1960, respectively, for each of the six racial categories. As indicated in the legend, the bars for 1960 are black and the bars for 1950 are crosshatched. The

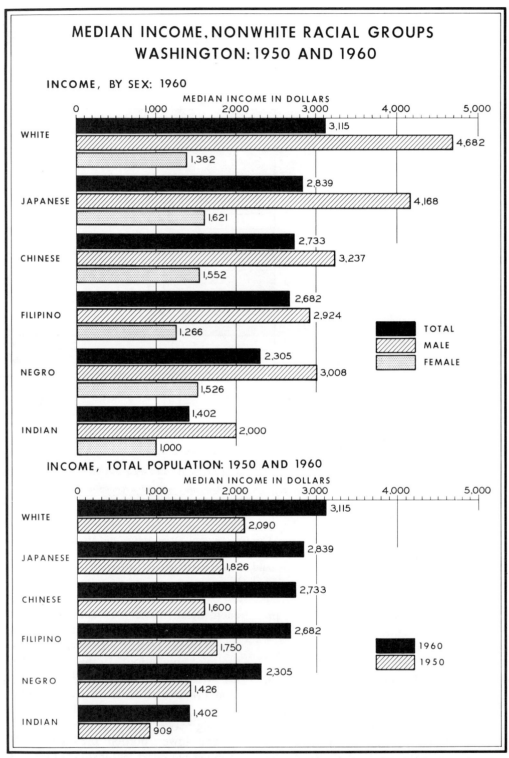

MEDIAN INCOME, NONWHITE RACIAL GROUPS
WASHINGTON: 1950 AND 1960

INCOME, BY SEX: 1960

MEDIAN INCOME IN DOLLARS

| | 0 | 1,000 | 2,000 | 3,000 | 4,000 | 5,000 |

WHITE
3,115
4,682
1,382

JAPANESE
2,839
4,168
1,621

CHINESE
2,733
3,237
1,552

FILIPINO
2,682
2,924
1,266

NEGRO
2,305
3,008
1,526

INDIAN
1,402
2,000
1,000

■ TOTAL
▨ MALE
▢ FEMALE

INCOME, TOTAL POPULATION: 1950 AND 1960

MEDIAN INCOME IN DOLLARS

| | 0 | 1,000 | 2,000 | 3,000 | 4,000 | 5,000 |

WHITE
3,115
2,090

JAPANESE
2,839
1,826

CHINESE
2,733
1,600

FILIPINO
2,682
1,750

NEGRO
2,305
1,426

INDIAN
1,402
909

■ 1960
▨ 1950

Figure 4–9. Illustration of grouped–bar charts. The chart portrays income data for nonwhite racial groups in the state of Washington. The upper portion of the chart shows groupings of three bars—median income for male, female, and total population in 1960—whereas the lower portion shows groupings of two bars—median income for total population in 1950 and 1960. (From Calvin F. Schmid, Charles E. Nobbe, and Arlene E. Mitchell, Nonwhite Races, State of Washington, Olympia: Washington State Planning and Community Affairs Agency, 1968, p. 126.)

rank order of the bars is based on the 1960 data. Also, it will be noted that to maintain comparability between the upper and lower series of bars, the scales are identical.

Figure 4–10 is another example of a grouped-bar chart, but with an additional feature not incorporated in Figure 4–9. Each of the bars is subdivided on the basis of nativity. Since this chart is both a grouped-bar chart as well as a subdivided bar chart it can be categorized as a "grouped–subdivided-bar chart."

The upper portion of the chart portrays the actual number of males and females classified by native born and foreign born for each of the five major nonwhite racial groups in the state of Washington. The lower portion of the chart portrays corresponding data in terms of percentage distribution. The fourfold classification by sex and nativity is represented by a simple shading scheme. The actual figures for each of the 40 categories included in this chart in addition to the two scales help to clarify and improve the accuracy of the various comparisons. The rank order of the bars is based on the size of the total population for each of the five racial categories.

Bilateral-bar Charts

There are three types of bilateral or two-way bar charts: (1) paired-bar chart, (2) deviation-bar chart, and (3) sliding-bar chart. In this type of chart the bars extend to the left and to the right of a common referent line or division. Bilateral-bar charts are well adapted to comparisons of two contrasting groups or attributes or to the presentation of positive and negative deviations from normal, increases and decreases, and gains and losses.

Paired-bar Chart

Figure 4–11 is a paired-bar chart showing a comparison of average monthly salaries received by both teachers and nonteachers employed by local governments in 1972. The ordering of the bars is based on groupings of SMSAs according to size. It will be observed that for both groups of employees there is a fairly consistent positive relationship between average monthly salaries and the size of the SMSAs. A comparison of monthly salaries for each of the respective major categories shows that

teachers rank higher than other employees. More precise and more readily interpretable comparisons could be made from this chart if the basic divisions on the scales were $200 rather than $300 and if ticks or points were indicated for each $100.

Figure 4–12 is a paired–grouped-bar chart that combines two distinct variables—income and taxes—for eight groupings of 79 of the 100 largest companies in the United States. The twofold source of income—United States and foreign countries—and the corresponding amount of taxes and tax credits represent the basic divisions of the data. All major nations of the world have a network of systems designed to avoid excessive double taxation of income earned abroad. In the United States the method used for avoiding double taxation is a tax-credit system. The foreign tax credit affects only income earned in some foreign country through activities conducted in that country. The comparative foreign and domestic incomes of these large corporations, which run into the billions of dollars, along with the amount of tax credits and taxes paid, are clearly portrayed in Figure 4–12. Because of several (nine) explanatory labels and legends, the scale was placed at the bottom of the chart.

Deviation-bar Chart

A bilateral bar chart showing percentage changes in dairy-product sales between 1965 and 1972 is exemplified by Figure 4–13. The various items are arranged in percentage rank order beginning with the highest positive deviation. The last item on the chart is the highest negative deviation. The scale on either side of the zero line normally covers the range of plus and minus values. However, it will be noted that since the top bar in Figure 4–13 represents a "freak" or highly erratic value it is broken and the figure (121.9%) is indicated at the end of the bar. The style used to show a break in the bar is not as clear as it should be. Accordingly, it is recommended that a style of break where the bar is actually separated as in Figure 4–5 be used instead. The stubs for the positive bars are indicated in the blank space to the left of the zero line and similarly, the stubs for the items with negative values are shown on the positive side. The fact that the scale figures are placed at the bottom is of no special significance. It would have been just as appropriate to have placed the scale figures at the top.

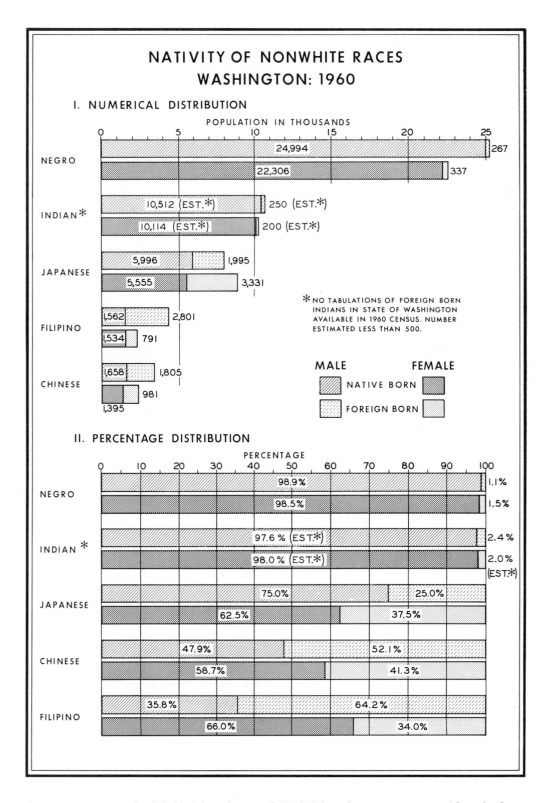

Figure 4–10. Grouped subdivided–bar charts. Subdivided–bar charts may portray either absolute numbers or percentages. This chart includes both types. The upper portion indicates the numerical distribution of nonwhite races in the state of Washington according to nativity, and the lower portion represents comparable data in percentages. (From Calvin F. Schmid, Charles E. Nobbe, and Arlene E. Mitchell, Non-white Races, State of Washington, *1968, p. 92.)*

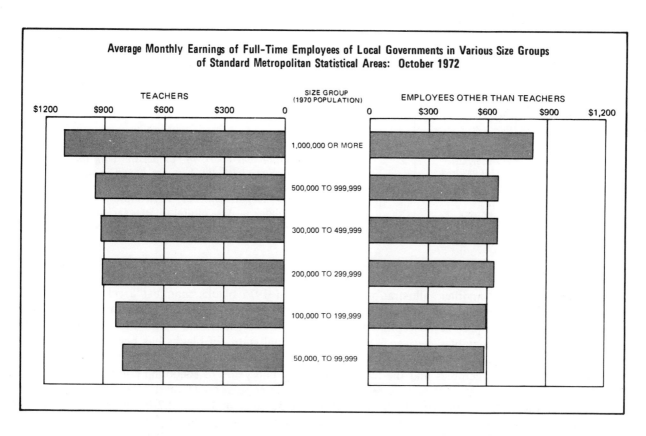

Average Monthly Earnings of Full-Time Employees of Local Governments in Various Size Groups
of Standard Metropolitan Statistical Areas: October 1972

Figure 4–11. A paired–bar chart. (*From United States Bureau of the Census,* Graphic Summary of the 1972 Census of Governments, *Topical Studies No. 5, Washington: Government Printing Office, 1974, p. 37.*)

Figure 4–12. A paired grouped–bar chart that combines two distinct variables—income and taxes (*From* 1974 Annual Report of the Secretary of the Treasury, *p. 504.*)

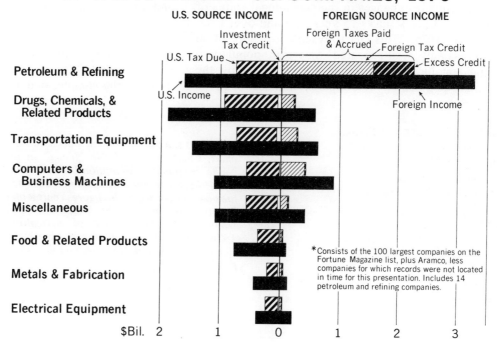

INCOME AND TAXES PAID,
OF THE 79 LARGEST U.S. COMPANIES,* 1970

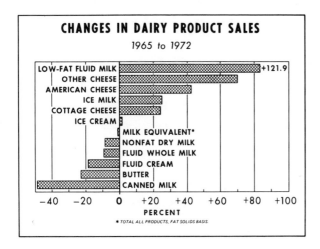

Figure 4–13. Another illustration of a deviation–bar chart. In comparison with the preceding chart, the bars are boxed in with clearly labelled scale lines. (From United States Department of Agriculture, 1973 Handbook of Agricultural Charts, Agriculture Handbook No. 455, October 1973, p. 84.)

Figure 4–14 is another illustration of a deviation-bar chart divided into two distinct parts. Both parts indicate changes in per capita consumption of processed vegetables between 1960 and 1975. The upper portion of Figure 4–14 portrays changes for canned vegetables and the lower portion, for frozen vegetables. It will be readily observed that the basic design of Figure 4–14 different from most of the bar charts presented in this chapter, especially with the absence of a scale, including scale figures, scale lines, scale points, and a scale legend. The value represented by each bar is indicated by a figure placed at the end of the bar.

Bar charts designed in this manner seem to be acceptable, although we do not believe they possess any special merit or advantage. A carefully designed bar chart with scale figures, scale lines, scale points, and a scale legend is much clearer and more readily interpreted.

Figure 4–15 is a grouped–deviation-bar chart that compares changes in the educational status of white and black males 25 years old and over from 1970 to 1975. This chart presents a picture of an increasingly well-educated American population. Incidentally, similar trends are exhibited by the female population. It is apparent that between 1970

and 1975 blacks manifest a relatively greater increase in educational attainment than whites. However, it should be pointed out that the educational status of blacks has been and still is considerably lower than that of whites. For example, the median years of schooling completed for the white male population 25 years of age and over are 9.3 in 1950, 10.7 in 1960, 12.2 in 1970, and 12.5 in 1975. Corresponding figures for black males are 6.4 in 1950, 7.9 in 1960, 9.6 in 1970, and 10.7 in 1975. It will be observed that the figures in parentheses for each of the bars indicate the number of persons included in the 1975 sample. The total number of persons for all of the categories is approximately 55,000. The 1970 sample is of comparable size. Estimates based on samples may differ somewhat from figures that would have been obtained if a complete census were taken using the same schedules, instructions, and enumerators. There are two types of error possible in an estimate based on a sample survey—sampling and nonsampling. Sampling variabilities are variations that occur by chance because a sample rather than the whole of the population is surveyed. Nonsampling errors can be attributed to many sources such as, inability to obtain information about all the cases in the sample, definitional difficulties, differ-

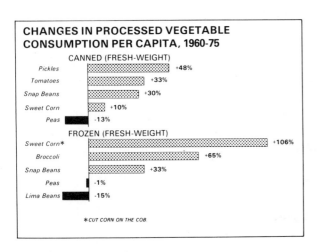

Figure 4–14. An illustration of a deviation–bar chart. Chart shows relative changes in per capita vegetable consumption between 1960 and 1975. Sometimes the scale in a bar chart may be omitted when the figures represented by the bars are clearly indicated. (From United States Department of Agriculture, 1976 Handbook of Agricultural Charts, Agricultural Handbook No. 504, October 1976, p. 153.)

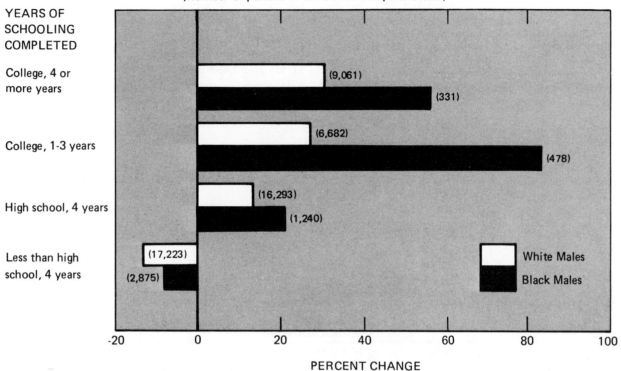

Percent Change in Years of Schooling Completed by
Males 25 Years Old and Over: 1970 to 1975
(Number of persons in 1975 shown in parentheses)

Figure 4–15. A grouped deviation–bar chart. (From United States Bureau of the Census, **Educational Attainment in the United States: March 1975,** *Current Population Reports,* **Series P-20, No. 295, 1976, p. 2.)**

ences in the interpretation of questions, inability to recall information, and errors in the processing of data.[4]

Sliding-bar Chart

Figure 4–16 is an illustration of a relatively simple sliding-bar chart consisting of two series of bars with only two components. The two components indicate the proportion of crimes "cleared" and the proportion "not cleared." The two series of bars pertain respectively to crimes against the person and crimes against property. Law-enforcement agencies "clear" a crime when they have identified the offender, have sufficient evidence to charge him, and actually take him into custody. The arrest of

one person can clear several crimes or several persons may be arrested in the process of clearing one crime. It will be observed that one component of each bar extends to the left (not cleared) and the other component to the right (cleared) of a common referent line. In more complicated sliding-bar charts the two major components may be subdivided into two or more segments; thus it is strongly recommended in a chart of this kind that the two major components not be subdivided into more than three or, at most, four segments.

Another illustration of a sliding bar chart is shown in Figure 4–17. It will be readily observed that this chart is considerably more complex than the preceding one. It portrays monthly salary differentials for certain professional and technical occupational categories in the state of New York in the spring of 1973. There are seven primary occupational groups with a total of 30 subgroups on this chart. The salary of each of the 30 subgroups is presented as a bar and positioned in relation to a

---

[4] United States Bureau of the Census, *Educational Attainment in the United States: March 1975,* Current Population Reports, Series P-20, No. 295, 1976, pp. 65–71.

horizontal scale. The length of each bar has been determined by the first (D_1) and the ninth decile (D_9) values, which embodies 80% of the cases. In addition, the median (Q_2), the first quartile (Q_1), and the third quartile (Q_3) are scaled off on each of the bars. The distance from Q_1 to Q_3 includes 50% of the cases. It will be seen from the legend that the portion of the bar from Q_1 to the median is cross-hatched with a fairly heavy single line and the por-

tion from the median to Q_3 by stippling. The portions of each bar from the first decile (D_1) to Q_1 and from Q_3 to the ninth decile (D_9) are left blank. For example, it will be observed from Figure 4–17 that the median monthly salary for attorneys IV and V are $2,166 and $2,749, respectively, and the corresponding middle-range salaries (Q_1 to Q_3) are $1,755 to $2,499 and $2,517 to $2,940. Engineers VIII report a median monthly salary of $2,331,

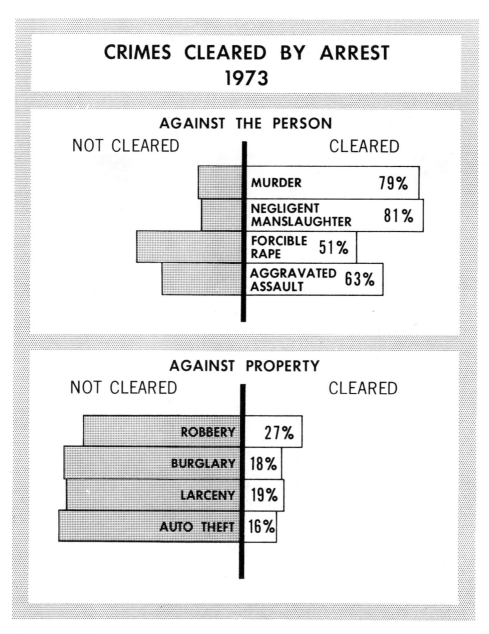

Figure 4–16. Effective application of sliding–bar chart to two simple dichotomous series. Chart shows the proportions of the various crimes against the person and crimes against property that are "cleared" and "not cleared." Law enforcement agencies "clear" a crime when they have identified the offender, have sufficient evidence to charge him, and actually take him into custody. (From Federal Bureau of Investigation, Crime in the United States: 1973, Washington: Government Printing Office, 1974, p. 29.)

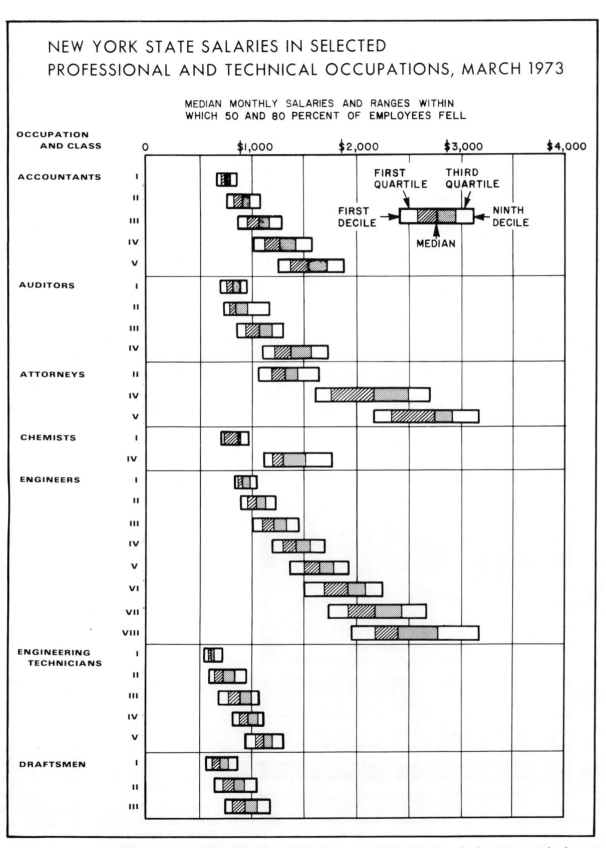

Figure 4–17. A sliding–bar chart (Redrawn from U.S. Department of Labor, Bureau of Labor Statistics, Professional, Administrative, Technical and Clerical Pay in New York, 1973, New York: Regional Report No. 36, March 1974, p. 15.)

with a middle range (Q_1 to Q_3) of \$2,175 to \$2,855. On the other hand, the respective median monthly salaries of draftsmen I and draftsmen III are \$755 and \$1,000, with middle salary ranges (Q_1 to Q_3) of \$685 to \$826 and \$910 to \$1,121.

Area-bar Chart

A variation of the 100% subdivided or component bar chart includes area as an essential feature. The areas of the bars for the major categories are drawn in proportion to the overall values that they represent; the areas of the subdivisions of the bars are based on the respective values of the subcategories. For example, the length of each of the five bars in Figure 4–18 is a constant, but the width of each bar is based on a specific proportion of a total. For example, since Mexicans comprise 59.3% of the total, Puerto Ricans 15.8%, Cubans 6.2%, and so on, the width of each of the bars is scaled accordingly. The area of each bar reflects its relative importance in comparison to the other bars in the series. The subdivisions, in turn, indicate the age composition of the different groups. The title,

labels, scale, and crosshatching are also, of course, essential features of this type of chart.

Figure 4–19 is another example of an area-bar chart whose basic design is considerably different from that represented by Figure 4–18. This chart was constructed to portray the relationship between the condition of dwelling units and the amount of rent paid. According to their condition, dwelling units are classified into four categories: (1) good condition, (2) needing minor repairs, (3) needing major repairs, and (4) unfit for use. The proportion of dwelling units in each of these four categories is indicated by a vertical percentage scale. The number of dwelling units in each of eight rental categories is the basis for dividing the chart horizontally. For example, for the city of Minneapolis the area of the segment representing the 23,029 dwelling units renting for \$30–\$49 per month is in pronounced contrast to the area comprising the 226 dwelling units renting for \$100 and over. Furthermore, the relationship between the condition of dwelling units and the amount of rent can be readily interpreted from this chart. In general, the proportion of units in good order increases in direct relation to the amount of rent paid. For example, only

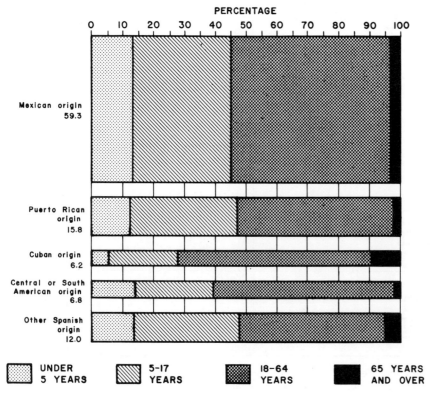

*Figure 4–18. Illustration of an area–bar chart. (**Redrawn from United States Bureau of the Census,** Persons of Spanish Origin in the United States: March 1976, **Current Population Reports, Series P-20, No. 302, 1976, p. 4.**)*

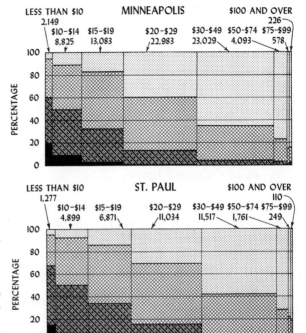

CONDITION OF RENTED DWELLING
UNITS BY MONTHLY RENT
MINNEAPOLIS AND ST.PAUL : 1934

Figure 4–19. Two area–bar charts arranged for comparison. It will be observed that the vertical scales indicate the percentage of dwelling units in each of the four categories—(1) "good condition," (2) "minor repairs," and (3) "major repairs" and "unfit for use"—according to the proportion of dwelling units in each of eight rental categories for Minneapolis and St. Paul, respectively. (From Calvin F. Schmid, Social Saga of Two Cities, *Minneapolis: Minneapolis Council of Social Agencies, 1937, p. 216.)*

5.7% of the dwelling units in Minneapolis and 5% of the dwelling units in St. Paul that show a monthly rent of less than $10 are considered to be in "good condition." Also, the respective proportions in this rental category that are "unfit for use" are relatively high. By contrast, the quality of housing in the higher rental classifications is progressively better.

Preprinted Hatching and Stippling Tapes and Sheets for Bar and Column Charts

In preparing bar and column charts it will be found that preprinted hatching and stippling patterns in the form of sheets and tapes will save a substantial amount of time and labor. The tapes are available in various widths such as $\frac{1}{4}$ in., $\frac{3}{8}$ in., $\frac{1}{2}$ in., and $\frac{5}{8}$ in. In addition to hatching and stippling patterns, the

tapes and sheets are printed in a wide variety of colors. Both the tapes and sheets have a self-adhesive backing and can be readily applied to a drawing.[5]

Unfortunately, some of the hatching and stippling on the tapes as well as on the larger preprinted sheets are poorly designed and ill adapted to bar and column charts. To use inappropriate or poorly designed hatching or stippling patterns could seriously detract from the quality of a chart. In this connection, the caveat made earlier deserves repeating: the selection of hatching and stippling patterns should be made with the most careful discrimination. This admonition applies not only to bar and column charts but to maps, pie charts, surface charts, and any other kind of chart where hatching and stippling might be used.

COLUMN CHARTS

As has been pointed out previously, the main difference between the bar and column charts is the

---

[5] For examples of these materials that are available commercially, see at least two or three of the catalogs listed in Chapter 2, footnote 4.

arrangement of bars; the bars are arranged horizontally in the bar chart and vertically in the column chart. However, with respect to emphasis and application, the column chart is especially valuable in portraying time series, if the number of plotted values is not very large. In comparison to the line chart, the column chart can provide greater emphasis in portraying amounts in a single time series and greater contrasts in portraying amounts in two or three time series. On the other hand, it can be said that the arithmetic line chart is more appropriate than the column chart if the period covers many years and plotting points.

Types of Column Charts

Eight different forms of the column chart are illustrated in Figures 4–20 and 4–21. The following statements summarize the names and salient characteristics of these eight variations of the column chart.

Simple Column Chart. In several basic features the simple column chart has much in common with the simple bar chart. The baseline of the column chart is drawn horizontally, and under no circumstances should it be omitted. The simple column chart is particularly valuable for showing time series.

Connected-column Chart. This type of chart possesses characteristics of both the simple column chart and staircase surface chart. Although all the columns are distinct, there is no space between them. The connected-column chart may be particularly valuable as a space-saving device.

Grouped-column Chart. This chart is comparable to the grouped-, multiple-, or compound-bar chart. Two or occasionally three columns representing different series or different classes in the same series can be grouped together. In grouping the columns they may be joined together or separated by a narrow space.

Subdivided-column Chart. The subdivided-column chart, like the subdivided-, segmented-, or component-bar chart, is used to show a series of values with respect to their component parts. The subdivided-column chart is also similar to the subdivided-surface chart. Crosshatching is

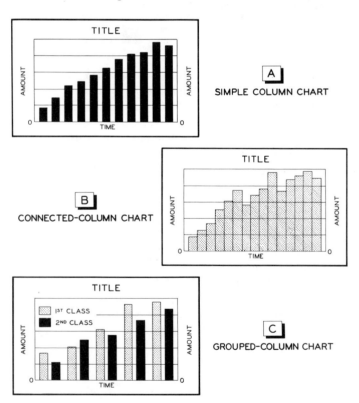
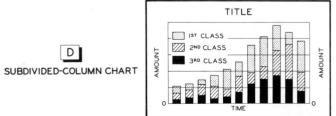

Figure 4–20. Illustrations of different types of column charts.

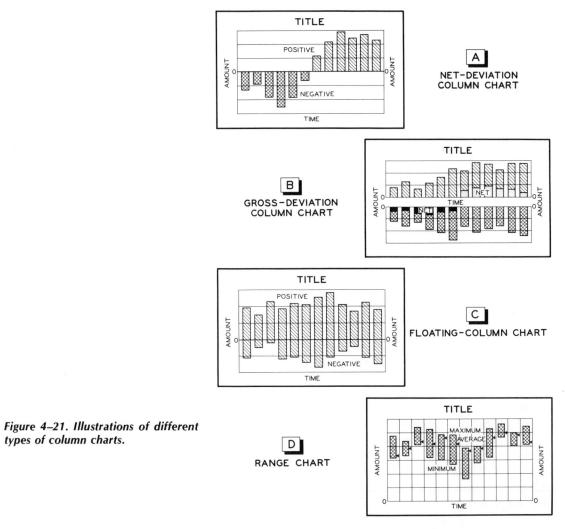

Figure 4–21. Illustrations of different types of column charts.

ordinarily used to differentiate the various subdivisions of the columns. The scale may be expressed in terms either of absolute or relative values.

Net-deviation-column Chart. The net-deviation- and the gross-deviation-column charts are similar to the bilateral-bar charts. They emphasize positive and negative numbers, increases and decreases, and gains and losses. In the net-deviation chart the column extends either above or below the referent line, but not in both directions.

Gross-deviation-column Chart. The columns in this type of chart extend in both directions from the referent line. By means of crosshatching, both gross and net changes can be readily portrayed.

Floating-column Chart. The floating-column chart is a deviational or bilateral chart with 100%

component columns. The deviations from the referent line represent positive and negative values or differential attributes.

Range Chart. The range chart shows maximal and minimal values in time series. This chart has been referred to as a "stock-price" chart, since it is extensively used in plotting highest and lowest daily, weekly, or monthly stock quotations. Average values also can be readily indicated on the columns.

Standards, Specifications, and Problems of Design

The standards as well as most of the characteristics and procedures discussed in connection with the bar chart are directly applicable to the column chart. The columns should be of uniform width and evenly spaced. The spacing between columns may vary from one-half to the same width as the columns. Sometimes, the columns may actually be connected with no space at all between them, and in the case of grouped column charts the columns may be drawn so they overlap. In the simple column chart the columns are usually blackened in, although stippling and crosshatching sometimes may be found appropriate. The vertical scale always begins with zero and covers the range of the data to be plotted.

Figure 4–22 clearly demonstrates the consequences of omitting the zero baseline. This is one of the most common as well as flagrant errors in constructing column charts. The column graph on the right (B) is drawn correctly with an ordinal scale running from zero to 7000. The chart on the left side (A) has a vertical scale ranging from 2000 to 7000. The differences in the relative size of the columns give an exaggerated and distorted impression. In A the height of the largest column is more than 18 times that of the smallest. Actually, the tallest column is about 3.5 times that of the smallest column in the correctly drawn chart.

Figure 4–23 illustrates additional standards, specifications, and problems in the design of column charts. Panel A shows four different grid patterns for column charts. In general, there are fewer grid rulings in column charts than in arithmetic line charts. Although the four different patterns portrayed in panel A are acceptable, we consider the completely boxed-in grid with full horizontal scale lines (b) as most desirable. It will be observed from the various illustrations of column charts in Figure 4–23 and the other illustrations of column charts in this chapter that the grid lines are not drawn through the columns. Panel B illustrates the importance of column width and spacing in laying out a chart of this kind. Panel C further emphasizes the necessity of care and good judgment in designing a column chart. Columns that are too

wide or too narrow can result in a clumsy and amateurish chart. Panel D offers a simple solution to the problem of too many columns in a limited amount of space. In such instances, the spaces between the columns may be omitted and the columns connected. Panel E indicates how the proportions of a column chart can affect the width of the columns as well as their spacing. The choice of proportions for a column chart should never be arbitrary, but rather adapted to the data at hand. Panel F points out that for emphasis, and only in exceptional cases, the plotted values may be shown directly above the columns [see sketches (a) and (b)]. Normally, the standards for locating and placing scale numerals and captions are the same for column charts as for line charts. Sketch (c) shows how to label a column for an incomplete period. Panels G and H illustrate good and poor shading patterns for column charts. Hatching and stippling patterns should not be either too coarse or grotesque or too fine or light.

Simple Column Chart

Figure 4–24 is an illustration of a simple column chart. Although it fulfills most of the standards and specifications of simple column charts, it embodies a few additional features not ordinarily included in a chart of this kind. To make the chart more meaningful, comparative decennial data for 1950, 1960, and 1970 are included. The three columns representing these statistics have been differentiated from the annual series by spacing and, of course, by appropriate labels. Also, another special feature of this chart is the percentages enclosed in circles, which represent the proportion national health expenditures comprise of the gross national product (GNP). Normally, a well-designed chart of this kind should have a vertical scale with scale lines running horizontally.

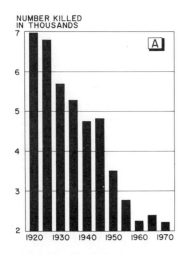

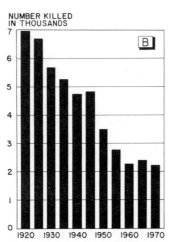

Figure 4–22. Column chart with and without zero base line. A. Erroneous omission of zero base line. B. Correct technique in designing an arithmetic scale for a column chart. Data represent number of railroad fatalities (passengers, employees, trespassers, and others) from 1920 to 1970. (Chart drawn from original data in U.S. Bureau of the Census, Historical Statistics of the United States, Colonial Times to 1970, Bicentennial Edition, Part 1, *Washington: Government Printing Office, 1975, Series Q 398–409.)*

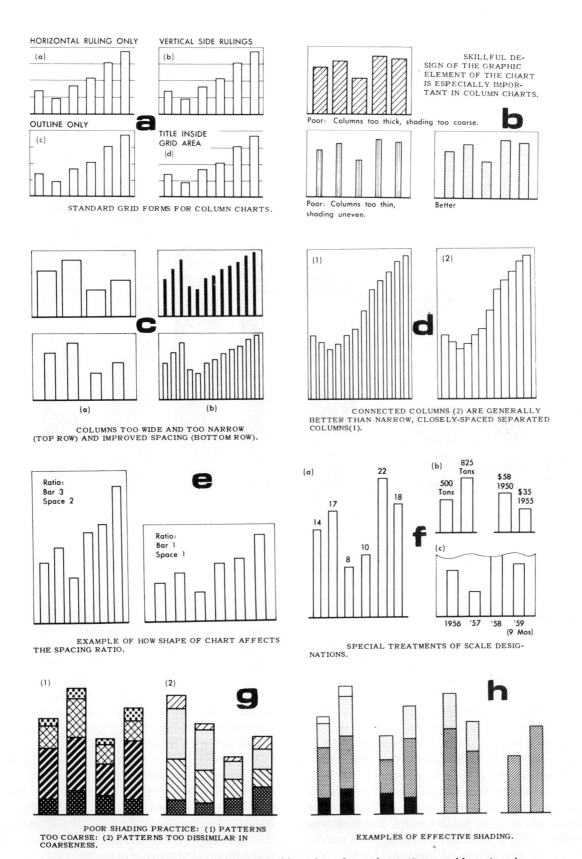

Figure 4–23. Some design specifications and problems for column charts. (*Extracted from* American Standard Time–Series Charts [ASA Y15.2–1960], *with the permission of the publisher, The American Society of Mechanical Engineers, 245 E. 47th Street, New York, N. Y. 10017.*)

NATIONAL HEALTH EXPENDITURES AND PERCENT OF GROSS
NATIONAL PRODUCT, SELECTED FISCAL YEARS 1950-75

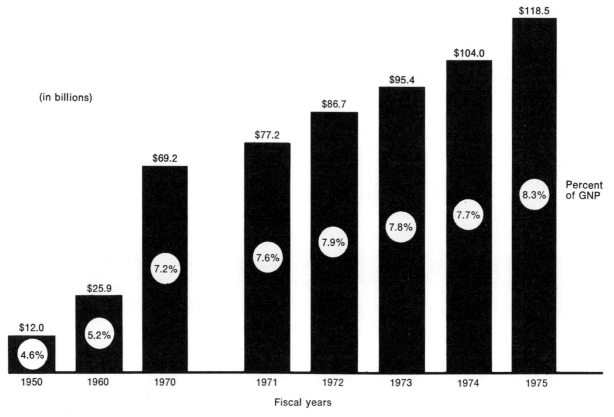

Figure 4–24. Simple column chart. [From Marjorie Smith Mueller and Robert M. Gibson, "National Health Expenditures, Fiscal Year 1975, Social Security Bulletin, 39, (2), February 1976, pp. 3–20.]

Connected-column Chart

Figure 4–25 is a combination of a connected-column chart and special type of symbol chart. Two simple connected-column charts are found at the extreme left and right sides of the grid. The connected-column chart on the left portrays the range of illiteracy in 1900, 1930, and 1960 for four regions consisting of combinations of geographic divisions as defined by the U.S. Bureau of the Census. For example, the region described as the South, which ranks highest in illiteracy for each of the specified years includes the following geographic divisions: South Atlantic, East South Central, and West South Central. The connected-column chart on the right shows the percentage of illiteracy for the entire United States in 1900, 1930, and 1960. The percentage of illiteracy for the population 15 years and over

(14 years and over in 1960) was reported to be 11.3 in 1900, 4.8 in 1930, and 2.4 in 1960. The lines and symbols represent the percentage of illiteracy for the nine geographic divisions for 1900, 1930, and 1960. The six columns and the nine lines with symbols have been superimposed on the vertical scale so that all are comparable with one another. Figure 4–25 represents considerable originality and summarizes simply and effectively a large amount of data. However, we believe that this chart could be improved by: (1) including spaces between the vertical scale and columns both on the left and right sides, (2) adding more scale figures as well as scale divisions, (3) making the lines and symbols for the geographic divisions slightly heavier, and (4) including a notation either on the chart or in the text that the data for the column chart on the left includes a combination of geographic divisions, not single divisions.

PERCENT ILLITERATE AMONG PERSONS 15 YEARS OLD AND OVER, BY GEOGRAPHIC DIVISION: 1900, 1930, AND 1960

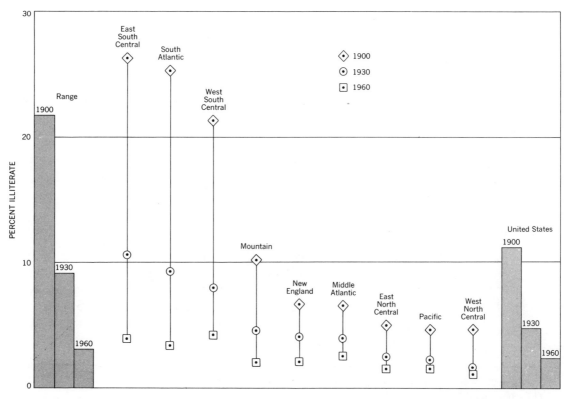

NOTE: Data for 1960 are for the population 14 years old and over. Data for the Pacific Division exclude Alaska and Hawaii.

Figure 4–25. A connected column chart combined with special symbols showing percentage of the population 15 years of age and older classified as illiterate for the entire United States and for each geographic division. (From John K. Folger and Charles B. Nam, Education of the American Population, Washington: Government Printing Office, 1967, p. 120.)

Grouped-column Chart

The grouped-column chart is used to compare two or three series of statistics by grouping together the columns for each specified period of time. In each grouping the columns may be: (1) connected, (2) separated by a relatively small space, or (3) over-lapped. Figure 4–26 is an illustration of a grouped-column chart in which there are groupings of three connected columns. The basic data pertain to trends in world cotton exports from 1967 to 1975 expressed in millions of bales. The three columns for each year represent exports by: (1) the United States, (2) other noncommunist countries, and (3) communist countries. Each of the three columns are differentiated by shading and hatching. It will be observed that cotton exports for the

United States ranged from 2.8 million tons in 1968 and 1969, respectively, to 6 million tons in 1973. The corresponding figures for other noncommunist countries ranged from 9.4 million tons in 1974 to 12.4 million tons in 1969 and 1974, respectively, and for communist countries from 2.4 million tons in 1968 and 1969, respectively, to 3.8 in 1974 and 1975, respectively.

Figure 4–27 is a grouped-column chart that portrays trends in homicide and suicide in the United States from 1960 and 1972 as measured by rates per 100,000 of total population. It will be noted especially that in the spacing of the groups of columns, there is a break in the yearly time sequence between 1960 and 1965 and between 1965 and 1967. The two breaks in the continuity of the series are indicated by wider spacing between the

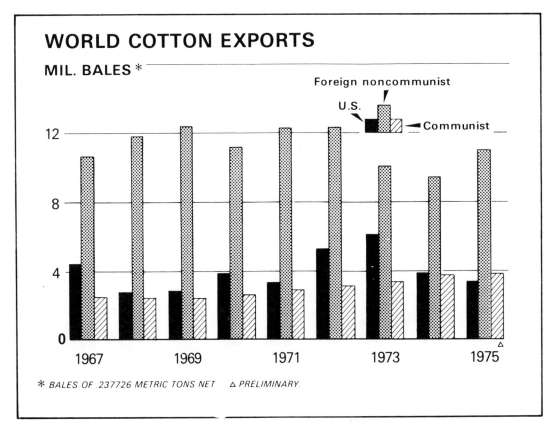

Figure 4–26. Another illustration of a grouped–column chart. This chart exhibits groupings of three columns. (From United States Department of Agriculture, 1976 Handbook of Agricultural Charts, Agricultural Handbook No. 504, October 1976, p. 141.)

groups of columns. It is very important that appropriate adjustments be made in the horizontal scale as a consequence of omissions or other factors that might cause breaks in the continuity of the data. In practice, the time scale in a column chart should possess the same significance as well as govern the spacing of data as the horizontal scale in the rectilinear coordinate chart.

Technique for Constructing Overlapping Type of Grouped-column Chart

This paragraph, including Figure 4–28, is a short digression designed to explain a simple step-by-step procedure for laying out overlapping columns. Incidentally, the procedure for drawing overlapping bars for a bar chart is very similar, except, of course, the bars are arranged horizontally:

Step A. For a grouping of three columns the first step is to draw five equidistant vertical pencil lines, the width of the spacing representing one-half the width of each column.

Step B. After determining the height of each of the three columns, pencil in the portion of each column that will be shown on the chart.

Step C. Ink in the three columns in accordance with the outline in step B.

Step D. Erase all pencil lines and shade each of the columns with a gradation intensity from light to dark as shown in Figure 4–28.

Subdivided-column Chart

The subdivided-column chart portrays the size of component parts of a series of totals, expressed either in absolute figures or in percentages. Figure

Homicide and Suicide Rates: 1960 to 1972

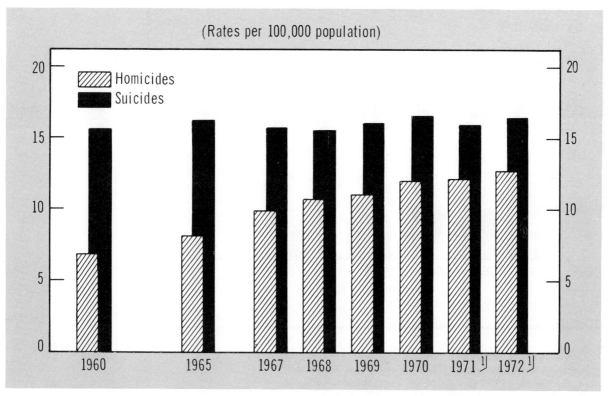

(Rates per 100,000 population)

Homicides
Suicides

1960   1965   1967   1968   1969   1970   1971 ¹⁾ 1972 ¹⁾

¹Estimated
Source: Chart prepared by U.S. Bureau of the Census. Data from U.S. Public Health Service.

Figure 4–27. A grouped–column chart with columns partially superimposed on each other in order to save space and to facilitate comparison. (From United States Bureau of the Census, Statistical Abstract of the United States: 1974, Washington: Government Printing Office, 1974, p. 144.)

4–29 is a subdivided-column chart with values expressed in absolute figures. It portrays the annual world production of wheat measured in millions of metric tons from 1966 to 1975. There are four subdivisions for each column representing the amount of wheat produced in: (1) Russia, (2) the United States, (3) four other major producers combined (Canada, France, Australia, and Argentina) and (4)

all other countries. The four subdivisions are differentiated by hatching and stippling patterns along with appropriate labels. Generally, in charts of this kind a key or legend consisting of appropriately labeled blocks of hatching and/or stippling is included on the chart. However, since there is ample space at the right side of the grid, which was designed for four additional years, the labels have

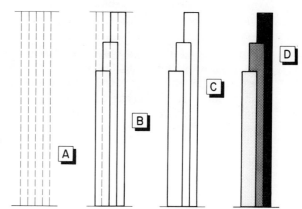

Figure 4–28. Technique for constructing overlapping type of grouped–column chart.

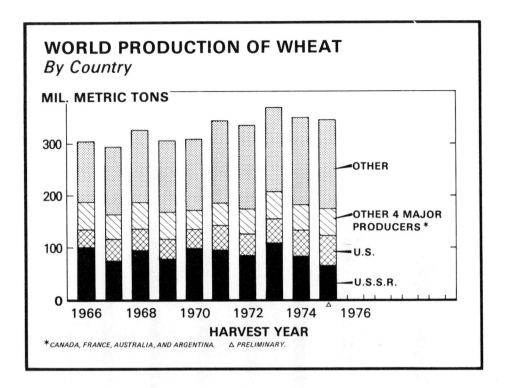

Figure 4–29. A subdivided–column chart with values expressed in absolute figures. (From United States Department of Agriculture, 1976 Handbook of Agricultural Charts, Agricultural Handbook No. 504, October 1976, p. 111.)

been placed directly contiguous to the subdivisions of the last column.

Figure 4–30 is a subdivided-column chart in which the components indicate the distribution of social-welfare expenditures, by program for each quinquennial fiscal year from 1950 to 1975. Social-welfare expenditures include cash benefits, services, and administration costs of all programs that are of direct benefit to individuals and families such as those pertaining to health and medical care, education, housing, welfare services, social insurance, and veterans' aid. In Figure 4–30 welfare expenditures have been classified into six categories, each identified by a special hatching pattern along with an appropriate label. The trends of expenditures for the six component categories are made more distinct by a series of connecting dashed lines. Proportionally, for example, during the 25-year period covered by the chart veterans' programs show a noticeable decline; health and medical programs show a slight decline; social insurance and housing and other social-welfare and public aid show increases; whereas education has evidenced some fluctuation, with the highest proportion reported in 1965.

Although the basic design of this chart conforms to accepted graphic standards and specifications, it lacks the forcefulness and impact of a well-constructed chart. This chart could have been greatly improved if more attention had been paid to a number of minor details. Concern or lack of concern for small and seemingly inconsequential details may spell the difference between a really superior and an ordinary chart. Figure 4–30 could be improved by: (1) a more discriminating selection of hatching patterns, (2) using larger letters and figures for both axes, (3) drawing somewhat lighter lines for the two scales, (4) making the lines outlining the columns heavier, and (5) extending the 100% line to the 1975 column.

Net-deviation-column Charts

Figure 4–31 depicts quarterly changes in the GNP from 1973 through June of 1976. The GNP changes are expressed in both current prices and in 1972 prices. The data representing the columns are changes from the preceding quarter in billions of dollars. For example, Quarter IV of 1974 recorded

PERCENTAGE DISTRIBUTION OF SOCIAL WELFARE EXPENDITURES, BY PROGRAM, SELECTED FISCAL YEARS 1950-75

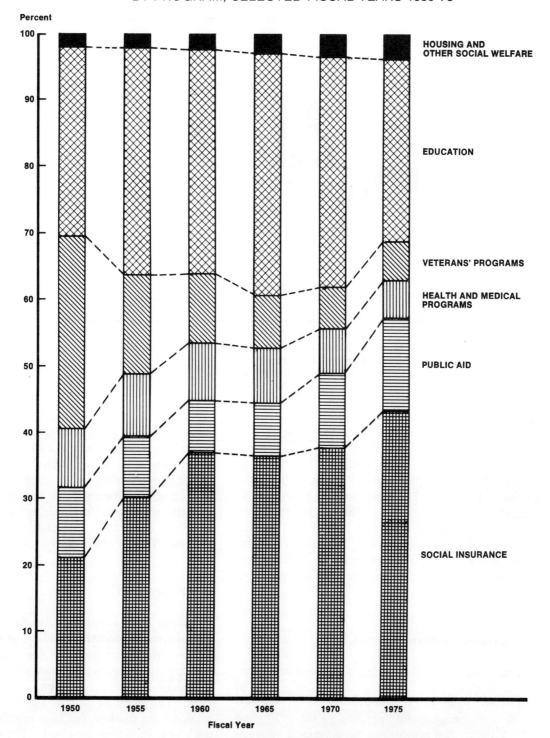

Percent

HOUSING AND OTHER SOCIAL WELFARE

EDUCATION

VETERANS' PROGRAMS

HEALTH AND MEDICAL PROGRAMS

PUBLIC AID

SOCIAL INSURANCE

Fiscal Year

Figure 4–30. One–hundred percent subdivided–column chart. See text for comments concerning the quality of this chart. [From Alfred M. Skolnik and Sophie R. Dales, "Social Welfare Expenditures, 1950–75," Social Security Bulletin, 39, (1), January 1976, pp. 3–20.]

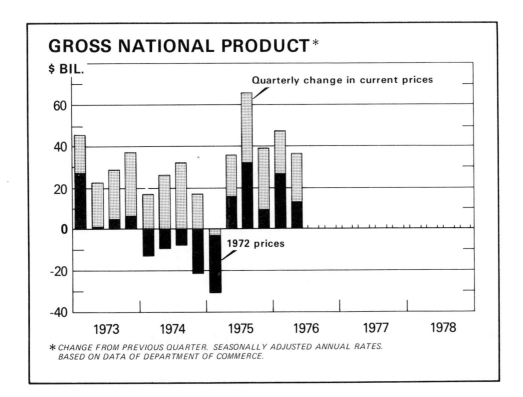

Figure 4–31. A net–deviation–column chart showing Gross National Product (GNP) by quarters. Quarterly changes in the GNP are shown both in current prices and in 1972 prices. (From United States Department of Agriculture, 1976 Handbook of Agricultural Charts, No. 504, p. 35.)

a GNP of 1449.2 billion dollars and Quarter I of 1975, 1446.2 billion dollars in current prices, indicating a change of −3 billion dollars. This figure is shown by the stippled portion of the column for Quarter I of 1975. The corresponding figures of the GNP in 1972 prices are as follows: Quarter IV of 1974, 1191.7 and Quarter I of 1975, 1161.1, which shows a quarterly change of −30.6 billion dollars. This figure of −30.6 billion dollars is indicated by the black portion of the column for Quarter I of 1975.

Gross-deviation-column Chart

Figure 4–32 is an illustration of a gross-deviation-column chart. It portrays in- and outmigration of persons 5 years of age and over by regions for two different quinquennial periods, 1965–1970 and 1970–1975. Net migration—the difference between the volume of inmigration and outmigration—is also indicated on the chart. The portion of the columns above the zero referent line represents inmi-

gration, and the portion of the columns below the zero referent line represents outmigration. Furthermore, the scale figures with plus signs designate inmigration and those with minus signs, outmigration. It will be observed that the regional migration patterns are similar for both periods. The South and West exhibit net inmigration, and the Northeast and North Central regions, net outmigration.

Range Chart

The range chart is particularly effective in showing fluctuations of monthly, weekly, or daily prices or stock-market quotations. For example, Figure 4–33 portrays the monthly range of the Dow Jones Industrial Average from January 1966 to January 1976. The length of each column indicates the fluctuation from the low and high monthly average for each year shown on the chart. The cross-line indicates the closing average for each month. Another important feature of this chart is the more than 60 explanatory legends and figures that make the chart

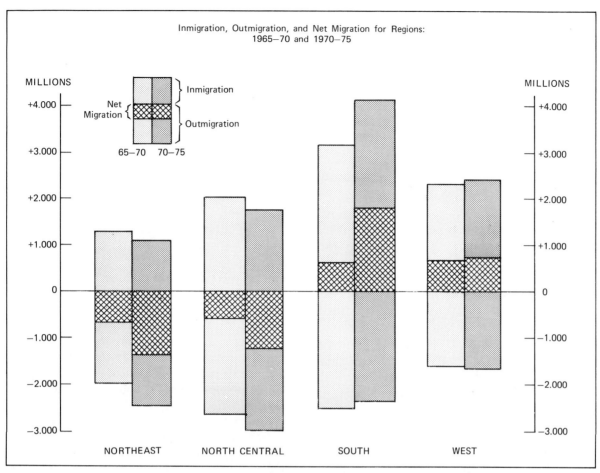

Figure 4–32. Gross–deviation column chart for portraying in– and outmigration of population. (From United States Bureau of the Census, Mobility of the Population of the United States: March 1970 to March 1975, Current Population Reports, Series P-20, No. 285, 1975, p. 3.)

Figure 4–33. A range chart showing monthly stock market fluctuations as indicated by Dow Jones Industrial Average. The length of each column is commensurate with the monthly range of fluctuation in the Dow Jones index. (From pamphlet published by Dean Witter and Company, Incorporated.)

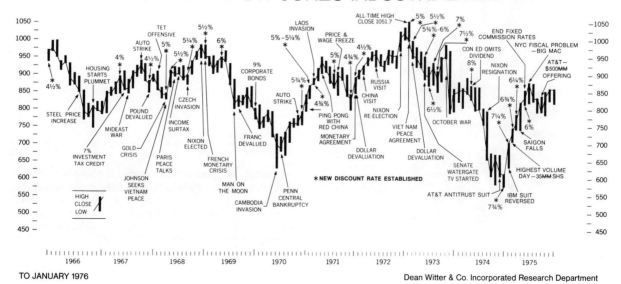

more readily interpretable as well as more meaningful.

Column Chart with Circular Baseline

To attract attention or achieve popular appeal, it is common practice to incorporate symbolic or pictorial features with basic graphic forms.[6] Figure 4–34, which shows the number of law-enforcement officers killed by hour of occurrence from 1966–1975, is a column chart with certain characteristics of a clock. Of course, other graphic forms could have been used in portraying this information. In fact, the Federal Bureau of Investigation in their 1976 annual report, *Crime in the United States, 1975,* from which the data for Figure 4–34 were derived, used a simple bar chart to depict this information. In the 1973 report the Federal Bureau of Investigation used a sector diagram in which degrees on a circle (sectors) corresponded to the number of deaths for each of the 24 hourly divisions.

As indicated in the preceding paragraph, Figure 4–34 was designed to present symbolically, if not pictorially, the diurnal cycle as it relates to the killing of law-enforcement officials. The length of each of the 24 columns is commensurate with the number of law-enforcement officials killed. The baseline is circular and is calibrated as a 24-hour clock, and the scale lines are represented by a series of concentric circles drawn equidistant from the

baseline. The first innermost circle carries a value of 10 deaths, the second 20 deaths, and each one thereafter with an additional value of 10 to the outermost circle with a value of 90 deaths.

Nontemporal Column Charts

Although column charts are used predominantly for portraying temporal data, there are some instances where this may not be the case. Characteristically, the column chart has two scales, the vertical scale indicating amount and the horizontal scale, time. Thus comparisons are made of a given item or several items over a period of time. On the other hand, the bar chart typically has only one scale, which is used to compare different categories at a given time. Because of the nature of the data, special objectives or purposes incorporated in the chart design or some other reason, the column chart may be adapted to portray comparisons at a given time without any implications of temporal change.

By the same token, bar charts are sometimes used to depict comparisons in which the temporal factor may be very explicit. In this connection, a question might be appropriately raised as to specifically when a temporal or nontemporal column chart or bar chart should or should not be used.

---

[6] See Chapter 9 for a more extended discussion.

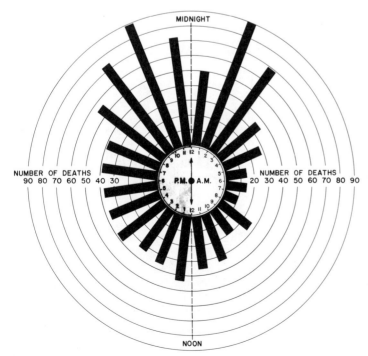

LAW ENFORCEMENT OFFICERS* KILLED
BY HOUR OF DAY: 1966-1975†

Figure 4–34. Another variation of the simple column chart, with circumference of a circle as the base line and series of concentric circles as scale lines. (Chart drawn from data in Federal Bureau of Investigation, Crime in the United States, 1975, *Washington: Government Printing Office, 1976, p. 229.)*

* DATA ON HOUR OF DAY NOT AVAILABLE FOR 8 OFFICERS WHO WERE KILLED
† TOTAL NUMBER OF OFFICERS KILLED: 1,023

There is no simple, capsuled prescription that will provide categorical answers to questions of this kind. Of course, there always is the danger of selecting an inappropriate graphic form, whether a bar, column, or any other kind of chart. Solutions to problems of this kind are largely dependent on knowledge and experience.

In this section several different types of column charts in which there is no time scale are presented. These charts may be described as follows: grouped-column chart, grouped–net-deviation-column chart, floating-column chart, and range chart.

Figure 4–35 is a grouped-column chart showing percentage changes in consumer prices in 1974 and in 1975 for 24 member countries of the Organization for Economic Cooperation and Development

(OECD). As will be observed from the explanatory legend, the black columns represent 1975 data and the outlined white columns, 1974 data. Symbolically, the columns simulate arrows, all of which point upward, further emphasizing the unprecedented inflationary trend. Incidentally, these data could have been portrayed by a bar chart with the arrows arranged horizontally, but in so doing some of the symbolic and graphic impact would have been lost.

Figure 4–36 is another illustration of a column chart that was designed to portray comparisons of three categories of enrollment in the 36 public and private colleges and universities in the state of Washington for a given point in time. The chart is simple, well balanced, and easily interpreted. If a bar chart, rather than a column chart, had been

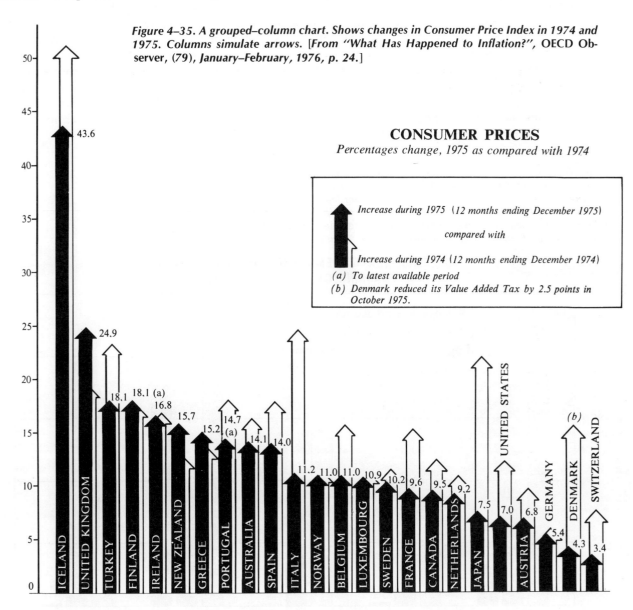

Figure 4–35. A grouped–column chart. Shows changes in Consumer Price Index in 1974 and 1975. Columns simulate arrows. [From "What Has Happened to Inflation?", OECD Observer, (79), January–February, 1976, p. 24.]

CONSUMER PRICES

Percentages change, 1975 as compared with 1974

Increase during 1975 (12 months ending December 1975)

compared with

Increase during 1974 (12 months ending December 1974)

(a) To latest available period
(b) Denmark reduced its Value Added Tax by 2.5 points in October 1975.

selected, the resultant design would have been somewhat clumsier and less effective. Figure 4–36 depicts the size and type of student enrollment in the five institutional groupings. For example, in the fall term of 1966 the University of Washington had 20,924, or 26% of the state total, of full-time academic students. Again, the 19 publicly supported community colleges combined enrolled 16,286 or 87.2% of the 18,677 nonacademic and noncredit students in the state.

Figure 4–37 is a grouped–net-deviation-column chart consisting of six relatively discrete comparisons of changes in public debt holdings for certain investor classes in 1965 and in 1966. The net-deviation-column chart is bilateral, indicating positive and negative changes. There is the characteristic baseline with plus figures above and minus figures below, expressed in billions of dollars. The columns in each pair are differentiated by hatching and stippling patterns. As illustrated by Figure 4–37, commercial bank holdings of government securities registered net declines in both 1965 and 1966. Similarly, corporations show declines for both years, whereas the remaining three investor classes indicated increases. The holdings for the five investor classes combined reported net in-

creases of 5.3 billion dollars in 1965 and 2.5 billion dollars in 1966. This chart emphasizes both temporal and nontemporal facts. However, it does not fit the typical pattern of the temporal column chart in which the horizontal scale represents a fairly continuous time sequence.

The floating-column chart is bilateral in basic design in which a series of columns consisting of two components portray deviations from a referent line. For example, Figure 4–38 shows the work status in 1973 of 1969 workers' age 62–67 in 1973. These data are based on a retirement-history study (RHS) of 11,153 respondents in 1969 and almost 9000 reinterviewees in 1973. It will be observed that each of the columns represent single-year age categories for men and for women, respectively. Each column is dichotomized in terms of proportions who are "working" and "not working" in 1973. A zero referent line differentiates the proportion of each age category in terms of work status. This chart reveals, among other things, a significant relationship between age and retirement for the 62–67 age group, slight differences in work status between men and women, and a very substantial proportion of this older age group who are still working.

Figure 4–36. A grouped–column chart. For this particular series of data, a grouped–column rather than a grouped–bar chart seems more appropriate. Since comparisons among different types of publicly supported institutions of higher learning are emphasized, the columns are not arranged in rank order. (From Calvin F. Schmid, Vincent A. Miller, and Willian S. Packard, Enrollment Statistics, Colleges and Universities, State of Washington, Fall Term: 1966, *Olympia: Planning and Community Affairs Agency, 1967, p. 9.)*

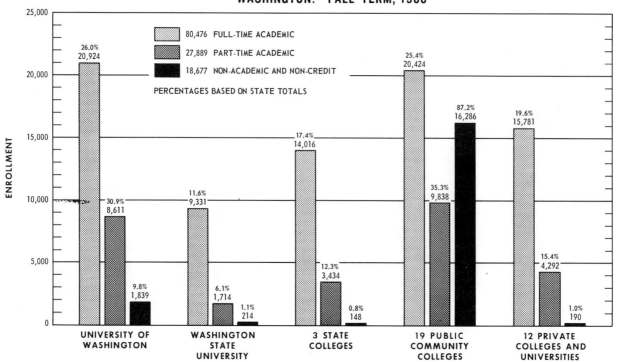

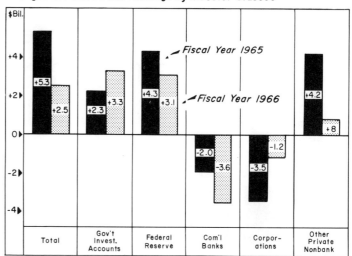

Changes in Public Debt Holdings by Investor Classes

Figure 4–37. Net–deviation column chart. (Redrawn from Annual Report of the Secretary of the Treasury, 1966.

Figure 4–39 is an example of a range chart designed to portray differences in the number of police department employees along with their corresponding averages per 1000 of population for groups of cities classified according to size. The length of each column is commensurate with the number of employees per 1000 of population, and the average for each of the columns is indicated by a distinctive horizontal line. The respective range values and averages have been printed directly on each of the columns. The sequence of the columns in Figure 4–39 is based on the relative size of the population categories beginning with the largest—cities over 250,000. The black column on the extreme left summarizes data for all of the cities combined.

Combining Features of Two of More Types of Charts

It is not an uncommon practice to combine features of two or more graphic forms in the same chart. Pragmatically, there is no reason why this should not be done, provided of course that such a technique represents the most appropriate and effective solution in the graphic portrayal of a given body of data. Figures 4–40 and 4–41 combine the essential features of both column and arithmetic line charts. In Figure 4–40 the three columns represent school enrollment and the three curves school expenditures, each corresponding to the three categories of (1) public schools, (2) private schools and (3) total.

Figure 4–38. A floating–column chart [From Lenore E. Bixby, "Retirement Patterns in the United States: Research and Policy Interaction," Social Security Bulletin, 39, (8), August 1976, pp. 3–19.]

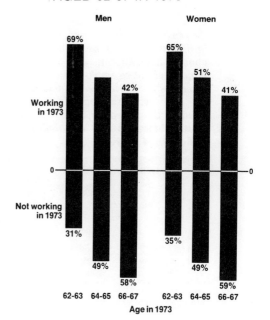

WORK STATUS IN 1973 OF 1969 WORKERS AGED 62-67 IN 1973

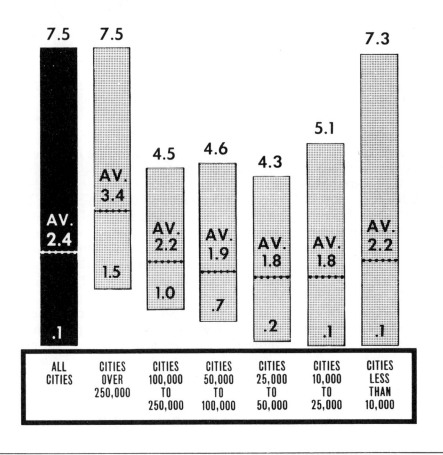

POLICE EMPLOYEE DATA

AVERAGE NUMBER OF POLICE DEPARTMENT EMPLOYEES, AND
RANGE IN NUMBER OF EMPLOYEES, PER 1,000 INHABITANTS

BY POPULATION GROUPS, OCTOBER 31, 1973

ALL CITIES	CITIES OVER 250,000	CITIES 100,000 TO 250,000	CITIES 50,000 TO 100,000	CITIES 25,000 TO 50,000	CITIES 10,000 TO 25,000	CITIES LESS THAN 10,000
7.5	7.5	4.5	4.6	4.3	5.1	7.3
AV. 2.4	AV. 3.4 / 1.5	AV. 2.2 / 1.0	AV. 1.9 / .7	AV. 1.8 / .2	AV. 1.8 / .1	AV. 2.2 / .1
.1						

Figure 4–39. Another illustration of the range chart. Although
the range chart is used most frequently to portray fluctuations
in time series, it can be applied effectively to other kinds of
comparative data. It will be observed that the average
number of police employees per 1000 persons for all American cities is 2.4. However, the range of rates, as well as average rates, vary substantially from one group of cities to
another. (From Federal Bureau of Investigation, Crime in the
United States: 1973, Washington: Government Printing
Office, 1974, p. 36.)

Public and Private School Expenditures and Enrollment: 1960 to 1974

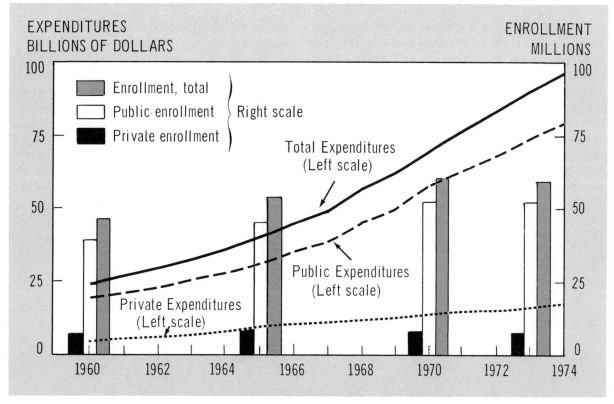

Source: Chart prepared by U.S. Bureau of the Census. Data from U.S. Office of Education.

Figure 4–40. A combination column and arithmetic line–chart with multiple scales. The purpose of this chart is to compare school enrollment for all levels of education in publicly and privately controlled institutions with corresponding expenditures for the period 1962 to 1974. (From United States Bureau of the Census, Statistical Abstract of the United States: 1974, *Washington: Government Printing Office, 1974, p. 107.)*

Figure 4–41. A combination of a grouped subdivided–column chart and arithmetic line chart. (From United States Department of Agriculture, 1976 Handbook of Agricultural Charts, Agricultural Handbook No. 504, *October 1976, p. 138.)*

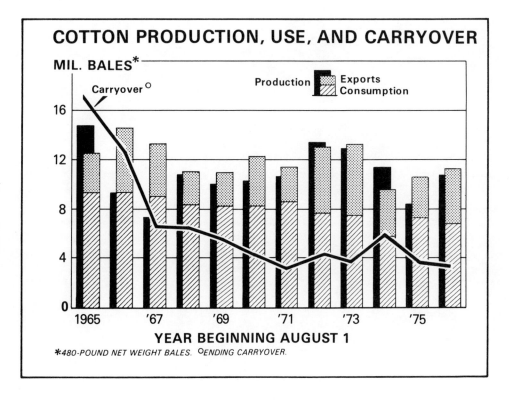

The two scales, the one on the left indicating expenditures in billions of dollars and the one on the right, enrollment in millions are well balanced and readily interpretable. The first three groups of columns are spaced apart every fifth year followed by the fourth group with an interval of four years. The three curves are plotted yearly. In designing charts of this kind, the hazards of multiple scales should be kept in mind.[7] In certain basic respects Figure 4–40 is similar to Figure 4–41. Figure 4–41 is a combination of a grouped-column chart and an arithmetic line chart. In Figure 4–41 there is only one ordinal scale representing millions of bales of cotton. Both the columns and the curve are plotted annually.

One of the columns (black) represents total annual production of cotton, and the other column (crosshatched and stippled) the amount exported and the amount consumed. Superimposed on the columns is a well-defined curve showing the amount of annual carryover of cotton during the 1965–1976 period.

---

[7] See Chapter 3, ''Rectilinear Coordinate Charts,'' for a more detailed discussion of the use of multiple scales.

CHAPTER FIVE

SEMILOGARITHMIC OR RATIO CHARTS

THE PURPOSE OF THIS CHAPTER IS TO describe the theory, construction, and use of the semilogarithmic chart. The semilogarithmic chart is unequaled for many purposes, especially in portraying proportional and percentage relationships. In comparison with the arithmetic line chart, it possesses most of the advantages without the disadvantages. This type of chart not only correctly represents relative changes, but also indicates absolute amounts. Because of its distinctive structure, it is referred to as a "semilogarithmic" or "arithlog" chart. The vertical axis is ruled logarithmically, and the horizontal axis, arithmetically. The continued narrowing of the spacings of the scale divisions on the vertical axis is characteristic of logarithmic ruling, whereas the equal intervals on the horizontal axis are indicative of arithmetic ruling. Because of its emphasis on proportional relationships, the semilogarithmic chart is sometimes referred to as a "ratio" chart.[1]

For the uninitiated, the term "semilogarithmic," as well as the characteristic ruling of the vertical axis, may seem formidable; but actually the theoretical principles on which this chart is based and its construction and use are comparatively simple. Prejudice and general lack of understanding unfortunately have resulted in considerable resistance to the use of semilogarithmic charts. Generally, rates of change are more significant than absolute amounts of change in statistical analysis and presentation. In using the ratio chart one can have confidence that relative changes are portrayed without distortion and uncertainty. An effective use of the semilogarithmic chart requires knowledge of only one or two elementary principles. Moreover, an understanding of logarithms is not at all necessary.

COMPARISON OF SEMILOGARITHMIC AND ARITHMETIC CHARTS

Thus far only charts with arithmetic scales have been discussed. In such charts equal spaces represent equal values—that is, equal amounts of change. In the semilogarithmic chart, the vertical scale is divided logarithmically so that relative changes can be represented accurately. The arithmetic chart emphasizes absolute changes; the semilogarithmic chart emphasizes rates of change. Although the semilogarithmic chart is extremely valuable in graphic presentation, it is not a complete substitute for the arithmetic graph.

The essential differences between arithmetic and semilogarithmic charts can be clarified readily by plotting two simple pairs of figures on each type of grid: in the first pair the value for one period is 90 and that for the succeeding period is 99, and in the second pair the corresponding change is from 10 to 11. In each instance there has been an increase of 10%. On an arithmetic chart the amount or increment of change for the first pair would be nine units, and for the second pair, one unit. In other words, the upward movement of the curve for the first pair on an arithmetic grid would be nine times as great as the upward movement of the curve for the second pair of figures. By contrast, the curves for these data when plotted on a semilogarithmic chart would have identical slopes, because the relative or percentage changes are the same.

Figure 5–1 illustrates more specifically the basic characteristics of both the arithmetic and semilogarithmic charts.[2] A series increasing at a constant amount—$10,000 per decade—is shown by a straight line on an arithmetic grid. This fact, of course, is readily understandable, since equal increments of change are represented by equal distances on an arithmetic scale, and accordingly the upward slope of the curve is constant at each period. The corresponding curve on a semilogarithmic grid is convex upward, which indicates an increase, but at a decreasing rate. This series is known as an arithmetic progression. It shows an increase by equal amounts from one period to another, but the rate of increase is a declining one. A series increasing at a constant rate is indicated by a curve showing a constant slope on the semilogarithmic grid, but on an arithmetic grid the curve is concave upward. This type of series is known as a "geometric progression" since each value differs from the preceding one by a constant ratio (rate, percentage, multiplier, or divisor). The two remaining illustrations on this chart indicate declining arithmetic and geometric series. A series decreasing by a constant amount is represented by a straight line on an arithmetic grid, whereas on a semilogarithmic grid it is convex downward, reflecting a decrease at an increasing rate. A constant rate of decrease is indicated by a straight line on a semilogarithmic chart and a concave downward line on an arithmetic chart.

Figure 5–2 further illustrates the advantages of the semilogarithmic chart and the limitations of the arithmetic chart, especially in the comparison of changes where relatively large and small quantities are involved. The arithmetic chart may be satisfactory for portraying comparative fluctuations if the quantities compared are of approximately the same value or size. On an arithmetic chart, the wider the range of scale, the greater the division between actual and relative changes. In a semilogarithmic

[1] The semilogarithmic chart must not be confused with the chart in which both axes are ruled logarithmically.
[2] William Addison Neiswanger, *Elementary Statistical Methods*, New York: Macmillan, 1943, pp. 186–189.

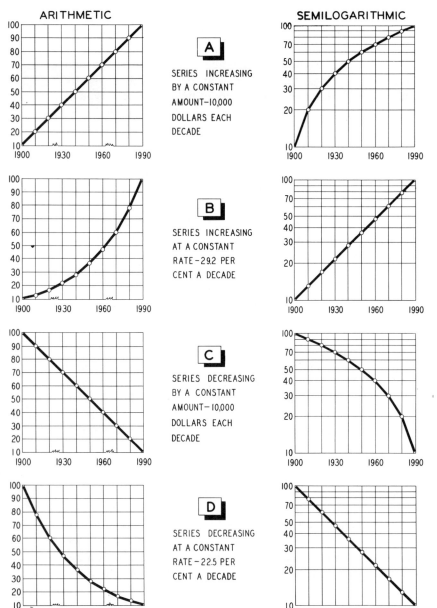

A

SERIES INCREASING BY A CONSTANT AMOUNT—10,000 DOLLARS EACH DECADE

B

SERIES INCREASING AT A CONSTANT RATE—29.2 PER CENT A DECADE

C

SERIES DECREASING BY A CONSTANT AMOUNT—10,000 DOLLARS EACH DECADE

D

SERIES DECREASING AT A CONSTANT RATE—22.5 PER CENT A DECADE

Figure 5–1. Comparison of arithmetic and semilogarithmic charts showing constant increments of change and rates of change, respectively.

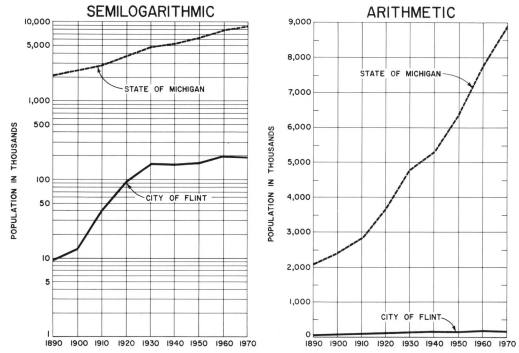

Figure 5–2. A comparison of arithmetic and semilogarithmic charts. Note especially the effectiveness of the semilogarithmic chart in portraying rate of change.

graph, on the other hand, it is possible to compare relatively small numbers with large ones without producing any misleading or inaccurate implications. It will be noted from Figure 5–2 that the ordinal axis on the arithmetic scale has a range from zero to 9,000,000 and the corresponding axis on the semilogarithmic grid ranges from 1000 to 10,000,000. Between 1900 and 1910, the population of the city of Flint, Michigan increased from 13,103 to 38,550, or 294.2%. On the arithmetic chart this increment is represented by approximately one-fourth of a scale unit, which is hardly detectable. The corresponding growth for the same decennial period for the entire state of Michigan was from 2,420,982 to 2,810,173, or 11.6%. It will be observed that this growth increment is registered by almost four units of the arithmetic scale. However, in comparing the differential rates of population growth for the two series, it is unmistakably indicated that the city of Flint greatly surpassed the entire state of Michigan. The relative increases in the two series are authentically portrayed on the semilogarithmic grid. On the arithmic grid, one is left with inaccurate and deceptive impressions. A comparison of the slopes of the two curves on the

semilogarithmic chart for any decennial period correctly indicates rates of growth.

CONSTRUCTION OF THE SEMILOGARITHMIC CHART

There are several different procedures that can be followed in constructing a semilogarithmic chart. Each procedure is discussed briefly, indicating its particular advantages and disadvantages. As pointed out in the foregoing discussion, equal vertical distances on a semilogarithmic chart always indicate equal percentages or rates of change. In other words, if the percentage change between two or more pairs of figures is constant, it will be found that the differences between the logarithms of these figures will be the same. Accordingly, a chart of this kind can be constructed either by plotting the logarithms of the items in a series on a natural scale or by laying out a logarithmic scale and plotting the natural numbers of the items in a series. The first method is not used very often since it is cumbersome and, of course, requires familiarity with the handling of logarithms. Moreover, since it is relatively simple to construct a logarithmic scale or to obtain specially prepared printed semilogarithmic paper, there seems to be no particular advantage in plotting logarithms of a series on plain coordinate paper or natural scale. Plotting data on a logarithmic scale is just as simple as plotting data on an arithmetic one.

Meaning of Logarithms

For those who are not familiar with logarithms, the following brief explanation may help to clarify a few points discussed in this chapter. A logarithm (common system of logarithms) is the power to which 10 must be raised to obtain a given number. For example, the logarithm of 10 is 1; of 100, 2; of 1000, 3; and of 10,000, 4. In other words, 100 is the second power of 10 (10^2), 1000 is the third power of 10 (10^3), and 10,000 is the fourth power of 10 (10^4). In case a number is not an exact power of 10, its logarithm is expressed as an approximation containing decimals. By consulting a table of logarithms, it will be found that the logarithm of 2 is 0.3010; of 3, 0.4771; of 4, 0.6021; of 20, 1.3010; of 200, 2.3010. There are two separate components of a logarithm: (1) characteristic and (2) mantissa. The characteristic is the integer of the logarithm and is located to the left of the decimal point. In the logarithm of 20, the characteristic is 1, and in the logarithm of 200, the characteristic is 2, and so on. The characteristic is always the number that is one less than the number of digits in the integer of the number. The mantissa is the decimal part of the logarithm. The antilogarithm is the number corresponding to a given logarithm. For example, since the logarithm of 3 is 0.4771, then 3 is the antilogarithm of 0.4771. It will be observed that in the construction of a semilogarithmic grid only the logarithmic values from 1 to 10 are required.

ADDITIONAL CHARACTERISTICS OF THE SEMILOGARITHMIC CHART

In addition to the characteristic logarithmic rulings on the vertical axis and the arithmetic rulings on the horizontal axis, there are other features of the semilogarithmic chart that should be mentioned. Undoubtedly, it has been observed already that there is no zero baseline on the semilogarithmic

scale. The logarithm of zero is minus infinity. Since there is no zero line, the bottom line of a chart on a logarithmic scale may represent any convenient value.[3] In general, it can be slightly less than the smallest value that is to be plotted on the chart. The highest value on a semilogarithmic chart should be a little more than the largest value in the series to be portrayed. As a matter of practice, it is recommended that the bottom line begin with 10 or some division or multiple of 10, such as 0.001, 0.01, 1, 10, 100, 1000, or 10,000. The value of each successive figure that might be added is 10 times that of the preceding one. As many figures as are required may be added above or below the original scale. The divisions on a logarithmic scale are referred to as "cycles," "decks," "banks," "phases," or "tiers." In practice it is found that more than five cycles are seldom needed. The highest and lowest values of the data to be plotted govern the number of cycles to be laid out on a chart.

Specific Techniques in Laying Out the Semilogarithmic Chart.

Before discussing the specific techniques in laying out the semilogarithmic chart, some comment should be made on the use of commercially printed semilogarithmic graph paper. In the preparation of charts, this type of graph paper possesses the shortcomings inherent in all graph paper. From a professional point of view, printed graph paper is inflexible and unattractive and should rarely be used in constructing charts for exhibit purposes or publication. The main value of printed graph paper is for administrative purposes and for preliminary and experimental sketching as a basis for ascertaining the more salient features of data and the most appropriate graphic design to be used for the final layout.

The first method of constructing a semilogarithmic scale is by means of a table of log-

---

[3] It is possible, of course, to show an arbitrary zero line, as well as relative values, on a semilogarithmic chart by recalibrating the scale. For example, the 100% line can be relabeled 0, and all other values of the scale relabeled correspondingly to represent percentage increase or decrease from this point. This technique is seldom used since it destroys the uniform labeling of scale values of the various decks, which are characteristic of the semilogarithmic chart. See Karl G. Karsten, *Charts and Graphs*, New York: Prentice-Hall, 1923, pp. 407–411.

arithms. Figure 5–3 portrays very simply the three major steps in the logical development of a logarithmic scale.[4] After the height of the scale is determined, the first step, A, merely shows a vertical line divided into 10 equal spaces from zero to 10. In step B the same distance is divided in proportion to the logarithmic values of 1 to 10. In step C the divisions thus derived are designated by their respective antilogarithms. Regardless of the desired height of a scale, it is relatively simple to lay out the divisions of the scale in proportion to the logarithmic values of a given height. For example, if the height of a scale is 4 in., then the first division will be the logarithm of 2 multiplied by 4, or (0.3010)(4) = 1.2 in. Similarly, the distance to 3 will be (0.4771)(4) = 1.91 in. A fractional division of the scale can also be derived in the same manner. For example, the distance to 3.5 is (0.5441)(4) = 2.18 in. Table 5–1 summarizes the cumulative distances from 1 to the respective divisions on a logarithmic scale 3 in., 4 in., 5 in., 6 in., and 7 in. in height. In calibrating a scale developed in this manner, a civil engineer's scale will be found useful in plotting the points. In case more than one deck is required for a chart, the original layout can be copied readily on tracing paper, tracing cloth, or plastic film.

A much easier and more practicable technique in laying out a logarithmic scale is to purchase four or five sizes of commercially printed semilogarithmic or logarithmic paper. Complete scales for plotting purposes can be prepared by cutting strips 0.75–1 in. wide from each of the sheets. Normally, these scales will be adequate for virtu-

ally all sizes of logarithmic charts that might be constructed. Moreover, a supply of this kind will last for years since additional strips can be cut from the paper in case any wear out. It is recommended that the strips of printed graph paper be mounted on thin cardboard (a filing folder is excellent for this purpose) to facilitate handling and reading of the scale and be sprayed with a coat of lacquer or plastic to preserve the scale. Each strip of paper prepared in this manner is an effective logarithmic scale. The standard statistician's scale mentioned in Chapter 2 has five logarithmic scales that will be found useful in constructing logarithmic charts. In light of the authors' experience, however, several scales prepared from printed semilogarithmic chart paper are more flexible and efficient.

Figure 5–4 illustrates how a logarithmic scale is used in laying out the vertical axis of a ratio chart. It will be observed that there are three cycles on this chart, and the procedure in plotting the points is the same as that for plotting points for grid lines on an arithmetic chart with a civil engineer's or some other equal-division scale. It is relatively simple to contract or expand a logarithmic scale with commercially printed graph paper. Figure 5–4 shows how a scale can be contracted, whereas Figure 5–5 illustrates how a scale can be expanded. From these illustrations it can be seen how a scale of any size can be constructed readily according to this technique and also how an assortment of several different sizes of paper will help to simplify work of this kind.

A third technique in constructing logarithmic scales is illustrated in Figure 5–6. The construction of a flexible scale of this kind is comparatively simple. Two logarithmic scales of different sizes are laid out several inches apart on a piece of paper,

[4] Neiswanger, *Elementary Statistical Methods* (op. cit.), pp. 189–190.

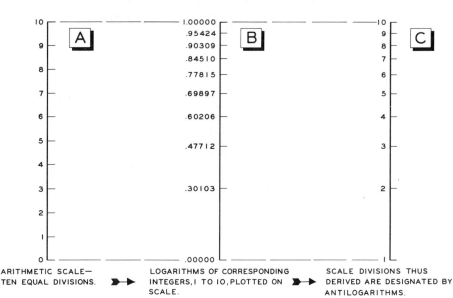

Figure 5–3. Basic technique in constructing a logarithmic scale.

drafting film, or tracing cloth. It is necessary to draw a horizontal center line so that the centers of the two scales will be exactly on the same level. The various points on the two logarithmic scales are then joined. If desired, the scale lines can then be extended in either direction to cover virtually any desired height. The flexible scale should be drawn on some relatively tough, transparent material, such as tracing cloth, drafting film, or heavy-rag tracing vellum. The scale can be used directly in the construction of logarithmic charts or can be reproduced first on black line or ozalid prints and then cut into strips according to required sizes. Another method in using the flexible scale is to overlay a strip of tracing cloth, drafting film, or vellum of the same height as the scale to be laid out. The various divisions can be marked directly on the overlay, which can be used as a scale for plotting points.

SPECIAL APPLICATIONS OF THE SEMILOGARITHMIC CHART

As a technique for showing proportional rates of change, the semilogarithmic chart is unquestionably the best. This fact has been emphasized through-out this chapter. The semilogarithmic chart makes possible direct and correct comparisons of relative increases and decreases. In addition, this type of chart has other special uses. First, in comparing rates of change among variables not expressed in the same units, the semilogarithmic chart has a unique advantage. In the case of an arithmetic chart, generally only one or possibly two scales can be indicated on the vertical axis. Under very special circumstances it is possible to use three different scales. In any case, multiple scales on arithmetic charts must be used with extreme caution and only under very limited conditions. There is no restriction of this kind in the case of a semilogarithmic chart, for it is possible to show several scales without complicating the chart or creating wrong impressions. In Figure 5–7 it will be observed from the grid on the left side that comparisons can be made readily among population growth, the number of telephones, the number of motor vehicles, and streetcar and bus passengers. Similarly, in the center grid, population growth is compared with water meters, electric light accounts, income from the city light department, number of electric ranges served by city current, the mileage of streets, and the mileage of sewers. On the grid on the right side of the chart, population growth is

Table 5–1

Size of Scale Intervals of Logarithmic Scales of
3-in., 4-in., 5-in., 6-in., and 7-in. Cycles

Scale Value	Logarithm	Cumulative Distance (Inches) from Scale Value 1				
		3-in. Cycle	4-in. Cycle	5-in. Cycle	6-in. Cycle	7-in. Cycle
1.0	0.0000	0.00	0.00	0.00	0.00	0.00
1.5	0.1761	0.53	0.70	0.88	1.06	1.23
2.0	0.3010	0.90	1.20	1.51	1.81	2.11
2.5	0.3979	1.19	1.59	1.99	2.39	2.79
3.0	0.4771	1.43	1.91	2.39	2.86	3.34
3.5	0.5441	1.63	2.18	2.72	3.26	3.81
4.0	0.6021	1.81	2.41	3.01	3.61	4.21
4.5	0.6532	1.96	2.61	3.27	3.92	4.57
5.0	0.6990	2.10	2.80	3.49	4.19	4.89
5.5	0.7404	2.22	2.96	3.70	4.44	5.18
6.0	0.7782	2.33	3.11	3.89	4.67	5.45
6.5	0.8129	2.44	3.25	4.06	4.88	5.69
7.0	0.8451	2.54	3.38	4.23	5.07	5.92
7.5	0.8751	2.63	3.50	4.38	5.25	6.13
8.0	0.9031	2.71	3.61	4.52	5.42	6.32
8.5	0.9294	2.79	3.72	4.65	5.58	6.51
9.0	0.9542	2.86	3.82	4.77	5.73	6.68
9.5	0.9777	2.93	3.91	4.89	5.87	6.84
10.0	1.0000	3.00	4.00	5.00	6.00	7.00

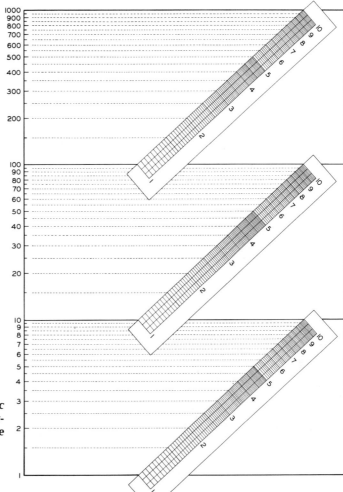

Figure 5–4. Technique for constructing logarithmic scale from commercially printed graph paper. Figure also illustrates how plotted scale can readily be reduced in size.

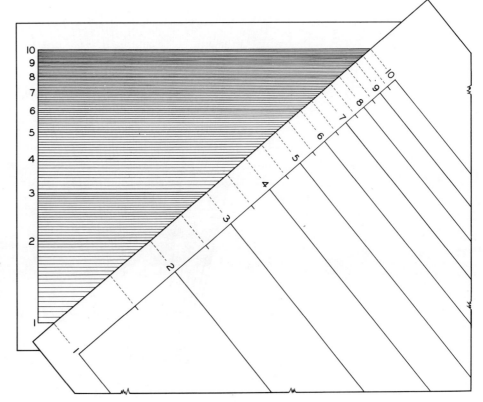

Figure 5–5. Another Illustration showing construction of logarithmic scale from commercially printed graph paper. Note in particular technique for expanding original scale.

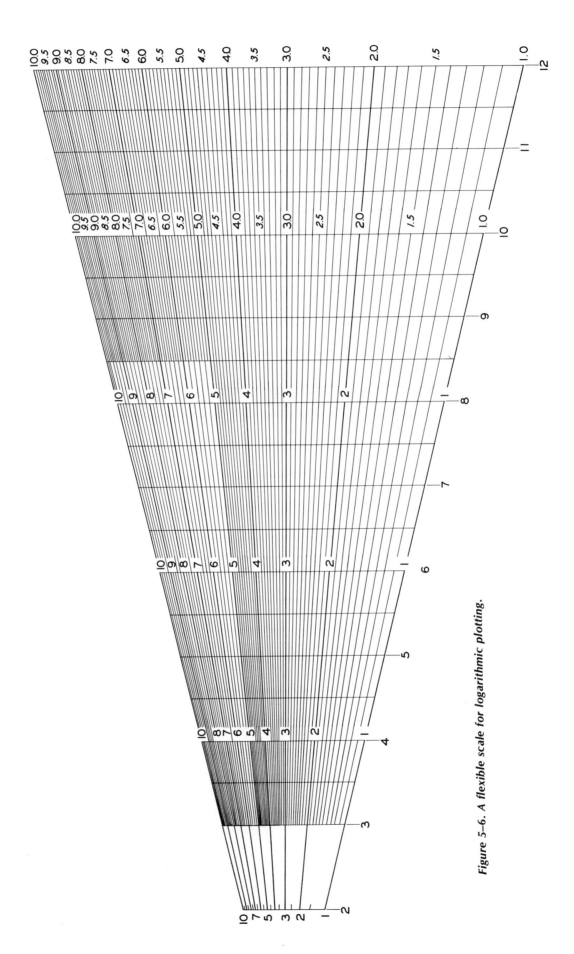

Figure 5–6. A flexible scale for logarithmic plotting.

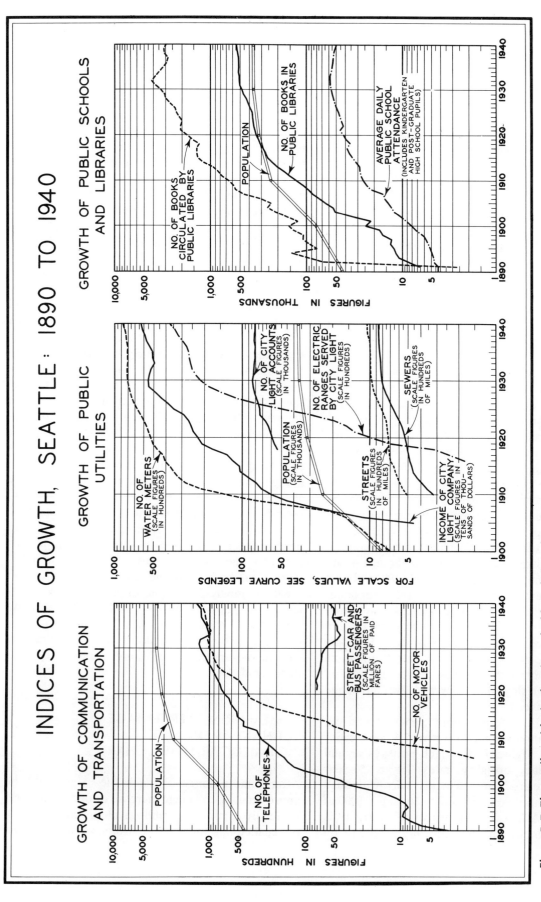

Figure 5–7. The semilogarithmic chart is a valuable technique for comparing rates of change among variables not expressed in the same units. (From Calvin F. Schmid, Social Trends in Seattle, Seattle: University of Washington Press, 1944, p. 38.)

compared with the number of books circulated by public libraries, the number of books in public libraries, and average daily public school attendance.

As indicated in connection with Figure 5–8, the semilogarithmic chart is particularly valuable in comparing two or more series of widely different magnitudes. The relative changes as indicated by the slopes of the curves are comparable no matter in what position they may be in the field. Equal rise or fall on the same scale represents the same ratio of change. Figure 5–8 indicates seven different series of data ranging in value from less than 25 to almost 50,000. The relative rates of change for each of these series are correctly indicated on the chart, and it is possible to make comparisons among them as well as among the segments of the same curve. In contrast, if these data had been plotted on an arithmetic grid, the results would have been worthless or actually worse than worthless, since it would have been impossible to interpret either relative rates of growth or absolute changes for most of the curves.

Another technique for comparing a large number of curves of widely different values is to place sections of a semilogarithmic scale one above the other according to any desired sequence. Figure 5–9 illustrates how a series of six age-specific fertility curves arranged chronologically according to age of female can be portrayed clearly by this method. The curve at the top represents the age group 15–19 years, followed in successive order by the five remaining age groups covering the normal reproductive period. It will be observed that the fertility rates vary markedly among the several age groups. For example, the rates for the age group 20–24 years range from approximately 100 to almost 300 per 1000 female population. On the other hand, the rates for the age group 40–44 years vary from less than 10 to approximately 30. Only that portion of the scale covering the range of rates for each respective age group is required. Trends and rates of changes among the various curves are readily reflected by the slope of the curves. This technique also saves space.

As an additional, but more elaborate and detailed, illustration similar to Figure 5–9, the reader is referred to Figure 5–10, which portrays annual age–sex-specific mortality rates for a 50-year period. There are 22 curves in this chart, with rates ranging from approximately 0.2 to 300.0 per 1000 of population. A half-century history of mortality is clearly, succinctly and authentically recorded by this chart. Again, it should be emphasized that the slope of the curve, either upward or downward, is indicative of the rate of change. First, mortality among females has almost without exception been below that for males and has shown a much greater average decline. Second, mortality for younger age categories has improved much more noticeably than for older ages. Third, by far the most pronounced and consistent decreases in death rates have been experienced by children in the first year of life. The rate for males in this age category dropped from 98.3 in 1910 to 27.2 in 1960. Comparable rates for females are 69.9 and 21.1. Fourth, in contrast to the younger age groups, there is a marked stability or actual increases for both males and females 65 years of age and over. For example, males 85 years and over show a rate of 188.9 in 1910 as compared to 242.9 in 1960.

It should be pointed out that the arithmetic and semilogarithmic scales approach each other as the maximal and minimal percentage changes among the values become increasingly smaller. If the relative difference between the highest and lowest values is around 25–50%, or sometimes even more, the arithmetic chart may be more appropriate than a semilogarithmic chart, but where the range of relative difference is much larger, the semilogarithmic chart is superior. Where there are several series of data lying on different portions of the scale, even though the percentage variations are extremely slight from one pair to another, the semilogarithmic chart is sensitive to these changes and depicts them correctly. The semilogarithmic chart may prove to be particularly valuable in studying relationships between one or more series of temporal data. Curves can be brought into close juxtaposition and readily compared. In this way it is possible to detect direct correlations as well as the absolute amount of "leads" and "lags." This procedure may frequently be a useful device as a preliminary step in the application of more elaborate correlational analyses.

MEASURING PERCENTAGE CHANGES ON A SEMILOGARITHMIC CHART

After some practice it is possible to estimate the approximate percentage increase or decrease represented by curves on a semilogarithmic chart. It will be recalled that the vertical distance of a curve on a

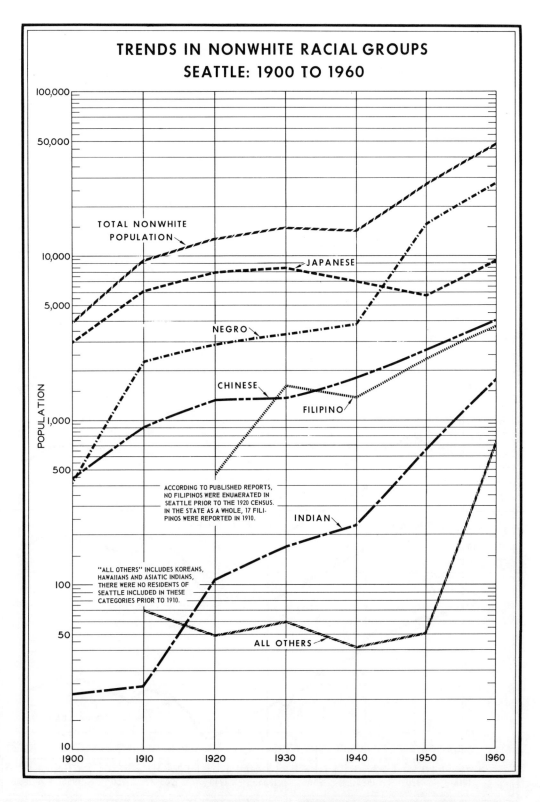

TRENDS IN NONWHITE RACIAL GROUPS
SEATTLE: 1900 TO 1960

TOTAL NONWHITE POPULATION

JAPANESE

NEGRO

CHINESE

FILIPINO

POPULATION

ACCORDING TO PUBLISHED REPORTS,
NO FILIPINOS WERE ENUMERATED IN
SEATTLE PRIOR TO THE 1920 CENSUS.
IN THE STATE AS A WHOLE, 17 FILI-
PINOS WERE REPORTED IN 1910.

INDIAN

"ALL OTHERS" INCLUDES KOREANS,
HAWAIIANS AND ASIATIC INDIANS,
THERE WERE NO RESIDENTS OF
SEATTLE INCLUDED IN THESE
CATEGORIES PRIOR TO 1910.

ALL OTHERS

100,000

50,000

10,000

5,000

1,000

500

100

50

10

1900 1910 1920 1930 1940 1950 1960

Figure 5–8. Four–deck semilogarithmic chart. There are seven different curves on this chart, with values ranging from less than 25 to almost 50,000. (From Calvin F. Schmid, Charles E. Nobbe, and Arlene E. Mitchell, Nonwhite Races, State of Washington, *Olympia: Washington State Planning and Community Affairs Agency, 1968, p. 50.)*

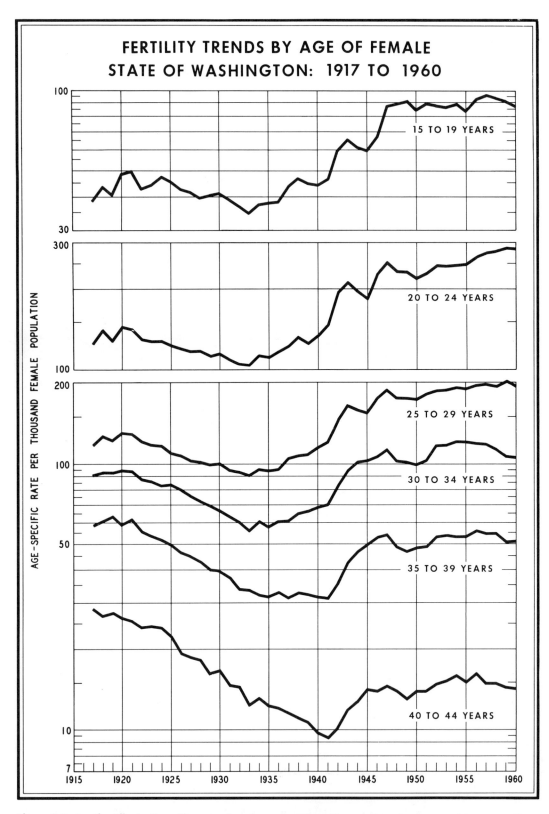

Figure 5–9. Another illustration of how a series of curves with a wide variation of values can be arranged in proper sequence, as well as in appropriate juxtaposition for ready comparison. (From Calvin F. Schmid et al., Population Forecasts, State of Washington: 1965 to 1985, *Olympia: Washington State Department of Commerce and Economic Development, 1966, p. 46.)*

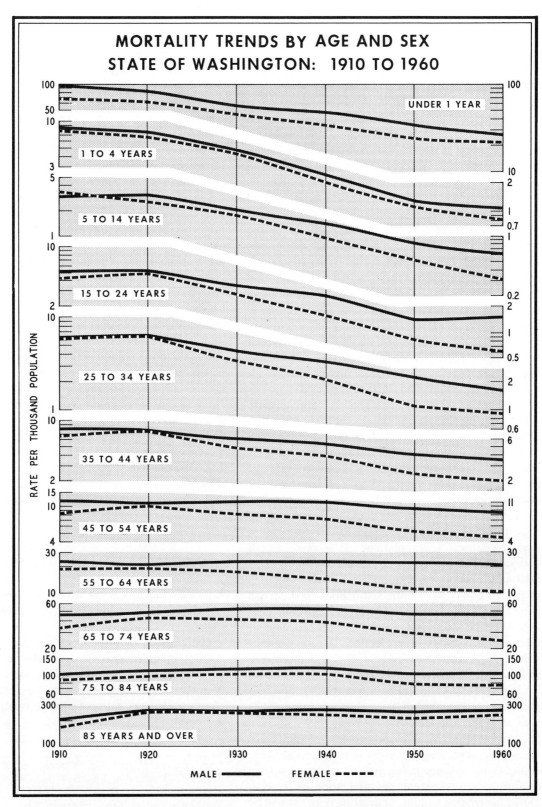

Figure 5–10. In order to conserve space as well as to facilitate comparison, several curves can be placed on one chart by including only small sections of a scale. Note by slope of curves the relatively greater decline in mortality in younger age–groups. Also, observe sex differentials in mortality. (From Calvin F. Schmid, et al., Population Forecasts, State of Washington: 1965 to 1985, Olymphia: Washington State Department of Commerce and Economic Development, 1966, p. 39.)

semilogarithmic chart is indicative of the percentage change regardless of the location of the curve on the grid. For example, the distances from 10 to 20, 100 to 200, and 1000 to 2000 represent increases of 100 percent, and all three curves indicating these changes will manifest the same slope.

Further implications of these facts are illustrated by Figure 5–11, which records the actual and projected growth of population in the state of Washington from 1870 to 1985. The decennial and quinquennial population figures, along with the corresponding incremental changes summarized in the tabular insert, are clearly reflected by the configuration of the curve. The steepest portions of the curve coincide with the first two intercensal periods of 1870–1880 and 1880–1890; the rates of change during these respective periods were 213.6% and 375.6%. In contrast, the relatively gradual slope of the curve during the 1930–1940 depression period is indicative of a slow rate of population growth. During this period the rate of population growth was 11.1%. It will be observed that the population figures for the forecast period are presented by quinquennial rather than decennial periods.

Perhaps as a word of caution, the forecast data presented by Figure 5–11 are not simple, mechanical extrapolations. Rather, they are based on an elaborate forecast model known as the "cohort-survival" technique involving large masses of statistical and other data and tens of thousands of computations.

Sometimes attempts are made to use the semilogarithmic charts for developing forecasts. This is done by simple extrapolation. It is possible, of course, to extrapolate from the arithmetic chart as well as the semilogarithmic chart. Extrapolations of this kind may have some justification, if the trend shows marked stability. However, extreme caution must be exercised. Arbitrary mechanical or mathematical types of projections are of dubious value. It is recommended that, if one is interested in forecasting, a more analytical type of procedure be used that would take into consideration the various components and basic elements involved as well as modifying factors.[5]

The most practicable and precise technique for measuring percentage changes is to trace the scale calibrations of the semilogarithmic chart on a strip of durable, transparent material such as tracing cloth, rag tracing vellum, or drafting film. It will be necessary, of course, to make a separate percentage

scale for each size of chart. Values corresponding to percentage changes should be marked carefully on the scale. The upper part of the scale of Figure 5–12 represents percentage increases, and the lower part shows percentage decreases. The scaling extends upward and downward from zero. The percentage increase from the beginning of a cycle to the first division is 100% (1 to 2, 10 to 20, 100 to 200, etc.). The increase from the beginning of the cycle to the third major division is 200% (1 to 3, 10 to 30, 100 to 300, etc.). The percentage increase from the beginning of the cycle to the end is 900% (1 to 10, 10 to 100, 100 to 1,000, etc.). The scale values below the zero point represent percentage decreases. For example, the decrease from the top of the scale to the bottom is 90% (10 to 1, 100 to 10, etc.). A change from a division to one immediately below, such as from 60 to 50, 3 to 2, 7000 to 6000, and so on, is 10%. Figure 5–12, which depicts Mexican immigration to the United States during 1905–1945, inclusive, illustrates the application of the percentage scale to the semilogarithmic chart. The section of the curve from 1915 to 1916 represents an increase in Mexican immigration from 12,430 to 18,425. The zero point of the percentage scale is placed on the level of the plotting point A. The distance to plotting point B (18,425) represents an increase of 48.2%. The percentage decline from 12,703 immigrants in 1930 to 3333 in 1931 can be read off the scale by placing the zero point on 12,703 and reading down to the scale value opposite 3333 (73.7%).

INTERPRETATION OF CURVES

Although the foregoing discussion on the characteristics, construction, and application of semilogarithmic charts touches directly on the subject of interpretation, it is the purpose of this section to present in more specific form the implications of typical curve patterns found on charts of this kind. It must not be forgotten that the semilogarithmic chart emphasizes rates of change, with the slope of the curve indicative of the rate of change. Rate-

---

[5] See Calvin F. Schmid, Vincent A. Miller, Kiyoshi Tagashira, Richard A. Engels, F. Jean Watson, *Population Forecasts, State of Washington: 1965 to 1985*, Olympia: Washington State Department of Commerce and Economic Development, 1966, passim.

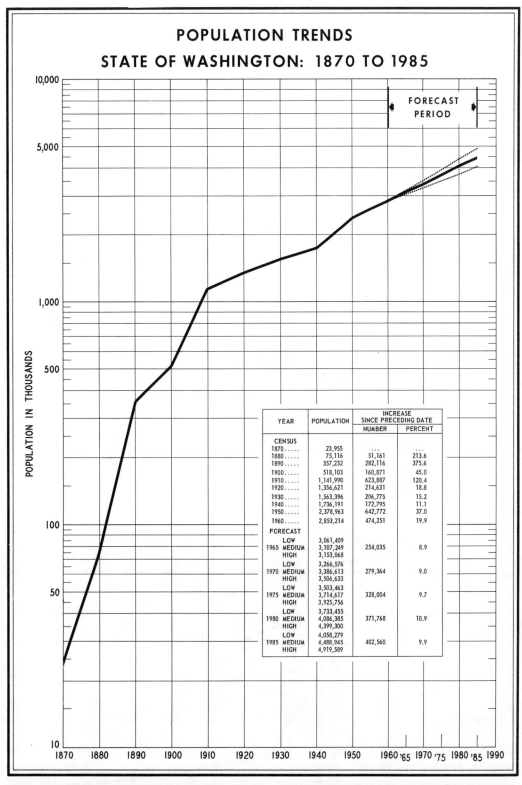

POPULATION TRENDS
STATE OF WASHINGTON: 1870 TO 1985

FORECAST PERIOD

YEAR	POPULATION	INCREASE SINCE PRECEDING DATE	
		NUMBER	PERCENT
CENSUS			
1870.....	23,955	...	...
1880.....	75,116	51,161	213.6
1890.....	357,232	282,116	375.6
1900.....	518,103	160,871	45.0
1910.....	1,141,990	623,887	120.4
1920.....	1,356,621	214,631	18.8
1930.....	1,563,396	206,775	15.2
1940.....	1,736,191	172,795	11.1
1950.....	2,378,963	642,772	37.0
1960.....	2,853,214	474,251	19.9
FORECAST			
1965 LOW	3,061,409		
MEDIUM	3,107,249	254,035	8.9
HIGH	3,153,068		
1970 LOW	3,266,576		
MEDIUM	3,386,613	279,364	9.0
HIGH	3,506,633		
1975 LOW	3,503,463		
MEDIUM	3,714,617	328,004	9.7
HIGH	3,925,756		
1980 LOW	3,733,455		
MEDIUM	4,086,385	371,768	10.9
HIGH	4,399,300		
1985 LOW	4,058,279		
MEDIUM	4,488,945	402,560	9.9
HIGH	4,919,589		

Figure 5–11. Rate of change on a semilogarithmic chart is clearly reflected by the slope of the curve. For corroboration of this fact, the statistics representing decennial and quinquennial percentage change in the tabular insert can be readily compared with the slope of the curve for each of the corresponding periods. (From Calvin F. Schmid and Stanton E. Schmid, Growth of Cities and Towns, State of Washington, *Olympia: Washington State Planning and Community Affairs Agency, 1969, p. 2.)*

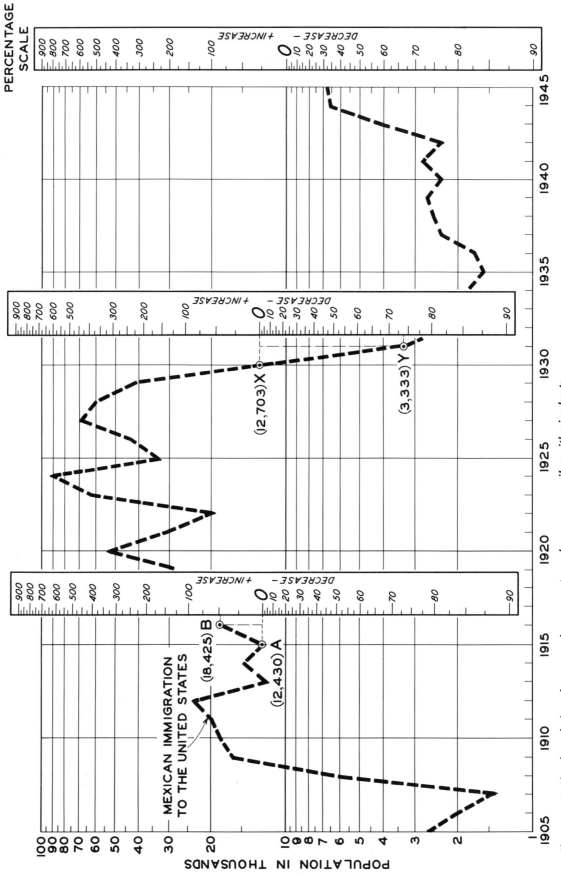

Figure 5-12. Simple technique for measuring percentage changes on semilogarithmic charts.

of-change comparisons can be made readily between different parts of a single series or between two or more series.

Figure 5–13 depicts certain generalized curve patterns found on semilogarithmic charts. First, a curve increasing at a constant rate takes the form of a straight ascending line. Correspondingly, a curve decreasing at a uniform rate is a straight descending line. Two or more curves or segments of curves on a semilogarithmic chart that are parallel indicate the same rate of change. Second, an ascending convex curve indicates an increase at a decreasing rate. This fact can be understood readily, since the relative steepness of the curve is indicative of the rate of change. The slope of the curve is steep at the beginning and becomes progressively less as the curve moves toward the top of the field. The configuration of a curve that is decreasing at a decreasing rate moves downward in concave fashion. Again, the implications of this pattern can be

ascertained readily since the relative slope of the various portions of the curve declines toward the bottom of the chart. Third, a curve increasing at an increasing rate moves upward in concave fashion. It will be observed that the relative slope of the line becomes more pronounced toward the top of the chart. If the curve is decreasing at an increasing rate, the curve pattern is convex downward. This is, of course, in conformity with the basic principle that the greater the slope of the line, the greater the rate of change. Since the declivity of the curve increases toward the bottom of the chart, the curve shows an increasing rate of change. Fourth, when the curve is horizontal, it is neither increasing nor decreasing.

To illustrate in greater detail the significance of curve patterns of a semilogarithmic chart, the reader is referred to Figure 5–14, which includes 37 curves manifesting a wide variety of configurations, ranging from a nearly constant horizontal level to

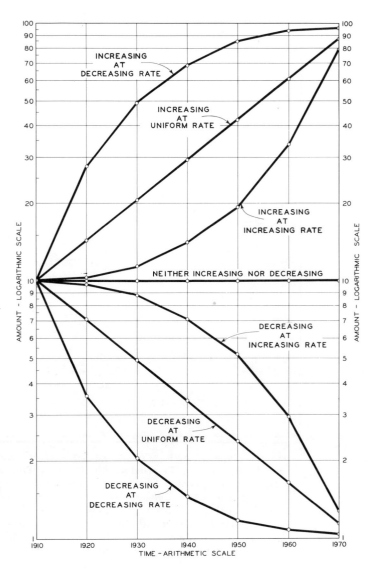

Figure 5–13. Curves illustrating the interpretation of semilogarithmic charts.

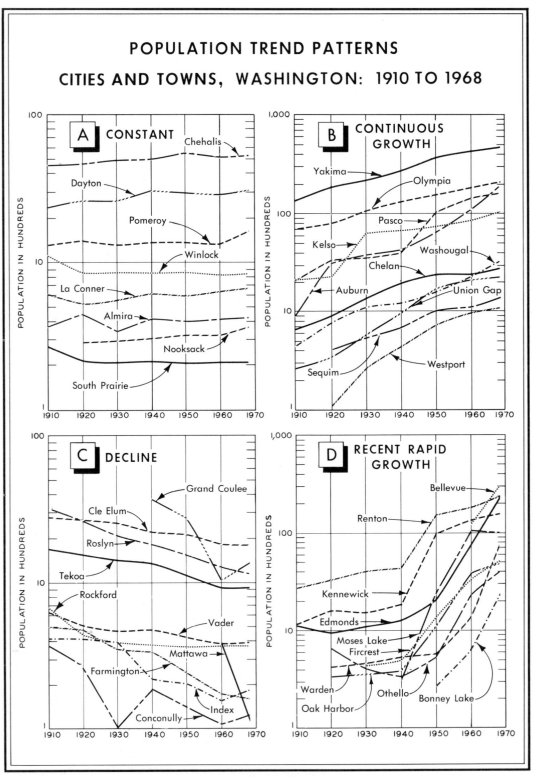

POPULATION TREND PATTERNS

CITIES AND TOWNS, WASHINGTON: 1910 TO 1968

A CONSTANT — Chehalis, Dayton, Pomeroy, Winlock, La Conner, Almira, Nooksack, South Prairie

B CONTINUOUS GROWTH — Yakima, Olympia, Pasco, Kelso, Washougal, Chelan, Auburn, Union Gap, Sequim, Westport

C DECLINE — Grand Coulee, Cle Elum, Roslyn, Tekoa, Rockford, Vader, Mattawa, Farmington, Index, Conconully

D RECENT RAPID GROWTH — Bellevue, Renton, Kennewick, Edmonds, Moses Lake, Fircrest, Warden, Othello, Bonney Lake, Oak Harbor

Figure 5–14. Basic patterns of change can be clearly and authentically portrayed by semilogarithmic charts. Population trends for a sample of 37 towns and cities with values ranging from 100 to almost 50,000 are shown on this chart. No other graphic technique could depict these data as effectively. (From Calvin F. Schmid and Stanton E. Schmid, Growth of Cities and Towns, State of Washington, *Olympia: Washington State Planning and Community Affairs Agency, 1969, p. 123.)*

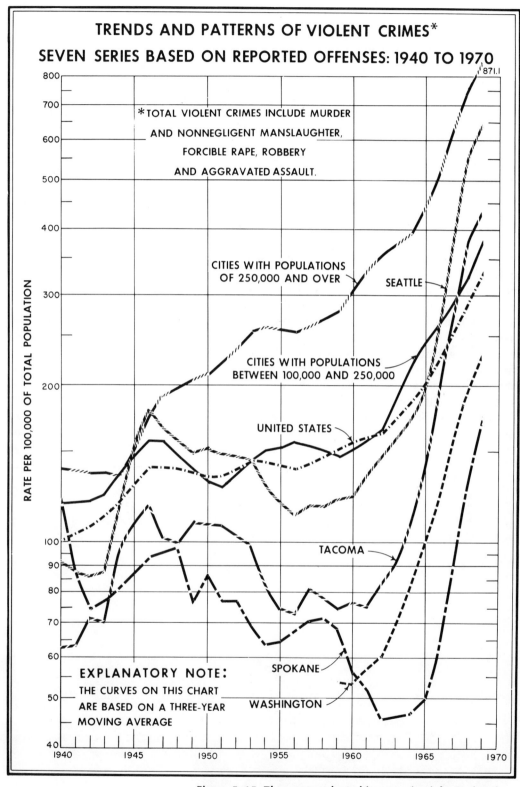

Figure 5–15. The unprecedented increase in violent crime in recent years is portrayed clearly and convincingly by the semilogarithmic chart (From Calvin F. Schmid and Stanton E. Schmid, Crime in the State of Washington, Olympia: Law and Justice Planning Office, Planning and Community Affairs Agency, 1972, p. 18.)

extraordinary upward and downward slopes. In general, the multiform curves in the four panels are reflective of a simple fourfold typology of population trends: (a) constant, with little or no change; (b) continuous upward movement; (c) more or less continuous decline; and (d) relatively recent accelerated rates of growth.

Another illustration of the significance of semilogarithmic curve patterns is the sudden and spectacular upward sweep of all the curves in Figure 5–15. These curves demonstrate most convincingly the unprecedented increase in violent crimes in recent years. No other graphic form could portray this fact as clearly, simply, and correctly as the semilogarithmic chart. Characteristically, from 1940 to the early 1960s most of the curves reflect relatively slight upward trends, frequently with minor fluctuations followed by a dramatic and accelerated increase to 1970. Although there are noticeable differentials in crime rates for the different areas and groupings, there is a striking parallelism among all the curves during the last 10-year period. For the seven areas and groupings the increase in violent crimes from 1960 to 1970 ranged from 126.4% to 483.7%. In an effort to minimize sharp and atypical irregularities in the curves, resulting from either fortuitous circumstances or discrepancies in the data, 3-year moving averages rather than original statistics were plotted on the charts.

OTHER GRAPHIC TECHNIQUES FOR SHOWING RATES OF CHANGE

Because of a possible lack of familiarity with the semilogarithmic chart, a desire for simplicity, or some other reason, a statistician may prefer to use some technique other than the semilogarithmic chart to portray rates of change. This can be done in at least two ways, neither of which is entirely satisfactory. These methods represent only a partial and frequently inadequate solution. Moreover, if simplification is the objective, more problems are actually created than solved. The first method is to portray relative changes by means of a percentage scale. Mere percentages fail to provide any indication of the actual values represented by the percentages on the curve. The semilogarithmic scale not only portrays relative changes correctly, but also exhibits accurately the numerical values of the series represented by the curve. Moreover, the semilogarithmic chart avoids the inevitable confusion resulting from the arbitrary selection of the base year or base period. The second alternate solution is to construct an arithmetic grid with two different vertical scales. This method is satisfactory if the scales are drawn in proper proportion and if the values do not vary too markedly from one another. Otherwise, the changes indicated by the curves will be distorted and misleading.

CHAPTER SIX

FREQUENCY GRAPHS AND RELATED CHARTS

IN THIS CHAPTER ARE DESCRIBED THE more important charting techniques that are used in portraying frequency distributions and similar forms of data. The presentation of this material is organized under the following major headings: (1) simple frequency graphs, (2) ogives, or cumulative frequency charts, (3) probability graphs, and (4) charts relating to distributions of age-specific rates.

SIMPLE FREQUENCY GRAPHS

Simple arithmetic frequency graphs represent the most common technique for portraying frequency distributions. There are three kinds of simple frequency graphs: (1) frequency polygon, (2) histogram, and (3) smoothed-frequency curve. These graphs are illustrated in Figure 6–1. It will be observed that they are based on data in Table 6–1.

Simple frequency graphs are usually drawn on rectilinear coordinates. The *Y*-axis always begins with zero and under no circumstances is it broken.[1] The horizontal scale does not have to begin with zero unless, of course, the lower limit of the first class interval is zero. In laying out the vertical scale, the range should be constructed to accommodate the maximum class frequency. Customarily, the highest value on the vertical axis is slightly higher than the maximal frequency. The scale intervals for the vertical axis are expressed in some convenient unit of round numbers, such as 5s, 10s, 25s, or some multiple thereof. The number of class intervals in the frequency distribution determines the range as well as the divisions of the horizontal scale.

In portraying frequency distributions, a distinction should be made between "continuous" and "discontinuous" variables. A continuous variable has an unlimited number of possible values ranging between the lowest and highest; a discontinuous variable represents discrete increments or complete units and hence is not capable of indefinite refinment. Each value of a discontinuous or discrete variable is distinct and separate, whereas the values of a continuous variable merge into one another by minute gradations. Age, weight, and temperature are examples of continuous variables; people, houses, and automobiles are examples of discontinuous variables.

Frequency Polygon

Normally, in laying out a polygon the appropriate frequency of each class is located at the midpoint of the interval, and the plotting points are then connected by straight lines. Of course, where the scale line itself identifies a specific value such as a single year of age in Figure 6–2, the plotting of the frequencies is located on each of the designated lines. Figures 6–1 (A), 6–2, 6–3, and 6–4 are illustrations of frequency polygons. As has been pointed out, the frequency polygon in Figure 6–1 (A) and also the histogram, step histogram, and smoothed-frequency graph are based on the same series of data found in Table 6–1. These data summarize the time required to complete the Fourth Annual Honolulu Marathon by 1456 participants. The abscissal axis indicates half-hour time intervals beginning with 2 hours and ending with 9 hours, and the ordinal axis shows the frequencies for each of the class intervals, which range from 1 to 348.

In Figure 6–2 there are two frequency polygons that portray grade retardation for two different periods, 1950 and 1960. It is obvious that neither curve can be characterized as either bell-shaped or symmetrical. Not infrequently, it is assumed by beginners that most, if not all, frequency distributions conform to a more-or-less symmetrical bell-shaped configuration. Actually, frequency distributions can take on almost any shape or form. Frequency curves may be highly skewed with a tail extending at either end. They also can be J-shaped or U-shaped. Two significant bodies of facts are emphasized by Figure 6–2: (1) the more or less characteristic age configuration of grade retardation; and (2) the marked reduction in retardation for the entire range of ages between 1950 and 1960. The U.S. Bureau of the Census definition of

Table 6–1

**Time Distribution of Participants
Completing Entire Distance, Fourth
Annual Honolulu Marathon:
December 12, 1976**

(Distance: 26 mi, 385 yd)

Time (Hours, Minutes, Seconds)	Participants	
	Number	Percentage
Total	1456	100.0
2.00.00–2.29.59	11	0.7
2.30.00–2.59.59	92	6.3
3.00.00–3.29.59	237	16.3
3.30.00–3.59.59	348	23.9
4.00.00–4.29.59	286	19.6
4.30.00–4.59.59	236	16.2
5.00.00–5.29.59	133	9.1
5.30.00–5.59.59	71	4.9
6.00.00–6.29.59	24	1.6
6.30.00–6.59.59	12	0.8
7.00.00–7.29.59	3	0.2
7.30.00–7.59.59	1	0.1
8.00.00–8.29.59	2	0.1

Data tabulated from individual listing of participants who finished the Fourth Annual Honolulu Marathon; printed in *The Honolulu Sunday Star-Bulletin and Advertiser* (December 26, 1976), p. F-3.

"normal" progress in schools permits a chronological age margin of 2 years; thus persons 7 and 8 years old in the second grade are "normal," 8 and 9 in the third grade, 9 and 10 in the fourth grade, and so on. Anyone older than normal in grade is defined as "retarded."

Figure 6–3 portrays the age distribution by single years of males and females who changed residence during a 1-year period. The horizontal axis represents age and the vertical axis, the percentage changing residence. The curves are differentiated by distinctive patterns and appropriately labeled. The chart could be noticeably improved by the addition of scale lines and ticks. It will be observed that men and women in the United States exhibit similar residential and migratory patterns, which is not surprising as most persons marry sometime during their lives, and most married couples live together and move as a pair. Most of the small differences between the residential and migratory patterns of men and women can be attributed to

differences in marital status, employment status, life-cycle stage, or labor-market opportunities from area to area, which may favor the employment of one sex over the other.

Additional illustrations of frequency polygons are exhibited in Figure 6–4. The upper panel portrays the age distribution for men and women at time of first marriage and the lower panel shows similar data at time of divorce after first marriage. The horizontal scale represents age and the vertical scale represents the percentage of cases in each age category. The basic data are country-wide samples of 51,453 men and 60,607 women for the series on first marriage, and 8282 men and 10,395 women for the series on divorce after first marriage. It will be observed that the most typical ages at first marriage are 20–23 years for men and 18–21 years for women. Approximately 42% of the men reported that they had been married for the first time between the ages of 20 and 23 years, whereas 48% of the women had married between 18 and 21. Most typical ages at divorce after first marriage are 25–29 for men and 20–24 for women. It will be noted that the respective median ages for all four distributions are indicated on the chart. The median as well as the mean and the mode are values on the abscissal scale.

Histogram

The typical histogram is constructed by erecting vertical lines at the limits of the class intervals and forming a series of contiguous rectangles or columns. The area of each rectangle represents the respective class frequencies. If the histogram is constructed over equal class intervals, the heights of the rectangles are proportional to the areas. In such cases the heights represent the class frequencies. For this reason histograms based on equal class intervals are much simpler to interpret than are those based on unequal intervals. Unequal class intervals are discussed in a subsequent section of this chapter. Sometimes all the vertical lines except the two at each end of the distribution are omitted, thus giving a step rather than a column

[1] The practice of breaking the vertical scale is frequently permissible in rectilinear time charts. For a more detailed discussion of this point as well as the basic theory and practice of constructing rectilinear coordinate charts, see Chapter 3.

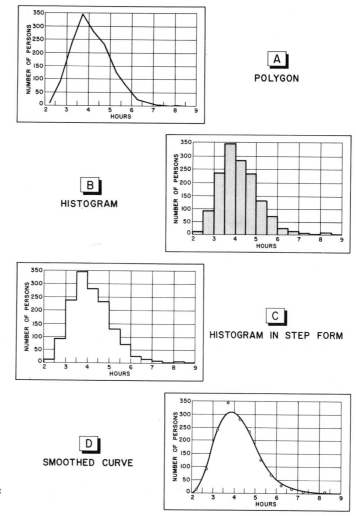

Figure 6–1. Four types of simple frequency charts (Based on data in Table 6–1.)

effect to the chart. This type of histogram is referred to as a "step-frequency" chart. Occasionally, the rectangles of the histogram are cross-hatched, stippled, or blacked. The histogram is particularly appropriate for depicting discrete series, although it can be used for continuous series. An examination of Figure 6–1 will reveal the conventional histogram as well as the step form of histogram.

Figure 6–5 is another example of a histogram. It is based on the data in Table 6–2. These statistics, which were derived from a country-wide sample survey of 22,803 persons, show the monthly wages of messengers.[2]

The distribution of monthly wages is summarized by twelve $50 class intervals ranging from $300 to $900. The frequencies vary from 68 to 4971. In designing a chart of this kind it is very obvious why the calibrations on the two axes must closely reflect the class intervals and frequencies of the statistical tabulation.

Smoothed-frequency Graph

The main purpose of smoothing a frequency graph is to iron out or eliminate the accidental irregularities resulting from sampling errors. As a rule, only frequency distributions based on samples should be smoothed. Accordingly, a smoothed-

---

[2] In this survey, "messenger" includes those who perform "various routine duties as running errands, operating minor office machines such as sealers or mailers, opening and distributing mail, and other minor clerical work. *Exclude* positions that require operation of a motor vehicle as a significant duty."

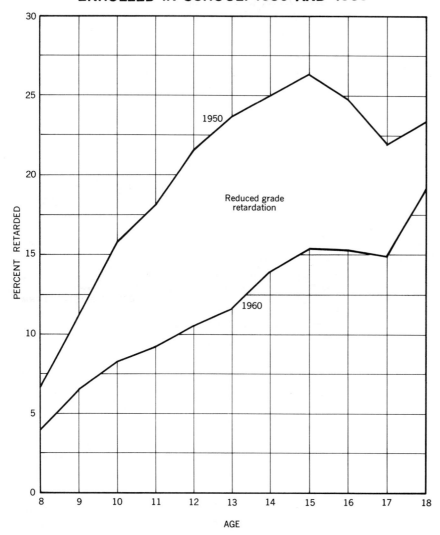

**GRADE RETARDATION OF PERSONS 8 TO 18 YEARS OLD
ENROLLED IN SCHOOL: 1950 AND 1960**

Figure 6–2. Two frequency polygons, expressed as percentages for comparative purpose, portray grade retardation for two periods, 1950 and 1960. (From John K. Folger and Charles B. Nam, Education of the American Population, Washington: Government Printing Office, 1967, p. 10.)

frequency curve represents a generalized characterization of the universe from which the sample was taken. Of course, only continuous series should be smoothed. In smoothing a curve it is important that the total area under the curve be equal to the area under the original histogram or polygon. Frequently, when a smoothed curve is constructed the plotting points of the original data are drawn on the grid to facilitate comparison with the original data.

Although there are several different procedures that can be used in smoothing frequency curves, the following simple graphic technique will be found satisfactory for most purposes:[3]

1. Construct a frequency polygon. The data used in developing this illustration are based on the distribution in Table 6–2. It will be observed

[3] L. L. Thurstone, *The Fundamentals of Statistics,* New York: Macmillan, 1938, pp. 39–44.

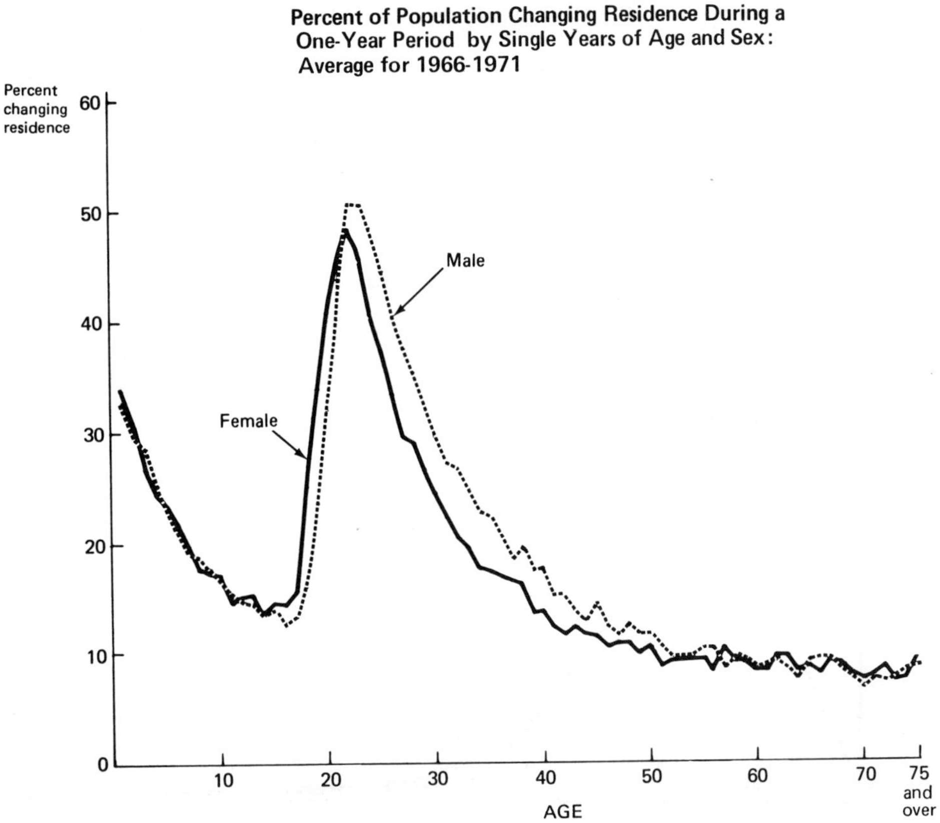

Percent of Population Changing Residence During a
One-Year Period by Single Years of Age and Sex:
Average for 1966-1971

Figure 6–3. A comparison of two frequency polygons. Data indicate ages by single years of males and females who changed their residence during a one–year period. This chart could be made more readily interpretable by the addition of scale lines and ticks. (From United States Bureau of the Census, A Statistical Portrait of Women in the U.S., Current Population Reports: Special Studies: Series P-23, No. 58, 1976, p. 11.)

from Figure 6–6 that the plotting points are shown by small open circles that are connected by light dashed lines. The plotting points are designated in alphabetical order, beginning at the lowest class interval.

2. Connect every other plotting point by straight lines, such as *AC, BD, CE, DF,* and so on.

3. Draw short lines, perpendicular to the *X*-axis, through each plotting point so that they cut the connecting lines *AC, BD, CE, DF,* and so on.

4. By inspection, indicate on the perpendicular lines the midpoints of the distance between the plotting points and the connecting lines *AC, BD, CE, DF,* and so on. The consecutive points thus determined are connected with a smooth freehand curve. The final smoothing is done with a French curve or other similar curve.

The most serious limitation of this technique for smoothing frequency curves is the tendency to reduce too much the height of the plotting point coincident with the modal interval. With a little experience and practice, however, adjustment can be made for this tendency.

Graphic Comparison of Frequency Distributions

There are several techniques for comparing graphically two or more frequency distributions. If the variables are continuous, the polygon or smoothed curve is usually most satisfactory. In constructing the polygons or smoothed curves, different line patterns can be used. One curve, for

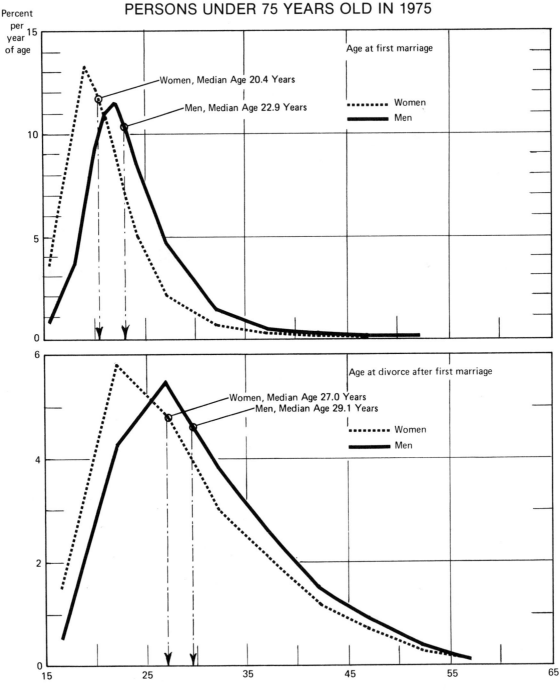

Figure 6–4. Additional illustrations of frequency polygons. The upper panel portrays the age distribution of men and women at first marriage and the lower panel similar data at divorce after first marriage. (From United States Bureau of the Census, Number, Timing and Duration of Marriage and Divorces in the United States: June 1975, Current Population Reports; Series P-20, No. 297, 1976, p. 9.)

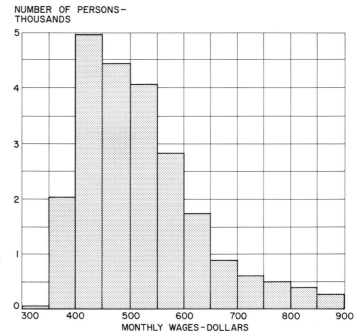

Figure 6–5. Histogram (based on data in Table 6–2.)

Table 6–2

**Monthly Wages of Messengers
United States (excluding Alaska and Hawaii)—March 1975**

| Monthly Wages in (Dollars) | Frequency | | Cumulative Frequency | | | |
| | | | Number | | Percentage | |
	Number	Percent-age	"Less Than"	"More Than"	"Less Than"	"More Than"
Total	22,803	100.0	22,803	22,803	100.0	100.0
300, under 350	68	0.3	68	22,803	0.3	100.0
350, under 400	2,052	9.0	2,120	22,735	9.3	99.7
400, under 450	4,971	21.8	7,091	20,683	31.1	90.7
450, under 500	4,424	19.4	11,515	15,712	50.5	68.9
500, under 550	4,059	17.8	15,574	11,288	68.3	49.5
550, under 600	2,828	12.4	18,402	7,229	80.7	31.7
600, under 650	1,733	7.6	20,135	4,401	88.3	19.3
650, under 700	866	3.8	21,001	2,668	92.1	11.7
700, under 750	616	2.7	21,617	1,802	94.8	7.9
750, under 800	502	2.2	22,119	1,186	97.0	5.2
800, under 850	410	1.8	22,529	684	98.8	3.0
850, under 900	274	1.2	22,803	274	100.0	1.2

Based on data from U.S. Bureau of Labor Statistics, *National Survey of Professional, Administrative, Technical and Clerical Pay, March 1975,* Washington, D. C.: Government Printing Office, 1975, p. 25. "Frequency" figures are sample data.

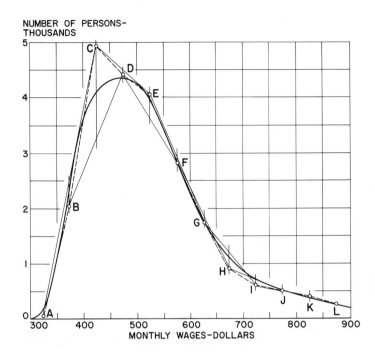

Figure 6–6. Technique for smoothing a frequency curve (based on data in Table 6–2.)

example, may be represented by a full line, another curve by a dashed line, another by a dot-and-dash line, or another curve by some other appropriate pattern. A discussion including illustrations of various curve patterns is found in Chapter 3. Figures 6–3 and 6–4 portray two frequency polygons on the same grid.

In comparing two or more series of data by means of frequency polygons or smoothed curves, either numerical or percentage values can be used. Numerical values should be used for comparison only when the total number of cases in each of the distributions are approximately the same. Where the number of cases in each of the series show considerable difference, it is generally advisable to use percentages. In this type of chart the vertical scale represents percentages rather than absolute frequencies, and the area under each of the polygons or smoothed curves is identical.

The histogram or step diagram also can be used for comparing two or more frequency distributions. Figure 6–7 illustrates the construction of histograms for comparing two series of data.[4]

The chart portrays a comparison of the distribution of rents for renter-occupied dwelling units located inside SMSAs with those outside SMSAs. The columns for each histogram are differentiated by distinctive shading patterns. Since the total number of dwelling units in each of the two major categories are not equal, the comparisons are ex-

pressed in percentages. The chart shows very clearly that rental levels are considerably higher within SMSAs in comparison with those outside.

Portrayal of Frequency Distributions by Column Charts

Figure 6–8 is an effective graphic form for depicting the four frequency distributions pertaining to age, sex, and racial differentials of hypertension. Although this chart manifests a superficial resemblance to a histogram, in actuality it is a grouped-column chart. In light of the implications of unequal class intervals, which will be discussed in a later section, and the manner in which the columns should be plotted, this chart fails to conform to the basic theoretical statistical criteria of a histogram. Nevertheless, pragmatic considerations may sometimes override theoretical principles as long as they do not violate accepted standards of graphic presentation. For example, in this instance, in the process of selecting a particular graphic form one should be guided largely by the fundamental question as to

---

[4] In a strict mathematical sense the design of Figure 6–7 does not meet the requirements of a histogram since no adjustments were made for the two "open-ended" intervals and the one unequal class interval. The implications of these facts are brought out more clearly in a subsequent section.

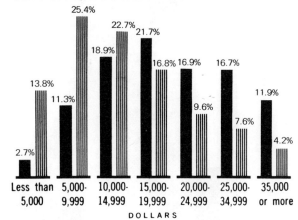

Occupied Housing Units: 1970

■ INSIDE SMSA's   ▥ OUTSIDE SMSA's
(SMSA's=Standard Metropolitan Statistical Areas)

VALUE: Percent Distribution
OWNER OCCUPIED ONE-FAMILY HOMES

CONTRACT RENT: Percent Distribution
RENTER OCCUPIED

Figure 6–7. Histograms designed for comparison of two series of data. (From United States Bureau of the Census, 1970 Census of Housing, General Housing Characteristics, United States Summary, Washington: Government Printing Office, pp. 1–7.)

what the most effective graphic technique is for portraying these data. Certainly, the grouped-column chart seems most appropriate. Among the many facts that Figure 6–8 portrays, the following might be cited: proportionately more women than men currently have hypertension. This sex difference is apparent among every age group except those aged 17–24 years. The prevalence of hypertension increases with advancing age. Proportionately more black persons than white currently have hypertension. White males have the lowest proportion of hypertensives and black females, the highest proportion of hypertensives.

Variant of Typical Frequency Histogram; Age–Sex Pyramid or Triangle

The age–sex pyramid, which is extensively used to portray certain types of population data, is fundamentally a two-way, or bilateral, histogram with the X- and Y-axes reversed. It will be observed from Figures 6–9, 6–10, and 6–11 that the class intervals are indicated by the vertical axis, and the numerical or percentage frequency, by the horizontal axis. The histogram rectangles to the left of the zero or baseline represent the male sex, and those to the

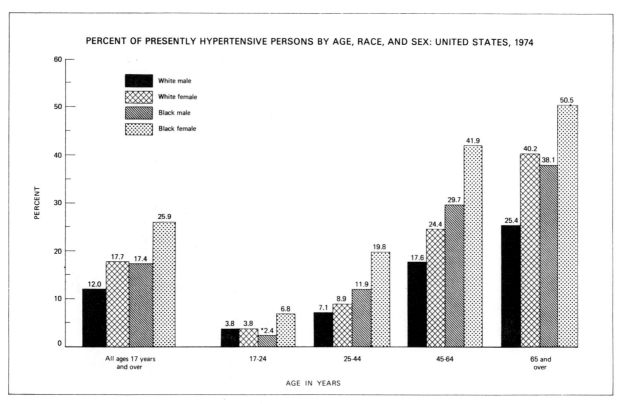

Figure 6–8. A grouped–column chart for comparing four frequency distributions. [*From "Hypertension: United States, 1974," Advancedata, HEW National Center for Health Statistics, (2), November 8, 1976, p. 2.*]

right, the female sex. The age divisions read from bottom to top, beginning with the youngest group. In a normally structured population the general configuration of this type of chart is pyramidal or triangular. This fact is clearly understandable as a consequence of the normal operation of fertility and mortality on the age and sex structure of the population. However, migration or some other factor may be responsible for extreme variations from the symmetrical triangle.

The series of nine age and sex pyramids in Figure 6–9 typifies the selective influence of various ecological and other factors on the age and sex structure of the population in different sections of a large city. It will be observed that this series of pyramids has been drawn as double histograms in step form. For comparative purpose, an age–sex pyramid for the total population of Seattle has been superimposed in a light dashed line on each of the nine pyramids. The nine pyramids typify the age and sex structures of the populations in certain urban subareas. For example, the pyramid for census tract M1, which embraces most of the central

business district (CBD), is markedly asymmetrical, indicating a pronounced excess of males (85.3%) and a very small proportion of children (0.4% under 5 years or 1.4% under 15 years of age). The proportion of the population in the upper age groups is considerably higher in the CBD than in the city as a whole. Census tract M3 is representative of a centrally located rooming-house and apartment-house area, characterized by a high proportion of females (59.3%) and a small proportion of children (2.4% of the population is under 15 years of age, as compared to 25.9% for the city as a whole). Another significant illustration is exemplified by census tracts O1, O2, and L5, which represent transitional areas contiguous to the CBD. Tract O1 is mainly a "Hobohemia," colloquially referred to as "Skid Road"; O2 includes Chinatown and smaller clusterings of Filipinos, blacks, and Japanese; and L5 is inhabited largely by a transient working-class white population. In all three tracts there is a heavy preponderance of the male sex, with 88.8% in O1, 75.6% in O2, and 72.5% in L5. The proportion of children under 15 years of age in these three tracts

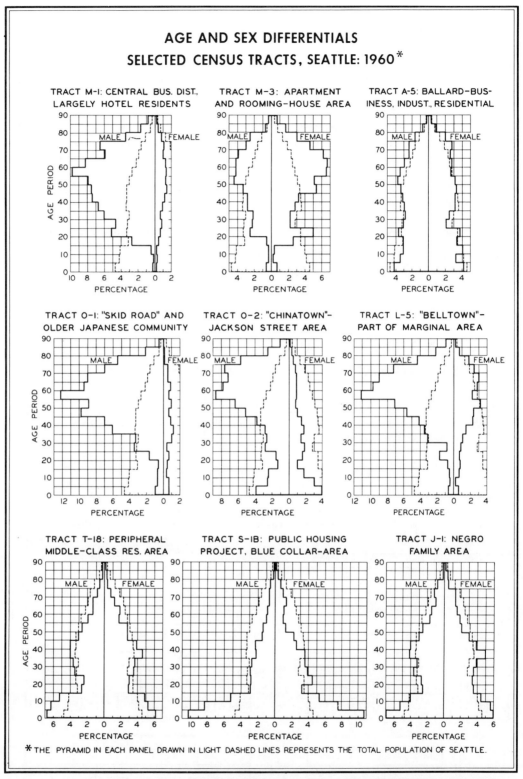

AGE AND SEX DIFFERENTIALS
SELECTED CENSUS TRACTS, SEATTLE: 1960*

TRACT M-1: CENTRAL BUS. DIST., LARGELY HOTEL RESIDENTS

TRACT M-3: APARTMENT AND ROOMING-HOUSE AREA

TRACT A-5: BALLARD-BUS-INESS, INDUST., RESIDENTIAL

TRACT O-1: "SKID ROAD" AND OLDER JAPANESE COMMUNITY

TRACT O-2: "CHINATOWN"-JACKSON STREET AREA

TRACT L-5: "BELLTOWN"-PART OF MARGINAL AREA

TRACT T-18: PERIPHERAL MIDDLE-CLASS RES. AREA

TRACT S-1B: PUBLIC HOUSING PROJECT, BLUE COLLAR-AREA

TRACT J-1: NEGRO FAMILY AREA

*THE PYRAMID IN EACH PANEL DRAWN IN LIGHT DASHED LINES REPRESENTS THE TOTAL POPULATION OF SEATTLE.

Figure 6–9. A series of age and sex pyramids. Age and sex pyramids are bilateral or two–way histograms, with frequencies represented by the horizontal, rather than by the vertical, axis. (From Calvin F. Schmid and Stanton E. Schmid, Crime in the State of Washington, Olympia: Law and Justice Planning Office, Planning and Community Affairs Agency, 1972, p. 100.)

is small. Also, it might be pointed out that these three tracts are characterized by a declining population, a large percentage of foreign-born persons, a high proportion of separated, divorced, and widowed, and low-educational-status individuals, a high proportion of unskilled laborers, and a high rate of unemployment.

Figure 6–10 depicts the extraordinary transformation of the age–sex structure of the Japanese population in the state of Washington during a 50-year period. In 1910 the overwhelming proportion of the Japanese population consisted of young adult male migrants 20–40 years of age. Over the years, with the migration of more females and the establishment of families along with the influence of fertility and mortality, the age–sex composition of the Japanese population has become similar to that of the white population. It will be observed that each bar of the pyramids has been fully outlined and stippled, and a dash line repre-

Figure 6–10. Age and sex pyramids, with the class–intervals of the histograms completely outlined and stippled. In contrast, the pyramids in the preceding chart are drawn in step–form. It will be observed that the sex and age structure of the Japanese population in the state of Washington is characterized by an extraordinary preponderance of males between 20 and 40 years of age. (From Calvin F. Schmid, Charles E. Nobbe, and Arlene E. Mitchell, Nonwhite Races, State of Washington, Olympia: Washington State Planning and Community Affairs Agency, 1968, p. 85.)

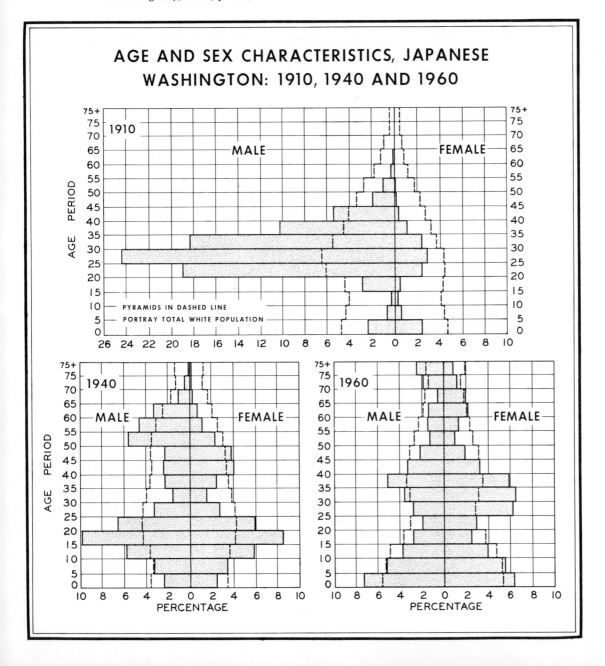

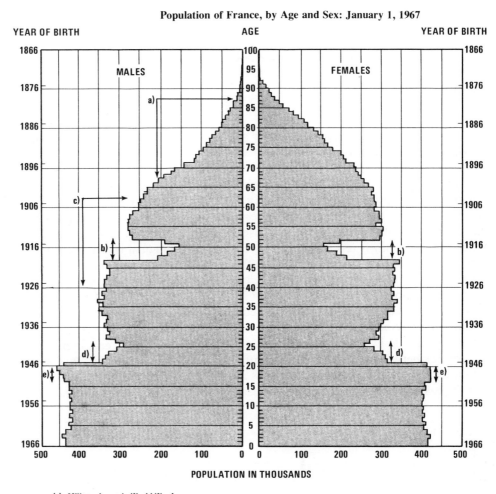

Population of France, by Age and Sex: January 1, 1967

(a) Military losses in World War I
(b) Deficit of births during World War I
(c) Military losses in World War II
(d) Deficit of births during World War II
(e) Rise of births due to demobilization after World War II

Figure 6–11. Age and sex pyramid of the population of France, with particular emphasis on age–sex–selective factors largely attributable to World War I and World War II. (From Henry S. Shryock, Jacob S. Siegel, et al., **The Methods and Materials of Demography,** *United States Bureau of the Census, Washington: Government Printing Office, 1, 1971, p. 242. Chart based on France, Institut national de la statistique et des études economiques,* Annuaire statistique de la France, *1967, 1968, p. 33.)*

senting the age–sex configuration of the white population for each of the respective years has been superimposed on the three pyramids.

Figure 6–11 is a detailed portrayal of the age–sex structure of the population of France covering a period of 100 years. The impact of World Wars I and II as indicated by the processes of mortality and fertility is emphasized in this chart. The vertical scale consists of 20 5-year class intervals, with each interval divided into 1-year units. The total span of the vertical scale is 100 years, which is synchronized with the year of birth of each cohort from 1866 to 1966. The horizontal scale is expressed in absolute numbers rather than percentages, as in the preceding sets of pyramids presented in Figures 6–9 and 6–10. The explanatory references in Figure

6–11 are very important since they clearly point out that the various gaps, irregularities, and asymmetrical deviations in the pyramid are attributable to both direct and indirect factors associated with the two world wars.

Charting Frequency Distributions with Unequal Class Intervals

It is a basic principle in the graphic presentation of frequency distributions that the frequency between any two points in the distribution is represented by the area under the curve between those points. When the frequency is represented by a percentage of the total, the area under the curve is unity and the mathematical expression of the area is called its "density function."

Empirical frequency distributions based on data obtained in discrete units may likewise be represented by curves having this areal relationship to frequencies between any designated points. If the data are grouped into class intervals, it is assumed that the cases in the interval are evenly distributed,

and hence each point between the class boundaries has the same frequency. Accordingly, the area of a rectangle in a histogram formed over any class interval represents the frequency in that interval. Since the area of a rectangle is the product of its width times its height, the width is the independent, arbitrarily chosen value, and the frequency depends on the observations, the height may be computed readily by dividing the frequency by the width of the class interval. If the class intervals are all of equal width, the width can be considered to be unity. In such instances, of course, the height of the rectangle is equal to the frequency in the class interval. However, if the class intervals are of unequal width, the same basic principle applies and the proper height is found by dividing the frequency by the width of each class interval. Any convenient interval may be chosen as unity, and the proper divisors can be computed from this interval. Using these divisors, the height for each rectangle of the histogram can then be computed readily for any combination of class width. For example, in part A of Figure 6–12 equal intervals of $5,000 were used. If $5,000 is then chosen as unity, in order to com-

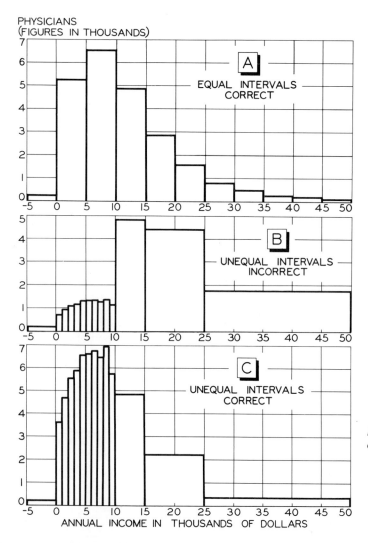

Figure 6–12. Histograms with equal and unequal class intervals. (Based on data in Table 6–3.)

pute the heights of rectangles of the histogram in part C of Figure 6–12, where the class interval is $1,000, the frequency must be divided by 1/5 (since $1,000 is 1/5 of $5,000); and, where the class interval is $10,000, the frequency must be divided by 2 (since $10,000 is two times $5,000); and so on. These data are shown in Table 6–3. To determine the divisor, divide the width of the class interval under consideration by the width of the class interval that has been chosen as unity.

A common error in constructing a histogram with unequal class intervals is to make the heights of the respective rectangles commensurate with the frequencies of the class intervals without taking into consideration the width of the class intervals. This practice leads to extreme distortion and misrep-

resentation (see part B in Figure 6–12). Errors of this kind can be readily avoided if the basic principles outlined in the foregoing paragraphs are followed.

Frequency Distribution Plotted on Logarithmic Scale

Sometimes it may be desirable to plot frequency distributions on a logarithmic scale, particularly if there is pronounced skewness. The results of plotting a series of figures on a logarithmic scale are the same as plotting the logarithms of the figures. If, for example, a frequency distribution shows marked positive skewness, it tends to be normalized when

Table 6–3

Distribution of Net Incomes of Major Independent Physicians

To keep the table as simple as possible, the two open-ended class intervals, −$5,000 or more (loss) at the lower extreme and $50,000 or more (gain) at the upper extreme, were omitted. There were only two cases in the interval −$5,000 or more, and 164 in the interval $50,000 or more. For the last column at the right, using interval of 5,000 as unity, divide number of physicians by 1,000/5,000, or 0.2, for intervals of 1,000; 10,000/5,000, or 2, for intervals of 10,000; and for intervals of 25,000, 25,000/5,000, or 5.

A. Equal Class Intervals		B. Unequal Class Intervals		
Annual Income (Dollars)	Number of Physicians	Annual Income (Dollars)	Number of Physicians	Height of Histogram Rectangle Adjusted to Preserve Frequency Area
Total	23,047	Total	23,047	
−5,000 to −0,001	206	−5,000 to −0,001	206	206
		0 to 999	726	3,630
		1,000 to 1,999	938	4,690
0 to 4,999	5,267	2,000 to 2,999	1,110	5,550
		3,000 to 3,999	1,177	5,885
		4,000 to 4,999	1,316	6,580
		5,000 to 5,999	1,323	6,615
		6,000 to 6,999	1,353	6,765
5,000 to 9,999	6,514	7,000 to 7,999	1,292	6,460
		8,000 to 8,999	1,395	6,975
		9,000 to 9,999	1,151	5,755
10,000 to 14,999	4,851	10,000 to 14,999	4,851	4,851
15,000 to 19,999	2,839	15,000 to 24,999	4,423	2,211
20,000 to 24,999	1,584			
25,000 to 29,999	795			
30,000 to 34,999	472			
35,000 to 39,999	249	25,000 to 49,999	1,786	357
40,000 to 44,999	173			
45,000 to 49,999	97			

Unpublished data compiled under direction of William Weinfeld for his study, "Income of Physicians, 1929–1949," *Survey of Current Business* (July, 1951), pp. 9–26. Special transcript of data furnished by Charles F. Schwartz, Assistant Chief, National Income Division, United States Department of Commerce.

plotted on a chart with a logarithmic horizontal axis. This fact is illustrated by Figure 6–13.[5]

In a subsequent paper C. B. Williams pointed out that:

When I converted some of Yule's tables into diagrams I was struck by their general resemblance to skew distributions with which I have recently been dealing in some entomological problems . . . which distributions, I found, became normal and symmetrical if the logarithm of the number was taken as a basis for subdivision into groups instead of the number itself.[6]

Mathematicians have done very little work on this normalizing procedure, and at the present time the mathematical implications of logarithmic transformation of frequency distributions are still obscure. Also, it should be pointed out that in plotting frequency distributions the vertical scale rather than the horizontal scale may be ruled logarithmically, or both the horizontal and vertical scales may be calibrated in this manner.

CUMULATIVE-FREQUENCY GRAPH OR OGIVE

For some purposes the cumulative-frequency curve, or ogive, is more valuable than the simple frequency graph. In the simple frequency distribution the number of cases for each class interval is indicated separately. In a cumulative-frequency distribution the frequencies of the successive class intervals are accumulated, beginning at either end of the distribution. If the cumulation process is from the lesser to the greater, it is referred to as a "less than" type of distribution; if the cumulation

[5] The original data for these frequency distributions were derived from G. Udny Yule, "On Sentence-Length as a Statistical Characteristic of Style in Prose: With Application to Two Cases of Disputed Authorship," *Biometrika,* **30** (1939), 361–390.
[6] A Note on the Statistical Analysis of Sentence-Length as a Criterion of Literary Style," *Biometrika,* **31** (1940), 356–361.

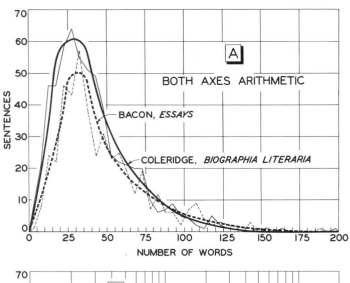
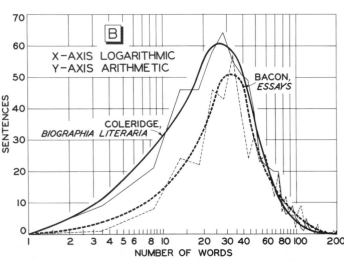

Figure 6–13. Plotting frequency distributions on arithmetic and semilogarithmic scales. In the upper panel both axes of the grid are arithmetic, whereas in the lower panel the horizontal axis is logarithmic, and the vertical axis arithmetic. The data show the numbers of sentences (vertical axis) having a specified length in words (horizontal axis) in Bacon's Essays and Coleridge's Biographia Literaria. (From G. Udny Yule, "On Sentence–Length as a Statistical Characteristic of Style in Prose: With Application to Two Cases of Disputed Authorship," Biometrika, 30, 1940, pp. 362–90.)

proceeds from the greater to the lesser, it is known as a ''more than'' type of distribution.

In constructing an ogive the cumulative frequencies are represented by the vertical axis and the class intervals, by the horizontal axis. Unlike the simple frequency graph, the range of the vertical scale covers the total number of cases in the distribution. In the upper panel of Figure 6–14, for example, the ordinal scale extends from zero to 25,000, which is 2197 more than the total number of cases.

Instead of plotting the cumulated frequencies at the midpoint of each class interval, as is done in the simple frequency graph, they are plotted either at

---

[7] In older terminology the word ''percentile'' was used instead of ''centile.'' ''Centile'' seems to be preferable since it is more consistent with general usage of terms describing other divisions of the scale, such as deciles, quintiles, and quartiles, but not ''perdeciles,'' ''perquintiles,'' or ''perquartiles.''

the lower or upper end of the interval, depending on whether the cumulation is of the ''less than'' or ''more than'' type. If the distribution is of the ''less than'' type, the cumulated frequency for each class is plotted at the upper end of the interval. When the cumulative frequencies are represented as percentages, as is often the case, the vertical axis covers the range from zero to 100%, whereas the horizontal axis is the same as for the numerical frequency graph. The percentage cumulative-frequency chart is also referred to as a ''centile graph'' or ''centile curve.'' The lower panel in Figure 6–14 illustrates this type of chart.[7]

Both the numerical and percentage cumulative-frequency curves are characteristically of the elongated S-shape. The ''less than'' type extends from the lower left to the upper right of the grid and the ''more than'' type, from the upper left to the lower right of the grid. The ''less than'' and ''more than'' types of curves intersect at the median value. It

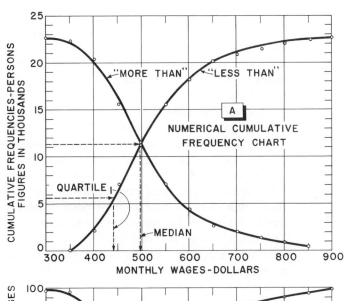

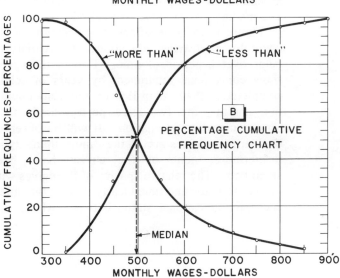

Figure 6–14. Cumulative frequency graphs or ogives. In the upper panel A, the figures on the vertical axis represent actual cumulative frequencies, whereas in the lower panel B, the figures on the vertical axis are cumulative percentages. Note especially the plotting points for both the "less than" and "more than" types of ogives and also the interpolation lines. (Based on data in Table 6–2. Portrays cumulative distribution of monthly wages of messengers.)

should be emphasized that the median, quartiles, deciles, and other similar measures represent values on the X-axis.

From the standpoint of graphic presentation, the ogive is especially adapted to two purposes. First, it is used to determine as well as portray the number or proportion of cases above or below a given value. For example, to estimate the number of messengers receiving monthly wages of $675, or less, a vertical line can be plotted at the midpoint of the interval 650–700 on the abscissal scale on Figure 6–14 (A). A horizontal line is then drawn from the intersection of the vertical line and the ogive to the ordinal axis, which indicates that approximately 20,750 of the messengers receive $675 or less per month. Second, the ogive is used to compare two or more frequency distributions. There is generally less overlapping when comparing several ogives on the same grid than when comparing several simple frequency curves in this manner. In comparing ogives, emphasis is placed on the number or proportion of cases above or below a given point, whereas in comparing simple frequency curves, emphasis is placed on maximal concentration and skewness. In this connection, however, it should be remembered that the maximal frequency or concentration of cases on an ogive is indicated by the steepest portion of the curve.

The median, quartiles, deciles, or some other measure of this kind can also be derived by simple interpolation. The first quartile (Q_1), for example, can be found by dividing the number of cases in a distribution by four ($N/4$); from this value on the vertical axis a horizontal line is drawn to the "less than" type of ogive, and from the point of intersection a vertical line is dropped to the horizontal axis. The point where the vertical line intersects the horizontal axis is Q_1. Figure 6–14 (A) illustrates the procedure in interpolating quartiles and median. The median, for example, is $495.50.

Figure 6–15 is an effective application of the ogive for portraying educational differentials by color over a period of time. Two of the ogives show educational attainment by years of school completed in 1940 and in 1960 for the white population, and the other two ogives portray similar facts for the nonwhite population. It will be observed that all four ogives are of the "more than" type; furthermore, none of the curves have been smoothed. The relative spacing of the ogives with respect to color and time clearly reveals the differences in educational status between whites and

nonwhites as well as changes in educational attainment in both groups that have occurred between 1940 and 1960. Specific values and indicators of educational attainment can be derived from the chart by simple interpolation. For example, by reading across the 50% scale line on the vertical axis it will be found that the median educational levels for nonwhites were 5.8 years in 1940 and 8.2 years in 1960, whereas the corresponding figures for whites were 8.7 years in 1940 and 10.8 years in 1960.

Lorenz Curve

A special type of cumulative-frequency graph known as a "Lorenz curve"[8] can be used effectively to portray such data as the distribution of wealth and income in relation to certain segments of the population, the productivity of farms in terms of cumulative proportions of farms, and the distribution of retail sales as related to various groupings of stores.

The first step in the construction of a Lorenz curve is to transpose the data into percentages and arrange them into "less than" types of cumulative-frequency distributions. The basic data for illustration of this type of curve are portrayed in Figure 6–16 and summarized in Table 6–4.

The next step is to construct a square-shaped grid with both axes ranging in value from zero to 100%. The horizontal axis represents the percentage of physicians cumulated from lowest to highest incomes, and the vertical axis represents the percentage of net income cumulated from lowest to highest income. The chart clearly portrays the relative amount of dispersion in frequency distributions. A curve of equal distribution would be a straight line extending diagonally from zero to 100. Such a curve would indicate that any specified proportion of physicians would earn precisely the same proportion of income. For example, 20% of the physicians would receive 20% of the income, 50% of the physicians would receive 50% of the income, 75% of the physicians would receive 75% of the income, and so on. Actually, this is not the

[8] Named after M. O. Lorenz, who first developed this type of curve. For further details, see his original paper entitled "Methods of Measuring the Concentration of Wealth," *Journal of the American Statistical Association,* New Series No. 70 (June 1905), 209–219.

case. There is a marked deviation from the line of equal distribution. The distance between the curve

and the diagonal line is indicative of the degree of deviation. It will be observed from Figure 6–16 that 50% of the physicians, beginning with those of lowest income, receive less than 20% of the income.[9]

Figure 6–17 is another example of the Lorenz curve. It shows how the total 1971 income received by "consumer units" in the United States was distributed. "Consumer units" include the civilian noninstitutional population of the United States and members of the Armed Forces in the United States living off post or with their families on post. The two types of consumer units are: (1) families and (2) unrelated individuals. It is obvious

---

[9] For detailed discussions of the statistical properties of the Lorenz curve as a measure of the extent of inequality of a distribution, especially its relation to the Gini index or coefficient, G, see Farhad Mehran, "Bounds on the Gini Index Based on Observed Points of the Lorenz Curve," *Journal of the American Statistical Association*, **70** (349) (March 1975), 64–66; J. L. Gastwirth, "The Estimation of the Lorenz Curve and Gini Index," *The Review of Economics and Statistics*, **54** (August 1972), 306–316; N. C. Kakwani and N. Podder, "On the Estimation of Lorenz Curves from Grouped Observations," *International Economic Review*, **14** (June 1973), 278–292.

Figure 6–15. An effective application of the cumulative–frequency graph or ogive. This chart clearly depicts educational attainment by school–year completed of the white and nonwhite population of the United States in 1940 and 1960. (From John K. Folger and Charles B. Nam, Education of the American Population, *Washington: Government Printing Office, 1967, p. 147.)*

PERCENT OF THE POPULATION 25 YEARS OLD AND OVER WITH INDICATED YEARS OF SCHOOL COMPLETED, BY COLOR: 1940 TO 1960

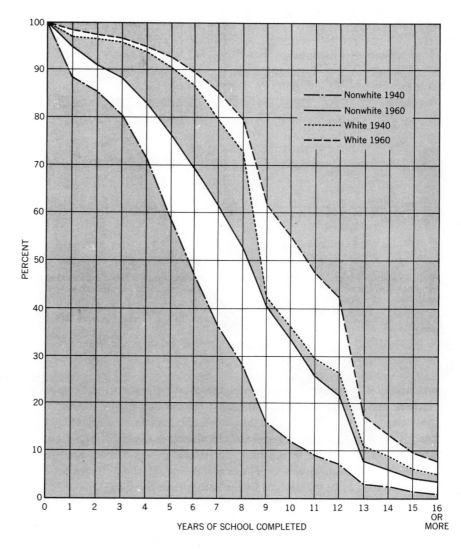

that the distribution pattern for family units is more equable than the one for unrelated individuals. By single graphic interpolation it is possible to measure fairly accurately the proportion of the income received by any specific proportion of the families or of unrelated individuals.

PROBABILITY GRAPHS

"Probability paper"[10] is the name given to the special arrangement of vertical and horizontal spacing of a grid that has the property of representing the cumulative normal function as a straight line. Since probability paper is widely used and represents a special class of grids used on charts for particular purposes, its characteristics and utility should be recognized. It is based on the normal frequency curve. The use of such a grid was early suggested by Francis Galton[11] and later developed by Allen Hazen. Although it is possible to reverse the axes, the usual grid is ruled arithmetically on the vertical axis and the horizontal axis is divided proportionally to the magnitude of cumulative normal ordinates.

Since the normal distribution is asymptotic to both the zero and the 100% values, the horizontal scale on probability paper cannot reach either zero or 100%, but must start with a small number, usually 0.01, and extend to a magnitude near 100%, such as 99.99, as is illustrated in Figure 6–18.

The characteristic shape of the cumulative graph, or ogive, of the normal distribution is an elongated S. When the axes of the graph are reversed to correspond with the probability paper

---

[10] Probability paper is produced commercially and can be obtained from stationers and drafting supply houses.
[11] Francis Galton, "A Geometric Determination of the Median Value of a System of Normal Variants, from Two of Its Centiles," *Nature,* **61** (November 30, 1899), 102–104; Allen Hazen, "Storage to be Provided in Impounding Reservoir for Municipal Water Supply," *Transactions of American Society of Civil Engineers,* **77** (December 1914), 1539–1669. In an earlier discussion the same year (p. 627), Mr. Hazen refers to the probability paper that he devised as follows: "A new kind of cross-section paper is made, in which the spacing of the lines in one direction is computed from tables of the probability curve, so that figures representing the summation of that curve plotted on it fall in a straight line."

CUMULATIVE PERCENTAGE DISTRIBUTIONS OF INDEPENDENT PHYSICIANS AND THEIR NET INCOME FROM MEDICAL WORK

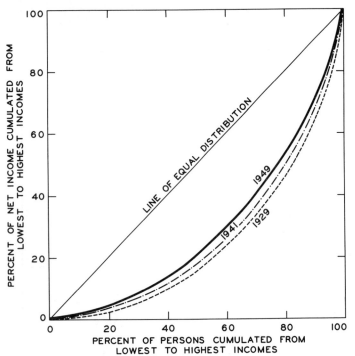

Figure 6–16. Lorenz curve. (Redrawn from William Weinfeld, "Income of Physicians, 1929–49," Survey of Current Business, July 1951, pp. 9–26.)

axes, the graph appears as in Figure 6–18. It is noticeable that the central part of the curve—from about the 25% point to the 75% point of the distribution—is almost a straight line. A grid that will straighten this central part has to be stretched only slightly from the equal arithmetic ruling, but in the sharply curved extremes a considerable amount of stretching or expansion of the grid is required. The probability grid is characterized by extremely wide spacing at the upper and lower ends of the scale, quickly decreasing spacing in the regions between 1% and 20% and between 80% and 99%, and almost equal spacing in the central part of the scale (see Figures 6–18 and 6–19.)

Table 6–4
Type of Data Required for Lorenz Curve
Distribution of Net Income of Major Independent Physicians

| Net Income (Dollars) | Midpoint of Income Class (1) | Number of Physicians (2) | Aggregate Income (000's omitted) (3) | Cumulative Frequencies | | | |
| | | | | Number | | Percentage | |
				Physicians (4)	Aggregate Income (000's omitted) (5)	Physicians (6)	Aggregate Income (7)
A. Loss:							
2,000 and over	3,500	22	−71	22	−71	0.1	(Under 0.05%)
1,000–1,999	1,500	42	−63	64	−134	0.3	0.1
1–999	500	144	−72	208	−206	0.9	0.1
B. Gain:							
1–999	500	726	363	934	157	4.0	0.1
1,000–1,999	1,500	938	1,407	1,872	1,564	8.1	0.6
2,000–2,999	2,500	1,110	2,775	2,982	4,339	12.8	1.6
3,000–3,999	3,500	1,177	4,120	4,159	8,459	17.9	3.1
4,000–4,999	4,500	1,316	5,922	5,475	14,381	23.6	5.2
5,000–5,999	5,500	1,323	7,276	6,798	21,657	29.3	7.9
6,000–6,999	6,500	1,353	8,794	8,151	30,451	35.1	11.1
7,000–7,999	7,500	1,292	9,690	9,443	40,141	40.7	14.6
8,000–8,999	8,500	1,395	11,858	10,838	51,999	46.7	18.9
9,000–9,999	9,500	1,151	10,934	11,989	62,933	51.6	22.9
10,000–14,999	12,500	4,851	59,574	16,840	122,507	72.5	44.5
15,000–19,999	17,500	2,839	48,790	19,679	171,297	84.8	62.2
20,000–24,999	22,500	1,584	35,118	21,263	206,415	91.6	75.0
25,000–29,999	27,500	795	21,566	22,058	227,981	95.0	82.8
30,000–39,999	35,000	721	24,439	22,779	252,420	98.1	91.7
40,000–49,999	45,000	270	11,960	23,049	264,380	99.3	96.0
50,000–59,999	55,000	91	4,968	23,140	269,348	99.7	97.8
60,000–69,999	65,000	30	1,940	23,170	271,288	99.8	98.5
70,000–99,999	85,000	36	2,900	23,206	274,188	99.97	99.6
100,000 and over	152,364	7	1,067	23,213	275,255	100.00	100.0
Totals		23,213	275,255				

Arranged from unpublished data compiled under direction of William Weinfeld for his study, "Income of Physicians, 1929–49," *Survey of Current Business* (July 1951), 9–26; special transcript of data furnished by Charles F. Schwartz, Assistant Chief, National Income Division, U.S. Department of Commerce.

Lorenz Curves of Families and Unrelated Individuals,
Family Personal Income, 1971

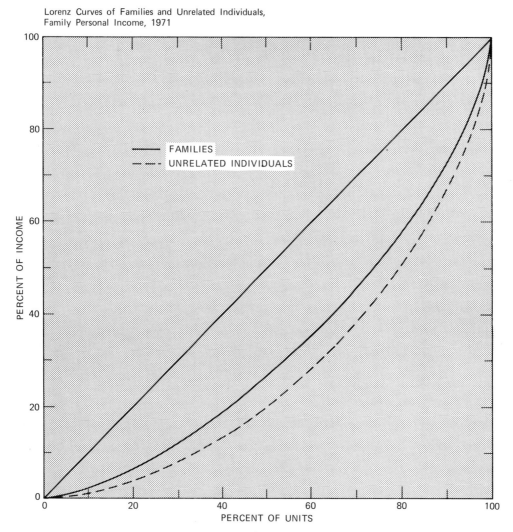

Figure 6–17. Another example of the Lorenz curve. Shows the distribution patterns of incomes of families and unrelated persons in 1971. [From Daniel B. Radner and John C. Hinrichs, "Size Distribution of Income in 1964, 1970, and 1971," Survey of Current Business, United States Department of Commerce, 54, (10), October 1974, p. 19.]

Because of the construction of the grid, then, the graph of the cumulative heights of ordinates of any perfectly normal distribution will appear as a straight line when plotted on probability paper. In demonstrating the normalcy of a distribution, it is much easier to detect and demonstrate deviations from a straight line than from any of the more complicated curves, such as the ogive. Figure 6–19 shows a comparison between the graph of the cumulative frequencies of an approximately normal distribution and the straight line that represents the normal distribution having the same mean and standard deviation.

tion. It is easy to see that the distribution is almost perfectly normal, except in the usually erratic extreme cases that violate the otherwise straight-line pattern on the probability paper.

The scale for the independent axis may be ruled either arithmetically or logarithmically. If the ogive is expressed as a straight line on arithmetic probability paper, the original frequency distribution can be considered symmetrical on an arithmetic projection. Similarly, if an ogive is represented by a straight line on logarithmic probability paper, the original frequency distribution can be considered

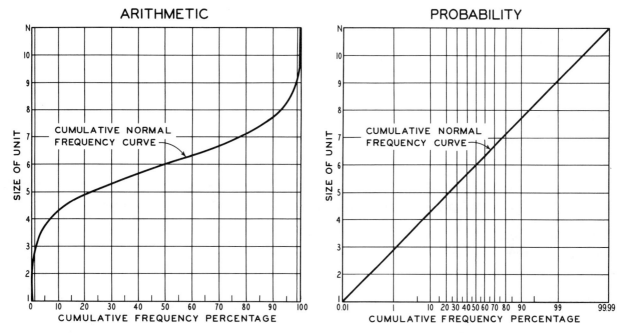

ARITHMETIC

PROBABILITY

Figure 6–18. Comparison of cumulative–frequency distribution plotted on arithmetic grid and on probability grid.

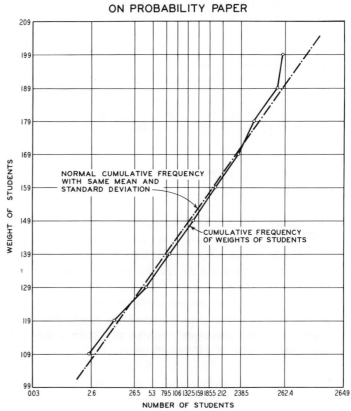

CUMULATIVE FREQUENCY OF WEIGHTS OF 265 FRESHMEN MALE STUDENTS AT THE UNIVERSITY OF WASHINGTON ON PROBABILITY PAPER

Figure 6–19. Illustration of use of probability paper in comparing cumulative frequency of weights of university students with normal cumulative frequency. (Data taken from Calvin F. Schmid, "Basic Statistical Concepts and Techniques," in Pauline V. Young, Scientific Social Surveys and Research, Englewood Cliffs, N. J.: Prentice–Hall, 1966, pp. 274–347.)

asymmetrical and can be made symmetrical by plotting on logarithmic projection. This provides a test for proportional asymmetry.

Probability paper also is a useful addition as a technique of statistical analysis, such as demonstrating comparisons between empirical and theoretical distributions and prediction. The rationale of using paper of this kind for prediction purposes is based on the law of probability as expressed by the normal frequency curve. For example, it can be used for predicting the longevity of telephone poles, freight cars, steel cable, cross ties, electric lamps, and pumps; probable weekly sales of certain items; probable proportions of defective units in testing or inspecting materials; probable attendance at expositions and fairs; probable variation in maturity of crops or stock; and human mortality.[12]

Special grids can be developed readily for the simplification of complicated curves, but it might be pointed out that extensive use of such techniques may result in criticism that the data are being distorted by graphic trickery. Probability paper and a few other special grids of this type have been found useful and may be considered above such criticism.[13] If the usefulness of a special grid can be demonstrated, there is no reason why it should not be adopted; but if clear advantage in its use is not present, the better understood, more conventional grids will make the presentation more acceptable and require less explanation.

The most satisfactory method of laying out a probability paper grid is by using a strip of commerical probability paper as a scale and proceeding as explained in detail in Chapter 5.[14]

CHARTING AGE-SPECIFIC RATES AND RATIOS

Distributions of age-specific rates often look like frequency distributions and as a consequence are sometimes mistaken for them. Like frequency distributions, distributions of age-specific rates may be more or less bell-shaped, U-shaped, J-shaped, or S-shaped; they may be relatively symmetrical or asymmetrical. Statistically, however, there is a basic difference between frequency distributions and distributions of age-specific rates.

Rates measure the relative frequency of occurrence of certain events and phenomena such as mortality, fertility, marriage, and crime. They are

proportions derived from frequencies as they relate to incidence or risk of occurrence of particular events. In deriving mortality rates, for example, the number of deaths during a given period is related to the population exposed to the risk of death. In computing an age–sex-specific rate, say, for suicide, the following formula would be used:

$$\left(\begin{array}{l}\text{Suicide rate for males,}\\\text{aged 35–39, United States: 1980}\end{array}\right)$$

$$= \frac{\left(\begin{array}{l}\text{Number of suicides, males}\\\text{aged 35–39, United States: 1980}\end{array}\right)}{\left(\begin{array}{l}\text{Midyear population, males}\\\text{aged 35–39, United States: 1980}\end{array}\right)} \times \frac{100,000}{1}$$

Figure 6–20 presents a series of age-specific rates for male and female "adult" arrestees—those 18 years of age and over—for a 3-year period 1968–1970 in the city of Seattle. The total number of "adult" arrestees during this 3-year period was 28,299. In instances where a person had been arrested more than once during 1968–1970, the basis of classification is the most serious offense charged. The relationship between age and sex in the commission of certain types of crimes is clearly re-

---

[12] See Walter E. Weld, *How to Chart Facts from Figures with Graphs,* Norwood, Mass.: Codex Book Co., 1947, pp. 88–92; Edwin Kurtz, "Replacement Insurance," *Administration,* **2** (November 1921), 41–69.

[13] A special grid known as "binomial paper" has become increasingly popular with theoretical statisticians. It has the property of making estimation of many of the answers required in binomial problems a matter of direct inspection of the graph on binomial paper.

[14] In developing the scale independently, it will be recalled that the range of normal probability is unlimited and the probability scale, expressed in percentage of a total, can never read zero or 100. However, all but 0.006% of the normal probability range is found between plus and minus four standard deviations from the mean, or within a range of eight standard units. The method of computing the probability scale, then, consists of locating the position of the cumulated normal percentage frequency in relation to a corresponding standard deviation unit. Tables of areas of the normal curve and other data are required to derive the values of a probability scale. A detailed step-by-step discussion of the construction of probability paper is perhaps too advanced for a text of this kind. Table III in George C. Whipple, "The Element of Chance in Sanitation," *Journal of the Franklin Institute,* **182** (July 1916), 37–59, would be found very useful if one were interested in constructing probability paper. It will be observed that Whipple uses "probable error" rather than "standard error." At the present time, the "standard error" concept has almost entirely supplanted "probable error."

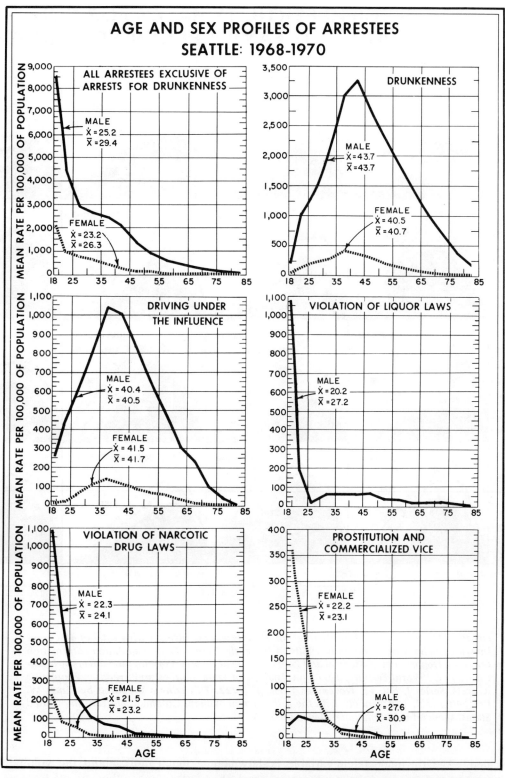

Figure 6–20. Graphic portrayal of several series of rates on arithmetic grids. Data represent 3–year means. (From Calvin F. Schmid and Stanton E. Schmid, Crime in the State of Washington, *Olympia: Law and Justice Planning Office, Planning and Community Affairs Agency, 1972, p. 205.)*

AGE-SPECIFIC FERTILITY RATES FOR COUNTRIES WITH VIGOROUS FAMILY PLANNING PROGRAMS

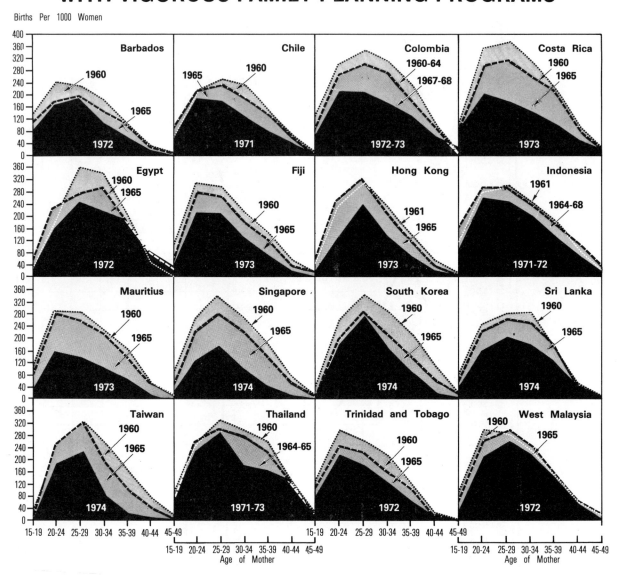

Figure 6–21. Age–specific fertility rates for 16 different countries, with a total of 48 curves showing declines from the early 1960s to the early 1970s. (From Population Information Program, Department of Medical and Public Affairs of George Washington University Medical Center, "World Fertility, 1976: An Analysis of Data Sources and Trends," Population Reports, Series J, No. 12, November 1976, p. J–222. This edition prepared by James W. Brackett and R. T. Ravenholt, with the assistance of William Goldman, all from the United States Agency for International Development.)

vealed. Age, the independent variable, is shown on the horizontal axis, and the incidence of arrest, the dependent variable, is plotted on the vertical axis. The rates for each sex are differentiated by two distinct curve patterns. Age-specific rates show much more about the volume of these particular phenomena than simple frequencies, since in series of this kind the frequencies are directly related to the number of people in each age group. The differentials in the age and sex behavior patterns for

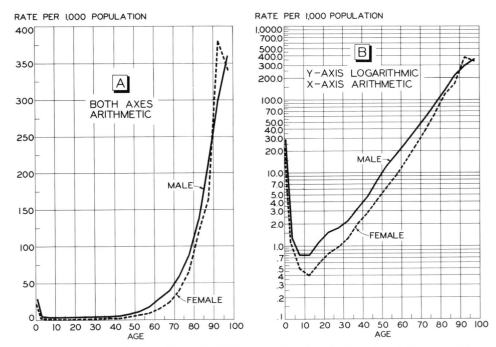

Figure 6–22. Same series of mortality rates plotted on arithmetic and on semilogarithmic grids.

the various crime categories are clearly portrayed by the curves in Figure 6–20. In addition, the median ($\dot{X}$) and the mean ($\overline{X}$) ages of arrestees for each crime category are shown on the chart.

Changes in age-specific fertility rates from the early 1960s to the early 1970s for 16 different countries are effectively portrayed by Figure 6–21. It will be observed that there are three sets of curves in each of the 16 panels. Distinctive curve patterns and shading have been combined to reveal the differential changes that have occurred. The resultant silhouetted effect provides special emphasis to the changing fertility profiles for these 16 countries. The family-planning programs in these countries are classified as "vigorous." The term "vigorous" reflects a qualitative judgment, based on the fact that family-planning services and supplies are con-

veniently available to a substantial portion of the population.

Generally, age-specific rates are plotted on arithmetic grids. Sometimes, however, the semilogarithmic grid will be found particularly appropriate. When rates vary widely in value the curves on a semilogarithmic grid are more readily interpretable by portraying differences more clearly and precisely. Figure 6–22 shows a comparison of two sets of age–sex-specific mortality rates from all causes plotted on both arithmetic and semilogarithmic grids. In the left panel both scales are arithmetic, whereas in the right panel the horizontal scale is arithmetic and the vertical scale is logarithmic. With respect to readability and significance, the semilogarithmic chart seems to be superior to that of the arithmetic chart.

CHAPTER SEVEN

MISCELLANEOUS GRAPHIC FORMS

THIS CHAPTER IS DEVOTED TO A DIS-cussion of certain miscellaneous graphic forms that, generally speaking, cannot be subsumed under the basic types included in the foregoing chapters. Furthermore, some of the charts in this chapter may be considered more specialized and perhaps not as widely used as many other graphic forms. It will be observed that among these miscellaneous forms, certain of them, such as the pie chart and the correlation charts, are more flexible and adaptable than the trilinear or the ranking charts, which have more limited application. Nevertheless, all charts presented in this chapter have distinctive advantages for certain types of problems. It is, therefore, essential for specialists in the field to be thoroughly familiar with as many graphic forms as possible, so that when the occasion arises the most appropriate design can be selected.

PIE CHART

Although the pie or sector chart ranks very high in popular appeal, it is not held in the highest esteem by many specialists in graphic presentation. Since the pie chart possesses more weaknesses perhaps than most graphic forms, it is especially important to observe proper discretion in its construction and application. The pie chart is used to portray component relations. The various sectors of a circle represent component parts of an aggregate or total.

Figure 7–1 shows three commonly used graphic forms for depicting component relations: (1) the pie chart, (2) the 100% bar graph, and (3) the simple bar chart.[1] These illustrations are all based on the same data, namely, the class status of students enrolled at the University of Washington in 1975. It will be observed that each of the three forms pos-sesses certain advantageous features. It is extremely difficult to state in an absolute sense which of the three forms is the "best" since the audience for whom a chart is designed and the purpose at hand are relative factors to be taken into consideration. Moreover, there are no detailed, accurate, systematic, and valid tests for evaluating the effectiveness of various types of graphs and charts. Such comparative evaluations of graphic forms that do exist are largely impressionistic and a priori. It must not be overlooked, of course, that a number of attempts have been made to determine objectively the relative merits and applicability of the pie, bar, and other simple graphic forms. The results of these investigations are suggestive but not conclusive.[2]

As a general rule, it is recommended that the bar chart be used for simple comparison, particularly if there are more than four to five categories. In constructing a pie chart the first step is to prepare the data so that the various component values can be transposed into corresponding degrees on the circle. Suppose there are four components in a series representing the following values: (1) 60%, (2) 20%, (3) 15%, and (4) 5%. Since 1% is equal to 3.6 degrees $(360/100 = 3.6)$, then the corresponding values of the four components in the illustration are $(60) (3.6) = 216°$; $(20) (3.6) = 72°$; $(15) (3.6) = 54°$; and $(5) (3.6) = 18°$. The second step is to plot a circle of appropriate size with a bow pencil or compass. Third, points on the circle representing the size of each sector are measured with a protractor. Protractors calibrated in percentages rather than degrees are, of course, much more efficient for chart work. With a percentage protractor it is possible to plot percentage values directly, thus obviating the intermediate step of transposing percentages to degrees. Printed chart sheets with circles divided into one hundred parts (percentages) are available commercially.

In laying out the sectors for a pie chart it is good practice to follow some logically arranged pattern or sequence. For example, it is a common procedure to arrange the sectors according to size, with the largest at the top and the others in sequence running clockwise. An essential feature of the pie chart is the careful identification of each sector with some kind of explanatory or descriptive label. If there is sufficient room, the labels can be placed inside the sectors; otherwise, the labels should be placed in contiguous positions outside the circle, usually with an arrow pointing to the appropriate sector. Sometimes the several sectors of a pie chart are identified by means of a key or legend directly below or on the side of the pie. But this method is more cumbersome than the other two described. Also, it is customary to indicate the percentages or other values represented by each sector directly below the identifying label. To clearly differentiate the sectors, it is recommended practice to hatch them according to a density sequence from dark to light or vice versa. For display charts color is appropriate. The pie chart may be made more

attractive by superimposing pictorial symbols or by laying out the chart in three-dimensional form. These techniques are discussed in Chapters 9 and 10.

Perhaps by pointing out certain weaknesses and dangers inherent in the basic design and application of the pie chart, more obvious mistakes can be avoided. First, it is generally inadvisable to attempt to portray a series of more than four or five categories by means of pie charts. If, for example, there are six, eight, or more categories, it may be very confusing to differentiate the relative values portrayed, especially if several small sectors are of approximately the same size. Second, the pie chart may lose its effectiveness if an attempt is made to compare the component values of several circles, as might be found in a temporal or geographical series. In such case the 100% bar or column chart is more appropriate. Third, although the proportionate values portrayed in a pie chart are measured as distances along arcs about the circle, there is actually a

---

¹ In Figure 7–1 the 100% bar chart is arranged horizontally, but it could have been placed just as well in a vertical position. Accordingly, when a chart of this kind is arranged vertically, it is referred to as a ''100% column chart.''

² See, for example, the citations in an annotated bibliography on graphic presentation: Barry M. Feinberg and Carolyn A. Franklin, eds., *Social Graphics Bibliography*, Washington: Bureau of Social Science Research, 1975, especially pp. 63–77.

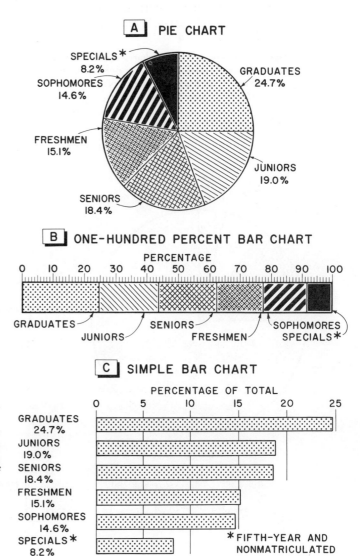

Figure 7–1. Comparison of different graphic forms for portraying components of a 100% total. A. Pie chart. B. 100% bar chart. C. Simple bar chart. Data show class status of student body at the University of Washington, 1975. (Chart drawn from original data.)

tendency to estimate values in terms of areas of sectors or by the size of subtended angles at the center of the circle.

Figures 7–2, 7–3, and 7–4 are three examples of pie charts, each with certain distinctive features, Figure 7–2 portrays four categories of aliens naturalized between 1960 and 1973. The pie on the left is based on an annual average for the 13-year period 1960–1972, and the one on the right is for the year 1973. The sectors are differentiated by shading patterns, indicated by a legend or key. The respective percentages are lettered directly on the chart. The average annual number of persons for the 1960–1972 period and for 1973 are also shown on the chart.

Figure 7–3 portrays expenditures of county governments totaling 24.4 billion dollars for 1971–1972 classified according to five categories. The "all other" category, comprising 5.4 billion dollars, is shown in detail by a special insert in the form of a simple bar chart. Also, three of the sectors—equipment, land and construction—are grouped together as "capital outlay," representing 3.3 billion

dollars. Unlike most pie charts, all of the figures are shown in absolute numbers, not percentages.

Figure 7–4 portrays comparisons of three different age groups—under 19, 19–64, and 65 and over—with respect to the source and amount of expenditures for personal health care. It is clear that age has a direct bearing on the size and nature of the nation's health-care bill. Americans spent an estimated 103.2 billion dollars for personal health care in the fiscal year 1975. Persons aged 65 and over, although one-fifth as numerous as those aged 19–64, had a health bill more than half as large. Persons under age 19—who comprise about a third of the total population—accounted for less than half of the 1975 health bill of those 65 years and over. For those under 65 years of age—largely the working population and their families—private funds in the form of health insurance and consumer out-of-pocket payments were the major source of financing for health care. For those under 19 years of age, 76% of the expenditures were private and 24% public, and for those 19–64 years of age 70% were classified as private and 30% as public. On the other

Figure 7–2. Pie or sector charts used in comparing data for two different periods. Chart portrays aliens who were naturalized in accordance with certain types of legal provisions. (From United States Bureau of the Census, Statistical Abstract of the United States: 1974, *Washington: Government Printing Office, 1974, p. 94.)*

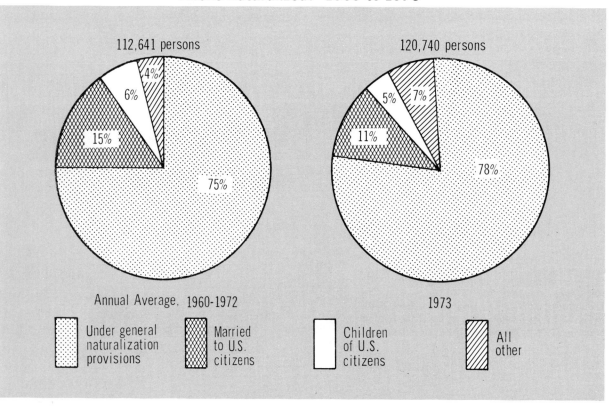

Aliens Naturalized: 1960 to 1973

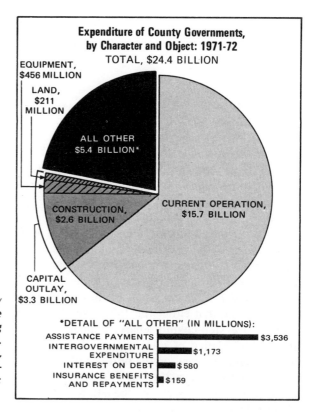

Figure 7–3. A pie chart with an explanatory bar chart insert. It will be observed that the bar chart depicts comparative data pertaining to the components of the "all other" category. (From United States Bureau of the Census, Graphic Summary of the 1972 Census of Governments, Topical Studies No. 5, Washington: Government Printing Office, 1974, p. 23.)

PERCENTAGE DISTRIBUTION OF EXPENDITURES FOR PERSONAL

HEALTH CARE, BY SOURCE OF FUNDS AND AGE GROUP,

FISCAL YEAR 1975

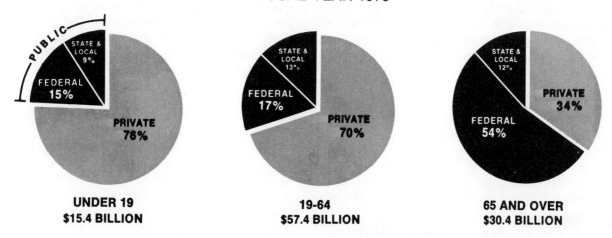

Figure 7–4. A series of pie charts used as a basis for comparing three age-groups. [From Marjorie Smith Mueller and Robert M. Gibson, "Age Differences in Health Care Spending, Fiscal Year 1975," Social Security Bulletin, 39, (6), June 1976, pp. 18–31.]

hand, for those 65 and over the public share of health-care expenditures totaled 66% and private, only 34%.

THE 100%–STEP-BAR CHART AND 100%–STEP-COLUMN CHART

Another technique for portraying components or divisions of an aggregate or total is the 100%–step-bar chart and the 100%–step-column chart. Although these charts may not possess the popular appeal of the pie chart, they are virtually free of the distortions and optical illusions of the pie chart. The basis of comparison is one-dimensional, and a linear scale is an integral part of the design. Figures 7–5 and 7–6 are examples of these charts. It cannot be said that either the 100%–step-bar chart or the 100%–step-column chart is superior to the other. The choice of one or the other of these charts should be based on the purpose of the chart, the audience to whom the chart is addressed, the other charts in the report, and the nature of the data being portrayed. Sometimes, perhaps both charts may be equally appropriate, and the choice becomes one of personal predilection. In charts of this kind, the data presented may be expressed either as absolute values or as percentages. Absolute numbers are used more frequently than percentages. Such is the case in both Figures 7–5 and 7–6.

Figure 7–5 represents the characteristic design of the 100%–step-bar chart in which the components are portrayed in actual numbers. The total or aggregate, normally consisting of from three to six components, is shown by a single bar at the top of the chart with a scale line placed slightly above or coincidental with the top of the bar. Sometimes a scale line is also placed at the bottom of the chart. The various components of the series are represented by separate segments of the total bar that are appropriately labeled. It will be seen from Figure 7–5 that the top segment portrays 8717 graduate students, the second segment 6701 juniors, followed by seniors (6474), freshmen (5341), sophomores (5138), and specials (2906).

Figure 7–6 is an example of a component-column chart, expressed in absolute figures. The basic features consist of: (1) a column representing a total and (2) separate sections of the column arranged in steps representing its component parts. The chart indicates the ownership of a total of 544.1 billion dollars of federal securities as of June 30, 1975. It will be observed that 147.2 billion dollars are in government accounts, 85 billion dollars are owned by the Federal Reserve System, 71.1 billion dollars are owned by commercial banks, 88 by individuals, 26.1 by savings institutions, 13.6 by corporations, and 113.1 by all others.

TRILINEAR CHART

The trilinear chart is used to portray simultaneously three variables expressed in the form of elements or components of a total. It is characteristically a 100% chart, since the sum of the three values indicated is equal to 100%.

The trilinear chart is drawn in the form of an equilateral triangle, each side of which is calibrated in equal percentage divisions ranging from zero to 100. The rulings are projected across the chart parallel to the sides in the manner of coordinates. For example, the lines indicating the scale divisions for the horizontal axis are drawn parallel to it and, similarly, the scale lines for the two other axes are parallel to their respective sides.

CLASS STATUS OF STUDENTS
UNIVERSITY OF WASHINGTON: 1975

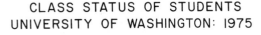

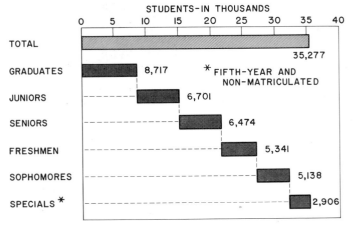

Figure 7–5. A 100% step–bar chart. (Drawn from original data.)

OWNERSHIP OF FEDERAL SECURITIES, JUNE 30, 1975

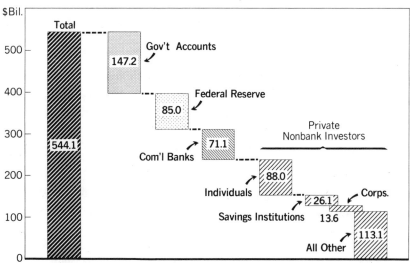

Figure 7–6. Component–column chart in step form. (From Annual Report of Secretary of the Treasury, 1975, p. 15.)

The trilinear chart is based on the geometric principle that in an equilateral triangle the sum of the three perpendiculars drawn from any point within the triangle to the sides is a constant and is equal to the altitude of the triangle. Therefore, as in the trilinear chart, the altitude represents 100%, and, accordingly, the perpendiculars from a given point within the triangle will represent the percentages of the three variables composing the whole.

The essential characteristics of a trilinear chart are portrayed in Figure 7–7. The scale lines and scale figures for each of the three axes are clearly indicated. For example, the baseline for component A is shown on the left, with the various scale lines drawn parallel to it. The baseline and other scale lines for component B are drawn correspondingly on the right side. The horizontal axis and the scale lines drawn parallel to it are referents for component C. The point X indicates a value for each variable: for component A, 20%; for component B, 30%; and for component C, 50%.

Trilinear charts are useful in portraying such data as the following: (1) properties of chemical compounds—mixtures and alloys composed of three elements or characteristics; (2) caloric values for different kinds of foods in terms of fats, proteins, and carbohydrates; and (3) operating, production, or other costs expressed by a threefold breakdown.

Although trilinear charts do not have a time scale, it is possible to plot the values of three or four series for different time periods on the same

Figure 7–7. Trilinear chart.

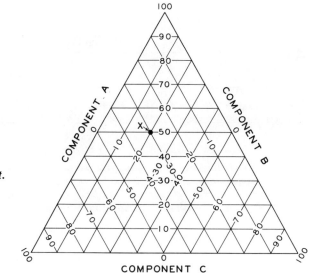

triangle, if the points are properly labeled. To avoid confusion, it is important not to plot too many values on the same chart.

Figure 7–8 is a discriminating application of the trilinear chart to a research project in the social sciences.[3] In fact, it is one of seven trilinear charts appearing in a study of adolescent subculture based on a survey of students in 10 different high schools. Figure 7–8 locates attitudinal values pertaining to interpersonal relations of both boys and girls with respect to three dimensions. The data portrayed in Figure 7–8 were derived from the following questions:

Suppose you had a chance to go out with either a cheerleader, a girl who is the best student in class, or the best looking girl in class. Which one would you rather go out with?

Cheerleader   Best student   Best looking

Suppose you had a chance to go out with either a star athlete, a boy who is the best student in class, or the best looking boy in class. Which one would you rather go out with?

Star athlete   Best student   Best looking

The chart shows very clearly that the brilliant girl student fares poorly as a date for boys. Less striking, but still evident, is the poor showing of the image of "brilliant boy student" as a date for girls. The best looking boy or girl ranks far above the "best student." Also, the boy athlete and the girl cheerleader are preferred as a dating partner to the "best student."

_____

[3] James S. Coleman, *Social Climates in High Schools,* Washington, D. C.: Government Printing Office, 1961, p. 14.

BOYS' AND GIRLS' CHOICE FOR A DATE: RELATIVE IMPORTANCE OF SCHOLARSHIP (BEST STUDENT), APPEARANCE (BEST LOOKING), AND ATHLETICS (STAR ATHLETE) OR ACTIVITIES (CHEERLEADER)

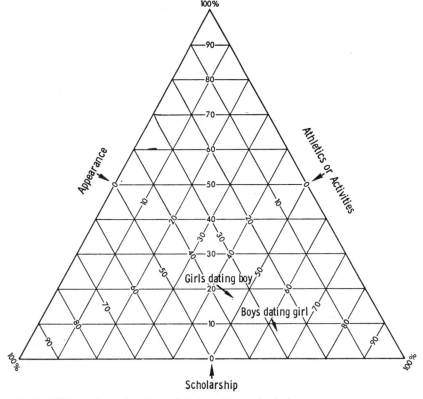

Figure 7–8. Trilinear chart showing relative rankings of scholarship, appearance, and athletics or activities among adolescent boys and girls. (From James S. Coleman, Social Climates in High Schools, *Washington: Government Printing Office, 1961, p. 14.)*

SCATTER DIAGRAM AND OTHER CORRELATION CHARTS

The scatter diagram (scattergram) and other types of correlation charts portray in graphic form the degree and type of relationship or covariation between two series of data. In statistical terminology the relationship between two or more variables is described as "correlation." The relationship or correlation between two variables may be either positive or negative. When one variable increases (or decreases) and the other changes by constant or nearly constant amounts in the same direction, the relation of the two series is positive or direct, but if the changes in the two variables are in opposite directions, the correlation between the two series is negative or inverse. For example, the height and weight of human beings are positively correlated, since taller people on the average weigh more than shorter people.

Figure 7–9 shows the correlation between land values and pedestrian traffic and vehicular traffic in the central business district of a large city to be positive. This fact is indicated by the patterning of the dots (more noticeable in the scatter diagram on the left), which is generally from the lower left corner to the upper right corner. On the other hand, if the dots tended to scatter diagonally in the opposite direction, the correlation would be negative. When there is a relatively low degree of correlation, the dots are widely scattered over the entire chart, with little or no tendency to align themselves diagonally either from left to right or from right to left. The precise degrees of relationship between land value and pedestrian traffic and land values and vehicular traffic are indicated by coefficients of correlation: $r = +0.840$ between land values and pedestrian traffic and $r = +0.469$ between land values and vehicular traffic. The product-moment or Pearsonian coefficient of correlation (r) is a pure number and ranges in value from positive one ($+1$) down through zero (0) to negative one (-1).

In constructing a scatter diagram the first step is to select suitable class intervals for the respective variables, so that each variable will have approximately 8 to 15 divisions. This procedure is similar to that for making a frequency distribution. Actually, the scatter diagram is a two-way or bivariate frequency distribution. Second, the axes representing the variables are laid out at right angles to

each other. Generally, it is immaterial which variable is considered independent (horizontal or X-axis) and which is dependent (vertical or Y-axis). Also, in choosing the size and number of class intervals for each variable, it is important that the space required be approximately the same for both series. A scatter diagram in the form of a square is much more satisfactory than one in the form of a rectangle with markedly unequal sides. Third, the spacing of the divisions on each axis for the class intervals should be large enough to accommodate the necessary lettering and tally marks or dots. Vertical and horizontal lines are drawn through the class-interval division points, thus forming a grid. Fourth, the class intervals for the X variable should read from left to right and, unlike the conventional frequency distribution, the intervals of the Y variable should read from bottom to top. Fifth, each entry that is recorded by a dot or tally mark in the proper cell should always represent two numerical values, one measured on the X-axis and the other on the Y-axis.

Figure 7–10 includes 15 scatter diagrams showing the relationship between various population and housing indices according to census tracts for 12 large American cities. It will be observed that some of the scatter diagrams indicate positive correlations and others show negative correlations. The coefficients of correlation and the regression lines measure the type and amount of correlation in each scatter diagram. A few of the scatter diagrams manifest curvilinear rather than rectilinear correlation. The constancy of the ratio of change of the two variables determines whether the correlation is rectilinear or curvilinear. If the amount of change in the two variables bears a constant ratio, the correlation is rectilinear; if it does not, the relationship is curvilinear.

Sometimes a scattergram plotted on a double logarithmic grid can be much more effective than one plotted on natural scales. The purpose of Figure 7–11 is to portray graphically the relationship between a series of population estimates for 238 incorporated towns and cities in the state of Washington for April 1, 1948 with figures derived in the subsequent decennial census taken as of April 1, 1950. If natural scales had been used in Figure 7–11, it would have been virtually impossible to include without extreme distortion the wide range of values from less than 50 people for Hatton to 467,000 for Seattle. All but a few of the dots representing the larger cities would have been concentrated in an

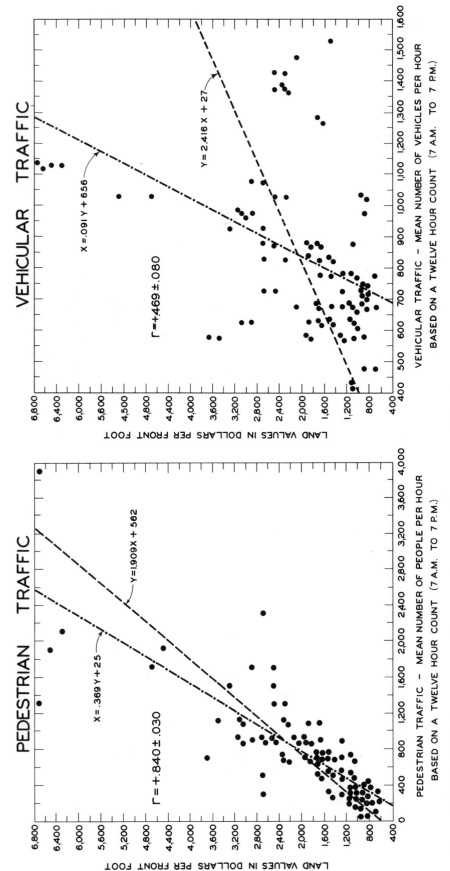

Figure 7–9. Correlation charts or scatter diagrams. These scatter diagrams were designed to show the relationship between land values and pedestrian and vehicular traffic in the central business district of Minneapolis. (From Calvin F. Schmid, "Land Values as an Ecological Index," Research Studies of the State College of Washington, IX, March, 1941, pp. 16–36.)

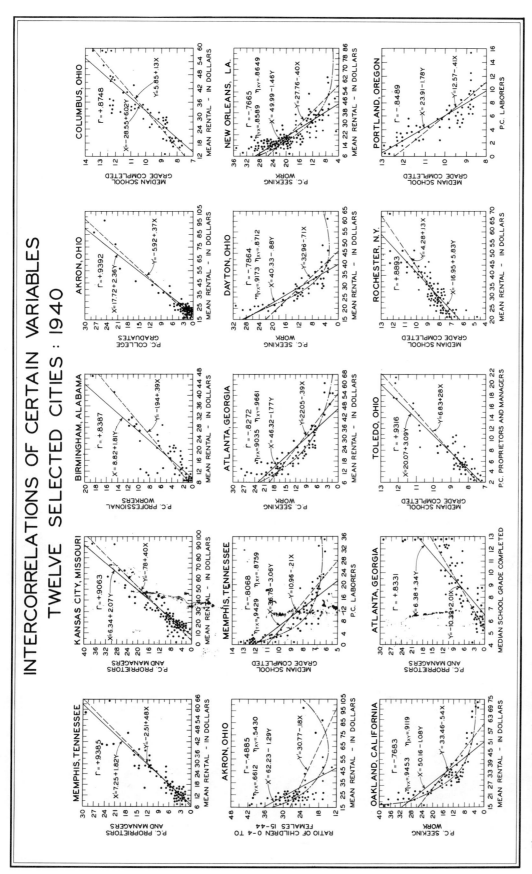

Figure 7–10. Another illustration of correlation charts. Note especially curvilinear relationship of several pairs of variables. [From Calvin F. Schmid, "Generalizations Concerning the Ecology of the American City," American Sociological Review, XV, (2), April 1950, pp. 264–81.]

indistinguishable, unintelligible mass in the lower left-hand part of the grid.

Figure 7–12 is another illustration of the log–log scatter diagram. As indicated previously, it would be impossible to portray meaningfully data manifesting relatively extreme variation in a scatter diagram with natural scales. For example, in Figure 7–12 the plotted values range from slightly more than 100 to well over 550,000 (population size of cities and towns) on the vertical scale, and from 1 to 263 on the horizontal scale (rank in population size). This chart is part of an analysis of the rank-size hypothesis for municipalities in the state of Washington. The rank-size principle was discovered in 1913 by Felix Auerbach, who discussed its application to German cities. Since that time, investigators have reported that it offers a simple descrip-

tion of city size distributions in various parts of the world.[4]

[4] The essential meaning of the rank-size principle may be explained by the following illustration. In the United States as a whole it has been observed that the second most populous city (rank 2) has a population approximately one-half of the largest; the third largest (rank 3), a population one-third of the largest; the fourth largest (rank 4), a population one-fourth of the largest; and so on down to the smallest, which in a list of N cities would have rank N and a population $1/N$th that of the largest. This phenomenon has been termed the *rank-size rule*, since it may be expressed in the terms "rank times size equals a constant." See Calvin F. Schmid and Stanton E. Schmid, *Growth of Cities and Towns, State of Washington*, Olympia: Washington State Planning and Community Affairs Agency, 1969, pp. 126–132; Felix Auerbach, "Das Gesetz der Bevölkerungskonzentration," *Petermanns Mitteilungen*, **59** (1913), 74–76.

Figure 7–11. A scatter diagram on double logarithmic ruling. Note the wide range of values shown on both the vertical and horizontal axes. (From unpublished study by Calvin F. Schmid.)

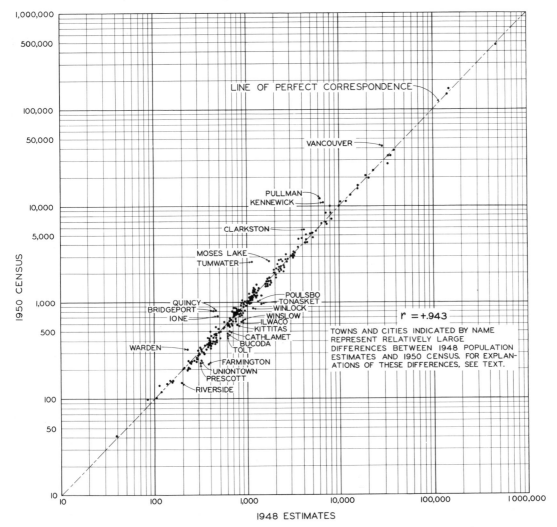

COMPARISON OF 1948 POPULATION ESTIMATES
WITH 1950 POPULATION CENSUS

$r = +.943$

TOWNS AND CITIES INDICATED BY NAME REPRESENT RELATIVELY LARGE DIFFERENCES BETWEEN 1948 POPULATION ESTIMATES AND 1950 CENSUS. FOR EXPLANATIONS OF THESE DIFFERENCES, SEE TEXT.

Correlation Surface

Although the scatter diagram is valuable for graphic and analytical purposes, it is not adequate to portray the three-dimensional qualities of a correlation surface. In scatter diagrams there are two dimensions of space scaled in accordance with a vertical and a horizontal axis that determine the location of each pair of variables as measured by their respective magnitudes. A correlation surface adds another dimension that provides greater meaning and insight to problems of correlation. Figures 7–13, 7–14, and 7–15 depict three basic steps in the development of a three-dimensional correlation surface. Figure 7–13 is the typical scatter diagram with its class intervals for the two variables, cell frequencies, total frequencies, and regression lines. The data indicate the relationship between scores on tests for general verbal ability and ability to comprehend scientific material for a sample of 231 freshmen in the College of Engineering at the University of Washington. The second step is exhibited by Figure 7–14. It will be observed that a series of rectangular prisms have been erected commensurate with the frequency in each cell. In a real sense these prisms are solid histograms analo-

Figure 7–12. Another application of a log–log scatter diagram. (From Calvin F. Schmid and Stanton E. Schmid, Growth of Cities and Towns, State of Washington, *Olympia: Washington State Planning and Community Affairs Agency, 1969, p. 127.)*

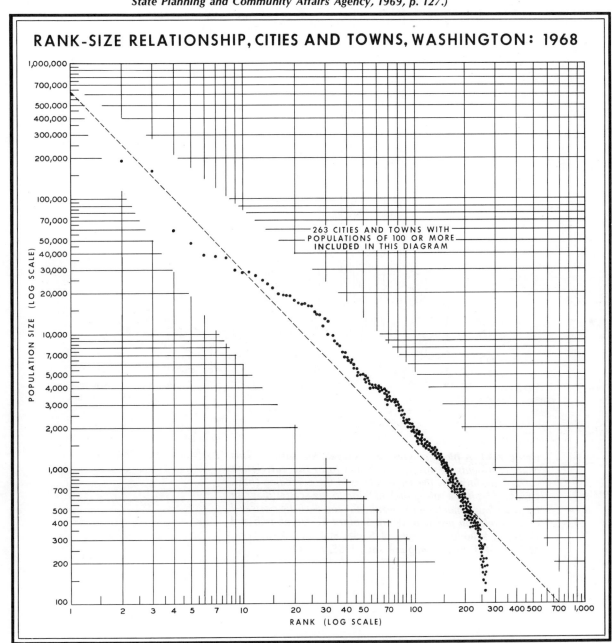

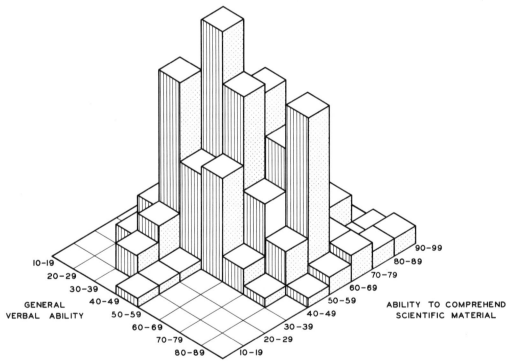

TEST I: GENERAL VERBAL ABILITY

TEST II: ABILITY TO COMPREHEND SCIENTIFIC MATERIAL

X\Y	10–19	20–29	30–39	40–49	50–59	60–69	70–79	80–89	f_Y
90–99									3
80–89									8
70–79									21
60–69									62
50–59									73
40–49									51
30–39									8
20–29									4
10–19									1
f_x	1	9	40	43	55	43	30	10	231

MEANS OF COLUMNS

MEANS OF ROWS

$Y' = .4956X + 30.41$

$X' = .7061Y + 13.37$

Figure 7–13. A scatter diagram showing the relationship between general verbal ability and the ability to comprehend scientific material for a sample of 231 freshmen in the College of Engineering, University of Washington. (From Sanford M. Dornbusch and Calvin F. Schmid, A Primer of Social Statistics, *New York: McGraw–Hill Book Company, Inc., 1955, p. 192.*

GENERAL VERBAL ABILITY: 10–19, 20–29, 30–39, 40–49, 50–59, 60–69, 70–79, 80–89

ABILITY TO COMPREHEND SCIENTIFIC MATERIAL: 90–99, 80–89, 70–79, 60–69, 50–59, 40–49, 30–39, 20–29, 10–19

Figure 7–14. A block diagram of a correlation surface. This chart represents in three–dimensional form the correlation surface produced by the same data as in the preceding chart. Graphically, it is a substantial addition to the scatter diagram by providing a much more meaningful and realistic portrayal of a correlation problem. (From Sanford M. Dornbusch and Calvin F. Schmid, A Primer of Social Statistics, *New York: McGraw–Hill Book Company, Inc., 1955, p. 193.*

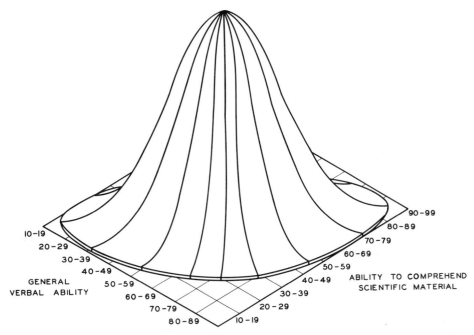

Figure 7–15. A smoothed correlation surface constructed from the preceding chart. (From Sanford M. Dornbusch and Calvin F. Schmid, A Primer of Social Statistics, *New York: McGraw–Hill Book Company, Inc., 1955, p. 193.*

gous to histograms in a univariate distribution. Also, like histograms in a univariate distribution, these solid histograms can be smoothed. It will be recalled from Chapter 6 that frequency curves portraying continuous variables based on samples are sometimes smoothed. Accordingly, as the third step, Figure 7–14 has been smoothed and the results portrayed in Figure 7–15.

GROWTH CURVES

Figure 7–16 also shows the relationship between two variables—age and weight of girls. However, the purpose and implications of this chart are very different from those of the simple correlation chart. Figure 7–16 portrays the growth in weight of girls aged 2–18 years indicated by seven smoothed centile curves. This chart is one of 14 growth charts for children prepared under the auspices of the National Center for Health Statistics. Figure 7–16, along with the other 13 charts, can show immedi-

[5] Peter V. V. Hamill, "NCHS Growth Charts, 1976," *Monthly Vital Statistics Report,* HEW National Center for Health Statistics, **25** (3) (Supplement) (June 22, 1976), 1–22.

ately how the growth of any child ranks in comparison with the rest of the U.S. population of like age and sex. Charts of this kind have very significant clinical application. The seven centile curves in Figure 7–16 are based on centile points of observed data grouped by age (5th, 10th, 25th, 50th, 75th, 90th, and 95th centiles) that were smoothed by a special technique in which computers were utilized. The basic scaling of the chart is metric, but for additional convenience, designations in pounds are also provided subordinately.[5]

THREE-VARIABLE CHARTS

Figure 7–17 is an example of a chart designed to portray three variables. It shows the percentage of eligible voters who registered to vote in relation to: (1) age and (2) education. There are three axes: (1) the vertical axis measures the percentage of voter registrants; (2) the horizontal axis represents age as designated by six class intervals; and (3) the longitudinal axis, shown on the left and right sides of the chart, indicates educational status as defined by five school-attendance categories. A glance at Figure 7–17 clearly reveals a close positive correspondence between voting registration and age and edu-

GIRLS WEIGHT BY AGE PERCENTILES: AGES 2 TO 18 YEARS

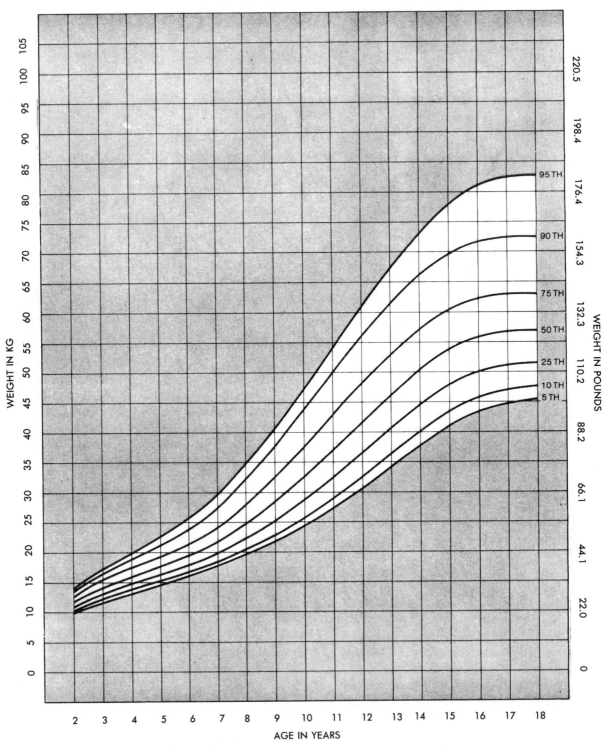

Figure 7–16. Growth curves, girls' weight by age centiles: Ages 2 to 18 Years. {From Peter
V. V. Hamill, et al., "NCHS Growth Charts, 1976," Monthly Vital Statistics Report, HEW National Center for Health Statistics, 25, [3 (Supplement)], June 22, 1976, p. 14.}

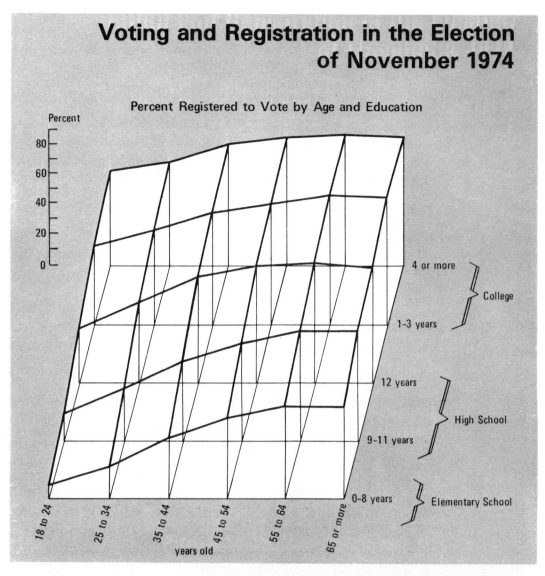

Voting and Registration in the Election of November 1974

Percent Registered to Vote by Age and Education

Figure 7–17. A three–axes chart showing percentage of eligible voters registered to vote in relation to age and education. (From United States Bureau of the Census, Voting and Registration in the Election of November 1974, Current Population Reports, *Series P-20, No. 293, 1976, cover page.)*

cation. The proportion of those who registered to vote in 1974 averaged 62.2%. However, it is obvious that there are wide differentials with respect to age and education. The proportion of those under 24 years of age who registered was a little over 40%, compared to over 75% for those 45 years of age and over. Similarly, there is a marked contrast between educational status and the proportion of voter registrants. However, when the two variables of age and education are combined with the percentage of voter registration as portrayed by Figure 7–17, the comparisons become more

significant and dramatic. For example, a combination of the younger age categories and low educational status clearly spells the lowest percentage of voter registration. On the other hand, as indicated by Figure 7–17, a combination of the older age categories and high educational status is associated with the highest percentage of voter registration.

Figure 7–18 is a more recent version of a three-dimensional chart that was first developed almost 100 years ago. In 1879, an Italian statistician, Luigi Perozzo, constructed a three-axes model, later called a "stereogram," in which Swedish census figures from 1750 to 1875 were used. The basic ideas for this model were developed earlier by Gustav Zeuner, a German statistician, who proposed the representation of population movements by a system of three coordinates, with the three axes as time, age, and number.[6] Since the time of Perozzo's stereogram other similar models and applications of three-dimensional representations of demographic movements have been developed. The three axes in Figure 7–18 are time, age, and frequency (percentage). The time axis extends from 1700 to 2100, age from birth to 100, and frequency from 0 to 4.5%. The emphasis of this chart is on changes in the age distribution of a population characterized by a transition from a "Malthusian" to a "stationary" type. It will be observed that the

pronounced changes in fertility from 1700 to 2100 are of crucial significance in this model.

FAN CHART

The purpose of the fan chart is to portray rates of change for two different periods either by percentages or index numbers. As many as 10 or 15 items may be shown on a chart of this kind, depending on the range and scatter of the values. If there are relatively large increases and decreases, the

---

[6] H. G. Funkhouser, "Historical Development of the Graphical Representation of Statistical Data," *Osiris*, **3** (1937), 351–354.

Figure 7–18. A three–dimensional chart or stereogram. A chart of this kind was first constructed in 1879 by an Italian statistician, Luigi Perozzo. [From the papers of Alfred J. Lotka, reproduced on the cover of Population Index, 42, (1), January, 1976.]

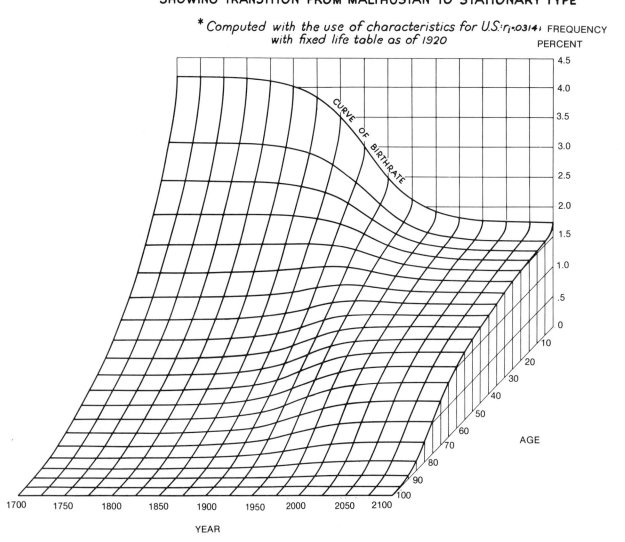

AGE DISTRIBUTION IN LOGISTIC POPULATION
SHOWING TRANSITION FROM MALTHUSIAN TO STATIONARY TYPE*

curves spread out from the base point in fanlike fashion. The base point is always zero if the figures are expressed in percentages, and usually 100 if expressed as index numbers.

Figure 7–19 shows the essential features of the fan chart. It will be observed that changes in per capita social-welfare expenditures under public programs from 1965 to 1974 are expressed in percentages. All the values are plotted from the 1965 zero base point. The specific rates of change can be interpreted from the vertical axis. All eight curves in the chart evidence increases. The chief advantage of this chart is its simplicity. Also, herein lies its most serious limitation. To measure rates of change merely by selecting two different dates may be unrepresentative and misleading. The selection of the base period as well as the later period frequently may be very arbitrary and atypical. Moreover, no intermediate values are taken into consideration. Again, the presentation of two percentages in graphic form without knowledge of the basic data from which they were derived could also lead to erroneous interpretation.

However, in the case of Figure 7–19 the base year is well chosen and the percentages reflected by the curves are statistically reliable. To some extent, 1965 is a benchmark year because of the increased tempo of social welfare since then, and also 1965 saw the beginning of the current inflationary cycle. All the 1965 base figures from which the percentages were computed are sufficiently consis-

tent and large to provide reliable measures of change.

Although the fan chart may be found useful for portraying rates of change for certain special purposes, it lacks the basic reliability, versatility, and wide application of the semilogarithmic chart.

ORGANIZATION CHARTS AND FLOWCHARTS

Unlike the other forms of graphic presentation discussed in this book, the typical organization chart as well as a large proportion of flowcharts is not used to portray or interpret statistical data. Nevertheless, these charts possess definite utility for certain kinds of research and administrative problems. With well-designed organization and flowcharts it is possible to present a large number of facts and relationships simply, clearly, and accurately without resorting to extensive and sometimes involved verbal description. Characteristically, the organization chart is used to present structural forms and logical and functional relationships, whereas flowcharts emphasize process and movement.

An organization chart portrays essential components of an organization in relation to other components. More specifically, it shows the relation of one official or department or function to another; titles and sometimes names of officials, and names

Figure 7–19. Illustration of a fan chart. [From Alfred M. Skolnik and Sophie R. Dales, "Social Welfare Expenditures, Fiscal Year 1974," Social Security Bulletin, 38, (1), January 1975, pp. 3–19.]

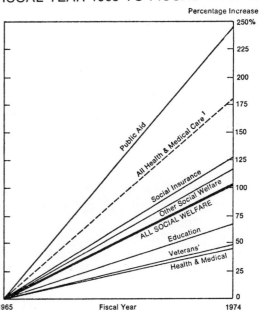

PERCENTAGE INCREASE OF CERTAIN WELFARE EXPENDITURES FROM FISCAL YEAR 1965 TO FISCAL YEAR 1974

of departments and their functions; and sources, lines, flow, and types of authority.

There are no standardized rules or practices that can be prescribed for the design and construction of organization charts. The major prerequisite for making a chart of this kind is a thorough understanding of the organization itself. The next step is to prepare several freehand, preliminary sketches of the chart to ascertain which design is most satisfactory in terms of accuracy, clarity, and detail. The various names, titles, and descriptive labels are generally enclosed in squares, circles, or other shapes that are connected by various kinds of lines.

Flowcharts portray, for example, the various steps in a series of operations; the specific processes and sequences involved in the planning, production, and distribution of some product; or the flow of income and expenditures as indicated by specific sources of funds and the manner in which they are disbursed.[7]

Figure 7–20 can be described as a typical organization chart. It clearly shows lines of authority and special functions and responsibilities of the various divisions and components, along with their interrelationships, of the Federal Deposit Insurance Corporation (FDIC). At the head of the FDIC is a three-member board of directors consisting of a chairman, the director of FDIC, and the comptroller of the currency. The board and its three members as individuals have a number of assistants and

committees that work under their authority and direction. There are two additional levels in the organizational structure representing specialized functional divisions and components. Each of these units has a director or chief who administers the program of the division.

Figure 7–21 portrays the basic organizational structure of the Organization for Economic Cooperation and Development (OECD), the membership of which includes over 20 noncommunist countries. (Yugoslavia participates in certain aspects of OECD work.) The Council, which consists of representatives of all member countries, is responsible for all OECD decisions. The executive committee consisting of 13 members designated annually, prepares decisions and recommendations for the council as well as coordinates the work of other bodies of OECD. The various committees indicated on

---

[7] Another type of chart similar to the flowchart is the "control" chart. Control charts are typically schedule or production charts used in planning and coordinating certain administrative, procurement, production, and distribution processes. Since these charts are so very specialized, with particular emphasis on operational control and coordination, they are not discussed in this book.

In this connection, it also should be pointed out that students of "sociometry" and "group dynamics" have developed the "sociogram" and other geometric techniques to portray various forms and patterns of social relationships. In some respects these techniques are similar to organization charts and flowcharts.

Figure 7–20. A typical organization chart. (From FDIC Federal Deposit Insurance Corporation, Annual Report—1975, Washington: Federal Deposit Insurance Corporation, 1975, p. iv.)

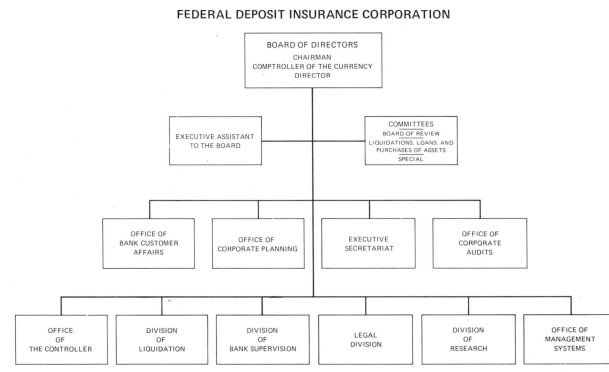

FEDERAL DEPOSIT INSURANCE CORPORATION

the chart, consisting of representatives of member countries plus those of special status countries in certain cases, prepare annual programs of work for council approval and set up working parties for the implementation of certain programs. The secretariat consists of the secretary general, two deputy secretaries, and three assistant secretaries along with a large permanent staff. The secretariat is responsible for preparing the work of the Council and executing the daily OECD work.

Figure 7–22 portrays the administrative structure of the Danish labor market in 1974. This structure reflects to a large degree an effort directed toward the alleviation of manpower problems that

Figure 7–21. Another illustration of an organization chart. This chart shows the basic organization structure of the Organization for Economic Cooperation and Development (OECD). (From a pamphlet published by OECD.)

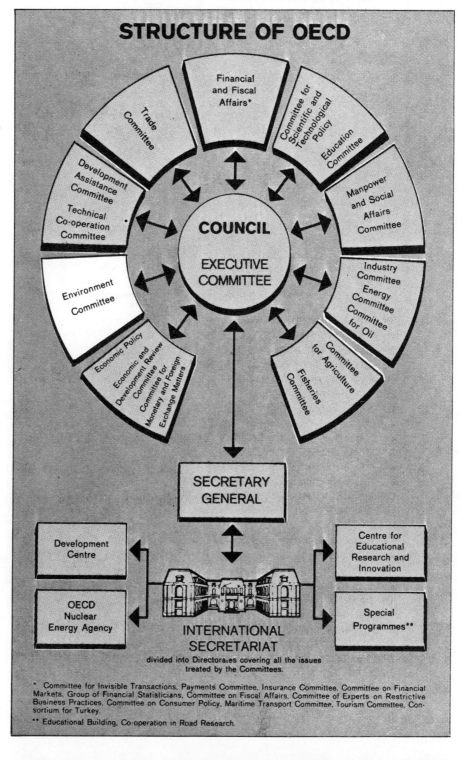

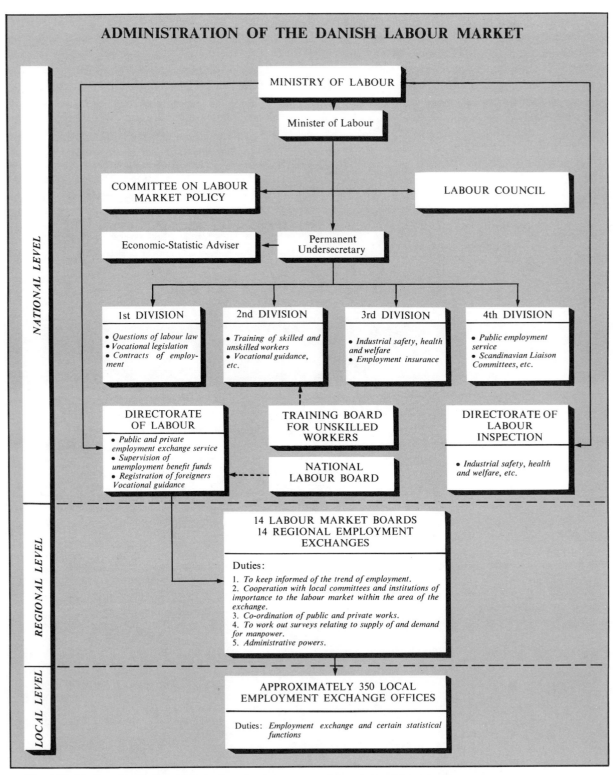

Figure 7–22. An organization chart portraying structure and functions of Danish labor market. [*From* OECD Observer, *(69), April 1974, pp. 5–7.*]

PAA Results for Burglary Offenses in Urban Areas
in terms of percent incarcerated at Superior Court levels

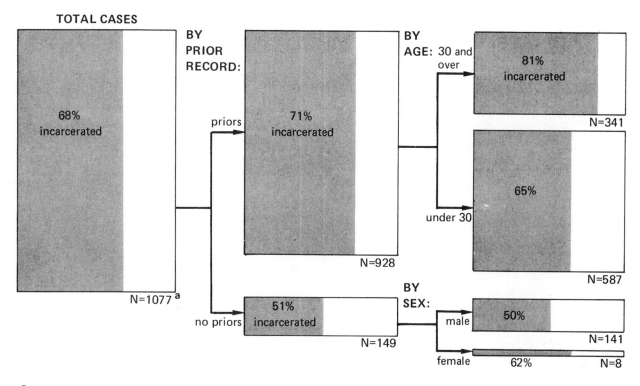

TOTAL CASES

68% incarcerated

N=1077 ᵃ

BY PRIOR RECORD:

priors

71% incarcerated

N=928

no priors

51% incarcerated

N=149

BY AGE: 30 and over

81% incarcerated

N=341

under 30

65%

N=587

BY SEX:

male

50%

N=141

female

62%   N=8

ᵃCases reported in subcells may not add up to the total number of cases due to missing values.

Figure 7–23. Flow chart portraying judicial processing of burglary offenders in urban areas. (From Carl E. Pope, The Judicial Processing of Assault and Burglary Offenders in Selected California Counties, *Washington: U.S. Department of Justice, Law Enforcement Assistance Administration, 1975, p. 23.)*

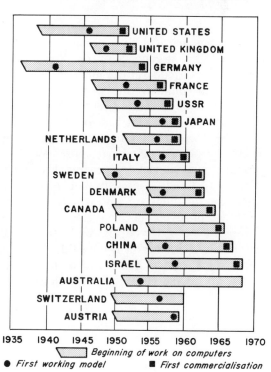

HISTORICAL LEAD-TIMES IN THE COMPUTER INDUSTRY

UNITED STATES
UNITED KINGDOM
GERMANY
FRANCE
USSR
JAPAN
NETHERLANDS
ITALY
SWEDEN
DENMARK
CANADA
POLAND
CHINA
ISRAEL
AUSTRALIA
SWITZERLAND
AUSTRIA

1935 1940 1945 1950 1955 1960 1965 1970

▱ *Beginning of work on computers*
● *First working model*   ■ *First commercialisation*

Figure 7–24. A "progress" chart depicting historical data. [From Nicolas Jequer, "Technological Gaps in the Computer Industry," OECD Observer, *(40) June 1969, pp. 31–37.]*

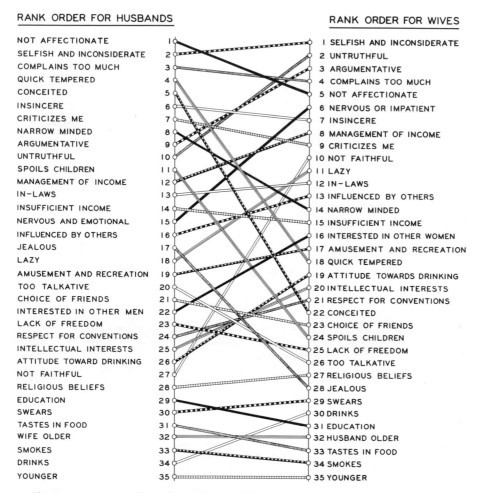

RANK ORDER FOR HUSBANDS

NOT AFFECTIONATE	1
SELFISH AND INCONSIDERATE	2
COMPLAINS TOO MUCH	3
QUICK TEMPERED	4
CONCEITED	5
INSINCERE	6
CRITICIZES ME	7
NARROW MINDED	8
ARGUMENTATIVE	9
UNTRUTHFUL	10
SPOILS CHILDREN	11
MANAGEMENT OF INCOME	12
IN-LAWS	13
INSUFFICIENT INCOME	14
NERVOUS AND EMOTIONAL	15
INFLUENCED BY OTHERS	16
JEALOUS	17
LAZY	18
AMUSEMENT AND RECREATION	19
TOO TALKATIVE	20
CHOICE OF FRIENDS	21
INTERESTED IN OTHER MEN	22
LACK OF FREEDOM	23
RESPECT FOR CONVENTIONS	24
INTELLECTUAL INTERESTS	25
ATTITUDE TOWARD DRINKING	26
NOT FAITHFUL	27
RELIGIOUS BELIEFS	28
EDUCATION	29
SWEARS	30
TASTES IN FOOD	31
WIFE OLDER	32
SMOKES	33
DRINKS	34
YOUNGER	35

RANK ORDER FOR WIVES

1	SELFISH AND INCONSIDERATE
2	UNTRUTHFUL
3	ARGUMENTATIVE
4	COMPLAINS TOO MUCH
5	NOT AFFECTIONATE
6	NERVOUS OR IMPATIENT
7	INSINCERE
8	MANAGEMENT OF INCOME
9	CRITICIZES ME
10	NOT FAITHFUL
11	LAZY
12	IN-LAWS
13	INFLUENCED BY OTHERS
14	NARROW MINDED
15	INSUFFICIENT INCOME
16	INTERESTED IN OTHER WOMEN
17	AMUSEMENT AND RECREATION
18	QUICK TEMPERED
19	ATTITUDE TOWARDS DRINKING
20	INTELLECTUAL INTERESTS
21	RESPECT FOR CONVENTIONS
22	CONCEITED
23	CHOICE OF FRIENDS
24	SPOILS CHILDREN
25	LACK OF FREEDOM
26	TOO TALKATIVE
27	RELIGIOUS BELIEFS
28	JEALOUS
29	SWEARS
30	DRINKS
31	EDUCATION
32	HUSBAND OLDER
33	TASTES IN FOOD
34	SMOKES
35	YOUNGER

Figure 7–25. A ranking chart. Shows differences between husbands and wives in ranking the seriousness of 35 grievances. From Louis M. Terman, (Psychological Factors in Marital Happiness, New York: McGraw–Hill, 1938, p. 105, Chart redrawn.)

have become particularly acute during the past two decades as a consequence of transition from a predominantly agricultural economy to one in which industry, the building trades, and service occupations play a major role. Unlike Belgium, France, and Germany, Denmark has specifically eschewed the large-scale importation of foreign workers, mainly because of its social consequences. The various organizational components directed by the Ministry of Labor along with their respective programs and functions are represented by three basic groupings or levels—local, regional, and national. It also will be observed that every significant aspect of the labor market is covered in this chart— employment service, health and welfare, industrial safety, vocational guidance and training, employ-

ment insurance, law and legislation, and records and statistics.

Figure 7–23 is a flowchart representing one aspect of judicial processing in our criminal justice system. It portrays the results of a "predictive attribute analysis" (PAA), a simple stepwise procedure used to extract those variables most closely related to the criterion variable. The criterion variable is the type of sentence. More specifically, this chart summarizes graphically the sentencing patterns of burglary offenders in urban areas processed through the superior court. It will be observed from Figure 7–22 that prior record of the offender was most highly correlated with the decision to incarcerate. Of those offenders with no prior record, 51% were sentenced to jail or prison, compared with

71% of those with a prison record—a difference of 20 percentage points. In the no-prior-record category sex was most highly correlated with the criterion variable, whereas for those with a prior record, age was most closely associated with the criterion. For those with no prior record, females (62%) were more likely than males (50%) to be incarcerated.[8]

Figure 7–24 is a simplified "progress" chart presenting significant historical data concerning the computer industry in 17 different countries. Each of the sliding bars representing a particular country has been superimposed on a time grid extending from 1935 to 1970. Below the grid there is a key or legend that explains the essential features of the chart design: (1) the bars signify the time span of work on the computer; (2) the circular symbol indicates the time when the first working model was constructed, and (3) the square symbol represents

---

[8] Additional illustrations of organization charts and flowcharts are presented in Chapters 9 and 10. These charts were included in Chapters 9 and 10 rather than in the present chapter because of the emphasis on pictorial and projection techniques.

the date when the commercialization of the computer occurred.

RANKING OR RATING CHARTS

In ranking or rating charts emphasis is placed on the position of certain items or categories, usually on the basis of magnitude or frequency. For example, states, cities, and other political units are often ranked for several different periods according to population size. In this type of chart emphasis is placed on rank-order position, rather than on the values themselves. An illustration of a ranking chart will be found in Figure 7–25. Thirty-five marital grievances are arranged in rank order by husbands and wives, respectively. It will be observed, for example, that the most common complaint of a husband is that his wife is "not affectionate." In the listing of complaints by wives this category ranks in fifth place. The connecting lines indicate the comparative ranking of the various categories for husbands and wives.

CHAPTER EIGHT

STATISTICAL MAPS

THE MOST EFFECTIVE TECHNIQUE FOR portraying spatial relationships is the map. Geographic data are sometimes arranged alphabetically or magnitudinally in tables and graphs, but the spatial character of the data when presented in this manner is largely obscured. The map provides the necessary medium for presenting areal relationships of spatial data clearly, meaningfully, and adequately.

Although the point of view and emphasis in this book are on the application of graphic techniques in presenting statistical data, it should not be overlooked that charts are also valuable for analytical purposes. This is particularly true of maps. Maps are often indispensable in locating problems, testing hypotheses, analyzing data, and discovering hidden facts and relationships.

There are many varieties of maps used in portraying statistical data. They can be grouped under the following basic types: (1) choropleth or shaded maps; (2) spot or point-symbol maps; (3) isoline maps; (4) maps with one or more types of graph superimposed (e.g., the bar, column, line, flow, or pictorial forms); (5) proportional maps; and (6) quasi- or nonstatistical historical and other schematic maps.[1]

BASE MAPS

Delineation of the base map is one of the first steps in the preparation of the various types of maps enumerated in the foregoing paragraph. The base map may be designed as a simple, outline map with a minimum of detail or may be laid out in relatively complex form with land-use patterns, topographical features, and other information. In either case the base map should be appropriate to the purpose at hand. In constructing a base map consideration should be given to the following points:[2]

1. The choice of the scale depends on such factors as the nature and amount of detail to be superimposed on the map, the purpose of the map, and the amount of reduction of the finished map.

2. The map projection should be such as not to create any marked distortions and in other respects be suitable for graphic presentation.

3. The amount of detail on the base map should be consistent with the purpose as well as the type and design of the finished map.

Figure 8–1 illustrates two relatively simple outline types of base maps for the state of Washington. Both show the boundaries and names of the 39 counties. The map at the top was designed for spots or point symbols, flow diagrams, and other graphic forms such as bars, columns, and curves. The county boundaries are drawn in light dot-and-dash lines, and the lettering is small and inconspicuous. The lower map is suitable for crosshatching purposes. The county boundaries are drawn in relatively heavy, full lines. The lettering of the names of the counties is relatively prominent and centered in each county division. Both base maps have space at the top for titles and space on the left side for legends and explanatory notes.

A more detailed base map is shown in Figure 8–2. This map provides an important background or framework for primary data that are superimposed on it. In constructing this map a careful selection was made of the features of the physical and man-made environment that are of fundamental importance in conditioning the spatial distribution of social phenomena. The facts are indicated by means of stippling, crosshatching, lettering, and other techniques. Characteristics of the physical environment often included on maps of this kind are rivers, lakes, hills, and other topographical features. Some of the factors of the cultural environment are railroads, railway yards, canals, main thoroughfares, industrial areas, vacant property, parks, and cemeteries. In actual practice, it may be necessary to forego a detailed presentation of all these characteristics, especially if the map is to be published in reduced form. A map cluttered with too many inconsequential details can be confusing and misleading. The base map represented by Figure 8–2 was designed for superimposing point symbols, flow diagrams, and other graphic forms.

The size of the original base map in Figure 8–2 is about 20 in. by 30 in. Since a large number of these maps, along with a similar one for crosshatching, were required for a series of studies of population, crime, and other subjects, a few hundred copies were photo-offset printed on high-grade vellum paper. By duplicating these two base maps in this manner, thousands of dollars in labor and materials were saved.

Another type of base without stippling and shading but showing in attenuated form the basic land-use pattern by dashed lines was designed for choropleth or crosshatched and shaded maps. It is obvious that the preceding base map—type A—would be entirely unsatisfactory for choropleth maps since the stippling and crosshatching on the base map would seriously conflict with the hatching or shading scheme devised to represent the primary data portrayed on the map. Accordingly, to obviate such confusion, vacant property and land devoted to parks, cemeteries, railroad yards, and industrial areas are left blank on the base map (Figure 8–3).

By preparing a base map like Figure 8–3 it is possible to crosshatch or shade only those areas of a city in which people actually reside (with minor exceptions). By carefully examining the point symbol and choropleth maps of Seattle in succeeding pages, the theory, purpose, and application of the two types of base map will become evident.

A third type of base map that exists per se as a special independent map is represented by Figure 8–4. Maps of this kind are constructed to serve as a reference source and guide in the analysis of ecological and sociological patterns and processes. For example, this particular map was designed for the purpose of analyzing crime differentials and social, demographic, and other correlates in a large urban community. A careful examination of Figure 8–4 will provide a meaningful orientation to the basic ecological and social structure of the city. Perhaps there are few cities of comparable size with a more varied topography and more intricate contour than Seattle. The city is characterized by many hills,

valleys, tidelands, lakes, canals, small streams, and one fairly prominent river. These physiographic irregularities have affected both land use and neighborhood patterns as well as the general morphology of the city. There are many segmental communities and neighborhoods of varying size and homogeneity that are readily identifiable not only by the residents of these respective areas, but also by the general population of the city. Figure 8–4 provides substance, clarity, and specificity to an analysis and understanding of the internal structuring of the city as well as its relationship to the spatial patterning of crime.

STATISTICAL AREAS

It is an obvious fact that essential prerequisites for the construction of statistical maps include reliable and meaningful data classified in accordance with specified geographical dimensions. Data of this kind may be compiled first hand by individual investigators or may be derived from such sources as published reports or special tabulations. Most of the data utilized in the construction of statistical maps are provided by governmental agencies. In terms of volume and variety, the United States Bureau of the Census is the most important source of information of this kind. Of course, other federal bureaus and agencies as well as state and local governmental offices and departments produce substantial amounts of valuable data. In the planning and construction of statistical maps it is not only essential to possess a genuine familiarity with the meaning, reliability, and sources of data, but it is also particularly important to have a clear understanding of the spatial referents used in the compilation of the data. Most of the data used in the construction of statistical maps are based on areas, but the type of area selected may spell the difference between a superior and an inferior map. As geographical and political entities, everyone is more or less familiar with states and counties, but for many types of statistical maps, areas of this kind may be too large and heterogeneous.

In recent years more homogeneous and frequently smaller areal units have been developed that serve as logical and pragmatic structures in research design while at the same time imparting greater meaning to the data. For research and analytical purposes, these areas have largely supplanted areas based on arbitrary and extraneous

[1] For additional discussion and examples of statistical maps, see Chapter 10.
[2] United Nations, Department of Social Affairs, *Modern Cartography: Base Maps for World Needs*, Lake Success, N. Y.: United Nations Publication, 1949, pp. 78–86.

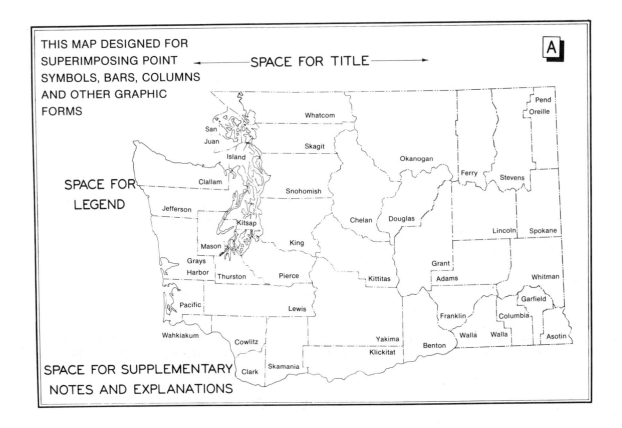

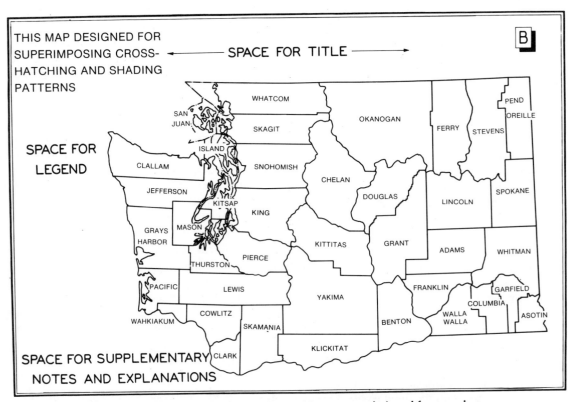

Figure 8–1. Examples of simple outline base map. A. This map was designed for superimposing various kinds of symbols, such as circles, spheres, columns, and bars. The county boundaries and county names are less conspicuous than in type B. B. This map was designed for crosshatching. Note relatively heavy lines representing county boundaries and also central position of county names.

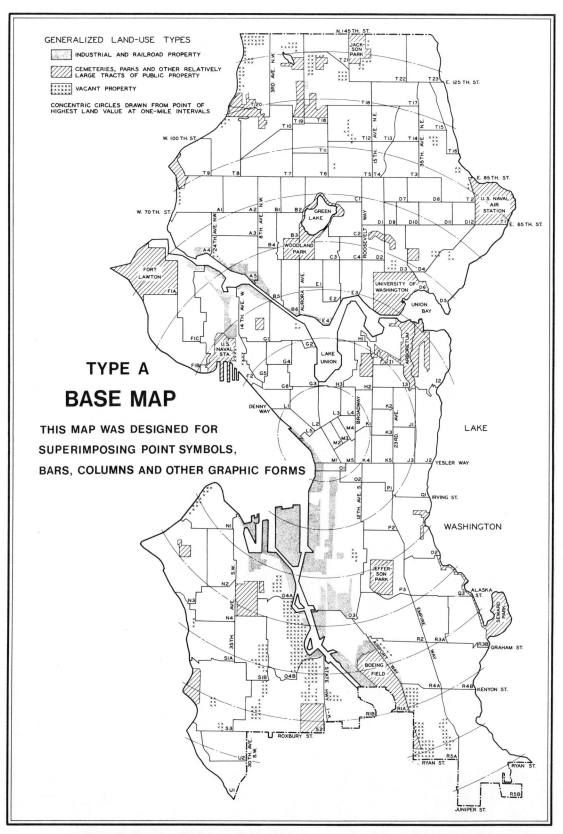

Figure 8–2. An urban base map designed for portraying point symbols, bars, columns, and other graphic forms. Note maps in this chapter in which two-and three–dimensional symbols and other point symbols have been superimposed on this base map. (Map designed by Calvin F. Schmid.)

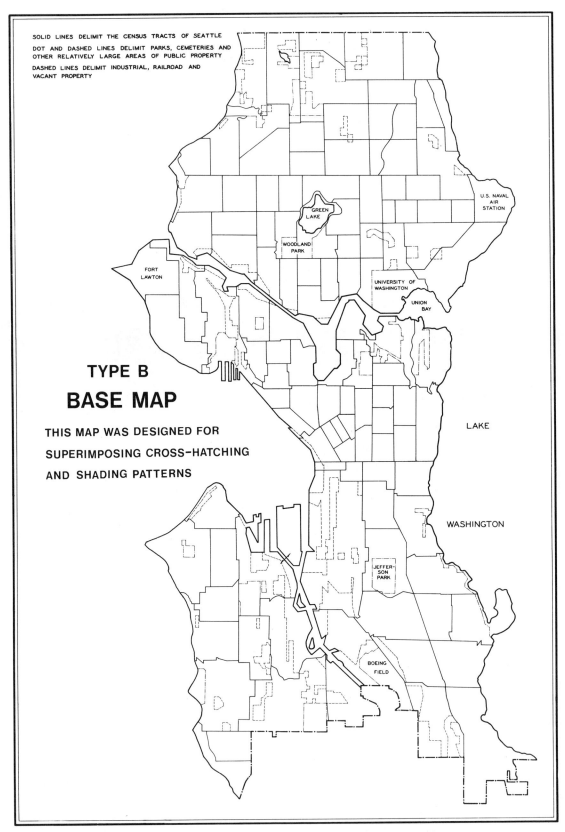

Figure 8–3. An urban base map designed for crosshatching. In order to obviate confusion with the superimposed crosshatching, stippling and other forms of shading have been omitted. It will be observed that this base map was used in the preparation of Figures 8–7 and 8–9. (Map designed by Calvin F. Schmid.)

Figure 8–4. A relatively detailed base map of a large city. This type of base map is used mainly as a reference source and guide in the discussion of ecological and sociological patterns and processes. (From Calvin F. Schmid and Stanton E. Schmid, Crime in the State of Washington, Olympia: Law and Justice Planning Office, Planning and Community Affairs Agency, 1972, p. 94.)

political and administrative considerations. Brief discussions of certain areas used in the construction of statistical maps are presented in the following paragraphs.

Census Tracts

Census tracts are small, permanently established geographical areas into which large cities and their environs have been divided for statistical purposes. Tract boundaries are selected by a local committee and approved by the Bureau of the Census. They remain the same for a long time, so that statistical comparisons can be made from year to year and from census to census. The average tract has over 4000 people and is originally laid out with attention to achieving some uniformity of population characteristics, economic status, and living conditions.

In each decennial census the Bureau of the Census tabulates population and housing information for each tract—hence the name "census tract." Local groups have increased the value of the census tract data by tabulating locally collected data by tracts.[3] Figures 8–2, 8–3, and 8–4 portray the census tract system for Seattle.

Census County Divisions

Census county divisions are statistical areas that were originated to serve as area subdivisions of counties in states where existing minor civil divisions were statistically inadequate. The inadequacies resulted from many factors but foremost and initially were boundaries that changed frequently and were difficult to identify and areas that were functionally obsolete and thus poorly known to their residents.

Census county divisions (or CCDs, as they became known) were first established in the state of Washington for the 1950 census. During the 1950s CCDs were established in 17 additional western and southern states for the 1960 census. Three additional states were added to the program for the 1970 census, bringing the total to 21.

The objective in delimiting CCDs was that each should represent a community or trading area, or a part of such area. Other factors such as land use or physiographic differences received some, but lesser, attention. In each state the entire area was subdivided into CCDs, using visible features as

boundaries except where CCD boundaries coincided with county or municipal boundaries.[4]

Enumeration Districts

Generally, enumeration districts are layed out within census tracts and CCDs as administrative expedients for controlling and directing the conduct of field enumerations. Also, they are used in subsequent tabulation processes. Because of their smaller size, data based on enumeration districts may be more appropriate for certain purposes than data based on census tracts or CCDs. Enumeration district data are available on a cost basis from the Census Bureau in the form of computer tapes and special tabulations.

Blocks

In recent decades the Census Bureau has tabulated and published a limited amount of data for hundreds of thousands of blocks. In addition to published statistics, block data are available on a contractual basis. Block data have proved extremely valuable, if not indispensable, for certain kinds of research and administrative problems. Because of additional published material as well as the ready availability of special tabulations and computer tapes, there has been an extraordinary proliferation of interest and demand for all kinds of small-area data. Also in this connection, with particular reference to statistical maps, the availability of small-area data in combination with computer-assisted cartography, there has occurred an unprecedented productivity of maps along with significant technological developments in this area.

---

[3] Quoted directly from Robert C. Klove, *Census Tract Manual*, U.S. Bureau of the Census, 5th ed., Washington, D. C.: Government Printing Office, 1966, p. 1 (this manual is now in the process of revision); see also, Calvin F. Schmid, "The Theory and Practice of Planning Census Tracts," *Sociology and Social Research*, **22** (January–February 1938), 228–238.

[4] Quoted directly from Robert C. Klove, *Census County Divisions, Past and Future*, U.S. Bureau of the Census, Technical Paper 30, Washington, D. C.: Government Printing Office, 1973, p. 1; see also Calvin F. Schmid, "Washington's State-Wide System of Census Tracts and Census Divisions," in *Studies in Population*, Princeton: Princeton University Press, 1949, pp. 39–45.

Political Areas

For conducting research on political issues as well as on a multitude of other problems, political areas are, of course, still indispensable. The Census Bureau, for example, compiles varying amounts and kinds of data by states, counties, minor civil divisions, incorporated places, wards, and congressional districts.[5] Outside of the United States political and administrative areas are sometimes identified by such labels as communes, departments, parishes (this term is also used in the state of Louisiana), and provinces.

Standard Metropolitan Statistical Areas

The general concept of a metropolitan area is one of an integrated economic and social unit with a recognized urban population nucleus of substantial size. The concept of "standard metropolitan statistical area" (SMSA) has been developed to meet the need for the presentation of general-purpose statistics about metropolitan areas by agencies of the federal government. A standard metropolitan statistical area always includes a city (cities) of specified population that constitutes the central city and the county (counties) in which it is located. A standard metropolitan statistical area also includes contiguous counties when the economic and social relationships between the central city and contiguous areas meet specified criteria of metropolitan character and integration. A standard metropolitan statistical area may cross state

lines. The criteria used to designate standard metropolitan statistical areas represent a reasoned judgment as to how metropolitan areas may be defined statistically in a uniform manner, using items that are: (1) widely recognized as indicative of metropolitan character (population, urban character, nonagricultural employment, population density, commuting ties) and (2) available from a body of federal statistics collected at the same time in all parts of the country and processed and tabulated according to consistent standards. The criteria used to designate standard metropolitan statistical areas are subject to continuing review, and further changes in the criteria may be expected in the future as additional statistical data become available and as the nature and structure of metropolitan areas themselves become better understood.[6]

Urbanized Areas

The major objective of the Census Bureau in delineating urbanized areas is to provide a better separation of urban and rural populations in the vicinity of the larger cities. An urbanized area includes a central city or cities of a certain population size plus contiguous territory, both incorporated and unincorporated, meeting specific criteria of population size and density.[7]

CHOROPLETH[8] MAPS

Characteristically, the choropleth map is used to portray rates and ratios based on clearly delimited areal units such as regions, nations, states, counties, or census tracts. In the case of spot or dot maps, emphasis is placed on absolute numbers or sizes, whereas in choropleth maps emphasis is on relative frequencies and proportions. In choropleth maps, value ranges or rates and percentages are represented by a graded series of crosshatchings, shadings, and sometimes colors.

A few more-or-less typical examples of data appropriate for choropleth maps are as follows: rates of marriage, divorce, birth, morbidity, mortality, and crime; percentage of total population classified according to age, sex, race, or nativity; percentage of population consisting of carpenters, college graduates, unemployed, and so forth; mean or median rent and mean or median value of dwelling

[5] William T. Fay and Robert C. Klove, "The 1970 Census," *The Professional Geographer,* **22** (September 1970), 284–289.
[6] Sentences taken verbatim from Office of Management and Budget, *Standard Metropolitan Statistical Areas: 1975,* Washington, D. C.: Government Printing Office, 1975, pp. iii and 1.
[7] For additional details, see U.S. Bureau of the Census, *Population of Urbanized Areas Established Since the 1970 Census, For the United States: 1970,* Supplementary Report, 1970 Census of Population, Washington, D. C.: Government Printing Office, 1976.
[8] In deference to cartographic terminology, we use the term "choropleth" map rather than "shaded" or "crosshatched" map, which was used in the first edition of the *Handbook*. Among American cartographers "choropleth" is generally accepted as standard usage in spite of the not infrequent confusion of other cartographic terms and their pseudo-Greek derivations.

units; median grade completed for population 25 years of age and over; population density; per capita income, sales, taxes, and so on; percentage of votes for particular candidates or issues; per capita consumption of coffee, beer, sugar, butter, or cigarettes; amount of wheat, corn, potatoes, or tobacco produced per acre; percentage of land in farms or forests; and rates of increase and decrease of population, income, sales, manufacturing, or agricultural production.

Crosshatched, shaded, or colored maps are occasionally constructed to portray simple chronological series or groupings of qualities or attributes that are basically nonstatistical. Since this book is devoted to graphic forms used in presenting statistical data, the qualitative type of crosshatched or shaded map is given only cursory treatment here.

The fundamental principle to be observed in the crosshatching technique is to arrange the density of lines in such a way as to give an optical effect from light to dark or dark to light with respect to intensity of tone or pattern. Each type of crosshatching or shading indicates a value interval in a series of rates or percentages. Generally, the smallest value is indicated by light stippling or crosshatching. Each successive interval is indicated by an increasingly heavy type of hatching, with the highest interval usually represented by black.

During the past several decades cartographers, psychologists, psycho-physicists, and others have devoted a considerable amount of research in shading values with respect to optical responses, esthetics, and practical applications. The results of these investigations are valuable, both in a theoretical and practical sense. However, there is still much to be learned. It is not a simple, perfunctory procedure in selecting shading patterns for a choropleth map. In this process both the map designer and the map user are involved since it is not easy to: (1) find shaded screens whose visual intensity is at least approximately proportional to the original data and (2) select patterns that make it possible for the user to distinguish and visually separate the values represented by the shading scheme.[9] As far as the human eye is concerned, it has been clearly demonstrated that in a gray spectrum the percentage of blackness perceived in relation to the percentage of the area that is inked conforms to a curvilinear, rather than linear, pattern. Furthermore, the problem of perception may be further complicated by the texture or patterning of the various intervals in the shading scheme.[10]

Construction of Choropleth Maps

The first step in the construction of a crosshatched or shaded map is to arrange the rates, percentages, averages, or other data into an array. If the number of cases is relatively large, say, about a hundred or more, it would be difficult to arrange the data into an array. A frequency distribution with relatively small, equal class intervals should be compiled. After a very careful study of the array or frequency distribution, the data should be grouped into from five to eight class intervals, with each interval represented by an appropriate hatching pattern. As previously indicated, the lightest hatching or stippling normally corresponds to the smallest magnitude, with increasing densities showing suc-

[9] Of course, the first obstacle can be technically resolved by programming an automatic line plotter to create a continuum of gray tones with any light intensity. See, for example, Jean-Claude Muller, "Statistical Accuracy and Map Enhancement in Choroplethic Mapping," in *Proceedings of the International Symposium on Computer-Assisted Cartography, 1975*, (op. cit.), pp. 136–148. It should be recognized, however, that the solution to this particular shading problem is not as simple as the preceding statement might seem to imply. In the first place, the average person does not have ready access to computer equipment, and second, from an esthetic point of view, computer-generated shading patterns are frequently substandard and inappropriate.

[10] See, for example, John K. Wright, Loyd A. Jones, Leonard Stone, T. W. Birch, *Notes on Statistical Mapping*, American Geographical Society and Population Association of America, New York and Washington, 1938; A. E. O. Munsell, L. L. Sloan, and I. H. Godlove, "Neutral Value Scales. I Munsell Neutral Value Scale," *Journal Optical Society of America*, 23 (1933), 394–411; George F. Jenks and Duane S. Knos, "The Use of Shading Patterns in Graded Series," *Annals, Association of American Geographers*, 51 (1961), 316–334; Robert Lee Williams, "Map Symbols: Equal-Appearing Intervals for Printed Screens," *Annals, Association of American Geographers*, 48 (1958), 132–139; Henry W. Castner and Arthur H. Robinson, *Dot Area Symbols in Cartography: The Influence of Pattern on Their Perception*, American Congress on Surveying and Mapping, Washington, D. C., 1969, Technical Monograph No. CA-4; S. S. Stevens and E. H. Galanter, "Ratio Scales and Category Scales for a Dozen Perceptual Continua," *Journal of Experimental Psychology*, 54 (1957), 377–411; Robert L. Williams, *Statistical Symbols for Maps: Their Design and Relative Values*, New Haven: Yale University Map Laboratory, 1956; Arthur H. Robinson and Randall D. Sale, *Elements of Cartography*, 3rd ed., New York: Wiley, 1969, pp. 250–260; George F. McCleary, Jr., "In Pursuit of the Map User," *Proceedings of the International Symposium on Computer-Assisted Cartography, 1975*, Washington, D. C.: U.S. Bureau of the Census, 1976, pp. 238–250.

cessively higher values. Generally, there should not be more than eight class intervals since more than eight hatchings are confusing and difficult to differentiate.

Experience shows that spatial series do not necessarily conform to symmetrical bell-shaped curves. Many series are skewed markedly or are U-shaped or J-shaped in varying degrees. Intervals of equal size are desirable, but the character of many distributions is such as to render this impossible. For some purposes the class intervals may be expressed in terms of standard deviations, quartiles, quintiles, deciles, or some other measure of a frequency distribution. Also, in population-density maps, for example, class intervals may be indicated in the form of an arithmetic or geometric progression. If in a geometric progression a series of density intervals begins with 0–49, the second would be 50–149; the third, 150–349; the fourth, 350–749; the fifth, 750–1549; and so on. In the determination of class intervals for choropleth maps it is not uncommon practice to rely on inspection by selecting natural divisions or breaking points in the distribution. Sometimes a distribution is divided arbitrarily into a predetermined number of class intervals. Ideally, any technique for determining class intervals should minimize the differences within classes and maximize the differences between classes. Jenks has suggested that this might be accomplished by analysis of variance.[11]

Use of Colors and Tints

Color is frequently used in the construction of maps and for certain purposes has distinct advantages. Color can make charts attractive and appealing but

[11] George F. Jenks, "Contemporary Statistical Maps, Evidence of Spatial and Graphic Ignorance," in *Proceedings of the International Symposium on Computer-Assisted Cartography*, Washington, D. C.: U.S. Bureau of the Census, 1976, pp. 51–60.
[12] David J. Cuff, "Conflicting Goals in Choosing Colors for Quantitative Maps," *Proceedings of the International Symposium on Computer-Assisted Cartography: 1975*, Washington, D. C.: U.S. Bureau of the Census, 1976, pp. 286–288.
[13] National Resources Committee, *Suggested Symbols for Planning Maps and Charts*, Washington, D. C.: Government Printing Office, April, 1937, p. A-4 (this same work is referred to in the next two footnotes).
[14] Robert C. Klove, "Census Statistical Mapping and the Users," ibid., pp. 175–182.
[15] Lloyd Kaufman, "The Uses of Color," ibid., pp. 270–276.

presents serious limitations as a substitute for the typical crosshatched map. First, the goal of a color scheme for choropleth maps is to achieve a strong and unambiguous sense of quantitative change—a clear and distinguishable gradation in value from one color to another.[12] However, there is no optical progression of colors that can identify variations in magnitude as precisely, logically, or with the same visually graded impression as crosshatching. A color gradation that manifests degrees of intensity is as follows: white, light yellow, golden yellow, orange, pink, light brown, dark brown, dark green, purple, and black.[13] In addition to intensity (chroma), color possesses two other dimensions—hue (actual color) and darkness or lightness (value). Even where only one color is used it is very difficult to develop a practical color density or intensity sequence. Generally, it is preferable to show intensity gradations for one color than to use a multicolor density scheme. Furthermore, "cartographers as well as others recognize that color and its use are a subjective matter and that people see colors differently."[14] Also in this connection, it is significant to note that "one male in eight suffers to some degree with some kind of color deficiency."[15] Second, the cost of printing in color is substantially more expensive than in black and white. Moreover, in the case of diazo and other relatively inexpensive types of black-and-white reproduction, colors in original charts are meaningless or actually a detriment since certain colors or color intensities do not reproduce clearly. Recently, the Xerox Corporation has marketed a machine that reproduces prints in color. Color can be used successfully to show areal distributions of attributive or chronological series. Maps of this type can be shown either in distinct colors or in tints. Political, geological, and soil maps are examples of nonquantitative distribution maps. In political maps, for example, where each country or other governmental unit is distinct, no color gradation is required. Geological maps frequently conform to a conventionalized color scheme very close to a chromatic scale of yellow, green, blue, violet, and red, supplemented with hues and patterns when necessary.

Shortcomings of the Choropleth Map

Although the choropleth map is a very valuable graphic technique, there are three shortcomings that should be recognized. First, an entire areal unit representing a single class interval is crosshatched or shaded uniformly regardless of the great differences that may exist within the unit itself. For example, one small corner of an area may be densely populated whereas other parts may be relatively sparse or entirely uninhabited, but the entire area is expressed as an average with uniform shading. Second, actually the transition in value from one spatial unit to another is usually gradual and not abrupt. Since data for choropleth maps are based on discrete areal divisions, an impression of definitive and abrupt change may be conveyed by maps of this kind. Third, the amount of crosshatching or shading is determined solely on the basis of geographic area and not by the number of cases each district contains. In terms of visual impression, it is a natural tendency to judge the larger geographic areas as being more important, but actually, in comparison to the number of cases, the smaller areas may be far larger and more significant from a quantitative point of view. Where some factor other than area is of determinative significance, the divisions may be drawn in proportion to the value of the factor rather than according to normal geographic size, thereby eliminating this objection.[16]

Crosshatching Techniques

There are two techniques that can be used in applying crosshatching to a map: (1) ruling pen and ink or (2) commercially prepared crosshatching or shading patterns.[17] Figure 8–5 illustrates a series of pen and ink hatchings which the authors have used in dozens of maps and other types of charts. It will be observed that the hatchings follow a visual gradation from light to dark, with each block representing a particular pattern. The spacing, weight, and other characteristics of hatching schemes should be adapted to the size and other significant features of the chart. If the chart is to be reproduced, consideration should be given to the type of reproduction as well as the amount of reduction. Crosshatching made with pen and ink is more flexible than commercially prepared crosshatching screens, since such factors as size of drawing, line thickness, spacing, and type of reproduction can be fully evaluated and allowed for in the design and execution of the chart. To achieve equal spacing of lines for crosshatched patterns, distances can be measured with

a scale or with a strip of printed graph or cross-ruled paper held in place with thumbtacks, drafting tape, or rubber cement. A section liner also may be found effective.

Figure 8–6 is a reproduction of a sample of commercially prepared hatching. The manufactured hatching screens are press printed on thin acetate.[18] The underside is coated with an adhesive. After the screen is cut out to the size and shape of an area, it is carefully applied to the chart with a burnishing instrument.[19]

Printed screens possess two main advantages: (1) no skill in tracing or drawing is required to use them; and (2) for certain purposes, they may save time and expense. The disadvantages of printed screens include: (1) they lack flexibility—the weight and spacing of lines of the various hatching patterns are not always adaptable to large-scale maps; (2) they are more costly and time consuming for some types of work; (3) they do not adhere satisfactorily to flexible material such as vellum, drafting film, or tracing cloth, especially when rolled, and they also tend to peel off stiff surfaces after a certain period of time, depending on room temperature, handling, and other factors; and (4) unless a heat-resistant adhesive is used or the tracing is protected by a layer of transparent acetate, it may be difficult to make inexpensive contact prints, such as blue- and black-line prints with printed screens. Frequently, the heat from the machine lights is great enough to melt the adhesive and cause the screen material to loosen.

A choropleth map depicting the distribution of robbery by census tracts for the city of Seattle is represented by Figure 8–7. The index for this map is based on cases of robbery reported to the police during an 11-year period, 1960–1970. Mean rates per 100,000 of population were computed for each of the tracts. It will be observed that there were

---

[16] See pp. 212–215, this chapter.
[17] Of course, in the case of computer-generated maps, crosshatching and other patterns may be superimposed by special auxiliary equipment.
[18] See Chapter 2 for listing of companies that manufacture hatching and shading screens.
[19] The idea of printing hatching patterns on paper and applying them to maps is an old one. More than 75 years ago William Z. Ripley described this technique, which he used in the preparation of the maps for his well-known work, *Races of Europe,* New York: Appleton, 1915; see William Z. Ripley, ''Notes on Map Making and Graphic Representation,'' *Quarterly Publication of the American Statistical Association,* **6** (1898–1899), 313–327.

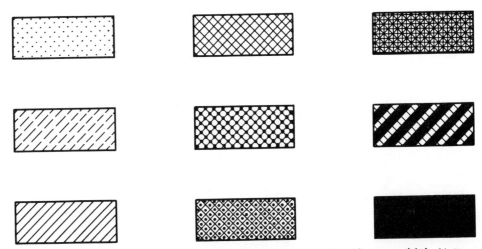

Figure 8–5. Hatching scheme made with pen and ink. Note use of these hatchings on several maps in this chapter.

11,614 cases of robbery reported to the police during this period, with the mean rate for the city as a whole as 194.1. The range in the incidence of this crime from one part of the city to another is extraordinary—from zero to 5350.3 per 100,000 of population. After careful study it was decided that nine class intervals would portray most satisfactorily the essential features of this series of rates. Although class intervals of uniform size may be desirable, it is usually impossible to conform to this

pattern. The extraordinarily skewed and irregular distribution of the data on robbery is a most convincing instance why equal class intervals may be impossible. The hatching for this map was executed with pen and ink. An examination of Figure 8–7 reveals a very high incidence of robbery in the inner city (the downtown portion of the central sector of the city) and contiguous tracts. Tract O1 (Skid Road) shows a mean rate of 5350.3 and M1 [central business district (CBD)], a mean rate of 3624.6 per

Figure 8–6. Illustration of a series of pre-printed hatchings. These examples were selected from Keuffel and Esser Company's "Normatone" patterns. Numbers identify type of hatching for ordering and filing purposes.

61 6487-298   61 6487-1157   61 6487-1160

61 6487-204   61 6487-214   61 6487-248

61 6487-272   61 6487-230   61 6487-943

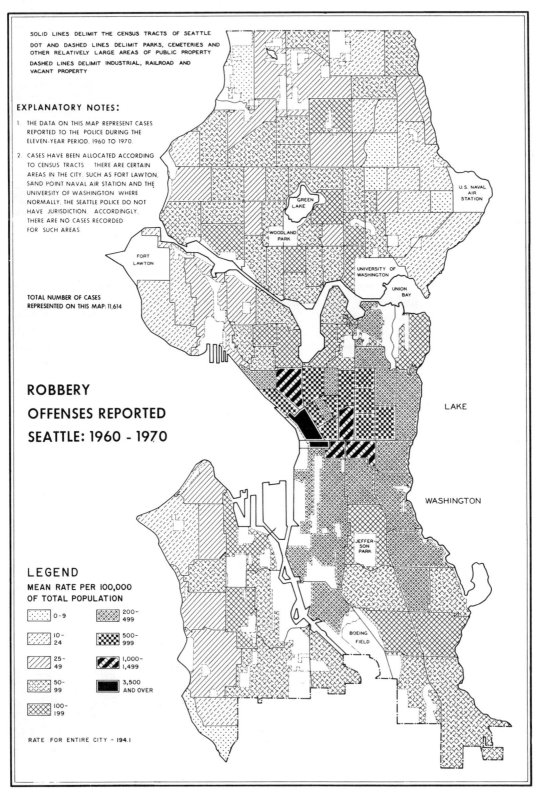

SOLID LINES DELIMIT THE CENSUS TRACTS OF SEATTLE

DOT AND DASHED LINES DELIMIT PARKS, CEMETERIES AND
OTHER RELATIVELY LARGE AREAS OF PUBLIC PROPERTY

DASHED LINES DELIMIT INDUSTRIAL, RAILROAD AND
VACANT PROPERTY

EXPLANATORY NOTES:

1. THE DATA ON THIS MAP REPRESENT CASES
   REPORTED TO THE POLICE DURING THE
   ELEVEN-YEAR PERIOD, 1960 TO 1970.

2. CASES HAVE BEEN ALLOCATED ACCORDING
   TO CENSUS TRACTS. THERE ARE CERTAIN
   AREAS IN THE CITY, SUCH AS FORT LAWTON,
   SAND POINT NAVAL AIR STATION AND THE
   UNIVERSITY OF WASHINGTON WHERE
   NORMALLY, THE SEATTLE POLICE DO NOT
   HAVE JURISDICTION. ACCORDINGLY,
   THERE ARE NO CASES RECORDED
   FOR SUCH AREAS

TOTAL NUMBER OF CASES
REPRESENTED ON THIS MAP: 11,614

ROBBERY

OFFENSES REPORTED

SEATTLE: 1960 - 1970

LEGEND

MEAN RATE PER 100,000
OF TOTAL POPULATION

0-9   200-499
10-24   500-999
25-49   1,000-1,499
50-99   3,500 AND OVER
100-199

RATE FOR ENTIRE CITY - 194.1

Figure 8–7. A choropleth or crosshatched map. In order to portray the essential details of this series of data, nine hatching categories were utilized. (From Calvin F. Schmid and Stanton E. Schmid, Crime in the State of Washington, Olympia: Law and Justice Planning Office, Planning and Community Affairs Agency, 1972, p. 128.)

100,000 of population. In contrast, comparatively low robbery rates are to be found in the newer, outlying residential areas. Only one tract, U1, a residential area located in the extreme southwest corner of the city, did not report a single robbery during the 11-year period. There were four tracts, all in the north end, with rates of less than 10 per 100,000 of population.

Figure 8–8 is another illustration of a choropleth map that portrays the percentage of nonwhite public elementary school children enrolled in the 86 elementary schools in the city of Seattle. The basic areal unit shown on this map is, of course, the elementary-school district (attendance area). The nonwhite category includes not only blacks, but also Japanese, Chinese, Filipinos, American Indian, and "all other." For the city as a whole, in 1962, when this map was prepared, 8067 (14.8%) of the 54,582 public elementary-school children were nonwhite. Statistically, the distribution of the percentages for the 86 districts is negatively skewed, with over 33% of the districts having less than 10% of the children classified as nonwhite. There are two districts without any nonwhite children. The proportions of nonwhite children enrolled in Seattle's most highly segregated elementary schools were 98.7% in Horace Mann, 95.1% in Leschi, 89.5% in Minor, 87.9% in Harrison, 87.2% in Colman, 87.1% in Bailey Gatzert, and 85% Madrona.[20] All these districts are located in the central area of the city. Characteristically, the school districts north of the Lake Washington Canal and along the western side of the city bordering Puget Sound show relatively small proportions of nonwhite children. The shading patterns were drawn in pen and ink. Also, there was sufficient room to indicate the respective percentage of nonwhite children for each district.

Unlike the two preceding choropleth maps, Figure 8–9 was designed to portray rates of change—the growth and decline of population by census tracts in the city of Seattle between 1950 and 1960. The hatching scheme reflects a continuum from relative high population decreases to relatively high population increases. It will be recalled that the

hatching in Figures 8–7 and 8–8 was done with pen and ink, but in Figure 8–9 the hatching represents preprinted commercial screens. Figure 8–9 typifies the growth processes of the large American urban community with outward movement of population. For more than half a century the peripheral growth of the corporate city of Seattle as well as the surrounding area has been most pronounced, whereas the central part has shown a consistent and continuous decline.

Figure 8–10 was selected to illustrate how the crosshatching technique can be used effectively to portray highly detailed and complex data. The basic data represent the front-footage assessed valuation of every tract of land in the corporate city of Minneapolis. In attempting to map data of this kind, one is confronted with two complex problems: (1) the areas for which the data are given are exceedingly small and numerous; and (2) the range of values is very wide. After careful study was made of the basic data, 11 class intervals were selected, and the front-footage value of every lot and every larger tract of land in the city was transferred from original records to a work map in accordance with a color scheme corresponding to the 11 class intervals. The smallness of the areas, as well as the large number of class intervals, made it particularly difficult to work out a system of graded hatching patterns and to draw these patterns on the map. The problem of reduction for printing also had to be taken into consideration. A careful examination of the map will reveal further details of planning and construction and also the relative effectiveness of the map in portraying graphically the essential patterning of land values in a large American city. All work on this map was done in pen and ink.

Figure 8–11 illustrates the application of the crosshatching technique in portraying nonquantitative data on maps. It will be observed that the various parcels of land annexed to the city of Seattle are differentiated by a series of hatching patterns. Each pattern represents the annexations recorded during certain intercensal periods, beginning in 1869. Detachments and accretions are noted by explanatory statements. Sometimes it may be found expedient to arrange the hatching density in a gradation to conform to a chronological sequence; for example, the lightest pattern might indicate the earliest period, with increasingly darker patterns for successive periods. Commercially printed hatching patterns were used on this map.

---

[20] In this connection, it might be noted that statistically valid and reliable measures of ecological segregation were formulated and empirically demonstrated in 1947; see Julius Jahn, Calvin F. Schmid, and Clarence Schrag, "The Measurement of Ecological Segregation," *American Sociological Review*, **12** (June 1947), 293–303.

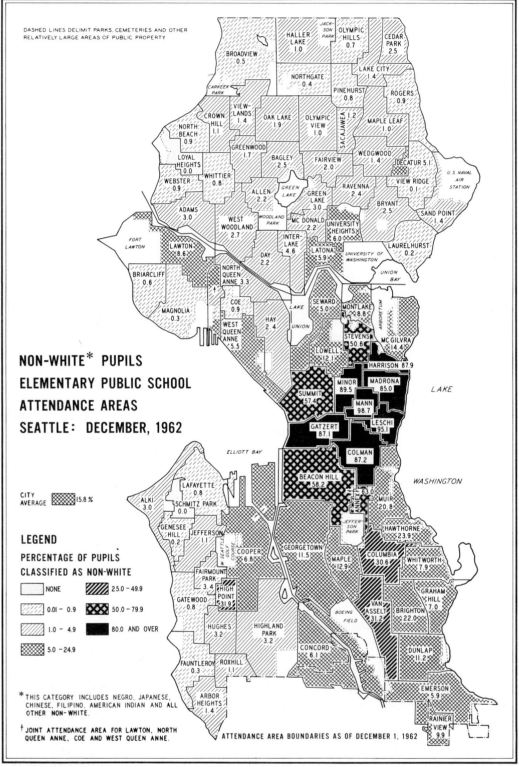

Figure 8–8. A choropleth or crosshatched map portraying distribution of nonwhite children by elementary school districts (From Calvin F. Schmid and Wayne W. McVey, Jr., Growth and Distribution of Minority Races in Seattle, Washington, Seattle: Seattle Public Schools, 1964, p. 37.)

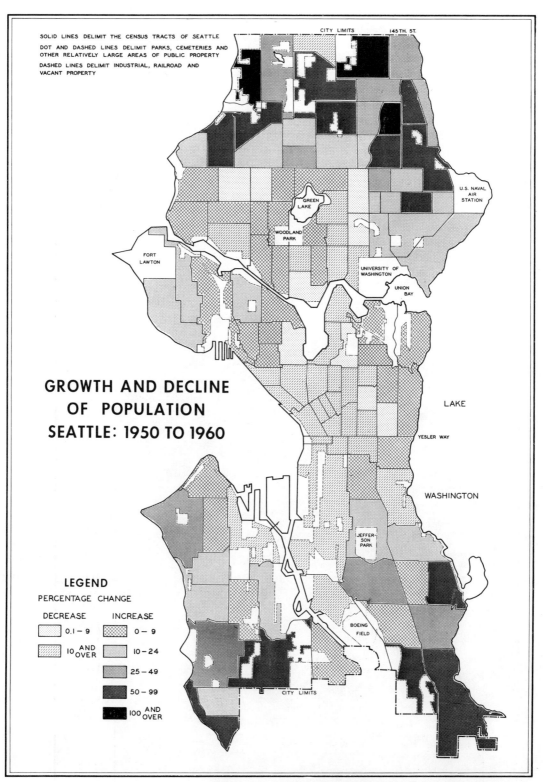

SOLID LINES DELIMIT THE CENSUS TRACTS OF SEATTLE

DOT AND DASHED LINES DELIMIT PARKS, CEMETERIES AND OTHER RELATIVELY LARGE AREAS OF PUBLIC PROPERTY

DASHED LINES DELIMIT INDUSTRIAL, RAILROAD AND VACANT PROPERTY

CITY LIMITS   145TH. ST.

U.S. NAVAL AIR STATION

GREEN LAKE

WOODLAND PARK

FORT LAWTON

UNIVERSITY OF WASHINGTON

UNION BAY

LAKE

YESLER WAY

WASHINGTON

GROWTH AND DECLINE OF POPULATION SEATTLE: 1950 TO 1960

JEFFER-SON PARK

BOEING FIELD

CITY LIMITS

LEGEND

PERCENTAGE CHANGE

DECREASE   INCREASE

0.1 − 9   0 − 9

10 AND OVER   10 − 24

                25 − 49

                50 − 99

                100 AND OVER

Figure 8–9. Another illustration of a choropleth or cross-hatched map showing growth and decline of population by census tracts. The hatching and shading on this map are commercial preprinted patterns. (From Calvin F. Schmid and Stanton E. Schmid, Growth of Cities and Towns, State of Washington, *Olympia: Washington State Planning and Community Affairs Agency, 1969, p. 150.)*

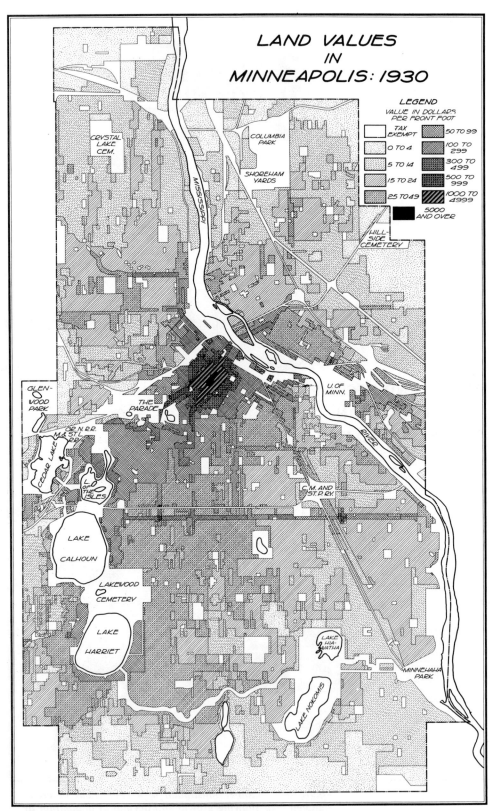

Figure 8–10. Another application of crosshatching technique. Note especially fine gradation of density for ten different categories. (From Calvin F. Schmid, "Land Values as an Ecological Index," Research Studies of the State College of Washington, IX, March 1941, pp. 16–36.)

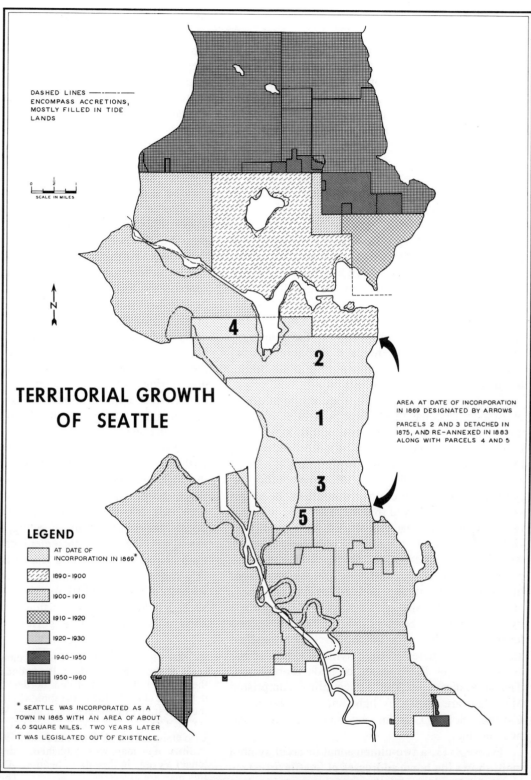

DASHED LINES ─ · ─ · ─
ENCOMPASS ACCRETIONS,
MOSTLY FILLED IN TIDE
LANDS

0   1/2   1
SCALE IN MILES

← N ↑

TERRITORIAL GROWTH
OF SEATTLE

4

2

AREA AT DATE OF INCORPORATION
IN 1869 DESIGNATED BY ARROWS

PARCELS 2 AND 3 DETACHED IN
1875, AND RE-ANNEXED IN 1883
ALONG WITH PARCELS 4 AND 5

1

3

5

LEGEND

AT DATE OF
INCORPORATION IN 1869*

1890 - 1900

1900 - 1910

1910 - 1920

1920 - 1930

1940 - 1950

1950 - 1960

* SEATTLE WAS INCORPORATED AS A
TOWN IN 1865 WITH AN AREA OF ABOUT
4.0 SQUARE MILES. TWO YEARS LATER
IT WAS LEGISLATED OUT OF EXISTENCE.

Figure 8–11. Crosshatched map portraying historical data. The hatching patterns on this map were cut from commercial, preprinted sheets. (From Calvin F. Schmid and Stanton E. Schmid, Growth of Cities and Towns, State of Washington, Olympia: Washington State Planning and Community Affairs Agency, *1969, p. 153.)*

SPOT, DOT, OR POINT-SYMBOL MAPS

Emphasis in spot, dot, or point-symbol maps is placed on frequencies or absolute amounts rather than on rates or proportions. Although there may be a certain amount of overlapping, spot maps can be differentiated into four types on the basis of the symbols used. Symbols may stress: (1) size, (2) number, (3) density, or (4) form.

Spot or Dot Maps with Areal and Cubic Symbols

In the first type of map the size of each symbol is proportional to the frequency or magnitude of the phenomena represented. Symbols may be either two- or three-dimensional and are usually in the form of circles or spheres rather than rectangles, cubes, or irregular forms. If circles are utilized, the respective areas are in proportion to the value represented. Similarly, in the case of spheres the respective volumes are drawn in accordance with the frequency or magnitude portrayed.

Figures 8–12 and 8–13 illustrate the application of two-dimensional (areal) symbols in portraying the spatial distribution of two entirely different types of social phenomenon. Figure 8–12 shows the size and type of hospitals in Metrolina.[21] There are two legends on the map, one representing the type of hospital and the other, the size of the hospital. It will be observed that there are four different types of hospital, each identified by a particular shading pattern. In the original publication, colors were used to differentiate the types of hospital— pastel blue for general, dark blue for long-term care, orange for rehabilitation, and red for eye, ear, nose, and throat. The size of the hospital, as measured by the number of beds, is indicated in the second legend by a series of eccentric circles of specified size. The diameter of each symbol varies as the square root of the number of beds represented. The boundaries of the 12 counties comprising Metrolina are shown by light lines and the North Carolina–South Carolina boundary by a much heavier line.

Figure 8–13, a two-dimensional or areal symbol map, shows the home addresses of Seattle arrestees charged with drug violations who were taken into custody in the University District (Tract D6) during the 3-year period 1968–1970. During this period 164 arrestees were residents of Seattle, while in addition, there were 91 nonresidents and 35 whose residence was "unknown." The male arrestees are represented by a black symbol and the female arrestees by a stippled symbol. The diameter of each symbol varies as the square root of the cases represented. The primary purpose of this map was designed to show the relationship of residential address of arrestees charged with drug law violations to the place where the arrest took place. It is significant to note that of 290 persons arrested in the University District (Tract D6) only 20 actually resided in this tract.

Another form of the two-dimensional symbol map is illustrated by Figure 8–14. It will be seen that the symbols are divided into sectors. In a basic sense they are a series of pie charts of varying size as determined by the number of cases represented. In Figure 8–14 the symbols are allocated by census tract and indicate the number of male arrestees for drunkenness classified by race.[22] The criterion for distributing the cases by census tract is place of arrest. There is not a single census tract in the city without at least one arrestee for drunkenness during 1968–1970. Tract M1, the CBD, shows the heaviest concentration of arrests, for both males and females charged with drunkenness. There were 2784 male arrestees. In attempting to explain the large number of arrestees for drunkenness in the CBD, the following questions might be raised. Can the high incidence of arrests be accounted for by the large number of drunkards who frequent the area? Or are the police less tolerant of public drunkenness in the main shopping, banking, professional service, and amusement center of the city than in areas such as Skid Road? Skid Road, Tract O1, ranks second in number of persons arrested, with 1638 males and 91 females. The size of the sectors indicates the proportion of male arrestees in each of the four racial categories. The incidence of

---

[21] "Metrolina" is a grouping of 12 counties located in the heart of the larger Southern Piedmont region, straddling the North and South Carolina border. Charlotte, which is located close to the geographic center of Metrolina, is the largest city in this area; see James W. Clay and Douglas M. Orr, Jr., eds., *Metrolina Atlas,* Chapel Hill: The University of North Carolina Press, 1972, pp. 3–9.

[22] Since this map was published, "drunkenness" is no longer a crime in the city of Seattle. The cases shown on this map are arrestees, not arrests. There were 101 male recidivists who were arrested 25 or more times in the city of Seattle for drunkenness during the 3-year period, 1968–1970.

drunkenness among Indians is out of all proportion to the number represented in the population. Among the 2784 male arrestees in Tract M1, 66.2% were white, 21.3% Indian, 7.8% black, and 4.7% all other.

Spherical or three-dimensional symbols are shown by Figures 8–15 and 8–16.   Figure 8–15

portrays changes (increases and decreases) in the number of blacks for each of the census tracts of Seattle during the 20-year period, 1950–1970.   In Seattle one of the most significant demographic trends in recent decades has been the heavy inmigration of blacks.   In 1940 there were only 3789 blacks residing in the city, but by 1950 this number

Figure 8–12. Map with two–dimensional symbols portraying size and type of hospitals in Metrolina. (From James W. Clay and Douglas M. Orr, Jr., Metrolina Atlas, *Chapel Hill: University of North Carolina Press, 1972, p. 204.*

SIZE AND TYPE OF HOSPITALS IN METROLINA

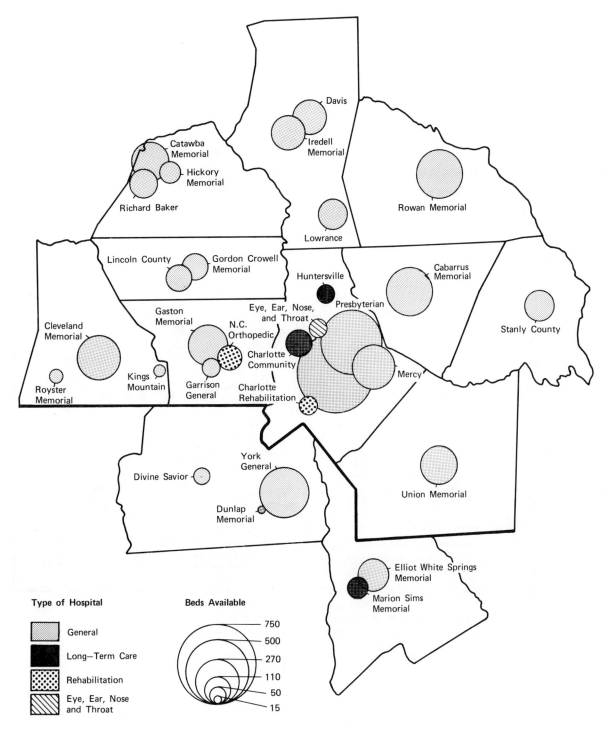

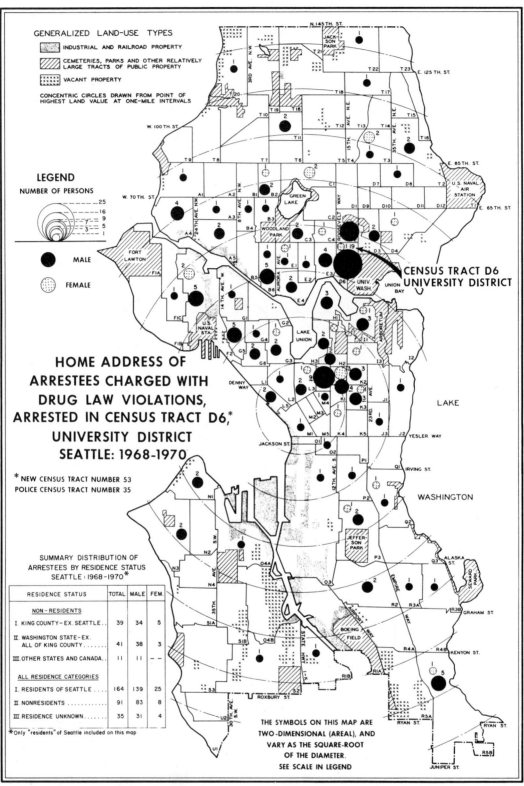

Figure 8–13. *A map with two–dimensional symbols. The residences of drug law violators arrested in the university district are portrayed on this map by two–dimensional symbols. Male arrestees are represented by black symbols, and female arrestees by stippled symbols. (From Calvin F. Schmid and Stanton E. Schmid,* Crime in the State of Washington, *Olympia: Law and Justice Planning Office, Planning and Community Affairs Agency, 1972, p. 249.)*

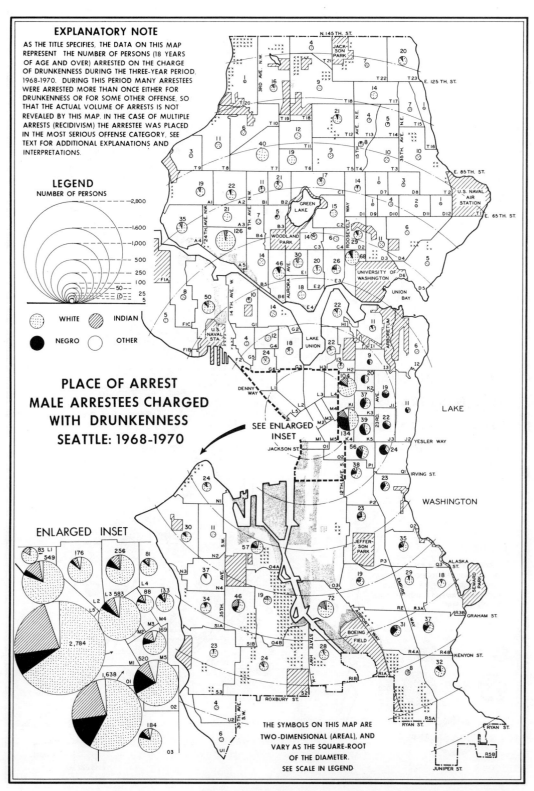

Figure 8–14. Map with two–dimensional segmented symbols. (From Calvin F. Schmid and Stanton E. Schmid, Crime in the State of Washington, *Olympia: Law and Justice Planning Office, Planning and Community Affairs Agency, 1972, p. 294.)*

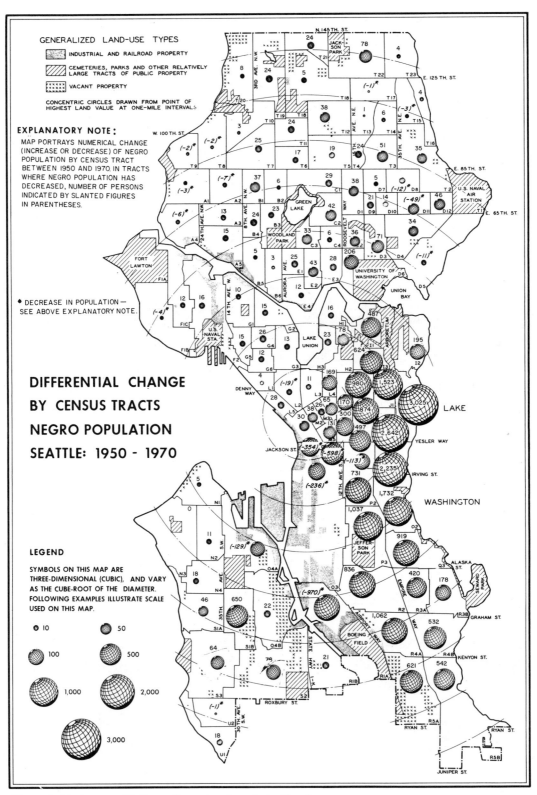

Figure 8–15. A map with three–dimensional symbols. The size of each symbol is drawn in relation to the numerical increase or decrease of the black population by census tract between 1950 and 1970. (From Calvin F. Schmid and Stanton E. Schmid, Crime in the State of Washington, *Olympia: Law and Justice Planning Office, Planning and Community Affairs Agency, 1972, p. 118.)*

INMIGRATION - ALL STUDENTS
PUBLIC AND PRIVATE INSTITUTIONS: 1963

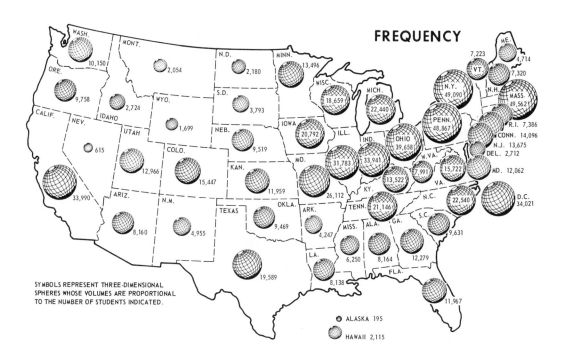

FREQUENCY

SYMBOLS REPRESENT THREE-DIMENSIONAL SPHERES WHOSE VOLUMES ARE PROPORTIONAL TO THE NUMBER OF STUDENTS INDICATED.

ALASKA 195
HAWAII 2,115

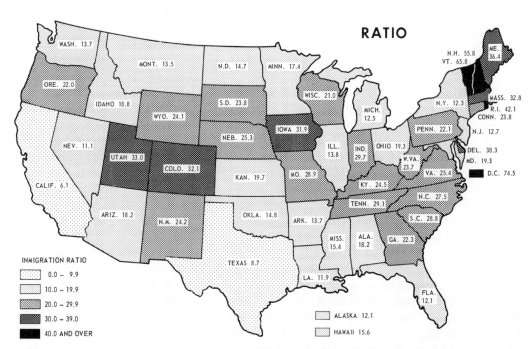

RATIO

INMIGRATION RATIO
- 0.0 – 9.9
- 10.0 – 19.9
- 20.0 – 29.9
- 30.0 – 39.0
- 40.0 AND OVER

ALASKA 12.1
HAWAII 15.6

Figure 8–16. Two complementary maps presenting inmigration of all college and university students for each of the 50 States. Sometimes it may be necessary to utilize two or more maps to present appropriately a series of data. It will be observed that the upper map portrays the actual number of inmigrants for each state, while the lower map indicates the proportion that inmigrants comprise of the total college and university enrollment in each state. (From Charles E. Gossman, Charles E. Nobbe, Theresa J. Patricelli, Calvin F. Schmid, and Thomas E. Steahr, Migration of College and University Students in the Stunited States, *Seattle: University of Washington Press, 1968, p. 17.)*

had grown to 15,666 and by 1970 to 37,868. At the present time (1977) there are over 50,000. Almost all of the census tracts exhibit increases in the black population. The largest decrease for a single census tract resulted from the demolition of warhousing projects. Significantly, large decreases also occurred in three of the tracts located in a marginal blighted area in proximity to the CBD. In the comparatively few tracts where the black population has decreased, the number of persons are indicated by a minus sign and slanted figures in parentheses. It will be observed that pronounced increases have occurred in many tracts located in the so-called central area and in southern Seattle.

The map with three-dimensional symbols in Figure 8–16 provides detailed information on the geographical distribution of inmigrant students attending public and private insitutions of higher learning. The pattern of concentration is readily discernible. Six of the 10 states that experienced the heaviest volume of inmigration are located in the Great Lakes Region and the Mideast Region. Massachusetts (49,562) shows the largest number of inmigrants, followed by New York (49,090), Pennsylvania (48,867), and Ohio (39,658). Those states having the fewest number of inmigrants, such as Alaska (195), Nevada (615), and Wyoming (1699), have few institutions of higher learning, have sparse populations, and occupy relatively remote locations.

To provide a more complete and well-rounded picture of college and university student migration, a choropleth map showing the proportion inmigrants comprise of the total enrollment in each state has been made an integral part of Figure 8–16. All states having the highest percentage of nonresident students are located in the Northeast, with the exception of Utah (33.0), Colorado (32.1), and Iowa (31.9). California (6.1) and Texas (8.7) have the lowest percentage of students enrolled from other states.

One of the main reasons for using three-dimensional symbols on maps is a very practical one. Where the range of values is very wide and the space on the map limited in size, it becomes necessary to use a type of symbol that can be properly fitted on the map. Also, where the number of symbols is large, the problem of available space becomes accentuated. For example, if two-dimensional symbols had been used in the construction of either Figure 8–15 or 8–16, the smallest values would have to be represented by points of microscopic size and the symbols representing the larger figures could not have been contained within the borders of the map, to say nothing of attempting to place them within the boundaries of the census tracts (Figure 8–15) or states (Figure 8–16). In spite of the shortcomings of three-dimensional symbols, they can serve an important function under certain circumstances. Three-dimensional symbols may be found particularly appropriate in constructing detailed population-density maps, which include both large and small cities as well as more widely distributed agglomerations of population.[23]

Procedure in Drawing Areal and Cubic Symbols

Correct drafting of circles as symbols for comparison of sizes is not difficult, if it is kept in mind that it is the *area* of the circle that represents the size being compared. The area of a circle is equal to its radius squared times the constant pi (π); that is, $A = \pi r^2$. Since the diameter, the dimension of the circle that is most useful in laying out a chart, may be expressed as twice the radius, the area of any circle may be expressed as $\pi(1/2 d)^2$, or $(\pi/4)d^2$. Expressing the constant $\pi/4$ as a unit of measurement, the area of the circle is found to be a function of the square of the diameter, or the area increases directly as the square of the diameter. That is, increasing the diameter of a circle to three times its previous length will increase the area of the circle to nine times its previous value. In laying out circles as symbols for comparison of sizes, then, the diameters of the circle symbols should be proportional to the square root of the sizes to which they correspond.

For example, to construct a series of comparable circles for the values 16, 25, 49, 81, and 144, the first step is to extract their respective square roots. Their square roots (4, 5, 7, 9, and 12, respectively) will determine the diameters of the circles. It is important to draw circles compatible with the general layout and dimensions of the chart. The initial

[23] See Sten de Geer, "A Map of the Distribution of Population in Sweden," *Geographical Review*, **12** (1922), 72–83. Maps of this kind will also be found in Calvin F. Schmid and Stanton E. Schmid, *Growth of Cities and Towns, State of Washington,* Olympia: Washington State Planning and Community Affairs Agency, 1969, pp. 10, 14, and 66–68.

step in this procedure is to determine the actual sizes of the largest and smallest circles in the series.

The smallest square root in the series will be used as a divisor for all of the others. If the most desirable size of the diameter (in inches) for the smallest circle is 0.3, then each derived quotient in the series is multiplied by 0.3. In the above illustration the quotients thus derived are as follows: 5/4 = 1.25; 7/4 = 1.75; 9/4 = 2.25; 12/4 = 3.00. If the diameter of the smallest circle is 0.3, the diameters for the remaining circles are

$$(1.25)(0.3) = 0.375$$
$$(1.75)(0.3) = 0.525$$
$$(2.25)(0.3) = 0.675$$
$$(3.00)(0.3) = 0.9$$

Similar considerations are encountered when the volume of spheres is used as a device for size comparison. The spherical symbol is outlined as a circle, the great circle of the sphere, and then shaded, or marked in some way to indicate the three-dimensional aspect of the symbol. Since it is the volume that is to be proportional to the sizes being compared, the relationship between the volume of a sphere and the diameter of its great circle must be considered. The volume of a sphere is found by the formula $V = (4/3\pi r^3)$, or the constant four-thirds of the number pi times the cube of the radius. Since the radius is one-half the diameter, this formula may be written $V = [4/3\pi(1/2d)^3]$, or $V = (1/6\pi d^3)$. As in the case of using circles for comparison by areas, the constant $\pi/6$ can be expressed as a unit of measurement, and the volume of the sphere is found to be a function of the cube of its diameter. Increasing the diameter of the great circle of the sphere to three times its original length will increase the volume of the sphere to 27 times its original value. To compare the sizes 8, 64, and 1000, circular symbols with respective diameters of 2, 4, and 10 units, when shaded or marked to indicate their spherical nature, will be correctly proportioned to represent the comparison by volume of spheres.

Examples of linear, areal, and cubic comparisons of the populations of six counties in the state of Washington in 1970 are shown in Table 8–1. An examination of Table 8–1 clearly reveals the specific steps for deriving comparable circles and spheres. For circles, the first step is to extract the square root of each figure in the series (column 3). Second, each square root is divided by the square root of the smallest figure (column 4). Third, a desirable diameter is selected for the smallest circle, which is used as a factor for all of the values in the series. For illustrative purposes 0.25 of an inch was chosen. If for some reason the factor chosen for a particular series turns out to be too large or too small, all of the derived figures can be divided or multiplied by any constant. In developing three-dimensional symbols the same procedure is followed, except, of course, cube roots of the values in the series are computed. It will be observed that, although the respective diameters of the circle and sphere were made identical for Pend Oreile County, the corresponding diameters for Clark County are considerably different in size. This fact further illustrates the significance of areal and volume symbols.

Table 8–1.
Linear, Areal, and Cubic Comparisons: Illustrations of
Techniques for Drawing Comparable Sizes of Circles and Spheres
POPULATION OF SIX COUNTIES IN WASHINGTON STATE IN 1970

The "factor" for columns 4 and 8 can be any desired size of diameter or radius of a circle or sphere representing the smallest value. In this table the "factor" selected was 0.25 in. (i.e., ¼ in.).

County (1)	Population (2)	Circles			Spheres		
		$\sqrt{\text{Col. 2}}$ (3)	Col. 3 $\div$ $\sqrt{6025}$ (4)	Col. 4 Mult. by Factor (Inches) (5)	$\sqrt[3]{\text{Col. 2}}$ (6)	Col. 6 $\div$ $\sqrt[3]{6025}$ (7)	Col. 7 Mult. by Factor (Inches) (8)
Clark	128,454	358.40	4.62	1.16	50.46	2.77	0.69
Grays Harbor	59,553	244.03	3.14	0.79	39.05	2.15	0.54
Kittitas	25,039	158.24	2.04	0.51	29.26	1.61	0.40
Klickitat	12,138	110.17	1.42	0.36	22.98	1.26	0.32
Lincoln	9,572	97.84	1.26	0.32	21.23	1.17	0.29
Pend Oreile	6,025	77.62	1.00	0.25	18.20	1.00	0.25

One of several methods can be used in extracting square roots and cube roots. Tables of these roots are available, perhaps the best known of which is *Barlow's Tables*. The logarithmic relationships of numbers can also be utilized in deriving square and cube roots. For example, one-half the log of a number is the log of the square root of the number, and one-third the log of a number is the log of the cube root of the number. Another method of extracting roots is by use of the binomial expansion. One of the most common techniques for deriving square roots is the mechanical method of successive divisions taught to pupils in junior high school.

Spot or Dot Maps Emphasizing Frequency of Symbols

In the second type of spot map the basic criterion is not size, but number or frequency of spots or point symbols. The spots are uniform in size, each representing a specific value. The design and arrangement of spots make them readily countable. With a well-constructed map of this kind it is possible to ascertain at a glance whether one geographic area contains more or fewer dots than another, and if one desires to make exact comparison between two or more areas, it is very easy to count the dots and compare the results. Usually the dots are distributed within statistical or administrative divisions such as counties, precincts, or census tracts. For example, the authors have prepared maps of this kind indicating the number of votes for a communist candidate by precincts, the number of substandard housing units by enumeration districts, and the number of robberies and other crimes by census tracts. As a general rule, the smallest geographic area on the map will determine the size of the dot and the number of units of frequencies to be represented by each dot. Figure 8–17 is an illustration of this type of map. The exact location of each house of prostitution is indicated, and the general pattern is related to the natural areas and to the census tracts of the central segment of the city.

Spot or Dot Maps Emphasizing Density of Symbols

The third type of map is also of a multiple-dot variety, but instead of emphasizing countable frequencies, comparative density and distribution are emphasized. Actually, of course, the map stressing numbers or frequency of spots may also at the same time indicate density of distribution, but not as exactly or characteristically as one designed with that purpose in mind. The spots used in density maps are invariably small black dots.

The size of the dots should be made commensurate with the overall size of the base map as well as with the number and distribution of dots. Also, if the map is to be reproduced, the amount of reduction should be carefully considered. In planning a map of this kind the dot ratio must be carefully worked out. One dot may be equivalent to 1, 5, 10, 25, 50, 75, 100, 200, 500, 1000, or some other number of items. If the ratio shown is too small, the number of dots may be so large that they frequently coalesce or possibly they cannot even be included on the map. On the other hand, if the ratio is too large, the dots may be so few that a clear pattern of density cannot be developed.

In summary, procedural problems in constructing a spot map where simple repeated symbols are used, boil down to three questions:[24]

1. How many cases should each dot represent?

2. How large should each dot be?

3. How should the location of each dot be determined?

Several different techniques can be used in making dots of this kind. The bow pen and drop pen are used most frequently. For relatively small dots a Wrico, LeRoy, Rapidograph, Payzant, or similar type of lettering pen will be found quick and efficient. Sometimes it may be found convenient to use dry transfer symbols, which are available commercially.

Figure 8–18 portrays the distribution of the Japanese population of Seattle according to a density-dot system. The purpose of a map of this kind is to indicate overall spatial patterning. A mere glance at the map reveals pronounced clusterings of Japanese in certain areas as well as a complete absence in other areas. It will be observed that each dot represents 10 people. Although the map indicates a noticeable degree of spatial segregation among the Japanese, it is not nearly as

---

[24] A suggestive nomograph has been devised for the purpose of determining optimal dot size and unit value; see, J. Ross Mackay, "Dotting the Dot Map," *Surveying and Mapping*, **9** (1949), 3–10.

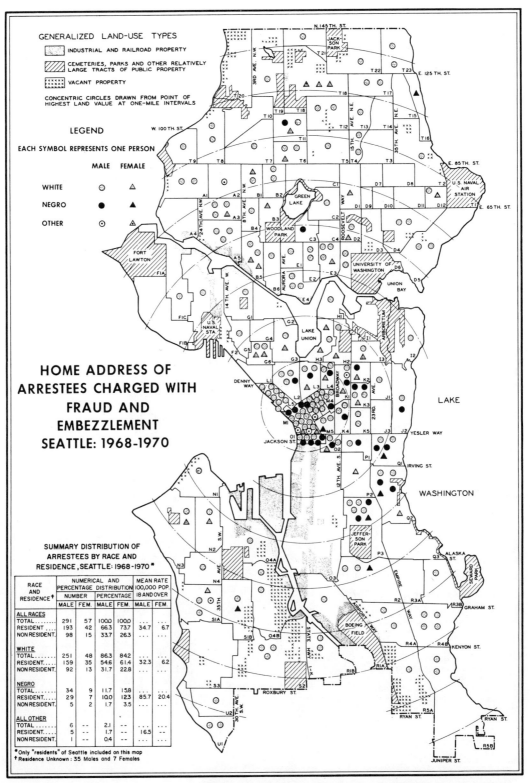

Figure 8–17. A spot map showing distribution of vice resorts in relation to natural areas in the central segment of a large city. (From unpublished study by Calvin F. Schmid.)

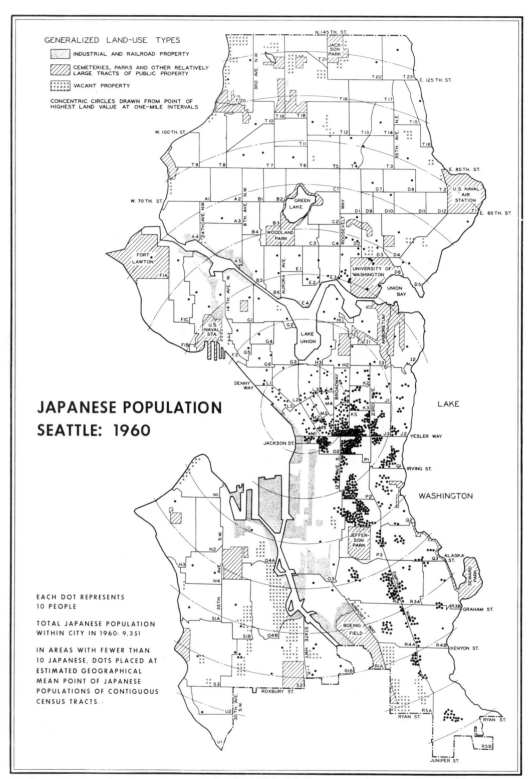

Figure 8–18. An example of a spot map emphasizing density of symbols. (From Calvin F. Schmid, Charles E. Nobbe, and Arlene E. Mitchell, Nonwhite Races, State of Washington, *Olympia: Washington State Planning and Community Affairs Agency, 1968, p. 64.)*

marked as it was a few decades ago. It will be recalled that Figure 8–8, a choropleth map, portrayed the spatial patterning of segregation among nonwhite children in elementary schools. As has been pointed out previously, alternate graphic techniques may be used to portray the same phenomena. In such instances it may be irrelevant to assume that one technique is necessarily superior to another, because the respective purposes of the charts may be entirely different. Crosshatched maps, for example, emphasize rates or proportions for specified areas, whereas density-dot maps show specific location and concentration of frequencies.

Spot Maps with Symbols Representing Qualities or Attributes

Unlike the three types of spot maps already discussed, the criterion for the symbol map is a qualitative one. The form of the symbol represents certain qualities or attributes. For example, if the male–female dichotomy is to be portrayed on a map, one type of symbol would represent male and another type, female. Likewise, if a number of different kinds of institutions such as churches, schools, hospitals, or factories are to be depicted, each type of institution would be represented by a different symbol.

Figure 8–19 is an example of a multiple-attribute map. The symbols were designed to differentiate according to sex and race a series of residents of Seattle who were charged with fraud and embezzlement during the 3-year period, 1968–1970. It will be observed that males are represented by cir-

cles and females, by triangles. For whites the symbols are stippled, for blacks they are black, and for the "all other" category a black dot is centered within the symbol. Each symbol represents one person. The location of each symbol was determined by the census tract in which the home address of the arrestee was situated. The tabular summary in the lower left-hand corner of the map provides additional specific information covering all of the arrestees for this crime. In addition to the 348 resident arrestees, there were 113 nonresidents and 42 whose residence was unknown.

ISOLINE MAPS

Isoline (from *isos*, meaning "equal") is a generic term describing a type of map widely used by geographers and other specialists to show the distribution of meteorological, physiographic, economic, demographic, and other data.[25] The basic data used in the preparation of isoline maps may be samples of absolute measurement for particular points or ratios for certain areas. In both instances, points having identical values are joined together by continuous flowing lines.

Some of the more familiar examples of isoline maps include those pertaining to a series of points of equal temperature, which are called "isotherms"; of equal rainfall, "isohyets"; of equal barometric pressure, "isobars"; of equal elevation, "isohypses" (or more commonly, "contour lines"); of equal magnetic variations, "isogenes"; and of equal time, "isochrones."

There are two fundamental types of isoline maps: (1) isometric map, in which the lines are drawn through points of equal value or intensity and (2) isopleth map, in which the lines connect equal rates or ratios for specific areas. In the isometric[26] map a sample of measurements is taken at different points on a map, and those of equal values or magnitude are connected by continuous lines. In contrast, the values used in the isopleth maps are rates or ratios computed on the basis of areal units, such as census tracts, townships, precincts, or counties. In this type of map the value for an area is reduced to a point. A topographic map is an example of the isometric type, and a population-density map with lines showing equal densities is an example of the isopleth type.

The isopleth map is particularly valuable for graphic presentation in the social sciences.[27] In the

[25] The beginner may find the terminology of maps of this type very confusing since there is little agreement concerning usage among cartographers. Instead of "isoline" some cartographers prefer "isogram" (equal-line), "isopleth" (equal measure), or "isorithm" (equal number). The terms "isometric" and "isontic" also have been used.

[26] The term "isometric" as used to describe a specific type of isoline map has an entirely different connotation from that used to describe a form of projection. See Chapter 10 for a discussion of isometric projection.

[27] The value of isoline maps both as a technique of analysis and presentation, is well exemplified in two recent publications. These studies include literally hundreds of isoline maps; see Ronald Abler and John S. Adams, *A Comparative Atlas of America's Great Cities: Twenty Metropolitan Regions*, Vol. 3, Association of American Geographers and University of Minnesota Press, 1976; Brian J. L. Berry and Quentin Gillard, *The Changing Shape of Metropolitan America*, Cambridge, Mass.: Ballinger Publishing Company, 1977.

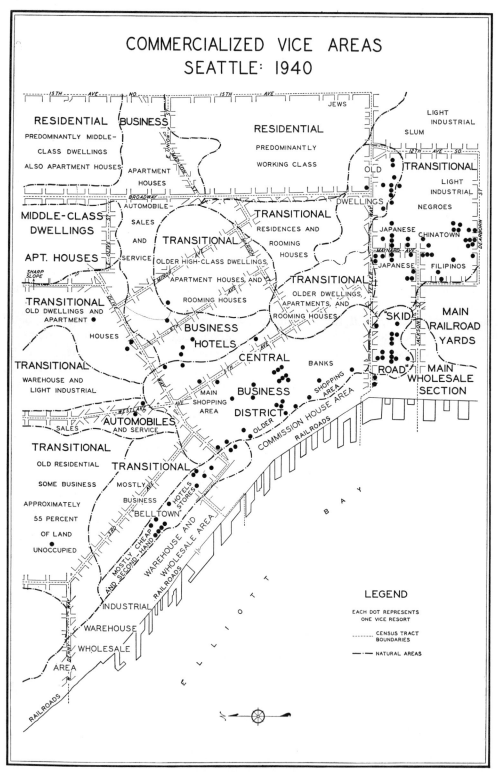

Figure 8–19. Spot map in which the form of the symbol is the basic criterion. (From Calvin F. Schmid and Stanton E. Schmid, Crime in the State of Washington, *Olympia: Law and Justice Planning Office, Planning and Community Affairs Agency, 1972, p. 237.)*

construction of isopleth maps, however, there are four basic considerations to be kept in mind. First, the areal units for which the data have been collected bear a close and significant relationship to the reliability, comparability, significance, and general appearance of the isopleth map. If the base areas are relatively large, meaningful variations are masked and the isopleths are extremely general. On the other hand, if the areas are relatively small, chance and possibly meaningless variations in the data will be recorded as myriads of tiny "islands" or "peaks" on the isopleth map. Most important, however, is the loss of measurability that occurs when adjacent base areas on a map are different in size. If one control point is based on a relatively large area and an adjacent control point on a relatively small area, the interpolation of values between them is subject to errors of interpretation that cannot be controlled statistically. If it is impossible or impracticable to use base areas of the same shape and size, extreme caution should be followed in interpreting the resulting isopleths. Data are usually available only for blocks, enumeration districts, census tracts, and political subdivisions. Since census or political subdivisions may not be identical in size and shape, the considerations mentioned here are particularly important. If the same data are available for more than one type of base area, selection should be determined mainly by the relationship and significance of the data to the size of the base area.

Second, in constructing an isopleth map a point is used to represent each areal unit. This point,

which is called the "control point" of the area, must be accurately located according to some specific assumption for each areal unit for which a rate or ratio has been derived. If the unit is symmetrical in shape and the distribution of the phenomenon is relatively uniform, the geographical center naturally would be chosen as the control point or "spot height." In actual practice, census tracts, precincts, counties, and other areas for which statistics are compiled are seldom symmetrical, and the patterns of distribution of most economic, social, and other phenomena are uneven. The problem is to determine the most typical or representative point in the area. This point in any type of area, with even or uneven distribution, is the center of gravity or pivot point where the distribution would balance if it were supported by a rigid and weightless plane.[28]

The third consideration[29] is the laying out of the isopleths drawn with reference to the values indicated by the control points in each statistical area. The procedure is largely one of interpolation and inference with reference to the various control points. Many mathematical interpolation methods could be used. But complicated interpolations cannot usually be justified by the data and technique of isopleth mapping, and linear interpolation should be used in most instances. On this question, the following quotation from Wright is pertinent:

Thus an isopleth representing a density of 20 to the square mile is made to connect figures "20" on the base and to pass halfway between a "15" and a "25", two-thirds of the way from an "18" to a "21", etc. The method is convenient and not misleading if the density figures are numerous and closely spaced, but it should always be remembered that an isopleth, although drawn in a similar manner, is not at all comparable to a contour line. One may determine the altitude of a point, but one cannot define the density of population at a point, since density can be measured with respect to areas (or volumes) only. Between the 20- and 40-foot contour lines the elevation is everywhere between 20 and 40 feet, but it is not true that the density of population within an area marked off by the 20- and 40-per-square-mile isopleths is necessarily between 20 and 40 to the square mile.[30]

The fourth consideration is the choice of intervals for the isopleths. The isopleth interval may be based on either a geometric or arithmetic progression or some division or multiple of 5 or 10, such as

[28] A discussion of techniques for locating control points for isopleth maps will be found in the following papers: J. Ross Mackay, "Some Problems and Techniques in Isopleth Mapping," *Economic Geography,* 27 (January 1951), 1–9; Ernest W. Mowrer, "The Isometric Map as a Technique of Social Research," *The American Journal of Sociology,* **44** (July 1938), 86–96; Fr. Uhorczak, "Metoda Izarytmiczna W. Mapach Statystycznych," *Polski Przeglad Kartograficzny,* 4 (G 1929), pp. 95–124.
[29] The third and fourth points are also relevant to the construction of the isometric-type map.
[30] John K. Wright, et al., "Notes on Statistical Mapping, with Special Reference to the Mapping of Population Phenomena," American Geographical Society and Population Association of America, 1938, p. 13; W. D. Jones, "Ratios and Isopleth Maps in Regional Investigation of Agricultural Land Occupancy," *Annals Association of American Geographers,* 20 (1930), 177–195; Calvin F. Schmid and Earl H. MacCannell, "Basic Problems, Techniques and Theory of Isopleth Mapping," *Journal of the American Statistical Association,* **50,** (March 1955), 220–239.

0, 5, 10, 25, 50, 100, 500, or 1000. The size of the interval should be adapted to each map, particularly in relation to the type of distribution, reliability, and other characteristics of the data. If the intervals are too large, the result may be an overgeneralized and meaningless map. On the other hand, if the isopleths are plotted in accordance with small class intervals or when a map has widely separated control points, an unwarranted impression of precision is conveyed. The value of each isoline is indicated on the map with the appropriate number, the significance of which is included in a supplementary legend.[31]

An illustration of the isometric type of isoline map is shown in Figure 8–20. This chart is a simplified contour map of Seattle. It will be observed that the contour lines are drawn at 50-ft intervals ranging from zero to 50 to over 500. The spaces between the isolines are crosshatched in accordance with the principles outlined in the section on crosshatched maps. There is a total of 11 different class intervals. The shading between the isolines focuses attention on the spaces between the contour lines and helps to make the map more readily interpretable and graphic.

Figure 8–21 is an isopleth map showing the educational status of the population of Chicago as indicated by the distribution of the median number of school grades completed by persons 25 years old and older. The various steps used in constructing this map are illustrated in Figure 8–22. This figure is an enlarged portion of the work map used in developing the isolines for Figure 8–21. The areal bases for the original data are census tracts, which are shown by stippled boundary lines and tract numbers. Control points indicated by circles, are located at the geographic center of each tract. The value for each control point represents the median grade completed for persons 25 years old and over within the tract. Each control point is connected by a straight line—an interpolation axis—with each adjacent control point. Adjacent control points are taken to mean the control points of tracts that have common boundaries. No interpolation axes are drawn between control points of tracts that touch only at corners. Equal linear divisions along interpolation axes have been laid out between each pair of control points. When suitable intervals have been determined—in this case, one school year—smoothed curves are drawn through points of equal value on each interpolation axis.

STATISTICAL THEORY AND ISOPLETH MAPPING

In attempting to clarify and improve the meaning of isopleth maps, it would seem particularly appropriate to examine the basic statistical assumptions and implications of this type of map.

Broadly speaking, the isopleth map, as well as certain crosshatched maps, is related to frequency distributions. In this general comparison the crosshatched area unit map is analogous to the histogram and the isopleth map, to the frequency polygon and smoothed-frequency curve.[32]

Both types of maps, however, are three-dimensional representations. Since these maps must be presented on a flat surface—excluding the use of three-dimensional models—and the two areal dimensions are given a surface orientation, the third or characteristic dimension is portrayed as a vertical projection on the surface. Thus the patterned map of areal subdivisions can be considered as the vertical projection of the surfaces of the tops of prismatic volumes over an area. If presented in isometric projection rather than vertical projection, the patterned map would appear as a block diagram (Figure 8–23).

The same assumptions and restrictions that apply to the histogram also apply to the patterned subdivision map. In the histogram it must be assumed that the frequency within a given class interval is uniform over the entire interval. This assumption is reflected by the horizontality of the line across the interval of a histogram at the height above the base that corresponds to this assumed uniform value. In the same way, it must be assumed that the distribution of a characteristic on a patterned map is uniform over the entire area of a subdivision in order to justify the use of a uniform hatching or color pattern.

The frequency represented by a histogram is proportional to the area under the curve ("curve" is

[31] Mackay, "Some Problems and Techniques of Isopleth Mapping" (op. cit.); J. W. Alexander and G. A. Zahorchak, "Population-Density Maps of the United States: Techniques and Patterns," *Geographical Review*, **33** (1943), 458–460.

[32] Figures 8–23, 8–24, and 8–25, along with the discussion in this section, are based on: Calvin F. Schmid and Earle H. MacCannell, "Basic Problems, Techniques and Theory of Isopleth Mapping," *Journal of the American Statistical Association*, **50** (March 1955), 220–239.

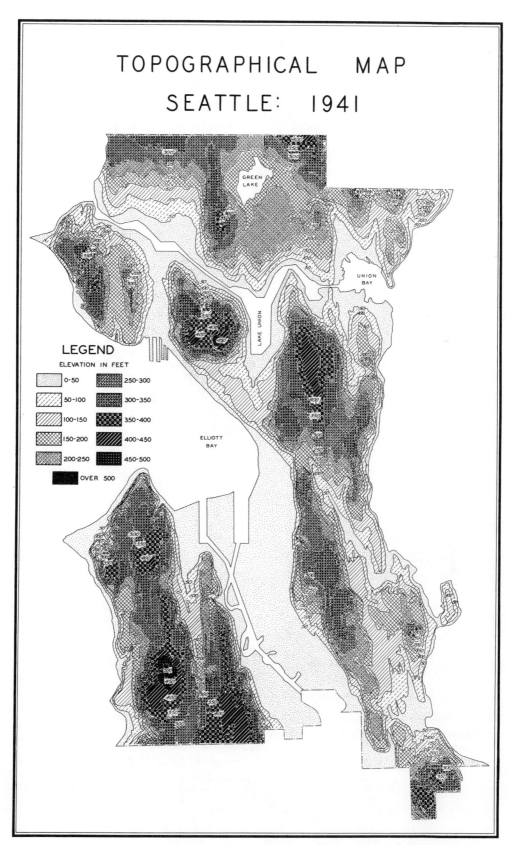

TOPOGRAPHICAL MAP
SEATTLE: 1941

GREEN
LAKE

UNION
BAY

LAKE UNION

LEGEND

ELEVATION IN FEET

	0-50		250-300
	50-100		300-350
	100-150		350-400
	150-200		400-450
	200-250		450-500
	OVER 500		

ELLIOTT
BAY

Figure 8–20. A contour map on which is superimposed a simplified crosshatching scheme for the purpose of differentiating elevations. (From Calvin F. Schmid, Social Trends in Seattle, *Seattle: University of Washington Press, 1944, p. 52.)*

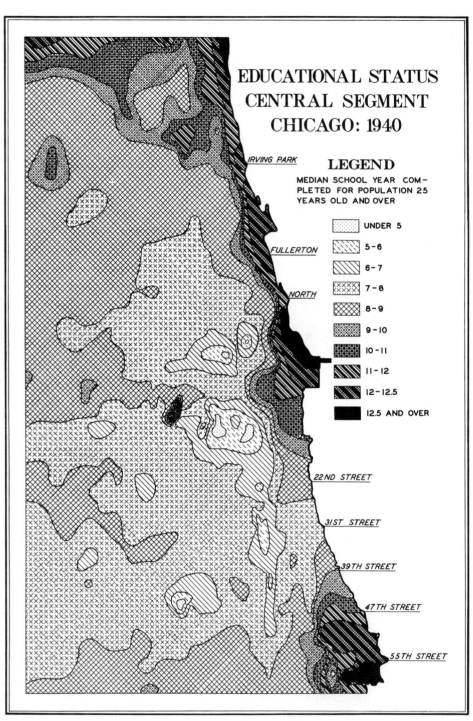

Figure 8–21. An isoline map constructed from census tract data.

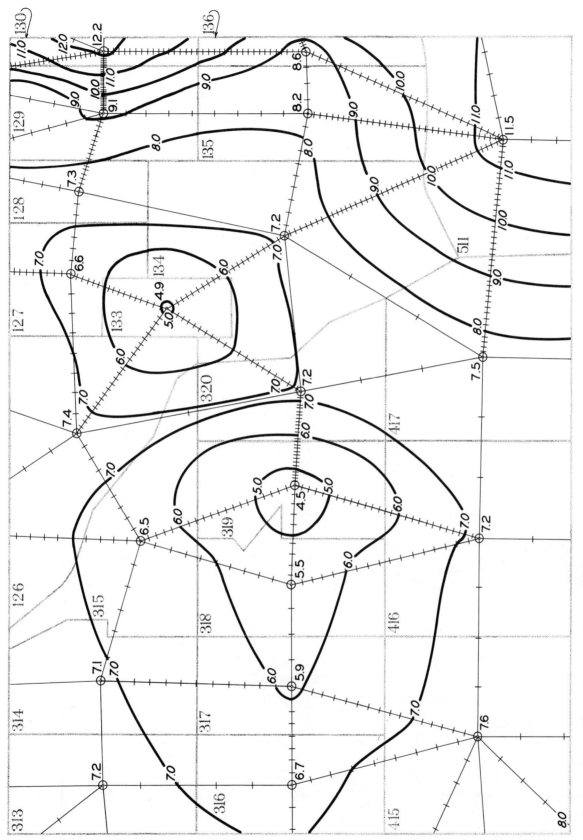

Figure 8–22. Procedure in constructing isolines from areal data. See text for specific directions.

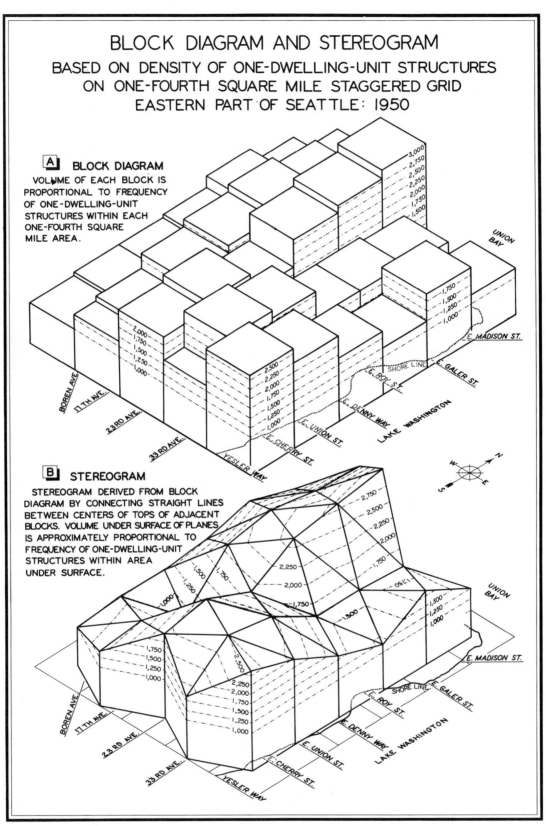

Figure 8–23. Illustration of the statistical surface concept as it relates to isopleth mapping. See text for further elucidation.

used here in the mathematical sense, referring to the vertical and horizontal "steps" of the histogram) as indicated in Chapter 6. If the class intervals are not equal, the height of the "steps" cannot be proportional to the frequencies of the several class intervals since in a histogram the height of a column divided by the length of its base is proportional to its frequency. It follows that the value of a subarea on a patterned map is proportional to the volume of a prismatic column under the subarea. Furthermore, unless all the subareas are of equal size, the heights of the columns above the base plane cannot be proportional to the values of the subareas. In actual practice, of course, the subareas are not usually equal, and hence the height is proportional to the value divided by the base area.

Although these assumptions are useful for certain purposes, there is another approach that approximates more closely most empirical conditions. This approach is based on the logic and assumptions of the frequency polygon rather than the histogram. The area under a frequency polygon that has been constructed by connecting the midpoints of the tops of histogram rectangles is approximately equal to the area under the histogram for any class interval, with the exception of a modal or antimodal interval.[33]

The relationship is also applicable to rate maps. It will be observed that the volume under the stereogram surface in Figure 8–23, for example, made up of planes connecting centroidal points on the top surface of the prismatic block diagram, is approximately equal to the volume of the block dia-

gram, and with the same exceptions of modal or antimodal intervals. It may be noted here that for each antimode there must be two modes (assuming a recession in values at the extremes) and that the biases tend to be compensating up to the limit of a single mode and antimode. A multimodal curve or surface is no more biased than a unimodal distribution. It follows that little distortion of the representation of values (i.e., statistical measurability) accrues if a block diagram is transformed into a stereogram by connecting the centroids of adjacent subareas with straight lines forming sloping planes. In addition, under the assumption that empirical agreement with data is improved by interpolation between centers, the surface of the stereogram is a better representation of the data than is the block diagram.

Although the stereogram devised on the basis of rates has no "real" or observable counterpart—as the "elevations" are hypothetical constructs designed to depict the varying rates and not the result of measurements at particular points—the hypothetical elevations on the surface of the stereogram may be represented on a vertical projection by a series of curves representing equal "elevations" or, actually, equal rates. If it is not smoothed, the stereogram surface is represented by a configuration of intersecting planes (Figure 8–23). Equal elevation is represented by a plane parallel to the base of the stereogram, and such a plane will cut the stereogram surface in a series of straight-line segments that form polygons in the vertical projection (Figure 8–24).

These polygons can be smoothed by precise techniques, but errors involved in the various assumptions leading to their construction are sufficiently great to make precise smoothing comparable to computations beyond the limit of significant digits in elementary mathematics (Figure 8–24).[34] To obviate a false appearance of accuracy and at the same time reduce chance fluctuations in the data, freehand smoothing can be used. As a test of the reliability, four draftsmen independently smoothed freehand a given polygon and the results were compared. The four curves drawn by the draftsmen were superimposed to show general agreement or disagreement, and the areas were measured with a planimeter. In light of this experiment, it was found that the variations were relatively small involving a maximum difference in area of less than 1%.

The vertical dimension on an isopleth map is as-

---

[33] The mode is a maximum. That is, any point, any area of uniform height, any histogram interval, or any other graphically described position surrounded on all sides by positions of lesser value is called a "mode." An "antimode" is a minimum in the same sense. An antimode is surrounded on all sides by greater values. Distributions may have any number of modes and antimodes. In two-dimensional presentation, if the data recede at both extremes, there is always one more mode than antimodes. If the data increase at the extremes there is one more antimode than modes, and if the data increase at one extreme and recede at the other, there are the same number of modes as antimodes. In three-dimensional presentation the same relationship between modes and antimodes usually obtains.

[34] The contour polygons need not be drawn in actual practice. The vertices can be connected with a smooth curve without first completing the edges of the polygons, which are not used in the final drawing anyway.

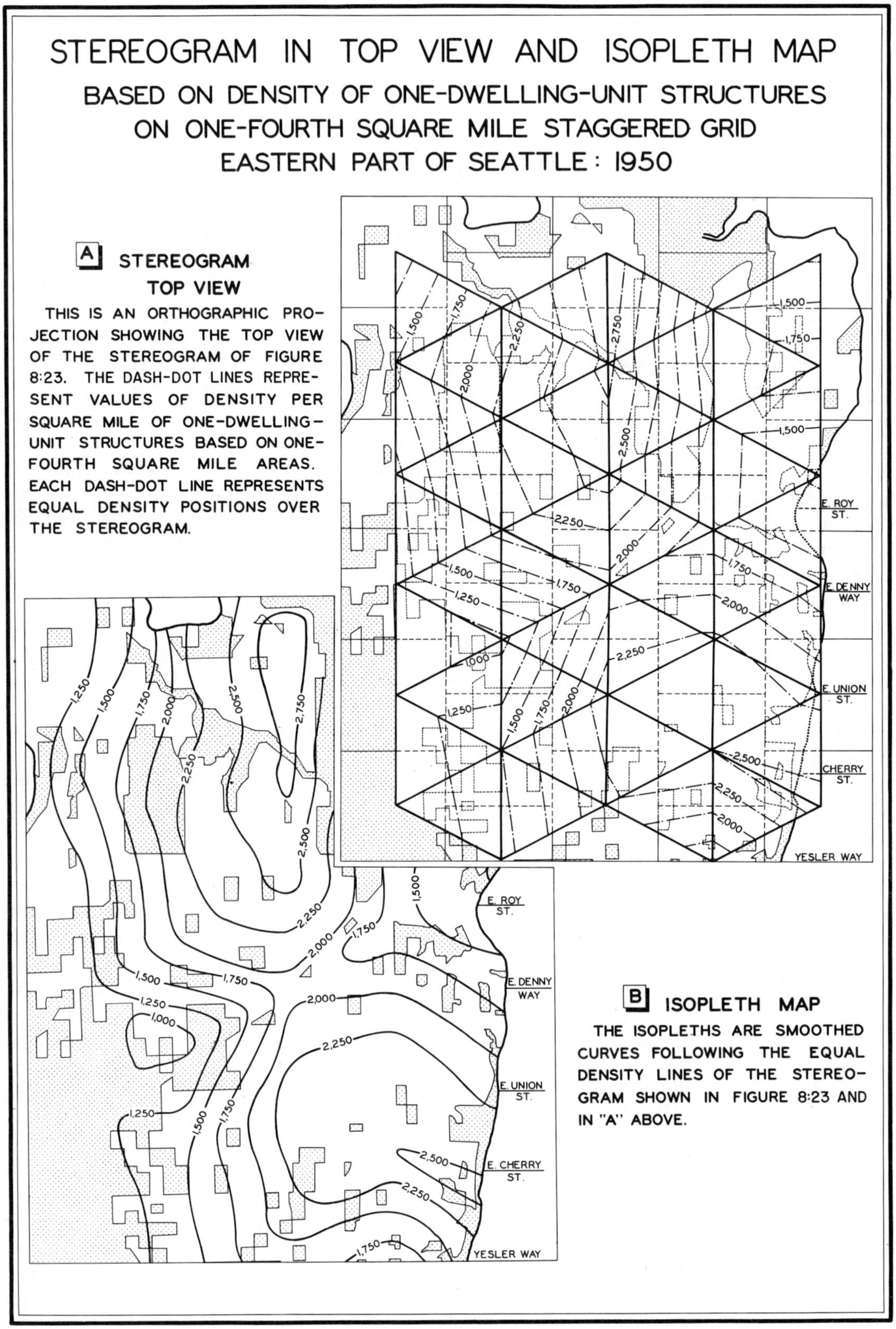

STEREOGRAM IN TOP VIEW AND ISOPLETH MAP
BASED ON DENSITY OF ONE-DWELLING-UNIT STRUCTURES
ON ONE-FOURTH SQUARE MILE STAGGERED GRID
EASTERN PART OF SEATTLE: 1950

A STEREOGRAM
TOP VIEW

THIS IS AN ORTHOGRAPHIC PRO-
JECTION SHOWING THE TOP VIEW
OF THE STEREOGRAM OF FIGURE
8:23. THE DASH-DOT LINES REPRE-
SENT VALUES OF DENSITY PER
SQUARE MILE OF ONE-DWELLING-
UNIT STRUCTURES BASED ON ONE-
FOURTH SQUARE MILE AREAS.
EACH DASH-DOT LINE REPRESENTS
EQUAL DENSITY POSITIONS OVER
THE STEREOGRAM.

B ISOPLETH MAP

THE ISOPLETHS ARE SMOOTHED
CURVES FOLLOWING THE EQUAL
DENSITY LINES OF THE STEREO-
GRAM SHOWN IN FIGURE 8:23 AND
IN "A" ABOVE.

*Figure 8–24. Top view of stereogram as presented in preceding chart and sequential devel-
opment of isopleth map.*

sumed to vary linearly from isoline to isoline and on the basis of this assumption, approximate values for any desired area of the map can be computed. By using a planimeter the desired areas can be measured and average heights determined. The value for a specified area is the area multipled by its average height in terms of the isolines that cover it.

Frequently, the characteristic portrayed on an isopleth map is expressed as a ratio of two nonareal units, such as dollars per person (income), persons per household, or some other combination of social or economic factors. When isoline maps are used to delimit these higher-ordered characteristics, the immediate relationship to area is obscured. The fact that a map is used implies some inherent association between the characteristics and their distribution over an area. The association can be expressed mathematically and hence manipulated statistically if each characteristic is related separately to the area. Since reciprocal values for any characteristic do not alter the isopleth placement, any line that represents a value per unit area can be said to represent also a unit area per unit value. That is, a line representing 100 persons per square mile can also be said to represent one one-hundredths square miles ($1/100$ mi^2) per person. Multiplication of isopleth line values is accomplished by superimposing the corresponding isolines on the same map. If one of the sets of isolines is then expressed as a reciprocal relationship with area, the superimposed lines will cancel out the areal unit, leaving the ratio as an expression between characteristics. To illustrate this point, a map may be prepared with isolines showing single-unit dwelling structures per square mile. A corresponding map might show number of dollars valuation of one-dwelling-unit structures per square mile. Both of these ratios are compatible with the usual concept of areal based, three-dimensional isopleth maps. If one of them, let us say, dwelling units per square mile, is designated as a reciprocal—square miles per dwelling unit—the intersection of an isopleth describing $100,000/per mi^2 with an isopleth indicating 0.085 mi^2 per dwelling unit represents 100,000 times 0.085 or $8,500 per one-dwelling-unit structure at that point. It should be pointed out that different-sized areal bases for calculating the location of isolines will give different patterns for

the same data. For the approximation to be as statistically measurable as possible, it is important that the areas used to compute the isolines for both characteristics be of the same size and shape. The isopleth map showing mean value of one-dwelling-unit structures in the eastern part of Seattle in 1950 (Figure 8–25) was constructed in this way.

MAPS WITH GRAPHIC FORMS SUPERIMPOSED[35]

Frequently, various graphic forms such as bars, columns, curves, flow lines, and pictorial symbols are superimposed on base maps. Where geographic location is of primary importance, one or more simplified graphs on a map may be very effective. Figure 8–26 presents a series of deviation-column charts that portray trends in urban suicide rates by nine "Geographic divisions" as defined by the United States Bureau of the Census. The baseline for all of the nine charts represents unweighted means of suicide rates for all 93 cities for six triennial periods from 1909–1911 to 1959–1961. Also, means were computed for the cities located in each of the nine geographic divisions. The differences between the means for all cities and the means for cities in each geographic divisions are portrayed by the nine deviation-column charts. It will be observed, for example, that large cities in the New England Geographic Division rank consistently below the national urban average in suicide, whereas cities in the Pacific Geographic Division rank consistently above. Cities in the East and West North Central Divisions deviate very little either above or below the national urban mean in suicide.

Figure 8–27 is a typical flow map showing the major streams of net migration of college and university undergraduates attending public institutions in eight regions as defined by the United States Office of Education. The thickness of the arrows from one region to another is proportional to the number of students. It will be observed that the Mideast Region is the source of seven large streams of net migration, with the heaviest streams going to the Great Lakes and to the Southeast Regions. Also, it will be seen that there is a large net movement of students to the Southwest from the following three regions: Mideast, Great Lakes, and Southwest.

---

[35] For additional examples of this type of map, see Chapter 10.

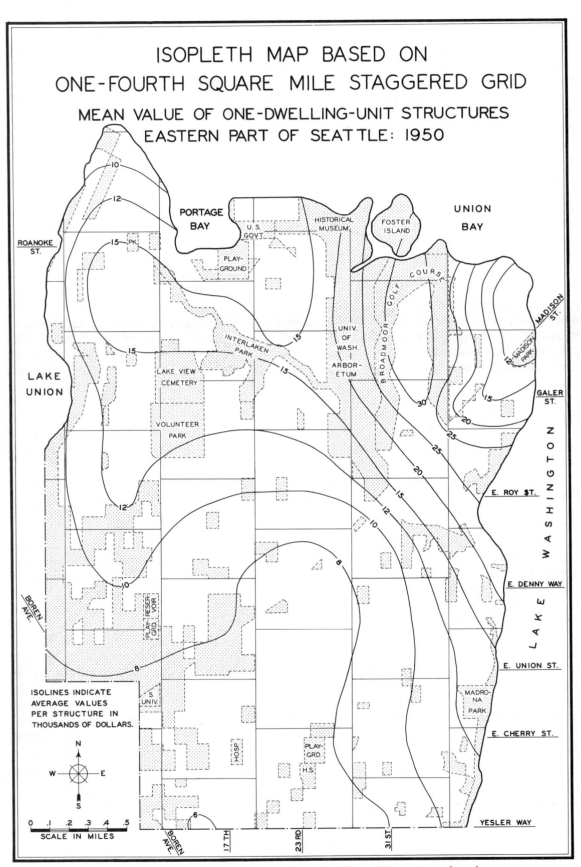

Figure 8–25. Isopleth map showing mean value of one–dwelling–unit structures based on one–fourth square mile staggered grid.

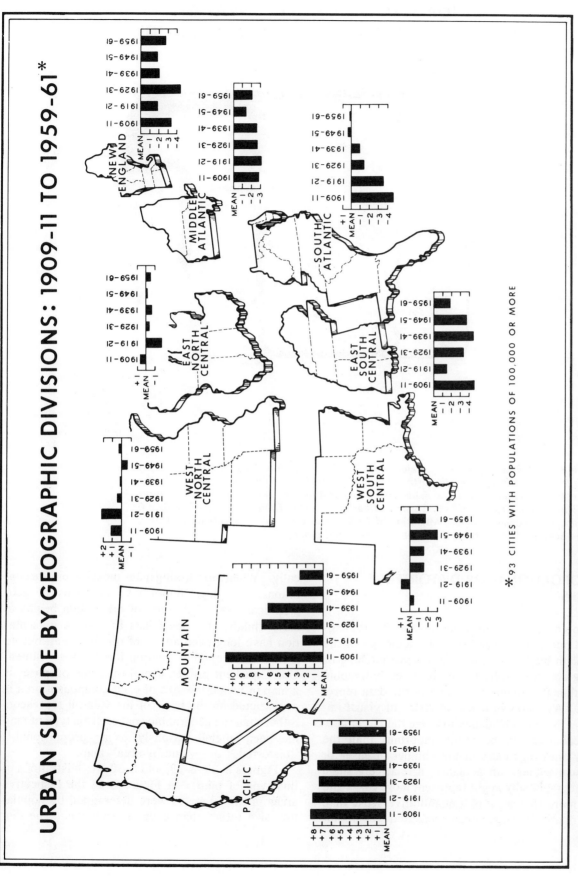

URBAN SUICIDE BY GEOGRAPHIC DIVISIONS: 1909-11 TO 1959-61*

Figure 8-26. Series of deviation-column charts superimposed on a map. (From Calvin F. Schmid and Stanton E. Schmid, Crime in the State of Washington, Olympia: Law and Justice Planning Office, Planning and Community Affairs Agency, 1972, p. 366.)

*93 CITIES WITH POPULATIONS OF 100,000 OR MORE

MAJOR STREAMS OF NET MIGRATION
UNDERGRADUATE STUDENTS - PUBLIC INSTITUTIONS: 1963

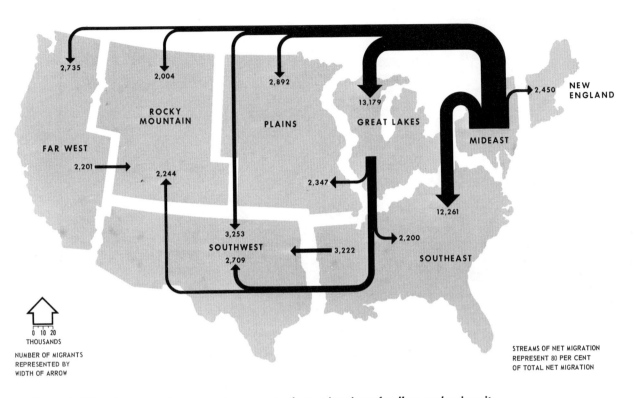

Figure 8–27. A flow map showing major streams of net migration of college and university undergraduates attending public institutions in eight regions of the United States. In this connection, a comparison can be made with a similar flow map in three–dimensional form. See Figure 10–38 (From Charles S. Gossman, Charles E. Nobbe, Theresa J. Patricelli, Calvin F. Schmid, and Thomas E. Steahr, Migration of College and University Students in the United States, *Seattle: University of Washington Press, 1968, p. 43.)*

PROPORTIONAL OR DISTORTED MAPS

It was pointed out in a previous section of this chapter that one of the three major shortcomings of the choropleth map is the practice of crosshatching or shading an area purely on the basis of geographic size rather than numerical value of the data represented. As a consequence, in terms of visual impression there is a tendency to judge the larger geographical areas to be more important than the smaller ones regardless of the number of cases or numerical values. In actuality, a relatively small area geographically might represent more cases and be far more significant in a quantitative sense than many relatively large areas measured geographi-

cally. When interpreting maps most people are conditioned to judge importance in terms of geographical size. This type of orientation begins in early childhood. Specialists in graphic presentation have long been aware of this problem, but no generally acceptable solution has been developed. One expedient proven useful for some purposes is a map in which the size of each component area is constructed on the basis of the value it represents rather than the geographic space. This type of map has been labeled variously, as a "proportional," "distorted," or "value-by-area" map.

Figures 8–28, 8–29, and 8–30 are illustrations of this type of map. In Figure 8–28 the respective areas of the 50 states were determined by population size rather than geographical size. The discrepancies between the conventional map and the one based on population are obvious. In 1975 California had a total area (land and water) of 158,693 mi² and a population of 21,185,000, whereas the corresponding figures for New York were 49,576 mi² and a population of 18,120,000. Montana had a total area (147,138 mi²) almost three times as large as New York. New York's population was over 24 times that of Montana. The area of Alaska was 3.8 times that of California, but California's population was over 60 times that of Alaska. Wyoming's area was almost twice that of New York, but New York's population was over 48 times as large.

Figure 8–29 is another example of a proportional map based on farm production (1974 cash receipts from farm products). Viewed in a geographic context, the outstanding size of Iowa, Illinois, and other Midwestern states contrasts significantly with the small size of New York, Pennsylvania, West Virginia, Nevada, Utah, Wyoming, New Mexico, and Alaska.

To facilitate comparison, a proportional map for the state of Washington based on population has been placed in juxtaposition with a map based on land area in Figure 8–30. Because of lack of familiarity with a state map, a proportional map even among residents could lose much of its impact if a conventional map were not made available for ready comparison. In the case of the United States a proportional map is almost invariably presented separately on the assumption that most people are reasonably familiar with the conventional geographical map of the United States. Washington State's King County, in which Seattle is situated, has by far the largest population of the 39 counties (935,014 in 1960 and 1,156,633 in 1970). Its land area is 2128 mi². King County comprised 32.8% of the population in 1960 and 33.9% in 1970. The total

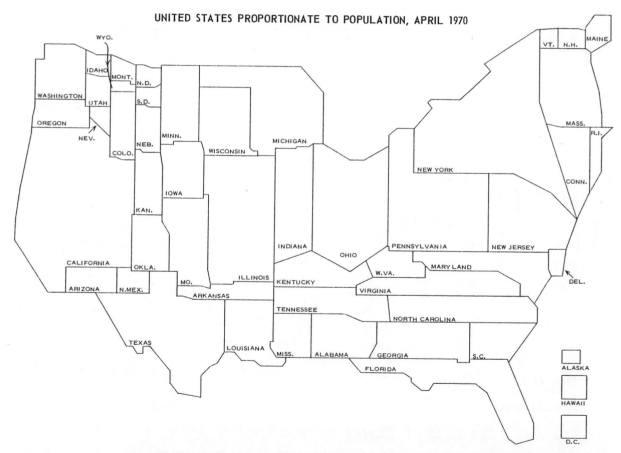

Figure 8–28. Illustration of a proportional map based on population. (Prepared by Division of Research and Statistics, State of Ohio Bureau of Employment Services, Columbus, Ohio, 1970.)

population of the state was 2,853,214 in 1960 and 3,409,169 in 1970. In land area it was 66,570 mi². King County has 3.2% of the land area of the state and approximately one-third of the population. By comparison, Okanogan County is the largest county in land area (5301 mi²), almost 2.5 times that of King County. King County had a population over 36 times that of Okanogan County (25,520) in 1960 and over 44 times in 1970 (25,867). To further illustrate this point, in 1970 the land area of Ferry County (2202 mi²) was about the same as that of King County (2128 mi²), but the population of King County was over 316 times as large.

Perhaps it should be noted that although the proportional map is an attempt to develop a rational adjustment to the problem of portraying areas on the basis of the numerical values they represent, rather than on the arbitrary basis of geographical size, it does not address itself at all to another serious shortcoming of the traditional choropleth map.

As indicated previously, although an entire area may be crosshatched or shaded uniformly, the distribution of cases within an area may be very uneven. Frequently, certain portions of an area may manifest extraordinary concentrations of cases whereas other portions may be virtually devoid of cases. All calculations in Figure 8–30 were based on counties regardless of the distributional patterns of population within each of the counties. There was an implicit assumption of homogeneity that in actuality did not exist. As a case in point, the 1,156,633 people residing in King County in 1970 were distributed very unevenly within this area. For example, in the entire eastern third of King County, which extends into the Cascade Range, there were only 1280 people, representing about $\frac{1}{10}$ of 1% (0.001%) of the total population. If the population were evenly distributed there would have been approximately 385,000 people residing in this area.

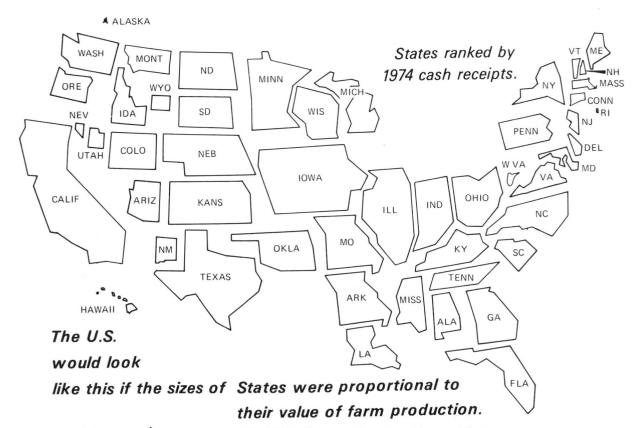

Figure 8–29. A proportional map of the United States based on the value of farm production. (From United States Department of Agriculture, Economic Research Service, The American Farmer, Washington: Government Printing Office, 1976, p. 25.)

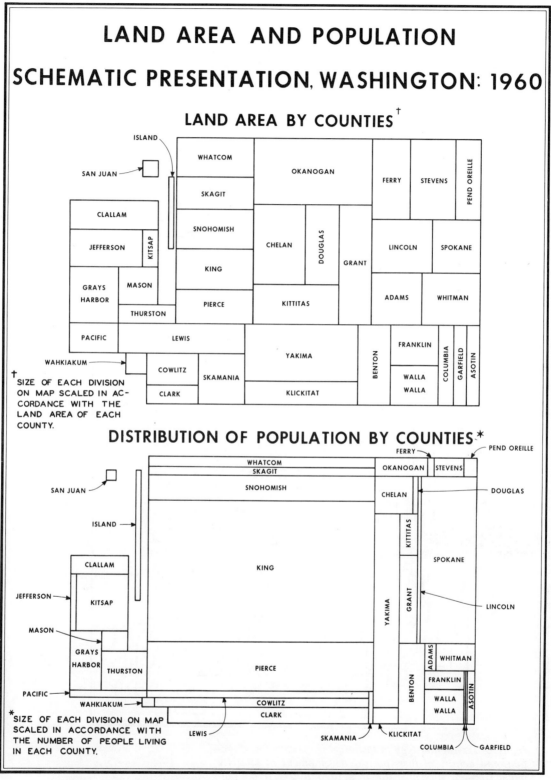

Figure 8–30. *Another illustration of a proportional map. (From Calvin F. Schmid and Stanton E. Schmid,* Growth of Cities and Towns, State of Washington, Olympia: Washington State Planning and Community Affairs Agency, *1969, p. 12.)*

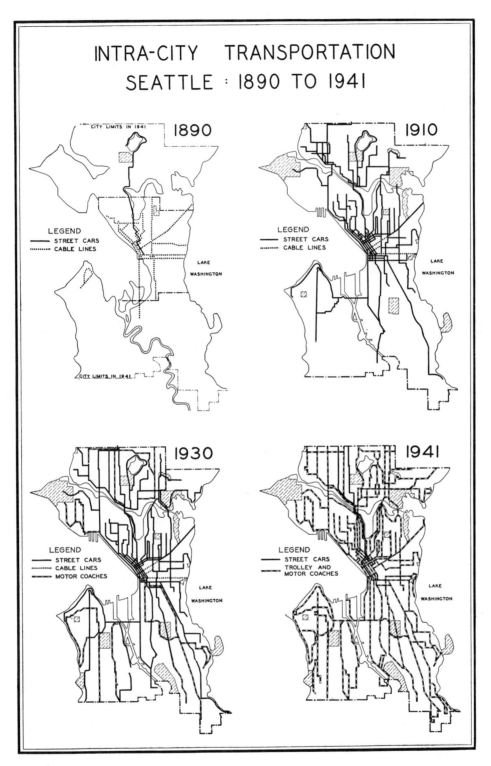

Figure 8–31. Another type of historical map. Patterns, direction, and density of lines portray development of intracity public transportation in Seattle from 1890 to 1941. (From Calvin F. Schmid, Social Trends in Seattle, *Seattle: University of Washington Press, 1944, p. 65.)*

PROMINENT METROLINA SITES AND ROUTES OF THE
AMERICAN REVOLUTION

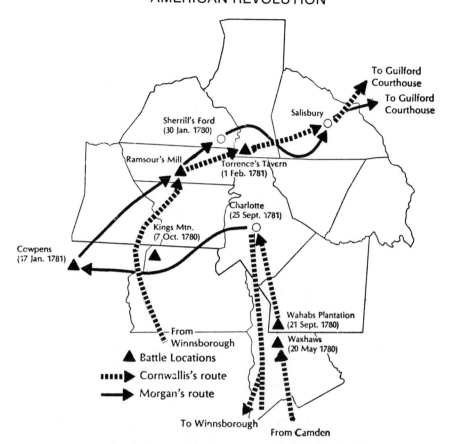

Figure 8–32. Historical map showing prominent sites and routes of troop movements in the American Revolution in Metrolina (From James W. Clay and Douglas M. Orr, Jr., Met-rolina Atlas, Chapel Hill: University of North Carolina Press, 1972, p. 16.)

NONSTATISTICAL HISTORICAL AND OTHER SCHEMATIC MAPS

Although historical and other types of schematic maps are typically nonstatistical, they nevertheless exemplify many of the characteristics and require many of the same design and construction techniques as the other maps presented in this treatise. For example, in a preceding section an historical chart (Figure 8–11) with most of the characteristics of the traditional choropleth map was discussed. This chart portrayed the territorial growth of a large city in which hatching and shading were dominant features. Figures 8–31 and 8–32 are examples of historical maps where lines and arrows rather than crosshatching are the distinctive characteristics. The emphasis in Figure 8–31 is on historical change. It shows the chronological development of intracity public transportation in Seattle from 1890 to 1941 by a series of four maps on which is superimposed a network of lines indicating the type and routes of public transportation for each of the four different dates. The different types of transportation—streetcars, cablecars, and trolley and motor coaches—are differentiated by distinctive line patterns.

Figure 8–32 shows battle locations and routes of American and British troop movements during the American Revolution in the Metrolina area of North and South Carolina.[36] The routes of troop movements are shown by arrows, the American troops by a full line, and the British by a broken line. The battles with specific dates are indicated by triangles. Three important events in this area that helped shape the outcome of the American Revolution were: (1) the early (June 13, 1780) defeat of Tories at Ramsour's Mill, (2) the defeat of the British at Kings Mountain (October 7, 1780), and (3) the American victory at Cowpens (January 17, 1781).

Figure 8–33 is a map portraying the ecological organization of a region. Specifically, it indicates

the basic patterns of metropolitan integration, including hierarchical dominance and subdominance. It will be observed that the major focal points are the supermetropolises of New York and Chicago along with the national metropolises of Kansas City, St. Louis, Cincinnati, Baltimore, and Philadelphia. Within the southern region are many less dominant but important centers. The several levels of metropolitan dominance are differentiated by distinctive symbols, and connecting lines emphasize the primary patterns of integration among all the metropolitan centers.

---

[36] See footnote 21 in this chapter for a more detailed description of Metrolina.

METROPOLITAN ORGANIZATION OF SOUTH
ORDERS OF DOMINANCE AND MAJOR LINES OF INTEGRATION

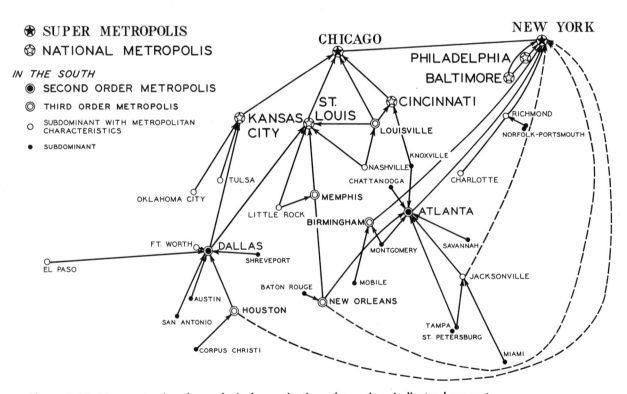

Figure 8–33. Map portraying the ecological organization of a region. Indicates how metropolitan communities are interrelated, including the various levels of dominance and subdominance (Map redrawn from Rupert B. Vance and Nicholas J. Demerath (eds.), The Urban South, *Chapel Hill: The University of North Carolina Press, 1954, Chapter 6 "Metropolitan Dominance and Integration.")*

SEVEN REPRESENTATIVE SERVICE AREAS
BATAVIA, NEW YORK

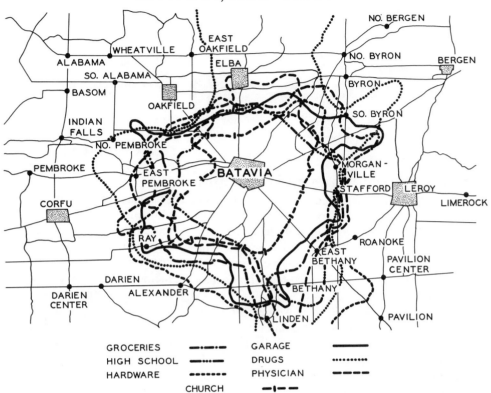

GROCERIES	—·—·—	GARAGE	———
HIGH SCHOOL	—···—	DRUGS	··········
HARDWARE	■■■■■■	PHYSICIAN	————
		CHURCH	—·■■—

Figure 8–34. A technique for delineating the rural community. (Map redrawn from Dwight Sanderson, Rural Sociology and Rural Social Organization, *New York: John Wiley and Sons, 1942, p. 277.)*

Figure 8–34 is an illustration of a useful and meaningful technique for delineating a rural community in terms of objective criteria. Every rural community has a focal center that extends its social and economic influence into the surrounding area. In a basic sense it is an integrating force since families in the area are oriented toward the center mainly because of the services it provides. The larger churches, schools, grocery stores, lodges, medical complexes, the one hardware store, drugstore, theater, and garage, are located there. Figure 8–34 delimits territorially the rural community of Batavia in terms of seven different service indexes.

CHAPTER NINE

PICTORIAL CHARTS

PICTORIAL GRAPHS ARE USED PRIMARILY because of their popular appeal. To the technically trained person they add very little or nothing to what might be conveyed by a well-designed conventional graphic form. To the layman or child who has only a slight understanding, perhaps even dislike, for statistical charts, pictorial techniques may be extremely effective.

Because of their simplicity as well as their dramatic and interest-creating qualities, pictorial charts are far superior to conventional graphic forms as a medium of popular communication. In addition, there seems to be some evidence that facts portrayed in pictorial charts are remembered longer than facts presented in tables or nonpictorial graphs.

More than for any other type of graphic form, the design and construction of pictorial charts demand both an artistic sense and a thorough understanding of the principles and rationale of charting statistical data. Furthermore, there are more serious pitfalls involved in preparing pictorial charts than most other types of charts. It is important to recognize at the outset that certain types of pictorial forms and techniques violate the basic standards of acceptable form and practice, and these, of course, should be carefully avoided.

In general, there are four basic types of charts in which pictorial symbols are used. The two distinguishing criteria for these four types of pictorial charts are purpose and emphasis. It is, of course, correct to say that the fundamental purpose of all types of pictorial symbols is to enhance the popular appeal of a chart as well as its effectiveness by means of artistic expression. In some pictorial charts, however, the symbols or pictures may represent units of measurement, whereas in other types they may function merely as embellishment.

The four types of pictorial charts are: (1) charts in which the size of the pictorial symbols is made in proportion to the values portrayed, (2) pictorial unit graphs in which each symbol represents a definite and uniform value, (3) cartoon and sketch charts in which the basic graphic form, such as a curve or bar, is portrayed as a picture, and (4) charts with pictorial embellishments ranging from a single pictorial filler to elaborate and detailed pictorial backgrounds.

PICTORIAL SYMBOLS OF PROPORTIONATE SIZE

The least satisfactory type of pictorial chart, but unfortunately one of the most common, is characterized by two or more symbols drawn in proportion to the values represented. For example, to compare the sizes of navies of two countries by this method, two symbols of warships drawn in proportion to the respective total tonnage of each navy are placed in juxtaposition. Seemingly, a chart of this kind possesses the virtues of simplicity, graphic appeal, and easy comparison. However, such is not the case. It is extremely difficult, if not sometimes impossible, to make intelligible comparisons based on varying sizes of complicated symbols, such as human beings, ships, automobiles, houses, domestic animals, and the like. As indicated in Chapter 4, the basis of comparing geometric forms may be either area or volume.

Paradoxically, if this type of chart were designed in accordance with correct mathematical principles, it would lose its more impressive and dramatic qualities, and as a consequence would seldom, if ever, be used. In other words, its use is confined almost exclusively to those instances based on incorrect standards of comparison.

There seem to be three classes of users who construct pictorial charts of this kind: (1) those unaware of the shortcomings of such charts, including the novice and dilettante as well as presumably trained and experienced statisticians, (2) propagandists who consider charts of this kind an effective technique for disseminating and implanting ideas, regardless of distortions and misrepresentations that might be involved, and (3) persons who may possess some degree of understanding of the weaknesses of such charts but carelessly assume, sometimes perhaps against their better judgment, that the qualities of simplicity and graphic appeal outweigh other considerations in popular presentation.

Illustration of Misleading Pictorial Chart

To point out the weaknesses and misuses of this graphic form, a chart appearing in the *Scientific American* is used for illustrative purposes. It will be observed from Figure 9–1 that the heights of the pictorial symbols are drawn in accordance with the values on the ordinal scale without regard to the resultant areas or volumes of the symbols.

The chart purports to show that the:

Size of the labor force with respect to the total population has gradually increased. The numbers at the left side of this diagram are millions of people. The large . . . [pictorial symbols] represent the total population; the smaller . . . [pictorial symbols], the labor force. Beside each of the figures is the number of people that it symbolizes. Beneath each of these numbers for the labor force is the percentage of the total population that it represents.

As pointed out previously, it is common practice in graphic presentation to construct geometric forms proportional to the values represented. The bases of comparison may be one-dimensional (distance), two-dimensional (area), or three-dimensional (vol-

ume). For example, the column chart is a one-dimensional graphic form, with the length of the columns indicating specific values of the categories represented. Although columns necessarily possess width, it is the respective length of each column that determines the magnitudes or values of a series of categories. Moreover, this in no way violates the areal character of the columns; since the width of each column is the same the lengths are directly proportional to their areas. It is much easier for the eye to appraise the comparative values of a one-dimensional form than of areal or cubic forms. Moreover, when two- and three-dimensional forms are irregular in shape, the problems of comparison become more complicated.

In Figure 9–1 the ordinal scale is virtually meaningless and irrelevant with respect to the areas or volumes of the symbols. Obviously, when the heights of pictures of this kind are increased, it is necessary to increase the widths in the same ratio in order to maintain "normal" proportions. But neither area nor volume bears a simple and direct relationship to height. For example, in 1900 the height of the larger symbol is 2.75 times that of the smaller one, but in area it is 7.56 times, and in volume 20.80 times that of the smaller one. Similarly, comparative discrepancies for the respective smaller and larger symbols for 1920, 1930, 1940, and 1950 are approximately the same as for 1900. Or, for example, if a comparison were made between the labor force symbols for 1900 and for 1950, it will

Figure 9–1. Originally designed chart in which the height of the symbols was the sole criterion. It is obvious that neither the area nor the volume of the symbols bears a simple and direct relationship to height.

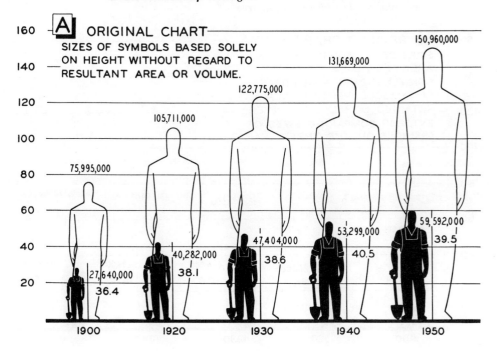

be observed that the one for 1950 is slightly more than twice as high but more than four times as large in area and eight times as large in volume.[1]

Mathematical Relationships Between Areas and Volumes of Pictorial Symbols

The relationship between the areas of comparable pictorial symbols can be expressed mathematically as follows.

First

$$Area = Height \times Width$$

To increase the area m times, keeping the same proportion between width and height,

$$mA = (kh)(kw) = k^2hw$$

Then

$$k^2 = (mA/hw) = m \quad \text{and} \quad k = \sqrt{m}$$

Hence, increasing the area m times while maintaining the same areal proportions requires increasing height by $\sqrt{m}$, irrespective of what the relation between the height and width might be. Also, increasing the height by k implies increasing width by k or increasing the area by k^2.

Similar logic and procedure are followed for increasing the volume of symbols while maintaining constant proportions.

$$Volume = Height \times Width \times Depth$$

To increase the volume m times and keep proportions constant,

$$mV = (kh)(kw)(kd) = k^3hwd$$

or

$$k^3 = (mV/hwd) = m$$

Therefore

$$k = \sqrt[3]{m}$$

Hence, increasing the volume m times and keeping the same cubic proportions requires increasing the height by $\sqrt[3]{m}$, irrespective of what the relations between height, width, or depth might be. On the other hand, increasing height by k also implies increasing the width and depth by k or increasing the volume by k^3.

It will be observed that the symbols in Figure 9–2 were reconstructed on the basis of comparable areas. First, square roots were obtained for each of the 10 figures in both series. Second, the square roots of all the figures in both the labor force and population figures were divided by the square root of the smallest figure (27,640,000) to establish a basis for deriving relative sizes of the symbols. By fixing the square root of 27,640,000 as one unit, then on a comparable basis 40,282,000 is 1.21 units,

---

[1] In case it might be assumed that this type of chart is seldom if ever, used at the present time, the reader will find a recent example in S. L. Blum, "Mapping Resources in Municipal Solid Waste," *Science,* **191** (4228) (February 20, 1976), pp. 669–675 (Figure 4).

Figure 9–2. Original chart redrawn so that all of the symbols are comparable with respect to area.

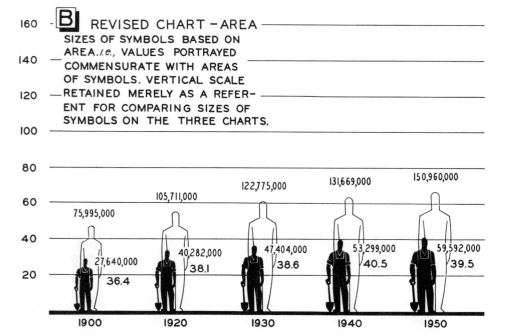

47,404,000 is 1.31 units, and so on; 75,995,000 is 1.66 units, 105,711,000 is 1.96 units, and so forth.

Similarly, the sizes of the symbols in Figure 9–3 were derived in accordance with the same procedure, but, of course, cube roots were derived first for each of the 10 figures in the two series. Second, the cube roots of each of the figures were divided by the cube root of 27,640,000 representing one unit. The ratios for the cube roots of the other figures are 1.13 for 40,282,200, 1.2 for 47,404,000, 1.56 for 105,711,000, 1.76 for 150,696,000, and so on.

Although the symbols in Figures 9–2 and 9–3 have been redesigned correctly on the respective bases of area or volume, they have lost much of their popular appeal and spectacular qualities. Moreover, even with the most meticulous scrutiny and mental effort, it is virtually impossible to interpret correctly comparative values for either series of symbols.

Appropriate Graphic Forms as Substitutes for Misleading Pictorial Charts

In charting data such as those discussed in the foregoing sections there are several appropriate and

[2] The preceding discussion, including Figures 9–1, 9–2, and 9–3, was extracted from Calvin F. Schmid, "What Price Pictorial Charts," *Estadistica, Journal of the Inter-American Statistical Institute,* **14** (50) (March 1956), 12–25.

"correct" graphic forms from which a selection could be made. They include: (1) grouped-column chart, (2) subdivided-column chart, (3) arithmetic line graph, (4) multiple-surface or stratum chart, (5) semilogarithmic graph, and (6) pictorial unit chart. Of course, in addition to these six different types of charts, there are others that could be used, but they either would require a transposition of the basic data into percentages or for some reason might be considered less satisfactory.[2]

Special Cases of Three-dimensional Objects Proportional to Values Represented

In spite of the caveats indicated in the preceding discussion, it is permissible to use pictorial symbols proportional to the values represented, when three-dimensional objects are treated as one- or two-dimensional objects. There are rare instances in which one or two of the dimensions in a three-dimensional object are constant or are perceived to be constant. Figures 9–4 and 9–5 are cases in point. Although a cigarette is a three-dimensional object, it is symbolized as one-dimensional in Figure 9–4. Two of the dimensions—width and depth (diameter)—in a cigarette are perceived to be constant while the only variable dimension is length. In Figure 9–4 the cigarette symbols of varying length simulate columns in a familiar and acceptable graphic form. Figure 9–4 may be categorized as a

Figure 9–3. Original chart redrawn so that all of the symbols are comparable with respect to volume.

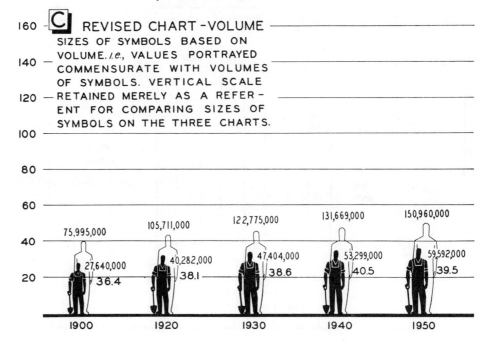

column chart or quasihistogram since it does not fulfill the essential statistical requirements of a histogram. It portrays the proportion of the population for certain age groups who smoke cigarettes. The length of each symbol is commensurate with the percentage indicated for each age group.

Another illustration of a three-dimensional object where one of the dimensions is perceived to be constant is shown by Figure 9–5. Although a metallic dollar is actually three-dimensional, most people perceive its thickness to be subordinated to areal size. As a mental image it becomes a disk—a two-dimensional object. The "shrinking" value of the dollar as a consequence of inflation implies a diminution in area, but not in thickness. Accordingly, the monetary symbols in Figure 9–5 are treated as two-dimensional objects. The areas of the four symbols have been drawn commensurate with the actual and projected purchasing power of the dollar.

PICTORIAL SYMBOLS PRIMARILY REPRESENTING COUNTING UNITS

The rationale of the second type of pictorial chart has a much more logical and, in terms of graphic presentation, more acceptable basis than the preceding type. Values do not vary according to the size of the symbol. In this type of pictorial chart

each symbol is of uniform size and of specified value. They are primarily counting units. If, for example, a chart of this kind were used to portray income and expenditures of an industrial corporation over a period of years, the basic monetary symbol could be designed to represent $100,000. Accordingly, in constructing the chart, two symbols would indicate $200,000; three symbols, $300,000; four symbols, $400,000; and so on.

The logical relationship between a pictorial chart of this kind and a simple bar or column chart is clear and direct. It will be recalled from Chapter 4 that in the conventional bar or column chart, values are measured by calibrations on a scale. In the bar or column chart, a more-or-less arbitrarily chosen distance is used to indicate a definite value. For example, if $\frac{1}{4}$ in. on the scale is equivalent to 100 people, then $\frac{1}{2}$ in. would indicate 200 people; $\frac{3}{4}$ in., 300 people; 1 in., 400 people; and so forth. It can be deduced readily that on the pictographic chart each symbol in a fundamental sense is analogous to a mensurational unit on the scale of a bar or column chart.

Historical Background of Pictorial Unit Chart

Perhaps more than any other single person, Dr. Otto Neurath has been responsible for the creation

Figure 9–4. A pictorial chart in which a three–dimensional object is treated as one–dimensional. Since the width and depth (diameter) of a cigarette are perceived as constant, the symbols are treated as one–dimensional (length). (From United States Department of Agriculture, 1973 Handbook of Agricultural Charts, *Agricultural Handbook No. 455, October 1973, p. 150.)*

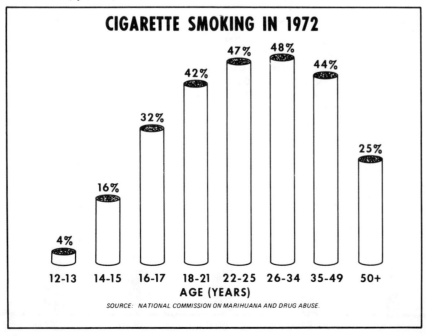

CIGARETTE SMOKING IN 1972

4% — 12-13
16% — 14-15
32% — 16-17
42% — 18-21
47% — 22-25
48% — 26-34
44% — 35-49
25% — 50+

AGE (YEARS)

SOURCE: NATIONAL COMMISSION ON MARIHUANA AND DRUG ABUSE.

THE SHRINKING DOLLAR

CONTINUING UPSWEEP OF INFLATION HAS DRASTICALLY
REDUCED FIXED RETIREMENT INCOMES

1950
100
CENTS

1970
62
CENTS

1960
80
CENTS

1980
46
CENTS

Figure 9–5. A pictorial chart in two–dimensional form. The respective areas of the four symbols are commensurate with the real value of the dollar. Since the item represented (metallic dollar) is essentially two–dimensional (disc-shaped), it is permissible to use areal symbols as a basis of comparison. Incidentally, since 1970, when this chart was published, the rate of inflation has been considerably greater than economists had forecasted at that time. (From Calvin F. Schmid, An Evaluative Survey of Faculty Retirement System, University of Washington, *Seattle: The Ad Hoc Committee on Retirement, 1970, p. 11.)*

and development of the modern pictographic technique for portraying statistical and other types of data. Dr. Neurath's endeavors date back to 1923, when he first developed a series of pictorial charts for a housing exhibit in the city of Vienna under the auspices of the Austrian Housing and Garden Plot Association. In 1924 this exhibition was transferred into the famous *Gesellschafts-und Wirthschaftsmuseum in Wien* (The Social and Economic Museum in Vienna).

In 1925, when discussing the Gesellschafts-und Wirtschaftsmuseum in Vienna, Neurath made the

following comments: ". . . .through its neutrality, and its independence of separate languages, visual education is superior to word education. *Words divide, pictures unite. . . . to remember simplified pictures is better than to forget accurate figures.*"[3] (Italics are Neurath's.)

It should be pointed out that Neurath was not actually the first person to use the pictorial unit type of chart. In 1914 Willard C. Brinton, in his *Graphic Methods for Presenting Facts* (pp. 39–40), presented illustrations of the pictorial unit chart. In illustrating the rationale of this type of chart, he selected an example showing the increase in passengers carried on American railroads from 1899 to 1911 and pointed out that "it was not a larger passenger, but more passengers, that the railroads carried." In his *Graphic Presentation,* published in 1939, Brinton reproduced three pictorial unit charts originally published in 1916 and 1917 (pp. 123–124). When

---

[3] Marie Neurath and Robert S. Cohen, eds., *Otto Neurath Empiricism and Sociology,* Boston: D. Reidel Publishing Company, 1973, pp. 217–220. This book includes a substantial amount of biographical material about Otto Neurath, excerpts from his writings, and a list of his works, as well as discussions of the Vienna Circle.

Neurath developed his system he was unaware of Brinton's work. The history of the pictorial unit chart is a good example of what the anthropologists call "parallel invention." Brinton, however, did not pursue the development of the pictorial graph technique beyond his initial exposition.

Besides creating an elaborate pictorial technique of portraying statistical and other data, Neurath later directed his energies toward the development of an auxiliary international picture language—"a helping language as he called it—to be used along with other languages according to circumstances."[4]

The basic symbols of his system were called "isotypes" (I-nternational S-ystem O-f TY-pographic P-icture E-ducation). From 1934, when he left Vienna, until his death, Neurath devoted much time to the development of his system and to the philosophy of international picture language.[5]

In addition to Dr. Neurath himself, several of his former associates, particularly Dr. Rudolph Modley, have exerted a strong influence in the popularization and diffusion of the pictorial unit chart in the United States. Dr. Modley's book *How to Use Pictorial Statistics* (1937) has proved to be a very useful manual in this field. With certain revisions and additions, portions of this book have been reproduced in another volume prepared in collaboration with Dyno Lowenstein, entitled *Pictographs and Graphs* (1952). Also, these men and their associates in Pictorial Statistics, Inc. (1934, renamed Pictographic Corporation in 1940), through the preparation of hundreds of pictorial unit charts on a commercial basis for governmental agencies, newspapers, magazines, and books, literally brought this type of chart into virtually every American home. During the past few decades the pictorial unit chart has lost the widespread popularity that it enjoyed in the 1930s.

Basic Principles in Designing a Pictorial Unit Chart

In the construction of a pictorial unit chart, certain basic rules and principles should be observed:[6]

1. The symbols should be self-explanatory. If the chart is concerned with ships, the symbol should be an outline of a ship.

2. All the symbols on the chart should represent a definite unit of value. Each symbol usually represents a convenient sum of individuals.

3. The chart should be made as simple and clear as possible. The number of facts presented should be kept to a minimum.

4. Pictographs should give only an overall picture; they should not show minute details.

5. Only comparisons should be charted. Isolated facts in themselves cannot be presented effectively by this method.

6. There are many facts that by their very nature cannot be shown pictorially. This is true of large bodies of data that require more refined and elaborate techniques of analysis.

In designing effective pictorial unit charts, the importance of clear, artistic, and meaningful symbols cannot be overemphasized. In general, symbols should meet the following standards:[7]

1. A symbol should be drawn in accordance with the principles of good design established by the fine and applied arts.

2. A symbol should be usable in either large or small size; it should be effective on a billboard as well as in a two-column newspaper chart.

3. A symbol must represent a general concept (such as ship, man, child) and not an individual of the species (not the "Queen Mary," George Washington, or Prince Charles).

4. A symbol must be clearly distinguishable from every other symbol.

5. A symbol should be interesting.

6. A symbol is essentially a counting unit, and must be clear as such.

7. A symbol must be usable in outline as well as in silhouette.

[4] Michael Twyman, "The Significance of Isotype," in J. A. Edwards and Michael Twyman, eds., *Graphic Communication through Isotype*, Reading, Mass.: The University of Reading Press, 1975, pp. 7–17. This publication contains bibliographies of both Otto and Marie Neurath as well as references by various authors concerning Otto Neurath and his work.
[5] Otto Neurath, *International Picture Language*, London: K. Paul Trench, Trubner & Co., 1936, passim.
[6] Rudolph Modley, *How To Use Pictorial Statistics*, New York: Harper, 1937, pp. 12–17; Rudolph Modley and Dyno Lowenstein, *Pictographs and Graphs* New York: Harper, 1952, pp. 24–28.
[7] Modley and Lowenstein, *Pictographs and Graphs* (op. cit.), p. 47.

The chart maker has the choice of making his own symbols or of purchasing them commercially. However, it should be pointed out that at the present time only a limited assortment of pictorial symbols are available commercially.[8] If a large number of charts is planned or if the symbols used are distinctive or unique, it is more economical to design and print them than to purchase them. Designing and printing can be done very simply, quickly, and inexpensively.

In making a set of symbols, even of different sizes, it actually is necessary to draw only a single symbol. A large number of photostatic or photographic positive copies of desired size can be made from this single original sketch. Generally, for flexibility of design, it is recommended that two or three different sizes of symbols be printed. The symbols thus reproduced can be cut out and aligned in rows with rubber cement or wax adhesive on 8.5-in. by 11-in. white mounting board. The completed copy is then printed by a photo-offset process in black ink on good quality, smooth-finish white paper. In constructing a pictorial unit chart, rows of symbols can be cut out and mounted with rubber cement or wax adhesive on relatively heavy cardboard.

Figure 9–6 is an example of a chart prepared in

the 1920s by Otto Neurath and his associates for the Gesellschafts und Wirtschaftsmuseum. It shows the number of births and deaths in Vienna for four successive quadrennial periods beginning in 1912–1915. Basically it is a grouped-bar chart, with the upper series of symbols for each quadrennial period representing births and the lower series, deaths. Each symbol of an infant represents 20,000 live births and each coffin represents 20,000 deaths. During the 1916–1919 period there was an excess of some 80,000 deaths over births, which is emphasized by a heavy vertical line.

Figures 9–6 through 9–12 illustrate several variations of pictorial unit charts, as well as certain standards and characteristics that should be observed in their design. Figure 9–7 is basically a simple bar chart in which a pictorial symbol represents the measuring unit. The chart shows the increased output per man hour from 1850 to 1960 as expressed in monetary value. Each symbol represents $0.20 worth of output at 1947 prices. It will be observed that the symbols are divided to show fractions of the basic unit. It is not an uncommon practice, however, to use only whole symbols. In this instance, if a fractional value to be portrayed is 50% or more, a whole symbol is added, but if the fractional value is less than 50%, nothing is added. The symbol of the workmen makes more visual and comprehensible the significance of the concept "man hour" in relation to the number of unit values produced.

Figure 9–6. An example of a pictorial unit chart constructed by Otto Neurath and his associates for the Gesellschafts—und Wirtschaftsmuseum in Wien. (From J. A. Edwards and Michael Twyman, et al., Graphic Communication through Isotype, *Reading: University of Reading, 1975, p. 8.)*

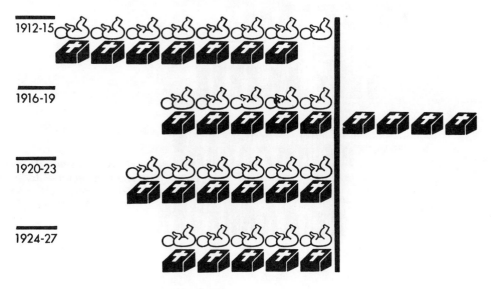

GEBURTEN UND STERBEFÄLLE IN WIEN

Jedes Kind = 20.000 Lebendgeburten Jeder Sarg = 20.000 Sterbefälle

Chart designed by the Isotype team in Vienna in the 1920s

OUTPUT PER MAN-HOUR:

Key to future welfare

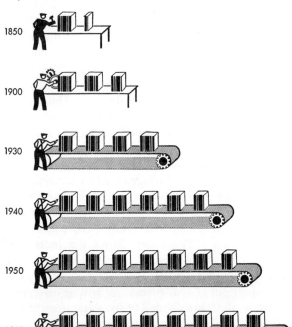

1850

1900

1930

1940

1950

1960

Each symbol represents 20 cents worth of output at 1947 prices

Figure 9–7. Horizontal bar chart in pictorial form portraying time series. (From Thomas R. Carskadon and Rudolf Modley, U.S.A.: Measure of a Nation, 1949, p. 99.)

OUR JOBS CHANGE

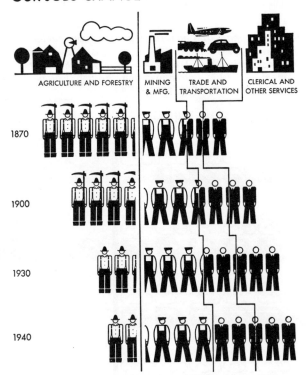

AGRICULTURE AND FORESTRY MINING & MFG. TRADE AND TRANSPORTATION CLERICAL AND OTHER SERVICES

1870

1900

1930

1940

Each symbol represents 10 per cent of all gainful workers

Figure 9–8. Illustration of a 100% sliding–bar chart in pictorial form showing time series. (From Thomas R. Carskadon and Rudolf Modley, U.S.A.: Measure of a Nation, 1949, p. 11.)

Figure 9–8 portrays changes in the occupational structure of the population of the United States from 1870 to 1940. The basic graphic form is a sliding 100% bar chart. There are four occupational categories shown on the chart: (1) agriculture and forestry, (2) mining and manufacturing, (3) trade and transportation, and (4) clerical and other services. Each type of occupational grouping is indicated by an appropriate symbol. The decreased proportion of farmers and the increased proportions of the three other categories are the main facts revealed by this chart. It will be observed that both Figures 9–7 and 9–8 were designed by Dr. Rudolph Modley.

Figure 9–9 includes three distinct but related pictorial bar charts concerning trends in American farming from 1940 to 1973. The upper panel shows changes in the number of people living on farms, the middle panel shows changes in the number of farms, and the lower panel shows changes in the average size of farms. A significant characteristic of this series of charts is the numerical scale for each of the charts. The customary practice for charts of this kind is to dispense with a scale and instead indicate by a brief statement or legend the number of cases each symbol represents. Of course, it cannot be said that the inclusion of a scale is necessarily incorrect or poor practice. It will be observed that although the total population of the United States increased from approximately 133 million in 1940 to 210 million in 1973, the farm population decreased from over 30 million in 1940 to less than 10 million in 1973. The number of farms declined from over six million in 1940 to less than three million in 1973. On the other hand, the average size of farms increased from 167 acres in 1940 to 383 in 1973.

Figure 9–10 is a simple bar chart apparently constructed in pictorial unit form. However, the dollar signs seem to be as much ornamental embellishments as distinct mensurational units. In spite of the ambiguous character of Figure 9–10, it does not make any real difference in terms of its quality and effectiveness. It is interesting to note that if Figure 9–10 were considered a pictorial unit chart, each dollar sign would represent about $26. It is common practice in constructing pictorial unit charts to represent the value of symbols with numbers ending in 5 or zero such as 5, 10, 25, 50, 100, and so on. Figure 9–10 portrays the average October earnings of full-time teachers according to enrollment size of districts. Average earnings varied from $663 in districts with less than 50 pupils to $977 in districts with 3000 or more pupils.

An example of a special type of bar chart in pictorial form is represented by Figure 9–11. This chart portrays school retention rates beginning with a cohort of 10 pupils in the fifth grade in the fall of 1961. As the chart indicates, about 96% of the fifth-graders in the fall of 1961 reached the ninth grade, 86% got as far as the eleventh grade, and 76% received a high-school diploma in 1969. In 1969 about 45% entered a degree-credit program in a college or university, and 22% can be expected to graduate from college with a 4-year degree. To make the chart more realistic, it will be observed that each of the grade levels is shown by a different type of symbol.

A pictorial unit chart in the form of a column chart is shown in Figure 9–12. This chart portrays trends in the monthly average value per person of bonus food stamps from 1968 to 1975. The height of each stack of monetary symbols is indicative of the monthly average value per person. It will be seen that average values have increased steadily from $6.52 in 1968 to $21.42 in 1975.

PICTORIAL CHARTS IN THE FORM OF SKETCHES OR CARTOONS

The third type of pictorial chart discussed in this chapter comprises various basic graphic forms designed as completed pictures, sketches, or cartoons. Charts of this kind are usually relatively simple, although occasionally they may be very elaborate. Figure 9–13 is an example of this type of chart. It is a 100% surface, band, or stratum chart drawn as a dollar bill. The pictorial fillers at the bottom are an attractive but not essential part of the graph itself. The vertical and horizontal axes of the surface chart, with scale points and scale figures, are clearly indicated. The dividing line representing the respective proportions of "marketing charges" and "farmer's share" is shown as a tear in the dollar bill.

Figure 9–14 is also drawn as a dollar bill, but the basic graphic form that it represents is a 100% component-bar chart. The various components, as well as the relative and absolute proportions of the total that they represent, are clearly indicated by explanatory legends and corresponding amounts in both dollars and percentages.

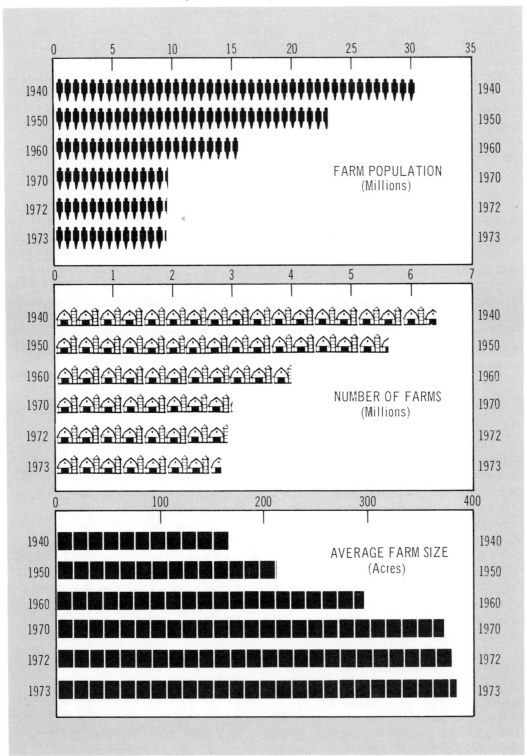

Changes in Farming: 1940 to 1973

Figure 9–9. Three pictorial unit charts representing different time series. The basic graphic form for all of these charts is the simple bar chart. (From United States Bureau of the Census, Statistical Abstract of the United States: 1974, *Washington: Government Printing Office, 1974, p. 592.)*

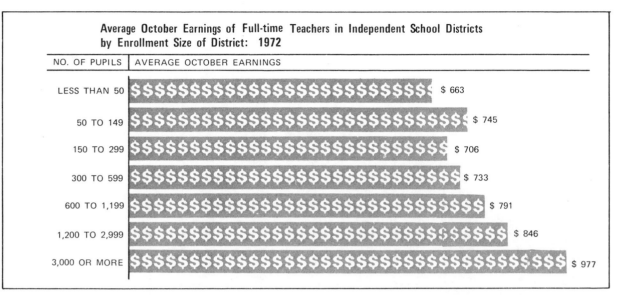

Average October Earnings of Full-time Teachers in Independent School Districts by Enrollment Size of District: 1972

NO. OF PUPILS	AVERAGE OCTOBER EARNINGS
LESS THAN 50	$ 663
50 TO 149	$ 745
150 TO 299	$ 706
300 TO 599	$ 733
600 TO 1,199	$ 791
1,200 TO 2,999	$ 846
3,000 OR MORE	$ 977

Figure 9–10. A simple bar chart with pictorial symbols. This chart has the basic characteristics of a pictorial unit chart, but apparently the symbols are used mainly for embellishment. (From United States Bureau of the Census, Graphic Summary of the 1972 Census of Governments, Topical Studies No. 5, Washington: Government Printing Office, 1974, p. 17.)

School Retention Rates

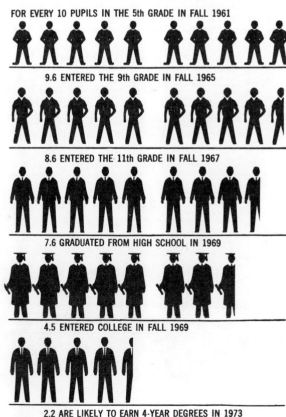

FOR EVERY 10 PUPILS IN THE 5th GRADE IN FALL 1961

9.6 ENTERED THE 9th GRADE IN FALL 1965

8.6 ENTERED THE 11th GRADE IN FALL 1967

7.6 GRADUATED FROM HIGH SCHOOL IN 1969

4.5 ENTERED COLLEGE IN FALL 1969

Figure 9–11. A pictorial unit chart portraying retention rates, fifth grade through college graduation, United States, 1961 to 1973. Note differences in symbols from one educational level to another. (From Kenneth A. Simon and W. Vance Grant, Digest of Educational Statistics, 1971 Edition, HEW, Office of Education, Washington: Government Printing Office, 1972, p. 8.)

2.2 ARE LIKELY TO EARN 4-YEAR DEGREES IN 1973

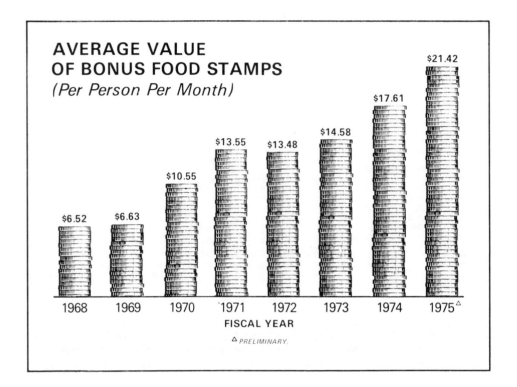

Figure 9–12. Column chart based on the pictorial unit concept.
The height of the several stacks of monetary symbols are
commensurate with the values represented. (From United
States Department of Agriculture, 1975 Handbook of Agricultural Charts, Agricultural Handbook, No. 491, October 1975,
p. 76.)

Figure 9–15 is similar to Figure 9–14 in that it is a 100% component type of chart. The divisions in Figure 9–15 are arranged vertically rather than horizontally, thus classifying it as a column chart. There are two weaknesses in the chart that should be pointed out. First, the actual 100% column comprises only that portion of the can below the rim around the shoulder of the can, whereas the portion above the rim, which is approximately one-third of the total height of the can, is supposed to be excluded with reference to the total or component values. Visually, this may be very confusing.

Figure 9–13. A pictorial chart in the form of
one–hundred percent surface or band chart. It
emphasizes the farmer's share of the consumer's food dollar from 1913 to 1951. (From U.S.
Bureau of Agricultural Economics, 1952 Agricultural Outlook Charts, p. 34.)

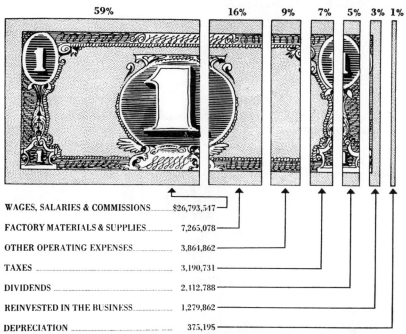

HOW WE USED THE $45,182,063 RECEIVED FROM OUR CUSTOMERS

59%	16%	9%	7%	5%	3%	1%

WAGES, SALARIES & COMMISSIONS $26,793,547

FACTORY MATERIALS & SUPPLIES 7,265,078

OTHER OPERATING EXPENSES 3,864,862

TAXES 3,190,731

DIVIDENDS 2,112,788

REINVESTED IN THE BUSINESS 1,279,862

DEPRECIATION 375,195

Figure 9–14. A one–hundred percent bar chart in pictorial form. (From Royal Typewriter Co., Inc., Annual Report, *1949, p. 4.)*

Second, a better-balanced chart might have been achieved if the largest components were placed at the bottom rather than at the top. Pictorial charts of this type have their place in graphic presentation, but extreme care must be taken to avoid optical illusions and other types of distortion.

Figure 9–16 is a good illustration of a pictorially designed column chart, the third type of pictorial chart discussed in this chapter. The phenomenal increase in the gross federal, state, and local debt from the turn of the century is portrayed as a series of stone columns figuratively extending into the

Figure 9–15. A simple one–hundred percent column chart presented in pictorial form. One feature of this chart that may tend to be misleading is the fact that only the part of the can below the handles actually represents the one-hundred percent total. (From H. W. Gilbertson, Educational Exhibits, *U.S. Department of Agriculture, Misc. Publ. No. 634, p. 24.)*

$273.6

$92.1

$39.1

$33.2

$3.4 $5.7

1902   1912   1922   1932   1942   1949

Figure 9–16. Pictorial column chart. (From the Tax Foundation, Facts and Figures on Government Finance, 1950–1951, p. 178.)

COST OF RECOMMENDED IMPROVEMENTS IN FACULTY RETIREMENT SYSTEM LESS THAN I CENT OF ANNUAL EXPENDITURE DOLLAR*

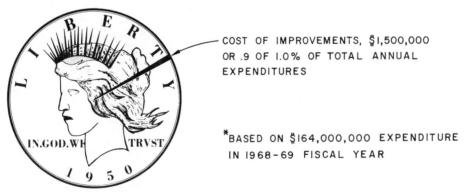

COST OF IMPROVEMENTS, $1,500,000 OR .9 OF 1.0% OF TOTAL ANNUAL EXPENDITURES

*BASED ON $164,000,000 EXPENDITURE IN 1968–69 FISCAL YEAR

Figure 9–17. A pie chart in pictorial form. (From Calvin F. Schmid, An Evaluative Survey of Faculty Retirement System, University of Washington, Seattle: The Ad Hoc Committee on Retirement, 1970, p. 19.)

clouds. The pictorial fillers representing Uncle Sam add to the appeal as well as the effectiveness of the design. The horizontal-scale figures and the values of each column are clearly indicated.

Figure 9–17 is an illustration of a simple pie chart shown as a silver dollar. Especially for popular appeal, a pictorial chart of this kind has a greater impact than a plain circle.[9] The obvious emphasis of this chart is to emphasize the relatively small expenditure that would be required to improve a university faculty-retirement system.

---

[9] See Chapter 10 for additional illustrations of pictorial pie charts constructed in isometric and perspective projection.

Figure 9–18 is a considerably more elaborate pictorialization of the pie chart. It is concerned with the alcoholic drinking habits of adults 65 years of age and over. It will be observed that Figure 9–18 summarizes data for three drinking categories for men and women separately and for both sexes combined. Men show a higher percentage of regular drinkers and a smaller percentage of abstainers than women. In general the proportion of drinkers, especially heavy drinkers, declines very noticeably with advancing age.

Figure 9–19 is a well-designed flowchart in which pictorial symbols and sketches are an integral part. It portrays the major flow of mercury within the biosphere beginning with such major emitters as

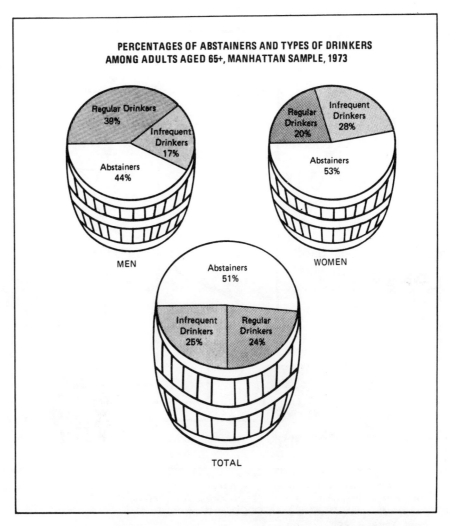

Figure 9–18. Pie charts constructed as part of pictorial sketches. (From Public Health Service, National Institute on Alcohol Abuse and Alcoholism, HEW, Alcohol and Health, Second Special Report to the U.S. Congress, Washington: Government Printing Office, 1974, p. 29.)

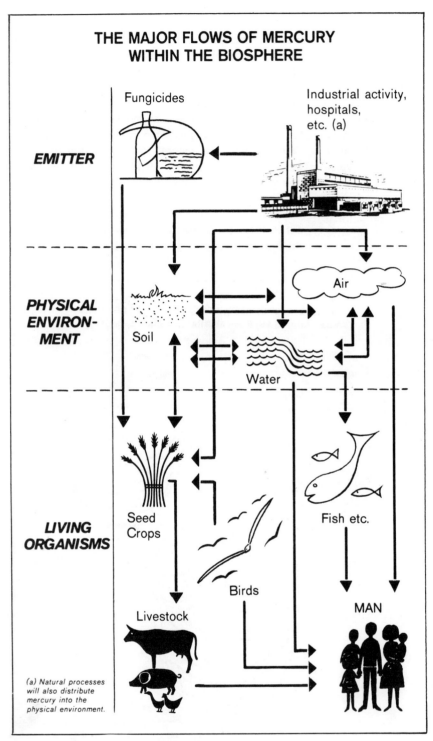

THE MAJOR FLOWS OF MERCURY
WITHIN THE BIOSPHERE

Fungicides

Industrial activity,
hospitals,
etc. (a)

EMITTER

*PHYSICAL
ENVIRON-
MENT*

Air

Soil

Water

*LIVING
ORGANISMS*

Seed
Crops

Fish etc.

Birds

Livestock

MAN

(a) Natural processes
will also distribute
mercury into the
physical environment.

*Figure 9–19. Flow chart in which pictorial symbols have been
effectively incorporated. (From Organization for Economic
Cooperation and Development, OECD at Work for Environment, 1973, p. 35.)*

industrial establishments and hospitals along with specific contaminants such as fungicides. From these sources, the physical environment—soil, air, and water—may be polluted. As a consequence, human beings may ultimately be affected either directly, through environmental pollution such as air and water, or indirectly, through living organisms, such as food from plants, livestock, fowl, and fish. The various interrelationships and direction of flow of the many elements involved in this process are indicated by arrows.

CHARTS WITH PICTORIAL EMBELLISHMENTS

The fourth type of pictorial chart discussed in this chapter represents more-or-less conventional graphic forms embellished with various kinds of pictures or symbols ranging from simple fillers to comparatively elaborate and detailed photographic or artistic backgrounds.

It will be recalled that a few of the charts presented in the preceding chapters were embellished with relatively simple pictorial fillers. Additional

illustrations of this kind will be found in Figures 9–20 through 9–27. The interpretation and significance of these charts are apparent. They are designed to arouse interest and provide visual association and emphasis to certain facts presented in the chart.

Figure 9–20 is a good illustration of how the forcefulness and appeal of a simple arithmetic line chart can be enhanced by the addition of a stereotyped sketch of a criminal with his facial mask, cap, gloves, and gun. The disproportionate thickness of the curve further accentuates the upward sweep in the number of serious crimes.

The design of Figure 9–21, both generally and in detail, is similar to that of Figure 9–20. The pictorial symbol is clearly indicative of the data presented by this chart.

Figure 9–22 also contains a symbolical filler like the two preceding charts, but in the form of a photograph rather than an artistic sketch. The statistical chart in Figure 9–22 is more formal and professional than the ones in Figures 9–20 and 9–21.

In Figure 9–23 the entire background of the grid is a photograph intended to symbolize the subject matter of the chart. It shows trends in the number

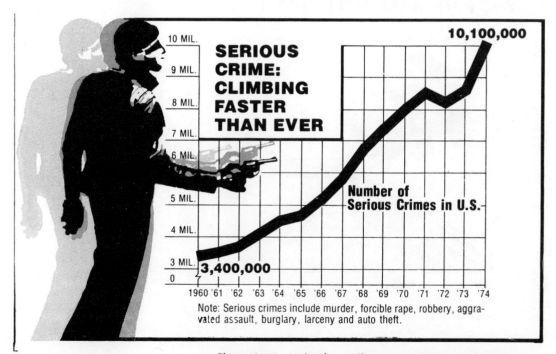

Figure 9–20. A simple rectilinear coordinate graph with an eye–catching pictorial symbol. Data from Federal Bureau of Investigation. (Chart reprinted from U.S. News and World Report, *April 7, 1975, p. 31. Copyright 1975, U.S. News and World Report, Inc.)*

970,000 —

DIVORCES:
REACHING NEW PEAKS
YEAR AFTER YEAR

850,000

750,000

650,000

610,000

550,000

Number of Divorces

450,000

350,000

0

1946 1950 1955 1960 1965 1970 1974 (est.)

Source: National Center for Health Statistics;
1974 estimates by USN&WR Economic Unit

Figure 9–21. Another example of a rectilinear coordinate graph with a pictorial symbol characterizing content of the chart. Normally the ordinal scale figures are placed on the left side of the grid. However, in view of the shape of the curve in this chart, it is acceptable to place the figures on the right side. (Chart reprinted from U.S. News and World Report, *January 13, 1975, p. 43. Copyright 1975, U.S. News and World Report, Inc.)*

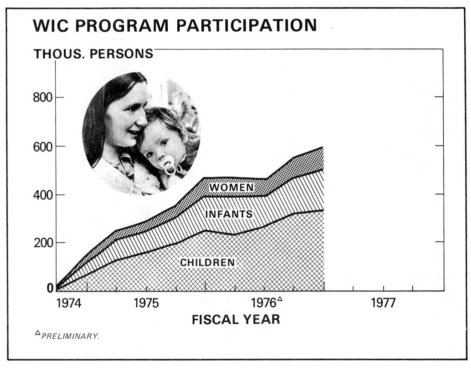

WIC PROGRAM PARTICIPATION

THOUS. PERSONS

800

600

400

WOMEN

INFANTS

200

CHILDREN

0

1974   1975   1976△   1977

FISCAL YEAR

△PRELIMINARY.

Figure 9–22. Subdivided or multiple–strata surface chart with a photographic filler symbolizing the data presented in the chart. (From United States Department of Agriculture, 1976 Handbook of Agricultural Charts, *Agricultural Handbook No. 504, October 1976, p. 80.)*

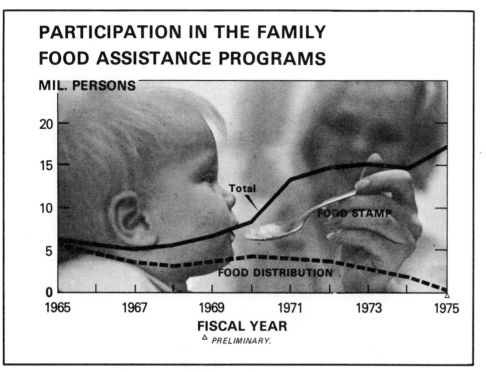

PARTICIPATION IN THE FAMILY FOOD ASSISTANCE PROGRAMS

MIL. PERSONS

Total

FOOD STAMP

FOOD DISTRIBUTION

FISCAL YEAR

△ PRELIMINARY.

Figure 9–23. Illustration of a rectilinear coordinate chart superimposed on photographic background. It will be noted that the two separate curves seem to indicate that this is a simple arithmetic line chart. Actually, however, it is a surface chart with one stratum representing persons on direct food distribution programs, and the other stratum persons on food stamp programs. (From United States Department of Agriculture, 1975 Handbook of Agricultural Charts, Agriculture Handbook, *No. 491, October 1975, p. 72.)*

Prices received by farmers for commodities – 1914-22 – 1939-47

PERCENT

INFLATION

CRASH

PRICES
World War I

PRICES
World War II

1909-14 = 100

FOR SALE

Figure 9–24. An arithmetic line chart with simple pictorial sketches superimposed. (From H. W. Gilbertson, Educational Exhibits, *U.S. Department of Agriculture, Misc. Publ. No. 634, p. 25.)*

of participants in government family food-assistance programs from 1965 to 1975. Briefly, the number of recipients of food-distribution programs declines as the number of those who obtain food stamps increases. Although Figure 9–23 looks like a simple arithmetic line chart, its interpretation is more consistent with that of a surface or stratum chart—the lower stratum representing those on food-distribution programs and the upper stratum, those on food-stamp programs. The unbroken curve indicates the total number of participants on both programs.

As illustrated by Figure 9–24, it may be appropriate to incorporate an element of humor into the pictorial fillers, depending largely on the type of data presented as well as the character of the audi-

ence to whom the chart is addressed. Techniques of this kind can add much human interest to statistical charts as well as reinforce their impact. It will be recalled from Chapter 3 that the basic design of Figure 9–24 is a special type of rectilinear coordinate chart with a multiple time scale, so that two temporal series, one for World War I and the other for World War II, are brought into close juxtaposition for comparative purposes.

Figures 9–25 and 9–26 are illustrations of two pie charts that have been embellished with pictorial fillers. Figure 9–25 portrays the proportion of gainfully employed women in each of eight occupational groups. Each of the eight corresponding sectors of the chart is not only properly labeled, but also is illustrated with a pictorial sketch. Figure 9–26

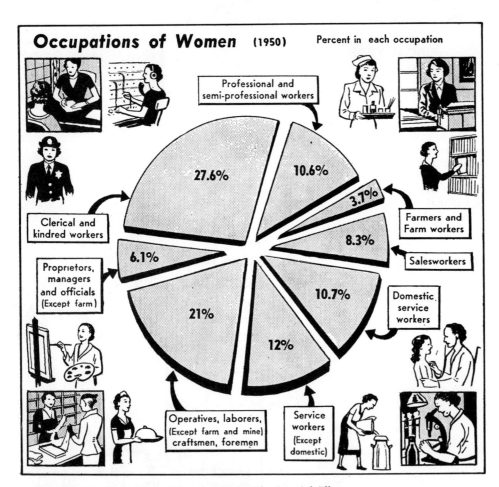

Figure 9–25. Illustration of the pie chart with pictorial fillers symbolizing the various occupational categories. Also, note the separation of sectors, which helps to emphasize quantitative differences among groupings as well as to facilitate comparisons. (Part of a Chicago Sun-Times "Graphichart" prepared by Tom P. Barrett.)

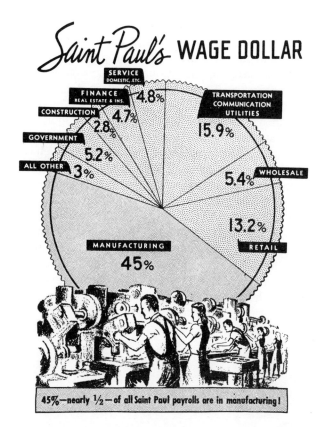

Figure 9–26. A pie chart in which the sector representing manufacturing is emphasized by a pictorial illustration. (From Saint Paul Assn. of Commerce, An Invitation to Industry, *p. 6.)*

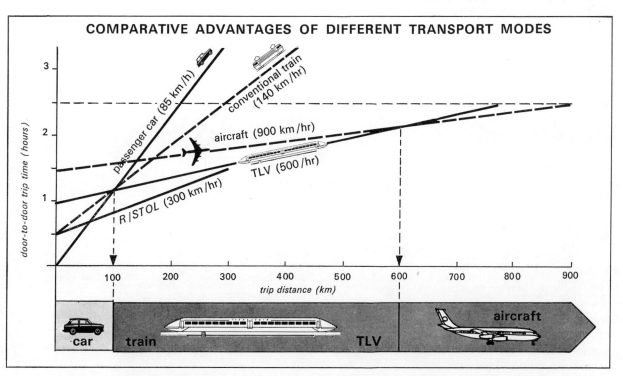

Figure 9–27. Pictorial symbols may also enhance the appeal, interest, and readability of charts that are more technical in character. [From C. Kenneth Orski, "The Future of European Intercity Transport," OECD Observer, *(60), October 1972, p. 29.]*

shows how the labor force of the city of St. Paul is distributed in various commercial, industrial, and governmental activities. The proportion in each sector is based on the amount of wages earned. It will be observed that 45% of the wage dollar is derived from manufacturing. Moreover, the pictorial sketch was designed to emphasize the importance of manufacturing in the economy of St. Paul.

Figure 9–27 presents a succinct as well as graphic evaluation of different modes of intercity transportation, including their potentials and limits. It is replete with fundamental technological, social, and economic implications. The basic structure of this chart is similar to the simple correlation chart discussed in Chapter 7, in which the relationship between two variables is presented. The vertical axis represents door-to-door trip time in hours and the horizontal axis, trip distance in kilometers.

The primary message conveyed by Figure 9–27 is a portrayal of the comparative advantages of the following types of intercity transportation: (1) passenger car, (2) conventional train, (3) the reduced and short takeoff and landing (R/STOL) aircraft, (4) high-speed tracked and levitated vehicles (TLV) using both air cushion and the magnetic suspension concepts, and (5) conventional aircraft.[10]

The pictorial symbols included in Figure 9–27 add substantially to its graphic impact by making it more appealing, more interesting, and more readable. The basic design of the chart has not been altered in the slightest by the pictorial symbols.

[10] C. Kenneth Orski, "The Future of European Intercity Transport," *OECD Observer*, No. 60 (October, 1972), pp. 27–33.

THE TECHNIQUES, AS WELL AS THE ADVAN-
tages and limitations, of presenting certain basic
types of statistical charts in three-dimensional pictorial form, are discussed in this chapter. During
the past two decades or so it has become common
practice to portray rectilinear coordinate graphs,
pie charts, bar and column charts, maps, and other
types of graphs and charts in axonometric, oblique,
or perspective projection. In fact, at the present
time the popularity of this form of presentation
seems to have surpassed, whether permanently or
temporarily, the pictorial unit chart so extensively
used during the decades of the 1930s and 1940s.[1]
Projection charts, with their depth and other pic-
turelike qualities, unquestionably possess definite
popular appeal. It will be found, however, that a
large proportion of three-dimensional charts are distorted and misleading because the designer has little
or no understanding either of the basic principles of
graphic presentation or of projection techniques.[2]

The specialist in graphic techniques should con-
stantly strive to improve the design of charts by
presenting them in more pleasing and intelligible
form. Oblique, axonometric, and perspective projection have proved especially valuable in attaining
these objectives. However, in attempting to
develop new graphic forms and techniques, standards of precision, good practice, or authenticity of
impression should never be sacrificed.

The value of any new technique in graphic presentation, or in fact the value of any specific graphic
form, should be judged in terms of its "communication efficiency," based on such criteria as clarity,
simplicity, forcefulness, relevance, reliability,
meaningfulness, and esthetic appeal. Unfortunately, no precise and objective instruments or
procedures have been devised to measure the
communication efficiency of graphic forms and
techniques. Evaluations of this kind at the present
time and for many years in the future must depend
on the judgment of knowledgeable and experienced
practitioners in the field of graphic presentation.

The design of three-dimensional pictorial
graphic forms should be based on accepted conventionalized principles of: (1) axonometric, (2) oblique, and (3) perspective projection. Sometimes
artists may delineate reasonably satisfactory charts
purely on an impressionistic basis, but inherent in
this practice is the danger of distortion and
inaccuracy.

The term "projection" as used in this discussion
pertains to certain widely used techniques in en-

CHAPTER TEN

PROJECTION TECHNIQUES IN GRAPHIC PRESENTATION

gineering, architecture, and art for describing the
shape and size of objects. The various forms of
projection and their relationships to one another are
summarized in schematic form in Figure 10–1. It
will be observed that the major interest of the
graphic specialist is in certain forms of one-plane
pictorial projection techniques rather than the customary orthographic projection where at least two
or three planes are used to describe three dimensions of an object, such as the front, side, and top
views of architectural or engineering drawings.

The differences among the various types of uni-
planar pictorial projection are determined in one of
two ways: (1) in the relation of the object to the
plane of projection or picture plane or (2) in the
angular relation of the lines (projectors) along which
points of the object are projected to the plane of
projection. Detailed consideration is given to the
implications of these criteria, particularly the manner in which they influence projection form and the
resultant type of picture. Figure 10–2 illustrates
how a cube looks when drawn in various types of
axonometric, oblique, and perspective projection.

AXONOMETRIC PROJECTION

To begin with, for the sake of simplicity and clarity,
a few basic terms used in the following presentation
should be defined: (1) "planes of projection" are
planes or surfaces on which the various views of the
object or picture are projected (drawn), and it is the

revolving of these planes that determines the location or arrangement of the view (the plane of projection as used in this discussion is analogous to the screen on which a motion picture is projected); (2) the "projection" of a picture (or drawing) is merely the projection of a myriad of points that form a familiar pattern referred to as the *picture* or *view;*[3] and (3) "projectors" are imaginary lines or visual rays drawn through every point of the figure intersecting a given plane of projection, thus forming a picture. Projectors may be parallel or they may converge according to some other rule of geometric projection.

Axonometric projection is a form of orthographic projection in which one plane of projection is used. In axonometric projection an object such as a rectangular solid is turned and then tilted so that with reference to the picture plane three faces in a single view are observed; the projectors are perpendicular to the picture plane (Figure 10–3).[4] Actually, of course, an object may be placed in any number of positions relative to the picture plane, making it possible to construct an infinite number of views with respect to general proportions, length of edges, and sizes of angles. A few of these possible positions have been classified into the following major divisions of axonometric projection: (1)

isometric, (2) dimetric, and (3) trimetric. It should be emphasized again that the position of the object relative to the plane of projection determines whether the projection is one of these three specific types.

---

[1] See Chapter 9 for a detailed discussion of the pictorial unit chart.

[2] To date very little has been published on the application of the principles of three-dimensional pictorial projection to graphic presentation. The first general discussion ever published on this subject appeared in the first edition of the *Handbook of Graphic Presentation,* prior to which (1954) there were two useful but brief articles dealing with special problems of three-dimensional presentation, both written by the same author, Kenneth W. Haemer. These articles are: "The Perils of Perspective," *The American Statistician,* **1** (December 1947), "The Pseudo Third Dimension," ibid., **5** (October 1951), 28.

[3] Frederick E. Giesecke, Alva Mitchell, Henry Cecil Spencer, and Ivan Leroy Hill, *Technical Drawing,* New York: Macmillan, 1974, pp. 153–202 and 497–566; Robert H. Hammond, Carson P. Buck, William B. Rogers, Gerald W. Walsh, and Hugh P. Ackert, *Engineering Graphics,* New York: Ronald Press, 1964, pp. 116–149 and 173–212.

[4] Figures 10–3, 10–8, and 10–9 have been redrawn from Warren J. Luzadder, *Fundamentals of Engineering Drawing,* Englewood Cliffs, N.J.: Prentice-Hall, 1971, pp. 252, 264, and 275.

Figure 10–1. Simplified classification of projection techniques. The types of projections most frequently used in graphic presentation are indicated in bold lettering. (Classification based mainly on Thomas E. French and Charles J. Vierck, Engineering Drawing, *New York: McGraw-Hill Book Co. 1966, pp. 97–206 and Frederick E. Giesecke, Alva Mitchell, Henry Cecil Spencer, and Ivan Leroy Hill,* Technical Drawing, *New York: Macmillan Publishing Co. Inc., 1974, pp. 9–11.)*

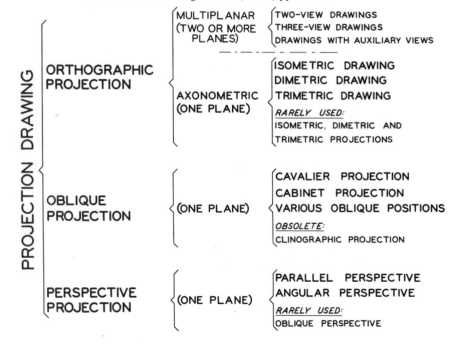

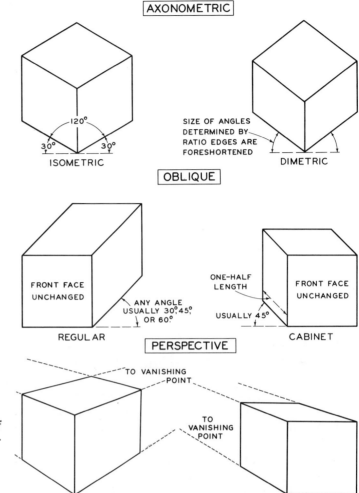

Figure 10–2. Simplified illustrations of types of one–plane pictorial projection used in graphic presentation.

Isometric Projection

The most common as well as simplest form of axonometric projection is isometric (equal-measure) projection. In isometric projection, for example, the three edges of a cube forming the corner nearest the plane of projection are so placed as to make equal angles with the plane of projection. The angles formed by these edges are represented by 120° angles in isometric projection (see Figures 10–4 and 10–5). Therefore, when one edge is vertical on the picture plane, the other two are represented by lines

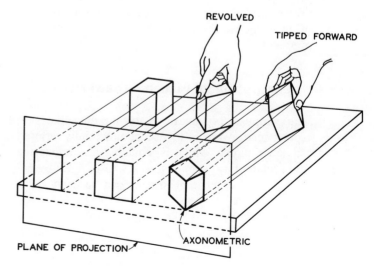

Figure 10–3. Axonometric projection.

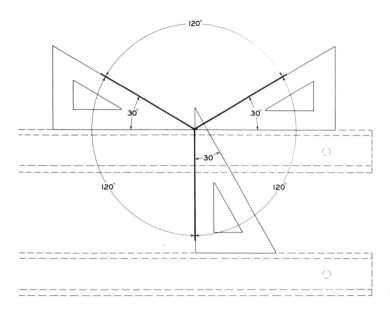

Figure 10–4. Isometric axes.

at angles of 30° to the horizontal, to right and left, respectively. To place a cube in isometric projection, it is necessary for the cube to be so aligned that the projector of the front corner extends through the rear corner.

The three faces of the cube in isometric position are foreshortened equally, which means, of course, that all edges of the cube are of equal length on the projection. Isometric lines (any line parallel to an edge of the cube) are foreshortened approximately 82/100 (0.8165) of their length (Figure 10–6). To make an isometric projection theoretically correct, Figure 10–6 clearly shows how an isometric scale can be constructed by a simple graphic method from a regular scale. Also, the difference between a "true isometric projection" and an "isometric drawing" will be found in this same illustration. The isometric drawing is larger than the isometric projection. The projections, however, are the same, and accordingly have no effect on pictorial projection. In actual practice, objects are seldom drawn in true isometric projection because the use of an isometric scale is both inconvenient and impractical.

Construction of Isometric Drawings

The simplest procedure in laying out charts in isometric drawing is to use commercially printed isometric paper, which is available at engineering and architectural supply stores. Also, a 30° by 60° triangle or isometric protractor can be used. For laying out circles in isometric projection, the simplest method is to use one of the commercially prepared templates, which are available in different sizes. If a template is not available, the four-centered approximation technique can be followed.[5]

Figure 10–7 shows the manner in which a grouped-column chart may be constructed by the utilization of commercially printed isometric paper.[6] The data indicate student enrollment by class and school according to sex for the 1976 autumn quarter at the University of Washington.

The width, position, spacing, and height of each column were governed largely by the rulings on the isometric paper. In actual practice printed paper of this kind possesses many advantages, but not in-

[5] See, for example, Giesecke, Mitchell, et al., *Technical Drawing* (op. cit.), pp. 508–511.
[6] In constructing charts in pictorial projection, particularly axonometric and perspective, printed grids and specially designed instruments will be found very useful as they help to eliminate a considerable amount of time-consuming and tedious mathematical computations and geometrical construction. Such items as the following are available commercially: printed isometric and dimetric grids, isometric protractors, isometric and other kinds of ellipses in the form of plastic templates, different kinds of printed perspective guides, perspective circles, and other special instruments for constructing isometric, dimetric, trimetric, and perspective drawings. Large art and drafting supply outlets stock many of these items. In case certain of the items are not available at a local outlet, they may be procured from: (1) Graphic-Standard Instruments Company, 15906 James Couzens Highway, Detroit, Mich. 48238; (2) Graphicraft, 112 Hoyt Street, Stamford, Conn. 06095.

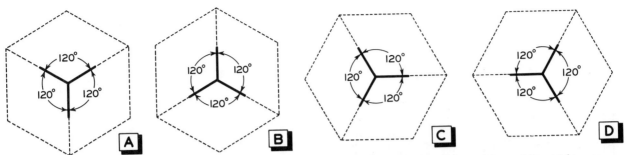

Figure 10–5. Various positions of isometric axes.

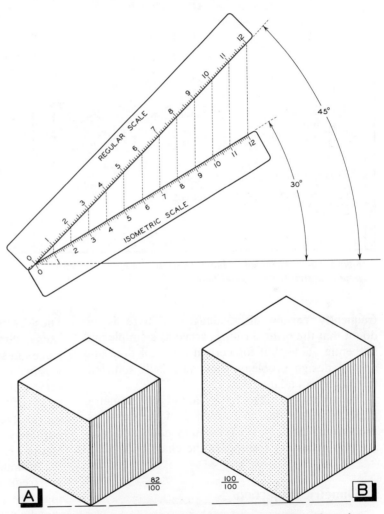

Figure 10–6. The relationship between a regular scale and an isometric scale. A. Cube is constructed by means of an isometric scale and is known as a true Isometric "Projection." B. Cube is constructed according to the conventional method, in which all foreshortening is disregarded. It is called an Isometric "Drawing."

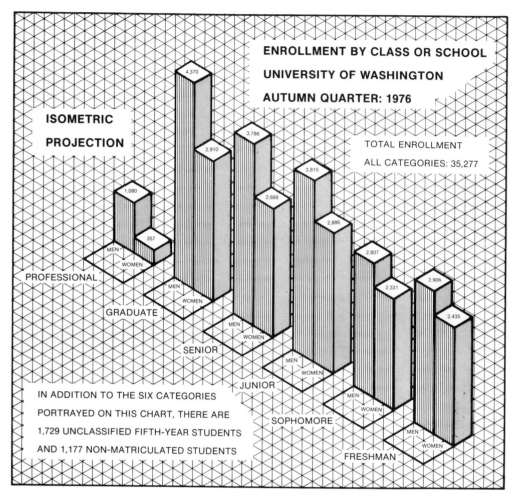

ENROLLMENT BY CLASS OR SCHOOL

UNIVERSITY OF WASHINGTON

AUTUMN QUARTER: 1976

ISOMETRIC

PROJECTION

TOTAL ENROLLMENT

ALL CATEGORIES: 35,277

IN ADDITION TO THE SIX CATEGORIES
PORTRAYED ON THIS CHART, THERE ARE
1,729 UNCLASSIFIED FIFTH-YEAR STUDENTS
AND 1,177 NON-MATRICULATED STUDENTS

*Figure 10–7. Grouped–column chart plotted on isometric
paper (drawn from original data).*

frequently certain disadvantages. There is no
doubt that the printed rulings serve as a simple and
authentic guide, but for certain types of data and
special design problems they may lack sufficient
flexibility and adaptability.

In addition to the basic layout on isometric
paper, the hatching and stippling of the columns,
the various labels, and explanatory notes and titles
are also necessary features of the chart.

Dimetric Projection

It will be recalled that in isometric projection all
three faces, or surfaces, of an object are equally
inclined and that all edges of an object are equally
foreshortened. In dimetric projection only two of
the faces, or surfaces, are equally foreshortened.

These facts must be kept in mind in laying out the
axes in dimetric projection. For example, a cube is
placed in such a position that two of the edges converging at the first corner are foreshortened at the
same ratio, and the other is foreshortened at a different ratio. In dimetric projection the object may
be revolved into many defined positions and, accordingly, an infinite number of dimetric projections is possible.

Although the dimensions of the original object
are frequently not specified in axonometric drawings, the positions resulting in dimetric projection
may be detected readily through the relationships of
the angles of the axes to the baseline. If, as is
usually the case, one of the axes is vertical, the
drawing is dimetric if the other two axes make equal
angles with the baseline and are not 30°. (It will be
remembered that the special case in which these

angles are 30° is the isometric position.) The drawing is also dimetric if one axis is vertical and the angle formed by the axis, which is to be in equal scale with the vertical, is 90° minus two times the other angle. In any other positions the drawing is trimetric.

It will be recalled that a distinction was made between isometric projection and isometric drawing. Similarly, the same general distinction obtains in both dimetric and trimetric projection. Dimetric drawing, for example, has the same shape as a dimetric projection, but the ratio between the object size and the projection is prescribed, whereas this relation does not hold between the object size and the drawing scales.

Trimetric Projection

The axes in trimetric projection are determined by placing the cube in such a position that all three edges converging at the front corner are foreshortened at different ratios. Each of the three axes thus constructed makes a different angle with the plane of projection. Also, this means that the scales of the edges are all different. Trimetric is the most general form of axonometric projection. Whenever an object is not placed in the position with respect to the projection plane that defines an isometric or dimetric projection, the resulting projection is trimetric.

Figure 10–8 illustrates the essential features of a chart delineated in trimetric projection. To make it comparable with Figure 10–7, which was drawn in isometric projection, the same data were used. It will be recalled that they represent student-enrollment statistics by class and college at the University of Washington for the autumn term of 1976–1977. Since both charts are representative of axonometric projection and are related generically they manifest certain similarities. The specific merits of the three forms of axonometric

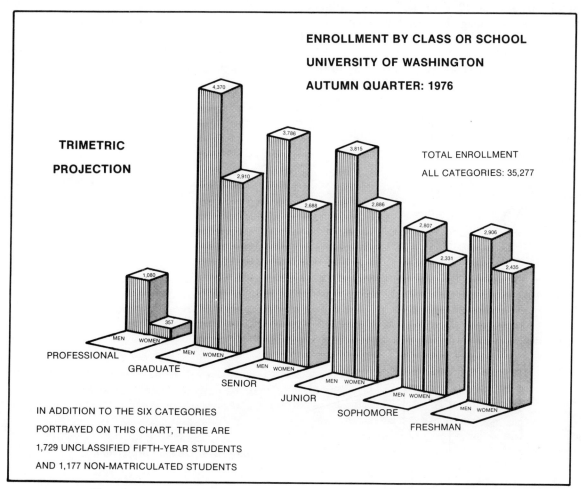

Figure 10–8. Grouped–column chart drawn in trimetric projection (drawn from original data).

projection—isometric, dimetric, and trimetric—are relative to the type of data presented and the purpose of the chart.

OBLIQUE PROJECTION

In the three forms of axonometric projection—isometric, dimetric, and trimetric—the projectors are at right angles to the picture planes, but in oblique projection the projectors strike the plane of projection obliquely. In other words, in oblique projection the angle of the projectors is less than 90° (Figure 10–9).

In oblique projection three faces of an object are visible, with the largest dimension parallel to the picture plane. Two of the axes are always at right angles to each other, and the third may be at any angle to the horizontal; 30° or 45° is generally used.

Oblique projection "is more flexible and has the following advantages over isometric drawing: (1) circular or irregular outlines on the front face show in their true shape; (2) distortion can be reduced by foreshortening along the receding axis; and (3) a greater choice is permitted in the selection of the positions of the axes."[7]

If the angle of obliquity of projectors to the picture plane is 45°, it is called "cavalier" projection. This is the most widely used type of oblique projection. To reduce the apparent distortion and appearance of excessive thickness of oblique projec-

tion, the actual length of the receding or lateral axis of the object is often shortened by one-half. Oblique projection with modification in this manner is called "cabinet" projection.

In cabinet projection the receding axis may be any angle, but is usually 30° or 45°. Figure 10–2 illustrates regular oblique projection, as well as the special cabinet type of oblique projection.

PERSPECTIVE

Of the several forms of pictorial projection, perspective is perhaps the most realistic. In perspective projection an object is represented as it is seen by the eye of an observer located at a finite distance from the object that is known as a "station point." If one were to look at an object through a window and trace an outline of the object on the glass, the basis of the projection on the glass would be perspective. In this illustration the windowpane represents the picture plane. In axonometric and oblique projections the projectors are parallel, but in perspective the projectors converge to a station point.

There are three types of perspective projection: parallel, or one-point; angular, or two-point; and oblique, or three-point. In parallel, or one-point,

---

[7] Luzadder, *Fundamentals of Engineering Drawing* (op. cit.), p. 264.

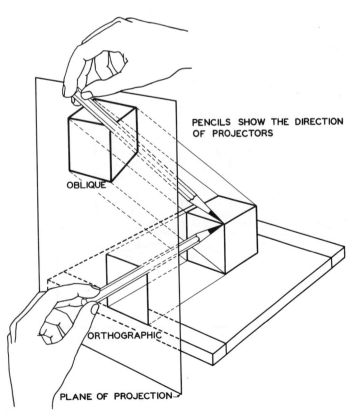

PENCILS SHOW THE DIRECTION OF PROJECTORS

OBLIQUE

ORTHOGRAPHIC

PLANE OF PROJECTION

Figure 10–9. Oblique projection.

perspective the principal face of the object is placed parallel to the picture plane. There is one set of parallel lines that vanish at a single point.

In angular, or two-point, perspective the object is so placed that its vertical faces are at an angle of less than 90° to the picture plane. There are two sets of parallel lines, one for each face, which require two vanishing points.

In the oblique, or three-point, perspective the object is placed so that none of its principal edges is parallel to the picture plane; that is, they are in angular relation to the picture plane; therefore, each of the three sets of parallel edges will have a separate vanishing point.[8]

Figure 10–2 illustrates the essential characteristics of the two more common types of perspective, namely, parallel, or one-point, perspective and angular, or two-point, perspective.

A more detailed portrayal of angular perspective will be found in Figure 10–10. To be proficient in perspective drawing, the student should familiarize himself with the meaning application of such concepts as: (1) point of sight, or station point, (2) picture plane, (3) horizon, (4) horizon plane, (5) vanishing point, (6) vanishing line, (7) ground line, (8) ground plane, and (9) cone of vision.

The actual construction of a simple column chart in angular perspective is illustrated in Figure 10–11. A printed grid, one of the mechanical aids referred to earlier, was used in the construction of Figure 10–11. An examination of this illustration will clearly convey some of the essential implications of perspective techniques in designing and interpreting statistical charts.

Perspective projection as applied to graphic presentation possesses serious limitations. Charts constructed in perspective are generally distorted;

they do not portray exact distance, shape, or size. Figure 10–12 shows an arithmetic line chart and a column chart drawn in conventional form along with variations in perspective and quasiperspective form.[9] The resultant distortions of the perspective and quasiperspective projections are obvious, and charts of this particular kind should be avoided. Wherever perspective projection is used, extreme caution should be taken to see that it enhances the value of the chart and does not create distortion or misrepresentation.

ADDITIONAL ILLUSTRATIONS OF CHARTS DRAWN IN VARIOUS TYPES OF PROJECTION

It will be observed from the illustrations in the following pages that most of the basic graphic forms, such as arithmetic line charts, band and silhouette charts, bar and column graphs, pie charts, frequency polygons and histograms, and maps, have been recast into axonometric drawing, oblique projection, and perspective. In addition, some of the examples do not conform precisely to theoretically correct standards of projection. Nevertheless, they may produce the desired effects. Rather than use merely impressionistic procedures in designing charts in one-plane pictorial projection, it is recommended that the theory and techniques of projection be mastered and followed carefully.

[8] Giesecke, Mitchell, et al., *Technical Drawing* (op. cit.), pp. 551–553.
[9] Figure 10–12 is based on ideas from Haemer, "The Perils of Perspective" (op. cit.).

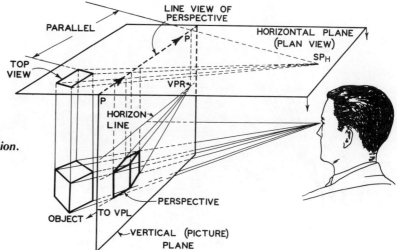

Figure 10–10. Angular perspective projection.

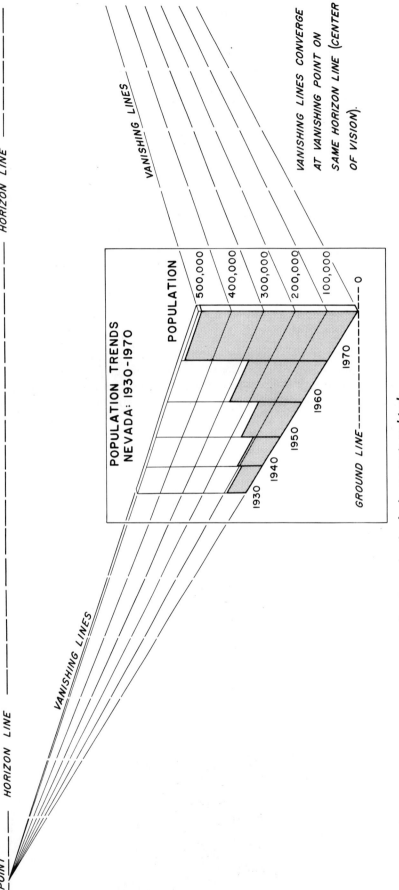

Figure 10–11. Column chart plotted on perspective paper showing basic concepts and techniques in perspective projection (drawn from original data).

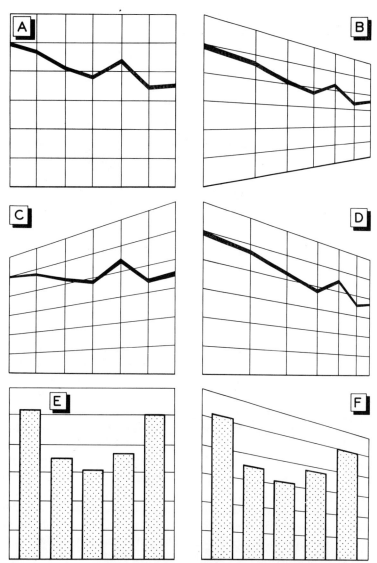

Figure 10–12. Comparison of conventional charts, Forms (A) and (E), with perspective and pseudo–perspective variations.

Examples of Charts in Axonometric Projection

Figure 10–13 is an example of a multiple 100% bar chart in axonometric projection (trimetric).[10] There are three components for each bar showing distribution of the International Harvester Company receipts for 1941, 1947, and 1948 to: (1) employees, (2) stockholders, and (3) funds for use in business.   The divisions of the bars are differentiated properly and explained by figures, legends, shading, and pictorial symbols.   A slight optical il-

lusion may be observed in the bar for 1941; this bar seems to be thicker at the right end, but actually this is not the case.

It will be observed from Figure 10–14 that the type of projection used is similar to that in Figure 10–13.   The chart form, however, is very different. Figure 10–14 can be described fundamentally

[10] Because of the manner in which several of the following charts have been drawn, it has been difficult to determine the precise form of projection.   Accordingly, the designations for such charts represent merely "approximate" descriptions.

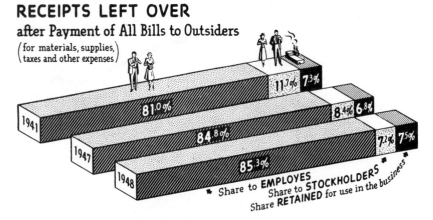

RECEIPTS LEFT OVER
after Payment of All Bills to Outsiders
(for materials, supplies, taxes and other expenses)

Figure 10–13. A one–hundred-percent bar chart shown in trimetric drawing. (From International Harvester Co., Annual Report, 1948, p. 8.)

as an arithmetic line chart or perhaps as a double single-surface chart. The data portray variations in net income and cash dividends for the International Harvester Company from 1940 to 1949. The basic features of the chart conform to accepted standards of graphic presentation, and the projection form seems to possess definite popular appeal.

It is both interesting and significant to compare Figures 10–14 and 10–15, since both represent identical graphic forms but different types of axonometric projection. Figure 10–15 is in isometric projection, whereas it will be recalled that Figure 10–14 is in trimetric projection.

Figure 10–16 is an illustration of six histograms drawn in isometric projection. These histograms portray the relationship between the percentage of

boys 14 and 15 years old and 16 and 17 years old not enrolled in school and their parents' educational and economic status. For example, 33.9% of the 16- and 17-year old group, whose parents had less than 8 years of schooling and an income of less than $3,000, are not attending school, in comparison to 5.8% whose parents had 12 or more years of schooling and an income of $7,000 or more. Similarly, but with differences not as pronounced, the corresponding figures for those 14 and 15 years old are 12.9% and 2.3%, respectively. The consistency of the relationships revealed by this series of statistics has made it possible to utilize pictorial projection with such clarity and simplicity. In delineating a chart of this kind, the most efficient and economic procedure is to utilize preprinted isometric paper.

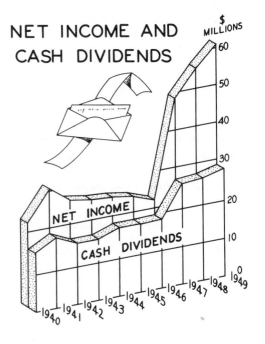

NET INCOME AND CASH DIVIDENDS

Figure 10–14. A surface chart showing two time series based on trimetric drawing. (Redrawn from International Harvester Co., Annual Report, 1949, p. 7.)

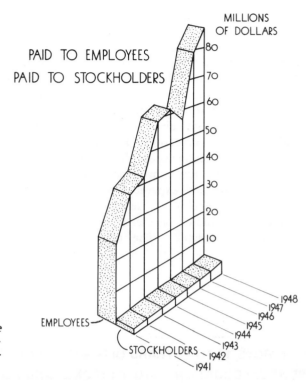

Figure 10–15. Another illustration of a surface chart in approximate isometric drawing. (Redrawn from Remington Rand, Inc., Annual Report, 1948, p. 6.)

Figure 10–17 represents a series of rectilinear coordinate line charts that seem to possess both trimetric and perspective projection characteristics. The chart portrays the amount and kind of assistance provided by the governments of countries that are members of the OECD Development Assistance Committee. The assistance went to so-called developing countries and multilateral agencies. The statistics cover the period 1964–1974. As will be observed, the total flow of financial resources increased from approximately 10 billion dollars in 1964 to almost 27 billion in 1974. The total flow is divided into five categories: (1) official development assistance, (2) private investment, (3) private export credits, (4) other official flows, and (5) grants by voluntary agencies. As indicated earlier, the type of projection utilized in the construction of this chart is not clear. Apparently, it shows both trimetric and perspective characteristics. In spite of the interesting design of this chart as well as its artistic appeal, it manifests certain ambiguities and distortions; the most obvious are the differences in the size of both the horizontal and vertical scale units. In the front portion of the chart the sizes of the scale units are larger than the corresponding ones in the back portion of the chart. Naturally, these discrepancies affect the size, proportions, and

other characteristics of the chart. If the designer of the chart had adhered consistently to trimetric or some other axonometric projection principles rather than resorting to perspective principles, these deficiencies would not have occurred.

Another artistic as well as effective illustration of a rectilinear coordinate chart drawn in trimetric projection is represented by Figure 10–18. This chart portrays trends in the proportion of single-parent families according to four age groupings of children. The age groupings are basically cumulative: under 3 years of age, under 6, 6–17, and under 18. The proportions of single-parent families portrayed by the chart represent percentages of all families with children in the four respective age groupings. An examination of Figure 10–18 clearly indicates that the proportion of single-parent families for each of the four series is increasing, with a maximum of almost 19% for the 6–17 age grouping.

Pie Charts Constructed in Pictorial Projection

Correct projection technique and skilled artistry, combined with a knowledge of constructing statisti-

cal charts, can produce an authentic and an esthetically appealing pie chart. In fact, carefully constructed three-dimensional pie charts can be made
superior to the conventional flat pie chart. Figures
10–19, 10–20, and 10–21 are examples of well-
constructed pie charts drawn in isometric and approximate isometric projection. It is sometimes difficult to differentiate circles drawn in axonometric
and perspective projection. For example, a circle
in isometric projection is an ellipse, whereas circles
drawn in perspective approximate an ellipse. The
most practical and expedient procedure in constructing an isometric ellipse is to utilize a plastic
isometric protractor or plastic isometric ellipses
guides or templates. The templates are constructed with mathematical precision and are available in many sizes with major axis diameters ranging up to 12 in. In dividing an ellipse into sectors it
is essential that an isometric protractor be used.
Obviously, the standard protractor will not do.
The crosshatching and shading in Figure 10–19
give depth and other picture-like qualities to the
chart.

Figures 10–20 and 10–21 include attractive and
meaningful pictorial fillers that add substantially to
the interpretability and forcefulness of these charts.
Figure 10–20 portrays the proportional distribution
pattern of the receipts of a large manufacturing corporation, expressed as parts of a dollar. There are
six categories. Figure 10–21 portrays the budget

PERCENT OF BOYS 14 TO 17 YEARS OLD NOT ENROLLED IN SCHOOL, BY PARENT'S EDUCATION, FAMILY INCOME, AND AGE. 1960

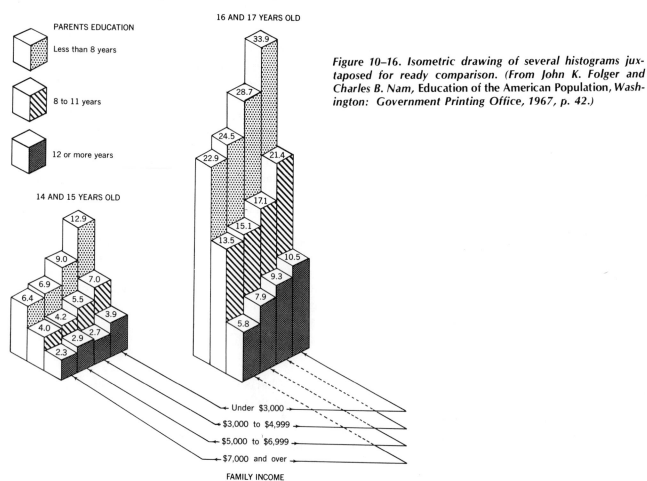

Figure 10–16. Isometric drawing of several histograms juxtaposed for ready comparison. (From John K. Folger and Charles B. Nam, Education of the American Population, Washington: Government Printing Office, 1967, p. 42.)

dollar of the federal government, including both sources of income and major categories of expenditure.

EXAMPLES OF CHARTS IN OBLIQUE PROJECTION

Oblique projection is particularly well adapted to the construction of column charts. In addition, oblique projection will be found effective for certain other types of charts such as the bar chart, rectilinear coordinate chart, and the surface chart. In this section examples are presented of all these graphic forms with special emphasis on column charts.

Column Charts

Figure 10–22 is a single-column chart showing variations and trends in enrollment at the University of

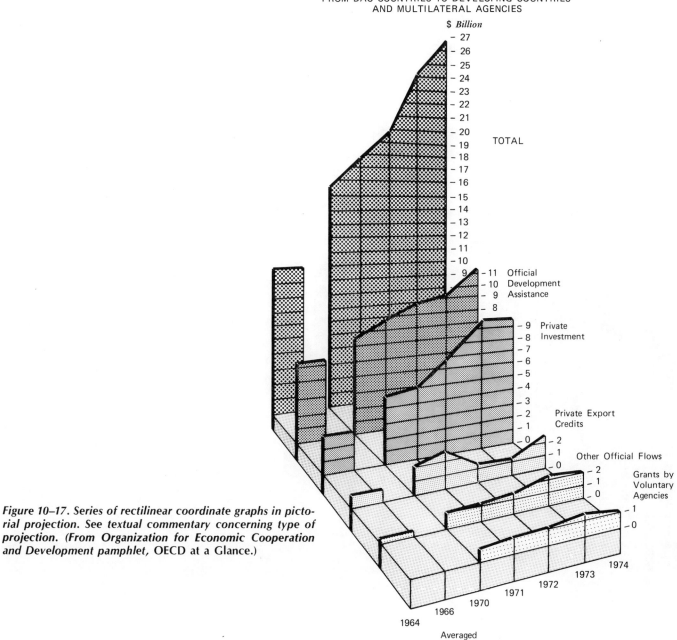

Figure 10–17. Series of rectilinear coordinate graphs in pictorial projection. See textual commentary concerning type of projection. (From Organization for Economic Cooperation and Development pamphlet, OECD at a Glance.)

Washington from 1966 to 1976. It will be observed that the front face of the column is black and the side face of the column is stippled. As indicated previously, the angle of obliquity may be any angle, but it is customarily 30° or 45°. The side face usually ranges from one-half to one-fifth the width of the front face. One of the more important considerations in designing a column chart in oblique form is to determine on what basis the height of the columns is to be measured. Figure 10–23 graphically illustrates this problem. It will be observed that

there are at least five different ways of measuring the height of a column chart drawn in oblique projection.[11] This apparently simple characteristic can cause much confusion. Furthermore, there does not seem to be any easy solution. The authors prefer the arrangement illustrated by B and D in Figure 10–23. Figure 10–22 is of this type. In oblique projection, outlines on the front face show their true

[11] The basic ideas for Figure 10–23 were taken from Haemer, "The Pseudo Third Dimension" (op. cit.).

Figure 10–18. Rectilinear coordinate chart drawn in trimetric projection [From "Early Childhood: An Integrated Policy for Growth and Development," in OECD Observer, (84), November–December 1976, pp. 19–22.]

SINGLE PARENT FAMILIES IN THE U.S.

as a percentage of all families with children under 3, 6, 18 and 6 through 17 years

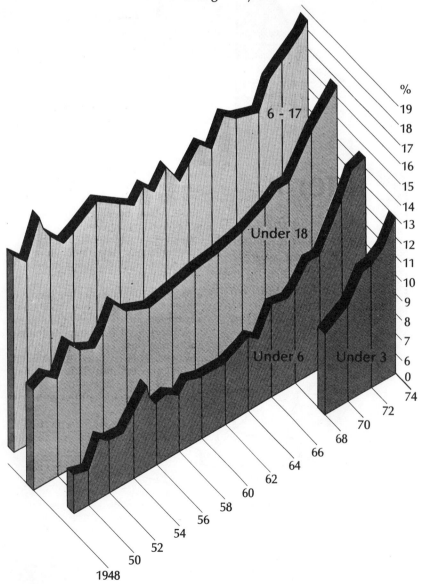

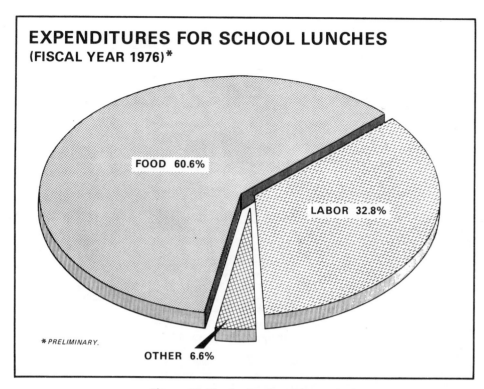

Figure 10–19. *A pie chart drawn in isometric projection. (From United States Department of Agriculture, 1976 Handbook of Agricultural Charts,* Agricultural Handbook No. 504, *October 1976, p. 83.)*

Figure 10–20. *A pictorial pie chart in approximate isometric projection. A circle in isometric projection is an ellipse, whereas a circle in perspective projection approximates an ellipse. (From International Harvester Co.,* Annual Report, *1949, p. 6.)*

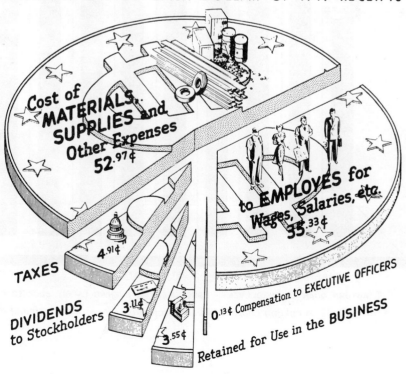

Figure 10–21. Another pictorial pie chart drawn in isometric projection. (From the President's Budget Message for 1953.)

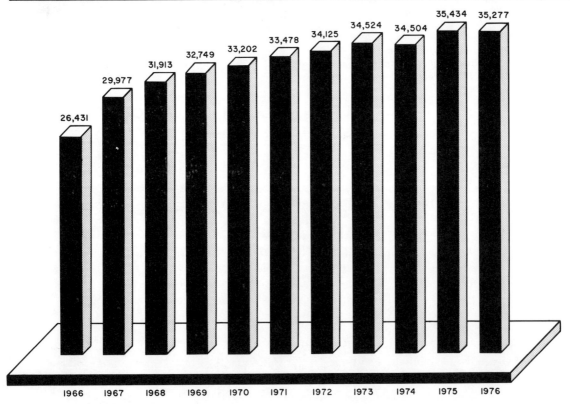

UNIVERSITY OF WASHINGTON ENROLLMENT TRENDS: 1966 TO 1976*

* AUTUMN QUARTER ENROLLMENT. ENROLLMENT IN EVENING CREDIT COURSES INCLUDED BEGINNING AUTUMN, 1967

Figure 10–22. A column chart in oblique projection (drawn from original data).

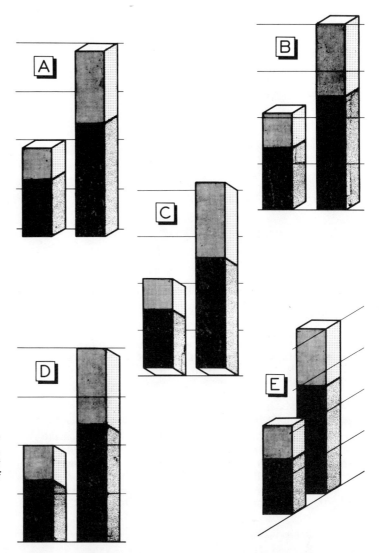

Figure 10–23. A common problem in pictorial projection techniques is to determine precise distances. As indicated by the above illustrations, there are at least five different ways of measuring the height of columns drawn in oblique projection.

size and shape. Moreover, the black face of the bars represents fundamentally a conventional column chart, and the sides and top are extraneous features designed to give depth to the chart for sake of pictorialization.

On the other hand, Figure 10–24 is very different. Instead of the face of the column, the back edge is chosen as the mensurational referent. Also, an actual scale is shown on this chart. It will be observed that Figure 10–24 is a grouped, subdivided-column chart, which compares earnings and cost of living for two different periods, for four personnel groups of the Du Pont Company.

Figure 10–25 is a subdivided-column chart in oblique projection showing trends in funding from 1969 to 1976 for food-assistance programs of the United States Department of Agriculture. The

three major programs are food distribution, food stamps, and child nutrition. The amount funded for each of these programs is shown on the columns by a distinctive hatching pattern. It will be observed that the category reflecting the greatest increase during this 8-year period is the food-stamp program. The funding for all three programs was less than two billion dollars in 1969 as compared to over eight billion dollars in 1976. The value represented by each of the columns is measured by the height of the front face.

Figure 10–26 is a series of 100%, subdivided-column charts constructed in oblique projection that show trends in racial integration by region and for the entire country for 1968, 1970, and 1972. Each column indicates the racial composition of children attending public schools in the three re-

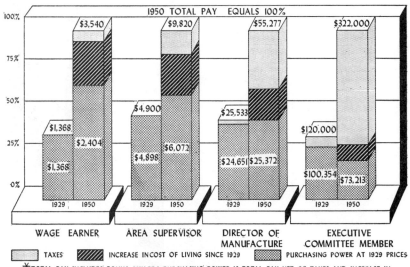

TOTAL PAY AND PURCHASING POWER*
1929 VS 1950

1950 TOTAL PAY EQUALS 100%

WAGE EARNER   AREA SUPERVISOR   DIRECTOR OF MANUFACTURE   EXECUTIVE COMMITTEE MEMBER

TAXES   INCREASE IN COST OF LIVING SINCE 1929   PURCHASING POWER AT 1929 PRICES

*TOTAL PAY INCLUDES BONUS AWARDS. PURCHASING POWER IS TOTAL PAY NET OF TAXES AND INCREASE IN COST OF LIVING SINCE 1929 ('SHRINKAGE IN VALUE OF THE DOLLAR') AS MEASURED BY U.S.B.L.S. CONSUMER'S PRICE INDEX.

Figure 10–24. A grouped–subdivided–column chart in oblique projection. (Redrawn from E. I. Du Pont de Nemours and Company, Annual Report, 1950, p. 30.)

Figure 10–25. Subdivided–column chart drawn in oblique projection. Normally, the ordinal scale should be placed on the left side, but because of the peculiar composition of this chart, there is justification in placing it on the right side. The columns are scaled from the front face. (From United States Department of Agriculture, 1976 Handbook of Agricultural Charts, Agricultural Handbook No. 504, October 1976, p. 75.)

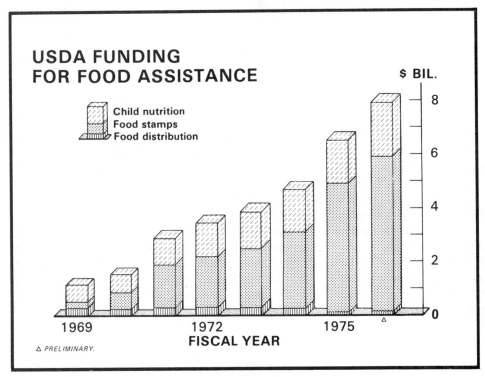

USDA FUNDING FOR FOOD ASSISTANCE

$ BIL.

Child nutrition
Food stamps
Food distribution

1969   1972   1975

FISCAL YEAR

△ PRELIMINARY.

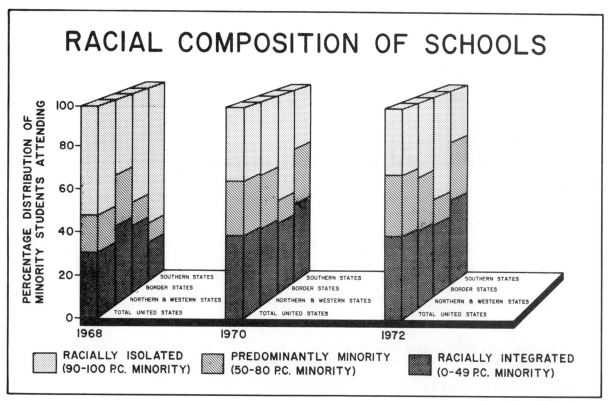

Figure 10–26. Grouped one–hundred percent column chart in oblique projection shows trends in racial composition of schools. (From National Center for Education Statistics, The Condition of Education: 1976 Edition, HEW, Office of Education, Washington: Government Printing Office, 1976, p. 67.)

gions and in the entire United States. Differentials in racial composition are defined in terms of the proportion of the children who are members of minority racial groups. There are: (1) "racially isolated" schools, where 90–100% of the children are members of minority races, (2) "predominantly minority," where 50–80% of the children are members of minority races, and (3) "racially integrated," where 0–49% are members of minority races. Each of these three categories is represented by a special hatching pattern on the columns. Since Figure 10–26 is a 100% column chart, the vertical scale is expressed in percentages ranging from zero to 100. The chart clearly reveals that the greatest increase in racial integration in the public schools occurred in the Southern states, especially between 1968 and 1970.

Figure 10–27 is a net-deviation-column chart delineated in oblique projection. It shows the percentage variation in mortality from all causes, for "standard ordinary policyholders" of the Metropolitan Life Insurance Company, from 1971 to

1976. The base from which the percentage deviations were derived, is the mean rate for the entire 1971–1976 period. The chart clearly shows that mortality was above the average for the first 3 years and below average for the last 3 years. The scale values, expressed in percentages, measure the front face of each column.

Although Figure 10–28 is a net-deviation-column chart constructed in oblique projection, it is substantially different from the preceding chart. It does not have a temporal axis. Its major categories emphasize comparative changes in consumption for specified kinds of vegetables. The bases for these comparisons are consumption patterns for two different 3-year periods, 1960–1962 versus 1972–1974. The differences between these two periods are expressed in percentages, which are measured on the chart by the length of the front face of each column. There is no vertical scale as in several of the preceding charts. The thin, simulated transparency of the platform from which the length of each column is measured is more definitive and precise, espe-

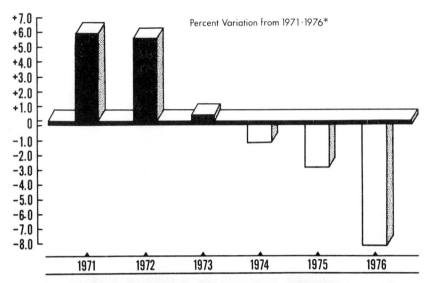

Percent Variation from 1971-1976*

Figure 10–27. A net–deviation–column chart drawn in oblique projection. Chart shows percent variation in mortality from 1971–1976 average for insurance policy holders. Death rates are adjusted to the 1976 distribution by age and sex. (From Metropolitan Life Insurance Company, Statistical Bulletin, October 1976, p. 12.)

Figure 10–28. A net–deviation–column chart drawn in oblique projection. It will be observed that the basic figures represent percentage changes in per capita fresh vegetable consumption between averages for two 3–year periods, 1960–1962 and 1972–1974. (From United States Department of Agriculture, 1975 Handbook of Agricultural Charts, Agriculture Handbook No. 491, October 1975, p. 150.)

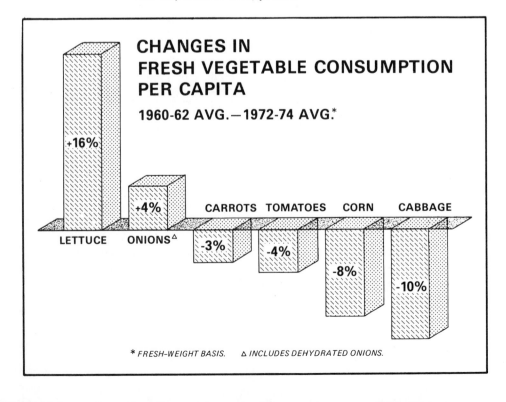

CHANGES IN FRESH VEGETABLE CONSUMPTION PER CAPITA

1960-62 AVG. — 1972-74 AVG.*

+16% LETTUCE
+4% ONIONS△
-3% CARROTS
-4% TOMATOES
-8% CORN
-10% CABBAGE

* FRESH-WEIGHT BASIS.   △ INCLUDES DEHYDRATED ONIONS.

cially for the negative deviations, than the thicker opaque platform in Figure 10–27.

A combination of a bilateral-column chart and an arithmetic line graph drawn in oblique projection is presented in Figure 10–29. The most unique features of this chart are the two grids depicted in oblique projection. Although both sets of columns are shown in oblique projection, emphasis is not placed on this fact. Visually, the columns possess very little depth except for a slight amount of shading. The vertical columns represent total purchases, and the "horizontal" columns, total sales. Curves superimposed on the two grids indicate sales and net purchases. Charts like this one, as well as others portrayed in this chapter, are basically very simple, and only a rudimentary knowledge of projection principles and techniques is required to construct them.

Bar Charts

Figure 10–30 is a subdivided-bar chart drawn in oblique projection. It is obvious that by repositioning the bars so they are arranged vertically, the basic design becomes readily transformed into a column chart. Of course, the years would have to be rearranged in chronological order to complete the transformation. In a series of this kind, where the temporal factor is of primary importance, a column chart would perhaps be more appropriate than a bar chart. Figure 10–30 portrays trends in the cost of the food-stamp program as reported by the United States Department of Agriculture. The scale representing cost in billions of dollars is located below

---

[12] Compare U.S. Department of Agriculture, *1975 Handbook of Agricultural Charts,* Agriculture Handbook No. 491, Washington, D. C., 1975, p. 75.

the bars, and the major cost categories are differentiated by a hatching scheme.

Surface Charts

Figure 10–31 is an example of a subdivided- or multiple-surface chart constructed in oblique projection. It shows trends in participation in the food-stamp program from 1969 to 1976. The ordinal scale indicates the number of participants in millions and, of course, the abscissal scale represents years (fiscal). There are two strata, the lower one comprising those on public assistance and the upper one, those not on public assistance.

Figure 10–32, like Figure 10–31, may be classified as a subdivided- or multiple-surface chart drawn in oblique projection. However, in Figure 10–32 the strata run parallel to each other, whereas in Figure 10–31 one stratum is above the other. Figure 10–32 depicts trends in the value of food stamps issued from 1969 to 1976. The stratum representing "total" figures has been placed in back and the stratum representing "bonus" figures, in front. Because of the visual distortion inherent in projections of this kind the location of the vertical scale has created a slight ambiguity. Should the vertical scale be placed in continuity with the front face or with the rear face of the chart? It is interesting to observe that this decision apparently may have created a dilemma in the mind of the delineator of the chart, since in contrast to the 1976 version of this chart, where the vertical scale was placed in line with the front face, in the 1975 version it was placed in alignment with the rear face of the chart.[12] The reproduction of the food coupon on the chart serves as a symbolical pictorial embellishment.

Figure 10–29. A combined column and line chart drawn in oblique projection. (From 1950 Annual Report of the Secretary of the Treasury, p. 289.)

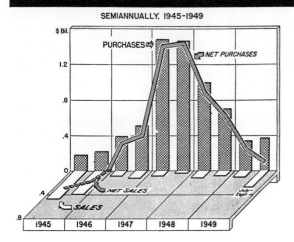

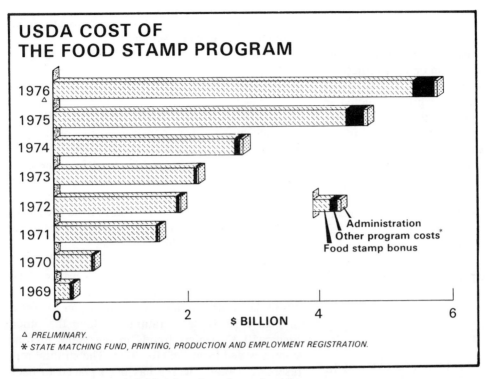

USDA COST OF THE FOOD STAMP PROGRAM

1976 △
1975
1974
1973
1972
1971
1970
1969

Administration
Other program costs*
Food stamp bonus

0   2   4   6
       $ BILLION

△ PRELIMINARY.
✱ STATE MATCHING FUND, PRINTING, PRODUCTION AND EMPLOYMENT REGISTRATION.

Figure 10–30. A subdivided–bar chart drawn in oblique projection. (From United States Department of Agriculture, 1976 Handbook of Agricultural Charts, Agricultural Handbook No. 504, October 1976, p. 77.)

Figure 10–31. A subdivided– or multiple–surface chart constructed in oblique projection. (From United States Department of Agriculture, 1976 Handbook of Agricultural Charts, Agricultural Handbook No. 504, October 1976, p. 76.)

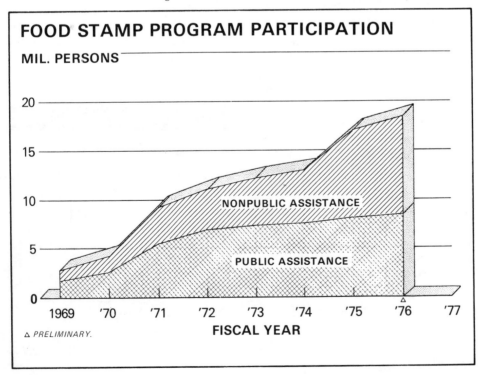

FOOD STAMP PROGRAM PARTICIPATION

MIL. PERSONS

20

15

10

NONPUBLIC ASSISTANCE

5

PUBLIC ASSISTANCE

0

1969   '70   '71   '72   '73   '74   '75   '76 △   '77

FISCAL YEAR

△ PRELIMINARY.

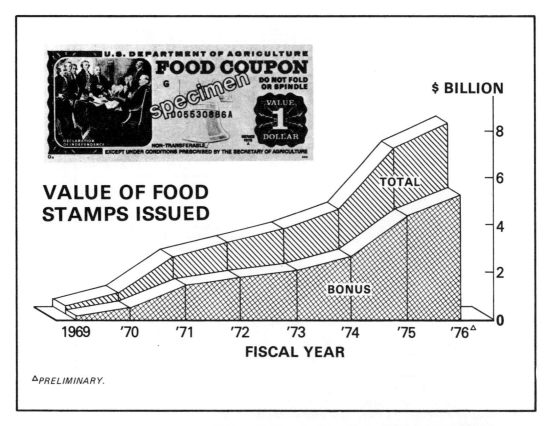

Figure 10–32. Another illustration of a subdivided– or multiple–strata–surface chart drawn in oblique projection. It will be noted that the basic design is different from the preceding chart. This chart consists of two separate juxtaposed surfaces, rather than one continuous surface that has been subdivided. (From United States Department of Agriculture, 1976 Handbook of Agricultural Charts, Agricultural Handbook No. 504, October 1976, p. 78.)

Organization Chart

Figure 10–33 is an organization chart whose basic components are plotted in oblique projection. The interrelationships of the various components are shown by artistically compatible connecting lines. The chart emphasizes the role of corporations in the structure of American farming. It will be observed that the 1,733,663 farms with sales of $2,500 or more are first classified by ownership or control. Corporations control 1% of these farms. The corporation-controlled farms are divided into two groups—those with more than 10 shareholders (8%) and those with 10 or fewer shareholders (92%). As an indicator of the importance of farms controlled by corporations, the amount of sales for each of

these two groups is shown on the bottom level of the chart.

EXAMPLES OF CHART IN PERSPECTIVE PROJECTION

Although perspective is the most realistic type of projection, it is the least satisfactory for graphic presentation. Perspective projection tends to distort objects to such a degree that it is virtually impossible to portray exact distance, shape, or size. It should not be implied, however, that perspective projection must never be used in the construction of statistical charts. Sometimes perspective projection can be used in pictorializing base maps and

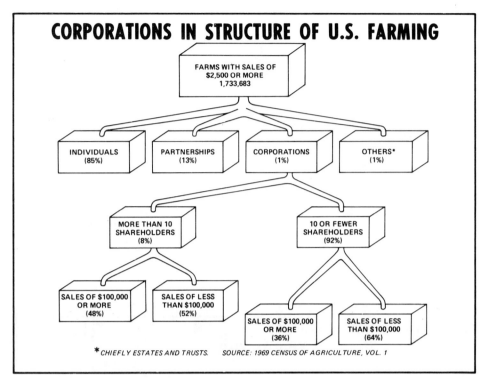

Figure 10–33. Organizational chart drawn in oblique projection. (From United States Department of Agriculture, 1973 Handbook of Agricultural Charts, Agricultural Handbook No. 455, October 1973, p. 28.)

ancillary elements in charts where exact mathematical relationships are secondary. However, where precise quantitative measurements are involved, as is the case for most statistical charts, it is not advisable to use perspective projection.

For example, Figure 10–34 illustrates a combination column-bar chart drawn in perspective projection. One axis indicates the amount of business and the other, the earnings of the Burroughs Adding Machine Company for 1937 to 1947. The grids for both the "vertical" columns and the "horizontal" bars are badly distorted as a consequence of the characteristic recession toward vanishing points. Accordingly, the width and height of the columns and bars are distorted to such a degree that even after a most careful examination the essential implications of the chart are almost impossible to interpret.

The reader will recall that Figures 10–10 and 10–11 further emphasize the deficiencies exemplified by Figure 10–34. Figure 10–10 demonstrates the consequences of recasting in perspective projection a simple, straightforward column chart. Every basic feature of the chart has been dis-

torted. The width of the columns and the calibrations of both the horizontal and vertical scales are so unequal as to render the chart almost impossible to interpret. There does not seem to be any justification for designing a chart of this kind. Figure 10–11 illustrates additional problems and weaknesses inherent in the application of perspective projection to graphic presentation.

MAPS CONSTRUCTED IN PICTORIAL PROJECTION

Frequently, maps drawn in pictorial projection may be more effective in presenting spatial data than the conventional flat, two-dimensional map. In the preparation of three-dimensional maps all of the basic projection techniques—axonometric, oblique, and perspective—may be used either singly or in combination. Most of the illustrations presented in the following pages represent combinations of perspective and oblique projection and perspective and quasiperspective projection. For example, the base maps depicted in Figures 10–35, 10–36, 10–37,

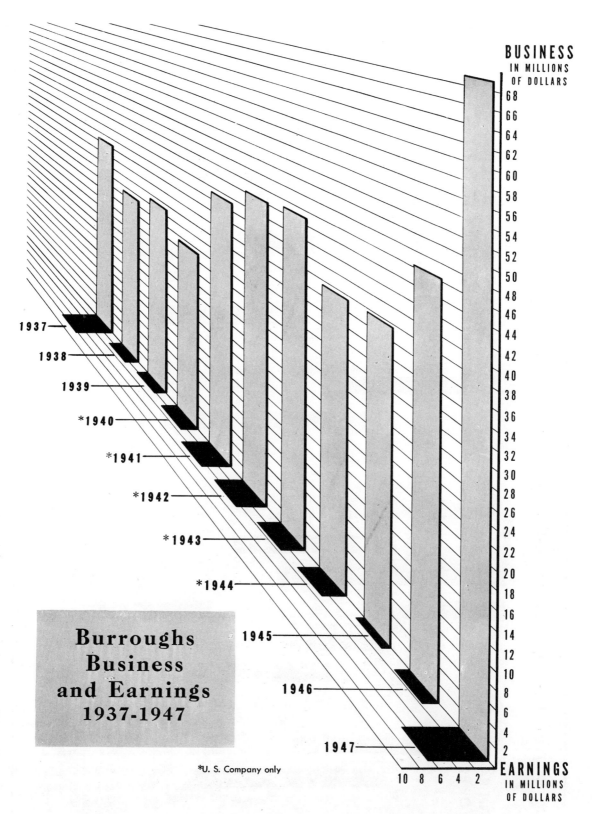

BUSINESS
IN MILLIONS
OF DOLLARS

68
66
64
62
60
58
56
54
52
50
48
46
44
42
40
38
36
34
32
30
28
26
24
22
20
18
16
14
12
10
8
6
4
2

1937
1938
1939
*1940
*1941
*1942
*1943
*1944
1945
1946
1947

Burroughs
Business
and Earnings
1937-1947

*U. S. Company only

10 8 6 4 2   EARNINGS
IN MILLIONS
OF DOLLARS

Figure 10–34. A combination column–bar chart drawn in perspective. Note that columns indicate total amount of business for each year from 1937 to 1947, and bars show corresponding earnings. (From Burroughs Adding Machine Co., Annual Report, 1947, p. 12.)

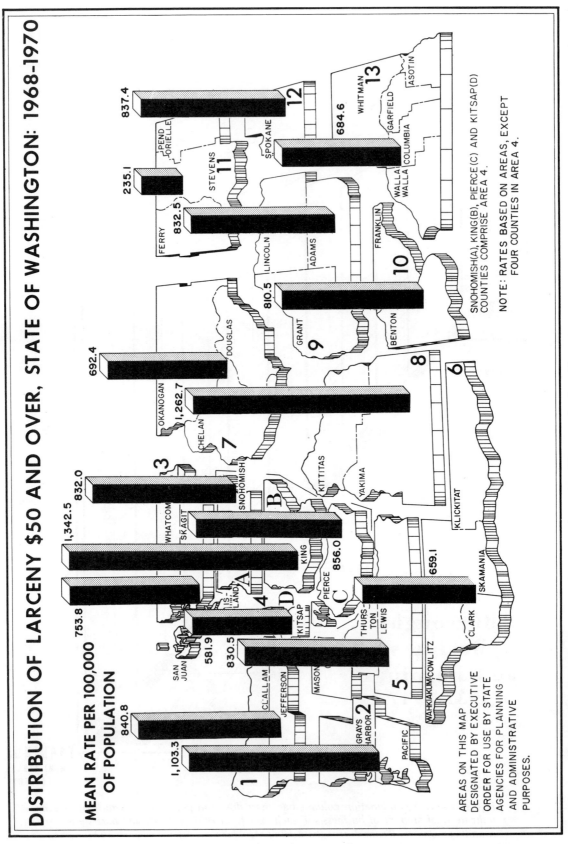

DISTRIBUTION OF LARCENY $50 AND OVER, STATE OF WASHINGTON: 1968-1970

MEAN RATE PER 100,000 OF POPULATION

Figure 10–35. A three–dimensional map. The columns are drawn in oblique projection. The base map, which was created photographically, is fundamentally in perspective projection. (From Calvin F. Schmid and Stanton E. Schmid, Crime in the State of Washington, Olympia: Law and Justice Planning Office, Planning and Community Affairs Agency, 1972, p. 56.)

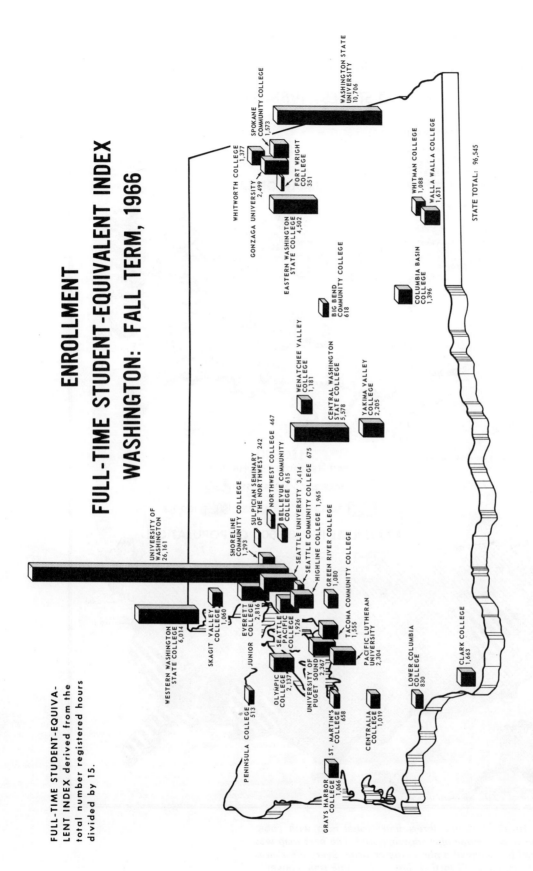

ENROLLMENT

FULL-TIME STUDENT-EQUIVALENT INDEX

WASHINGTON: FALL TERM, 1966

FULL-TIME STUDENT-EQUIVA-
LENT INDEX derived from the
total number registered hours
divided by 15.

UNIVERSITY OF
WASHINGTON
26,161

WESTERN WASHINGTON
STATE COLLEGE
6,014

SKAGIT VALLEY
COLLEGE
1,060

EVERETT COLLEGE
2,816

JUNIOR

SEATTLE
PACIFIC
COLLEGE
1,926

SHORELINE
COMMUNITY COLLEGE
1,293

SULPICIAN SEMINARY
OF THE NORTHWEST 242

NORTHWEST COLLEGE 467

BELLEVUE COMMUNITY
COLLEGE 615

SEATTLE UNIVERSITY 3,414

SEATTLE COMMUNITY COLLEGE 675

HIGHLINE COLLEGE 1,965

GREEN RIVER COLLEGE
1,080

TACOMA COMMUNITY COLLEGE
1,555

PENINSULA COLLEGE
513

OLYMPIC
COLLEGE
2,137

UNIVERSITY OF
PUGET SOUND
2,367

ST. MARTIN'S
COLLEGE
658

PACIFIC LUTHERAN
UNIVERSITY
2,304

CENTRALIA
COLLEGE
1,019

GRAYS HARBOR
COLLEGE
1,066

LOWER COLUMBIA
COLLEGE
830

CLARK COLLEGE
1,663

WHITWORTH COLLEGE
1,377

SPOKANE
COMMUNITY COLLEGE
1,573

GONZAGA UNIVERSITY
2,499

FORT WRIGHT
COLLEGE
351

WASHINGTON STATE
UNIVERSITY
10,706

EASTERN WASHINGTON
STATE COLLEGE
4,502

BIG BEND
COMMUNITY COLLEGE
618

WENATCHEE VALLEY
COLLEGE
1,181

CENTRAL WASHINGTON
STATE COLLEGE
5,578

YAKIMA VALLEY
COLLEGE
2,205

COLUMBIA BASIN
COLLEGE
1,396

WHITMAN COLLEGE
1,088

WALLA WALLA COLLEGE
1,631

STATE TOTAL: 96,545

Figure 10-36. Another example of a three-dimensional map. This map is similar to the preceding chart, but in more simplified form. (From Calvin F. Schmid, Vincent A. Miller, and William S. Packard, Enrollment Statistics, Colleges and Universities, State of Washington, Fall Term: 1966, Olympia: Planning and Community Affairs Agency, 1967, p. 7.)

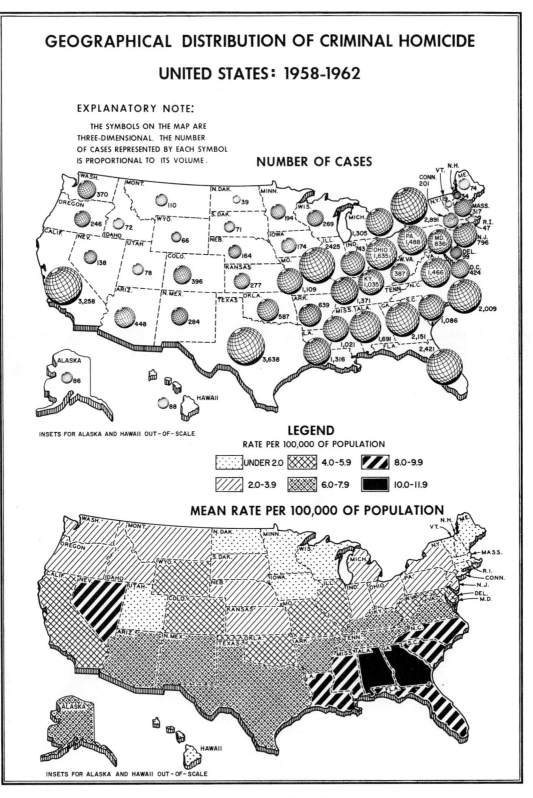

Figure 10–37. A simple three–dimensional map with cubic symbols and crosshatching superimposed. The base map was prepared by means of a photographic print. Every effort was made to minimize distortion, but at the same time convey a three–dimensional effect. (From Calvin F. Schmid and Stanton E. Schmid, Crime in the State of Washington, Olympia: Law and Justice Planning Office, Planning and Community Affairs Agency, 1972, p. 74.)

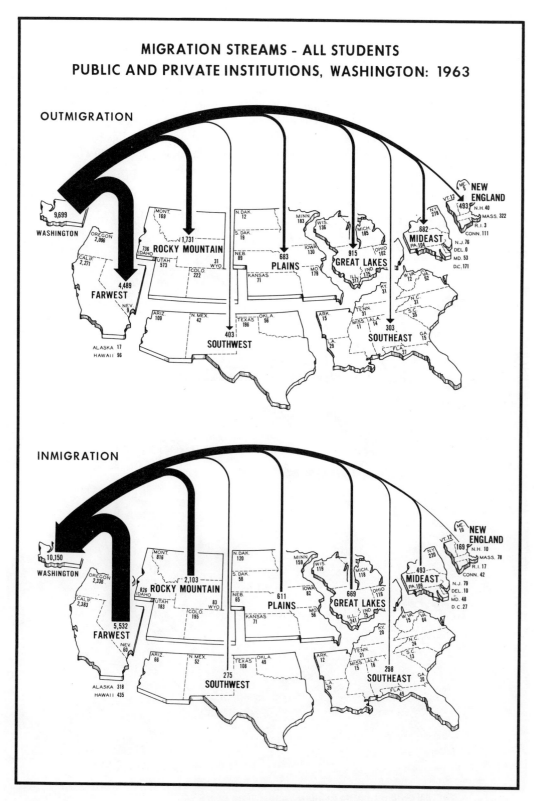

MIGRATION STREAMS - ALL STUDENTS
PUBLIC AND PRIVATE INSTITUTIONS, WASHINGTON: 1963

OUTMIGRATION

WASHINGTON 9,699

OREGON 2,096

CALIF. 2,271

MONT. 169

IDAHO 736

UTAH 573

COLO. 222

WYO. 31

ROCKY MOUNTAIN 1,731

FARWEST 4,489

NEV. 9

ALASKA 17

HAWAII 96

ARIZ. 109

N. MEX. 42

TEXAS 196

OKLA. 56

SOUTHWEST 403

N. DAK. 12

S. DAK. 19

NEB. 89

KANSAS 71

PLAINS 683

MINN. 183

WIS. 136

IOWA 130

MO. 179

GREAT LAKES 915

MICH. 185

OHIO 102

IND. 179

ILL. 317

KY. 31

ARK. 15

MISS. 11

TENN. 31

ALA. 14

LA. 29

SOUTHEAST 303

GA. 15

FLA. 27

W. VA. 12

VA. 52

N.C. 31

S.C. 35

MIDEAST 682

PA. 104

N.Y. 278

N.J. 76

DEL. 0

MD. 53

D.C. 171

NEW ENGLAND 493

ME. 5

VT. 12

N.H. 40

MASS. 322

R.I. 3

CONN. 111

INMIGRATION

WASHINGTON 10,150

OREGON 2,336

CALIF. 2,383

MONT. 816

IDAHO 826

UTAH 183

COLO. 195

WYO. 83

ROCKY MOUNTAIN 2,103

FARWEST 5,532

NEV. 60

ALASKA 318

HAWAII 435

ARIZ. 66

N. MEX. 52

TEXAS 108

OKLA. 49

SOUTHWEST 275

N. DAK. 120

S. DAK. 58

NEB. 65

KANSAS 71

PLAINS 611

MINN. 159

WIS. 119

IOWA 82

MO. 56

GREAT LAKES 669

MICH. 118

OHIO 116

IND. 75

ILL. 241

KY. 20

ARK. 12

MISS. 15

TENN. 21

ALA. 16

LA. 29

SOUTHEAST 298

GA. 20

FLA. 49

W. VA. 15

VA. 64

N.C. 24

S.C. 13

MIDEAST 493

PA. 109

N.Y. 220

N.J. 79

DEL. 10

MD. 48

D.C. 27

NEW ENGLAND 169

ME. 10

VT. 12

N.H. 10

MASS. 78

R.I. 17

CONN. 42

Figure 10–38. A flow–map drawn in three–dimensional form. This map shows streams of college and university student migration from (outmigration) and to (inmigration) the state of Washington. The width of the lines on the chart is indicative of the number of students. (From Charles S. Gossman, Charles E. Nobbe, Theresa J. Patricelli, Calvin F. Schmid, and Thomas E. Steahr, Migration of College and University Students, State of Washington, Seattle: Washington State Census Board, 1967, p. 3.)

and 10–38 have been constructed in perspective projection. Judged in terms of time, cost, labor, and reliability, we have found that in the construction of base maps in pictorial projection photographic reproduction techniques are far superior to the tedious and complicated drafting techniques. The photographic procedure in constructing pictorial projection base maps is very simple and straightforward. For example, in constructing a

base map of planning and administrative areas in the state of Washington, there were five steps: (1) a county outline map of the state showing planning and administrative areas was mounted on $\frac{3}{4}$ in. insulating board; (2) the planning and administrative areas along with Snohomish, King, Kitsap, and Pierce Counties (Area 4) separately were carefully cut out with a jigsaw; (3) after placing all the pieces in proper position on a flat surface, photographs were

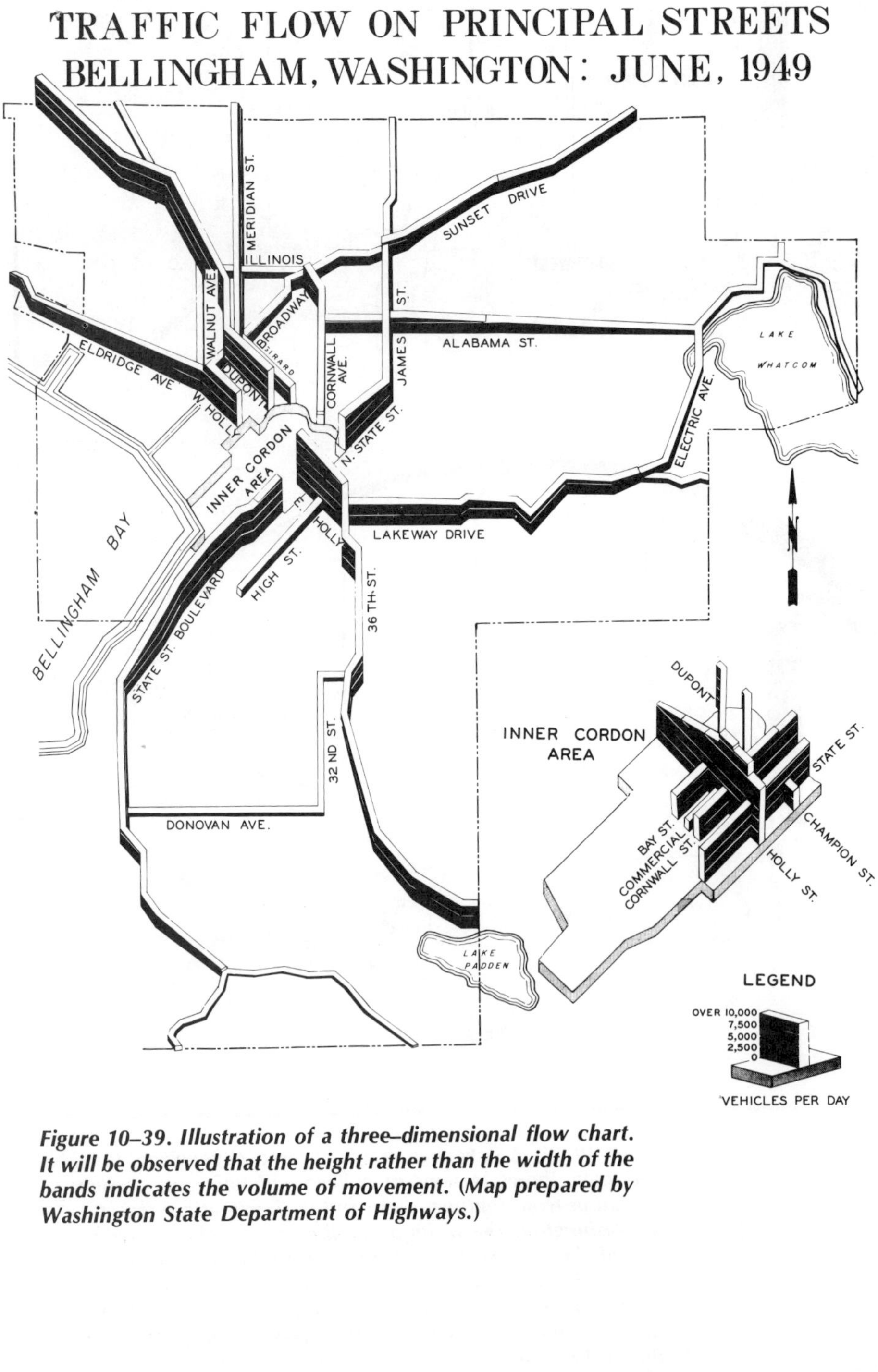

Figure 10–39. Illustration of a three–dimensional flow chart. It will be observed that the height rather than the width of the bands indicates the volume of movement. (Map prepared by Washington State Department of Highways.)

taken at different heights and angles; (4) a tracing with shading, lettering, border, and other features was drafted from the most suitable enlarged photographic print; and (5) several relatively inexpensive black-line prints were made from the tracing on which were superimposed different graphic forms, symbols, and lettering.

Figure 10–35 is an example of one of these charts. Altogether there are 20 maps in this series, which portray both the actual number of various crimes and rates per 100,000 of population.[13] It will be observed that Figure 10–35 shows mean rates per 100,000 of population for larceny of $50 and over for the 3-year period 1968–1970 according to planning and administrative areas in the state of Washington. The various columns are drawn in oblique projection, and of course, the heights of the columns are commensurate with the rates that are represented.

Figure 10–36 is in certain respects similar to Figure 10–35. Figure 10–36 portrays the approximate location and size of all the institutions of higher learning in the state of Washington as of the fall term of 1966. Enrollment is measured in terms of a full-time student-equivalent index, derived from the total number of registered hours divided by 15. In the fall of 1966 there was a total of 36 institutions of higher learning in the state of Washington. The enrollment of each institution is shown by a column drawn in oblique projection. Furthermore, the lettering contiguous to each of the columns indicates the name of the college or university and its exact enrollment. The enrollment ranges from 242 at the Sepulcian Seminary of the Northwest to 25,161 at the University of Washington. The total enrollment based on the full-time student-equivalent index for all institutions was 96,545.

Figure 10–37 portrays the geographic distribution of criminal homicide in the United States during the 5-year period 1958–1962. The actual

[13] Calvin F. Schmid and Stanton E. Schmid, *Crime in the State of Washington*, Olympia: Law and Justice Planning Office, Planning and Community Affairs Agency, 1972, pp. 38–69.

number of homicidal deaths as well as the incidence per 100,000 of population are included in this chart. It will be observed that the two base maps are identical and are shown in perspective projection. The symbols on the top map are in the form of spheres, and the number of cases represented by each symbol is proportional to its volume. Geometrically, the volume of a sphere varies as the cube root of its diameter. In the lower map the visual criterion for portraying rate differentials is based on a hatching gradation ranging from light to dark, with the darker the hatching, the higher the rates. A more extended discussion of the theory and practice of constructing statistical maps will be found in Chapter 8.

Figure 10–38 consists of two flow maps showing streams of college and university-student migration in and out of the state of Washington. In the fall of 1963 a total of 73,375 students enrolled in institutions of higher education in the United States reported Washington as their state of permanent residence. Of this total, 9699 migrated from Washington to colleges and universities located in other states. On the other hand, 10,150 students from other states were enrolled in Washington's colleges and universities. The volume and pattern of in- and outmigration are shown by the relative thickness and direction of the various flow lines. The eight groupings of states represent regional divisions delineated by the United States Office of Education. The base maps are in perspective projection, and the flow patterns have been superimposed by trial-and-error impressionistic sketching in quasi-perspective projection.

Figure 10–39 is another example of a flow map drawn in perspective. It shows the volume of traffic on the principal streets of a medium-sized city in the state of Washington. The relative height of the bands indicates the number of motor vehicles passing at various points on the main arteries of traffic. Although this type of map possesses unusual popular appeal, it is difficult to portray scale values accurately in many instances.

CHAPTER ELEVEN

ROLE OF THE COMPUTER IN GRAPHIC PRESENTATION

HERE THE PURPOSE IS TO INCREASE THE reader's awareness of the basic characteristics, applications, constraints, and potentials of computer-assisted graphic presentation. Obviously, because of limitation of space it is merely descriptive and informative and makes no pretense of serving as a guide or manual, even on the most elementary level. Any meaningful treatment of this kind with all its complexities and ramifications could hardly be encompassed in a single volume, to say nothing of a single chapter. Hopefully, this discussion will help the reader with little or no background in computer techniques to acquire a better understanding of the role of the computer in graphic presentation, as well as provide an incentive to pursue this subject further.

APPLICATION AND CONSTRAINTS OF THE COMPUTER IN GRAPHIC PRESENTATION

In recent years one of the most unprecedented developments in the field of graphic presentation has been the utilization of electronic computers and auxiliary equipment in the preparation of statistical charts. This development has occurred during a span of approximately 25 years, with the last 5–10 years representing a period of spectacular change.[2] In fact, "during the early 1970's computer graphic technology progressed far more rapidly than many of its most ardent proponents had hoped was possi-

ble."[3] Moreover, as far as the future is concerned, even more rapid application and development of computer technology in graphic presentation can be anticipated.

Although it has been convincingly demonstrated that computerized techniques occupy a very essential place in graphic presentation, it should be recognized that they possess certain constraints and limitations. Certainly, to assume at this stage that automation represents the ultimate solution for most of the basic problems in graphic presentation is mere fantasy. Without denigrating the importance of automation, an attempt will be made to evaluate its role, both present and future, from a realistic and objective point of view.

At the present level of technological development, two of the most significant constraints associated with computer-aided graphics are cost capability and performance quality. For example, the computer hardware system used by the United States Bureau of the Census in the production of graphics (discussed more fully in a later section of this chapter), including the three main units—the graphic terminal, the plotter, and the COM system—cost "about $570,000 . . . less sophisticated counterparts would run a great deal less."[4] In the case of the Census Bureau with its tremendous work load and massive collection, tabulation, and publication responsibilities, equipment of this kind is indispensable. It is obvious, however, that comparatively few public or private organizations or agencies can afford an expenditure of this magnitude, or one even considerably smaller.

However, in most large cities and university centers throughout the United States there are computer-service bureaus where it is possible to purchase time on computer equipment, including computer personnel. No doubt, in the future it can be assumed that more and improved computer installations will become available, and rental and other service charges should decline.[5]

In determining whether a particular chart or series of charts should be produced by computer or by the traditional hand method, there are two basic pragmatic considerations that should be carefully examined; namely, cost and quality. Occasionally, speed of production may be a secondary consideration. From the authors' perspective the process used in the production of charts—whether manual or automated—is not particularly relevant, provided there is little or no difference in the cost and quality of the charts. Under specified circumstances if one or the other basic technique is demonstrably superior in cost and quality, then that process should be chosen. Each case must be judged in light of existing facts and circumstances. Assuming that the cost and quality of the charts produced are the same, the context of a discussion concerning the comparative advantages and disadvantages of manual versus automated techniques becomes basically a question of mechanics.[6]

Not infrequently, it may be found expedient to combine automated and manual techniques for constructing certain types of charts. For example, where more tedious and complicated mathematical procedures are involved, a computer may be used for the basic layout, and a draftsman may prepare the final chart in more presentable form.[7]

As indicated previously, it is not possible to define in precise, quantifiable terms the concept of quality as applied to statistical charts. Nevertheless, there has developed over the years, among knowledgeable specialists in the field, a consensus of standards and criteria that can reliably categorize charts as "good" or "bad" and "acceptable" or "unacceptable." The ultimate criteria of quality in evaluating a statistical chart must be thought of in terms of forcefulness, integrity, and efficiency in communicating ideas. These criteria reflect the know-how, the expertise of the designer—in short, his professional competence. The mere mechanics of rendering the chart—whether manually or by electronic computer—represents an entirely different dimension. Chart design is a body of knowledge and expertise entirely different from drafting skills per se, or the ability to operate an electronic computer. The most skilled draftsman or the most experienced computer specialist, to say nothing of their run-of-the-mill counterparts, who do not possess extensive and well-rounded background and training in graphic design and supporting disciplines, are simply not competent to prepare superior statistical charts. Perhaps the most significant concern in the field of graphic presentation is production of statistical charts of the highest quality—charts that are effective, meaningful, attractive, and reliable. This implies higher standards of professional competence, which in turn are dependent on training and experience in graphic design. Although recognizably important the mechanics of chart making—whether manual or automated—are of secondary importance.

Although written from the point of view of the cartographer, the following quotation is applicable to the broader field of graphic presentation:

Too frequently there is evidence that systems to produce computer maps are the creation of cartographers lacking in computer knowhow or, possibly worse, computer scientists in ignorance of the niceties of cartography. If the subject is

[1] We are indebted to Mr. Jerry B. Schneider, Professor of Urban Planning and Civil Engineering of the University of Washington, and to Mr. Richard H. Schweitzer, Jr., Geographic Planning Specialist of the U.S. Bureau of the Census, for a critical reading of this chapter and for offering constructive suggestions.

[2] Apparently, the first computer maps were produced by a group of Swedish meteorologists in 1952. They were contour maps produced on a line printer; see Richard H. Schweitzer, "Micrographics: A New Approach to Automated Cartography and Graphics," *Proceedings of the 22nd International Technical Communication Conference,* Anaheim, California, 1975, pp. 305–316.

[3] Richard H. Schweitzer, *Mapping Urban America with Automated Cartography,* U.S. Bureau of the Census, Washington, D. C., 1973, p. 1.

[4] Vincent P. Barabba, "Automating Statistical Graphics: A Tool for Communication," American Statistics Association, *Proceedings of the Social Statistics Section,* 1976, Part 1. Washington, D. C.: 1976, pp. 82–88.

[5] United States Bureau of the Census, *Census Use Study: Computer Mapping,* Report No. 2, Washington, D. C.: Government Printing Office, 1969, p. 25.

[6] In this connection, it is interesting to note that some cartographers regard the introduction of automation to their field as nothing more nor less than another change of tools, whereas others hold an alternative viewpoint implying that automation can improve cartographic products over a wide range of applications and can produce map products that were hitherto impossible. The latter regard automation as a revolutionary rather than an evolutionary event; see David Rhind, "Computer-Aided Cartography," Institute of British Geographers, *Contemporary Cartography,* Transactions New Series, **2**, (1) (1977), 71–97.

[7] Recent examples of hundreds of charts prepared by a combination of both manual and computer techniques will be found in Ronald Abler and John S. Adams, *A Comparative Atlas of America's Great Cities: Twenty Metropolitan Regions,* Vol. 3, Published by the Association of American Geographers and the University of Minnesota Press, 1976:

Producing the atlas required the design and execution of over 1,000 maps and over 750 graphs that were to be spread over some 400 pages. . . . The numerous advances in computer graphics and cartography that have occurred in the last few years were barely on the horizon when the atlas was planned in 1971 and 1972. The advice the steering committee received from most people was to rely on manual production techniques. Therefore variables selected for mapping were converted to hard copy and then transferred manually to base maps. [p. 480]

to advance on a reputable basis it is essential that both types of specialist share their knowledge and experience.[8]

ROLE OF THE COMPUTER IN CARTOGRAPHY

The most significant and productive application of computer techniques in graphic presentation has been in the area of statistical mapping. This fact is evidenced by a proliferation of computer mapping systems and technologies, not only in the United States but in many other countries throughout the world.

Generally, with the exception perhaps of relatively simple line and bar charts, computer techniques—especially the design of software in graphic presentation—represent a highly skilled and complicated process. For example, in developing a computer mapping capability several prerequisites are essential.

1. A geographic base file, including street-address information and coordinates are required, except where only small volumes of data are involved and predefined areal units such as census tracts are used. In this latter case a geographic data set or boundary description file is required. Geographic coding of the data may turn out to be a time-consuming aspect of the computer mapping process.

2. Data to be used for computer mapping must be encoded with computer-readable addresses or areal codes that can be matched with the base file for the area from which the data have been drawn.

3. Access to mapping programs and computer equipment are essential. Fortunately, programs for the preparation of various types of statistical maps are available from a substantial number of computer centers. Particular programs are normally designed to fit certain types of electronic equipment.

4. To carry out the work involved in geographic coding, matching, and computer mapping operations, sufficient staff expertise is indispensable.[9]

William B. Overstreet has prepared a challenging case in favor of automation for cartographic work. Although in a general way these statements are relevant to the broader field of graphic presentation, it should be recognized that many statistical charts are small and simple in comparison to a substantial proportion of large, detailed, and complex maps produced by the cartographer. Furthermore, our interest in the present chapter is in the more inclusive aspects and applications of automated or computerized techniques in *graphic presentation*—the *graphic display* of all kinds of statistical data. To be sure, because of their importance, statistical maps, with their exclusive emphasis on spatial data and relationships, should occupy a significant part of any discussion of this kind, but maps are only one of several graphic forms. Accordingly, it cannot be assumed that automated techniques are equally applicable and valuable for all types of graphic forms and all kinds of graphic-display needs. From an economical and/or practical standpoint there are many graphic needs—perhaps most—that simply are not worth doing on a computer.

Computer techniques may be found advantageous for developing more elaborate and mathematically derived maps and charts, where extensive calculations and data processing are required. Also, electronic computers are especially valuable when a large number of charts of a particular type is required, inasmuch as the overwhelming proportion of the time and labor must be spent in preparatory work such as coding and manipulating the data to fit available equipment and programs. In such instances the computer could represent such advantages as speed, economy, accuracy, and flexibility.

The following represents a summary of Dr. Overstreet's argument in favor of computerized mapping techniques:[10]

1. To speed up the process of map making. Automation makes it feasible to translate large masses of digital data into a graphic medium with speed and clarity.

2. To improve the economics of mapping. Economy of operation is a real prime issue toward implementing automated techniques. De-

[8] R. S. Baxter, "Some Methodological Issues in Computer Drawn Maps," *The Cartographic Journal*, **13**, (2) (December 1976), 145–155.

[9] Quoted from U.S. Bureau of the Census, *Census Use Study: Computer Mapping* (op. cit.).

[10] William B. Overstreet, "Charge to the Conference," in *1975 Proceedings of the International Symposium on Computer-Assisted Cartography*, Washington, D. C.: U.S. Bureau of the Census, 1976, pp. 3–5. Another good discussion of the benefits as well as disbenefits of computer-aided cartography is included in Rhind, "Computer-Aided Cartography," (op. cit.).

spite continued higher costs of equipment and manpower, overall mapping costs have not risen because of increased efficiency.

3. To generate digital data for direct dissemination, and for rapid manipulation to produce, with a minimum of effort, maps at different scales and selected contents. A major advantage of cartographic data in digital form is the convenient interface with the geographically related information of management systems. Automated techniques can be applied to develop new and different forms of presentation.

4. To facilitate revision and updating of map making.

5. To reduce the incidence of errors. Each phase of mapping that can be removed from the frailties of human judgment and be automated is likely to become more error free.

A FEW COMMON TERMS IN COMPUTER-ASSISTED GRAPHIC PRESENTATION

To obtain a clearer understanding of the significance of certain procedures and problems associated with electronic computers, it is essential to acquire some grasp of at least a few basic terms. To the uninitiated, computer terminology may appear to be a bewildering jargon. The following are examples of a few of the more common terms used by computer specialists:

Hardware. Represents the combination of physical equipment needed to perform a given processing operation. Hardware comprises: (1) processing media (these are the computers); (2) data storage media (punched cards; tapes and disks); (3) transmission media for data and results; and (4) terminals.

Computer. Refers to that part of the hardware of an electronic installation which is essential for processing. It comprises: (1) the central processor; (2) the input/output units; and (3) memories, tape and disk units.

Software. Refers to all the programs involved in the functioning of a computer system. It is subdivided into three main categories: operating programs, library programs, and user programs.

Program. The set of ordered instructions enabling the computer to perform the processing or calculations desired upon a body of data.[11]

Binary. A numbering system based on 2 rather than 10 that uses only the digits 0 and 1 when written.

Bit. Abbreviation of binary digit. May be equivalent to an "on or off" condition, a "yes or no," and so on.

Byte. A group of binary digits usually operated upon as a unit. Usually 6 bits or 8 bits.

Digital Data. Information represented by a code consisting of a sequence of discrete elements.

Digitizer. A machine for converting an analog product (a map or other image) into its digital complement for further digital processing.[12]

Cathode-ray Tube (CRT). A vacuum tube in which a beam of electrons is projected onto a fluorescent screen (cf. "Television screen").

CRT Display. A display (e.g., text, linework) using a cathode-ray tube as the viewing element.

Alphanumeric. A contraction of the words "alphabetic" and "numeric."

Algorithm. A routine for solving a particular mathematical problem.[13]

Pen Plotters. A pen plotter physically moves a pen over a piece of paper or film, under program control, to produce graphical output. There are two basic types of plotter—flatbed and drum. Flatbed plotters, in which the pen moves over a flat sheet of paper or plastic, can produce maps ranging from $8\frac{1}{2}$ in. by 11 in. to 5 ft by 24 ft. Drum-plotter maps can be up to 120 ft long, which is the length of a roll of paper, and 11–30 in. wide.

Character-printed Maps. Maps produced by a standard high-speed computer printer prints typewriter-like characters and combinations of characters on standard computer printout paper.

Line-drawn Maps. Maps generated by a number of plotting devices, such as pen plotters, CRTs, and the geospace plotter. For example, pen

---

[11] Quoted from Organization for Economic Cooperation and Development, *The Evaluation of the Performance of Computer Systems,* OECD Information Studies, 1974, p. 38.

[12] Quoted from Thomas K. Peucker, *Computer Cartography,* Washington: Association of American Geographers, 1972, Resource Paper No. 17, p. 71.

[13] Quoted from British Cartographic Society, *Automated Cartography,* London: 1974, Special Publication No. 1, p. 145.

plotters actually draw lines to represent spatial arrangements described by the data. The CRTs and geospace plotters project images onto phosphorous screens, photosensitive paper, or film.[14]

GEOGRAPHIC BASE FILE

As indicated previously, four elements are involved in the computer mapping process: (1) selecting and specifying the data to be mapped, (2) linking the data file to a geographically structured file, (3) manipulating and organizing the data to fit available programs and equipment, and (4) exploring alternatives and then deciding how to display the data to emphasize their significant features.

This section is devoted specifically to characteristic procedures and implications of step (2), the geographically structured file. Generally, files of this kind are referred to as "geographic base files." The geographic entities—spatial units or areas—to be mapped must be described in digital form compatible to a coding system so they can be automatically matched to the geographical files the computer is referencing. The procedure of a geographic base file (GBF) to match coordinates to address information or other spatial referents is known as "geocoding." At present there is a large number of systems that can be used for geocoding. Nearly all these systems, except for the regular grid, are based on a system of Cartesian coordinates.[15]

The most difficult, laborious, and time-consuming aspects of the computer mapping process is the creation of geographic base file, or a geographically ordered data set. Without a complete, reliable, and proven GBF or geographic data set it is simply impossible to produce a satisfactory computerized map. A geographic data set is a digital representation of the boundaries of fixed geographic areas, each of which has a specific, unique code number.

To understand more fully how a GBF is created as well as its role in computer mapping, the GBF/DIME system of the Census Bureau is used for illustrative purposes. This is one of the best-known and most widely used systems at the present time.[16]

The code term GBF/DIME stands for geographic base file/dual independent map encoding. A GBF/DIME file contains local address information—street names, intersections, and ZIP codes, as well as the identification of geographic and political areas in which the local address falls (e.g., census blocks and tracts, townships, cities, counties). Other geographic identifiers can be added by users to include local statistical areas such as police precincts, school districts, transportation zones, and health-reporting areas.

The GBF/DIME *"system"* refers to maps used to create the GBF/DIME files (the U.S. Bureau of the Census Metropolitan Map series), the GBF/DIME files themselves, and the computer programs for establishing, maintaining, and using GBF/DIME files. The basic purpose of the system is to facilitate the conversion of administration records into statistical data, add a geographic identifier to them, and integrate and process national census data in urban areas.

The GBF/DIME technology is an outgrowth of the decision of the Census Bureau to conduct the 1970 Census of Population and Housing largely by mail. For the mail-back census to work, a standard set of maps of the SMSAs was prepared. Also, "address coding guides" (ACGs) were compiled. Each ACG contained an inventory of the address ranges between street intersections along with a set of codes that described the location of each mailing

---

[14] Quoted from United States Bureau of the Census, *Census Use Study: Computer Mapping* (op. cit.), pp. 2–12.

[15] Eric Teicholz, "Graphic Technology and the Display of Spatial Data," Cambridge: Harvard University Laboratory for Computer Graphics and Spatial Analyses, no date, pp. 1–10; Edgar M. Horwood and Charles E. Barb, "Geocoding Systems in the United States: 1970," Seattle: University of Washington Urban Data Center, 1970, pp. 1–12; Charles E. Barb, *Automated Street Address Geocoding Systems, Their Local Adaptation and Institutionalization,* University of Washington, unpublished doctoral dissertation, 1974.

[16] The following discussion on the GBF/DIME system is based on direct quotations from publications prepared by the U.S. Bureau of the Census: Morton A. Meyer, Richard Schweitzer, and Jacob Silver, *The Statistical Mapping and Geographic Base Files of the U.S. Bureau of the Census,* Washington, D. C.: Government Printing Office, 1973; U.S. Bureau of the Census, *Census Use Study: Computer Mapping,* Report No. 2, Washington, D. C.: Government Printing Office, 1969; U.S. Bureau of the Census, *Census Use Study: The Dime Geocoding System,* Report No. 4, Washington, D. C.: Government Printing Office, 1970; U.S. Bureau of the Census (text prepared by Maury Cagle) "GBF/DIME Dollars and Sense How Cities Can Improve Their Planning and Management Capacity Using a Bureau of the Census Geographic Data System," reprinted from *Nation's Cities,* 1976.

address. When work was well underway on the ACGs, it was realized that a much more useful set of files could be prepared utilizing DIME techniques, which were under separate development at that time.

The concept of DIME is derived from graph theory, in which a given point is described in terms of its location with regard to a vertical (Y) and a horizontal (X) axis (see Figure 11–1A, where the value plotted is Y_3 and X_6).

In the same way, the point on a map where a street or special feature such as a river intersects another street or feature, comes to an end, or changes direction, can be identified. Geographers refer to these intersections as "node points," and these are labeled with a dot and a unique identifying number. A line drawn between two nodes is a straight-line segment. For each segment of a street—the length between two node points—the file contains the following information: the "from" node, "to" node, street name, street type (boulevard, street, lane, etc.); and address ranges on the right and left sides of the street (Figure 11–1B). The census blocks and tracts are already uniquely numbered (or coded), and these are also included in the file (Figure 11–1C).

The "dual" part of DIME refers to the fact that the basic file is created by coding two separate sets of information—the nodes at the end of each line segment, and the areas enclosed by the nodes and line segments.

By applying graph theory and representing the node points as X and Y coordinates, the spatial relationships of the node points and the line segments may be determined. In this case, the points on the graph are intersections, the line segments are streets, and the X and Y coordinates, are respectively, latitude and longitude on a map. Once this is done, a computer is able to plot a complete replica of the source map, with streets at the proper angles and blocks the proper length.

The GBF/DIME system makes it possible to integrate different types of data records by relating address information to geographic identifiers. The problem is how to integrate files geographically.

Typically, local records are geographically defined as follows:

Record System	Geographic Locator
School enrollment	School district
Fire-department records	Fire district
Crimes	Police precinct
Building permits	Individual street address
Hospital patients	Home address

The blending or integration process is accomplished through a mechanism called "address matching." (ADMATCH), which is a widely available package of computer programs for address matching that geographically codes computerized data records containing street addresses with the spatial data included in a geographic base file. For example, it can be used to compare the addresses on input data records with address ranges in the GBF/DIME file. A match would occur when the street names are judged identical. When this occurs the desired geographical codes are assigned from the GBF/DIME record for this segment to the local data records. The result is a local data file based on standardized building blocks (Figure 11–1D).

To develop a more complete and accurate GBF/DIME file and provide for its maintenance and update on a continuing basis, the Census Bureau is implementing nationally a special package of programs known as the CUE program—the correction, update, and extension of the GBF/DIME files.[17]

COMPUTER PROGRAMS

Before a map or any other kind of graphic display can be produced by automated or computerized methods, a program, or set of ordered instructions, is prepared for the purpose of directing the computer to perform the processing or calculations desired on a set of data. The programs are normally written in computer language, of which there is a large number, the most common the FORTRAN (FORmula TRANslation).

Each mapping program (software) is designed to fit a particular type of computer equipment (hardware), especially the display characteristics of that equipment. Thus there are two general types of computer maps that can be produced—those asso-

[17] Morton A. Myers and Jacob Silver, "Present Status and Future Prospects of the Census Bureau's GBF/DIME CUE Program," U.S. Bureau of the Census, paper presented at the conference on Geographic Base File Systems—A Forward Look, April 16–17, 1974.

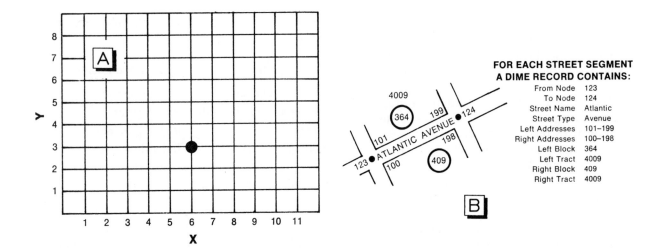

FOR EACH STREET SEGMENT
A DIME RECORD CONTAINS:

From Node	123
To Node	124
Street Name	Atlantic
Street Type	Avenue
Left Addresses	101–199
Right Addresses	100–198
Left Block	364
Left Tract	4009
Right Block	409
Right Tract	4009

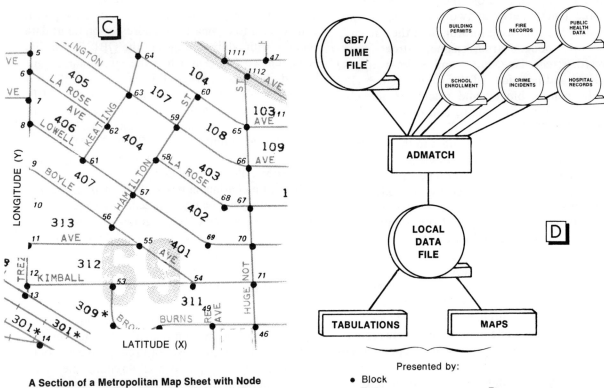

A Section of a Metropolitan Map Sheet with Node
Dots and Numbers (3-Digit Numbers Indicate Blocks
Within a Census Tract)

THE GBF/DIME SYSTEM

Presented by:
- Block
- Tract
- Etc.
- Districts (Fire, School, Others)

Figure 11–1. Illustration of basic characteristics and implications of GBF/DIME system. A. The concept of DIME is derived from graph theory, in which a given point is described in terms of its location with regard to a vertical (Y) and a horizontal (X) axis. B. For each segment of a street—the length between two node points—the file contains the information listed in the sketch. C. A section of metropolitan map sheet showing nodes and block numbers in a census tract. D. An overview of the GBF/DIME system indicating both the blending process of the DIME file with various kinds of local records through ADMATCH, and the resultant potentials for the preparation of tabulations and maps. (Sketches in this illustration taken from publications of the United States Bureau of the Census.)

ciated with "character-printing" equipment and those associated with "line-drawing" equipment. The first type of map uses a standard, high-speed printing device and prints typewriter characters (occasionally on top of one another) on a standard printer sheet. The second type of map is generated from lines drawn by pen plotters, CRTs, COM units, or electron beam plotters. This type of map is similar to that made by a draftsman.[18]

The best-known and most widely used mapping program at the present time is SYMAP (SYnagraphic MAPping system), which was developed in the early 1960s by Howard Fisher of Northwestern University Technological Institute, later of the Laboratory for Computer Graphics and Spatial Analysis at Harvard University.[19]

The SYMAP program produces maps on a standard line printer. It can create five basic types of maps, the three most common of which are conformant (choropleth), contour (isopleth), and proximal

(Figure 11–2).[20] The SYMAP program is written in FORTRAN IV and can be used on a wide variety of computers such as several IBM models and others from Burroughs, Honeywell, Siemens, and UNIVAC.

Figure 11–2 includes illustrations of three types of maps produced by the SYMAP program.[21] Characteristically, maps of this kind that are made on a line printer are relatively crude, wooden, and esthetically unattractive. Other programs besides SYMAP, such as LINMAP, GRIDS, CHORO, and CMAP, use the line printer and reflect the same characteristic crudity and coarseness. Line printers were never designed for graphic displays any more than a typewriter or similar machine was designed for the construction of statistical charts. Such machines were designed for printing words and figures. It will be observed from Figure 11–2 that the shadings are made from letters and other symbols on the line printer. In addition, the line printer suffers from other mechanical constraints such as size, spacing, and poor quality of lettering.[22]

Other programs available from the Laboratory for Computer Graphics and Spatial Analysis at Harvard University include the following: (1) CALFORM (CALcomp FORMs), initially written by Robert Cartwright in 1969 under the sponsorship of the University of Missouri, used to produce choropleth maps that are more precise and qualitatively superior to those produced by SYMAP and using a line (pen or CRT) plotter rather than a line printer (Figure 11–3) and (2) SYMVU computer mapping program, which, like the CALFORM, uses a line plotter, to represent gridded spatial data as a three-dimensional surface. In addition to SYMAP, CALFORM, and SYMVU there are other more specialized programs developed by the Laboratory for Computer Graphics and Spatial Analysis at Harvard University.

Various governmental agencies such as the Bureau of the Census and many universities including California (Berkley), U.C.L.A., Michigan, Minnesota, Idaho, Wisconsin, Washington, Kansas, Missouri, and others have developed a wide variety of computer programs for graphic display.

OTHER EXAMPLES OF COMPUTER-ASSISTED MAPS

Spot or Dot Map

Figure 11–4 is a good example of a spot or dot map prepared by means of an electronic computer. It is

---

[18] Quoted from George P. Leyland, "Computer Mapping—Here and Now," in U.S. Bureau of the Census, *Papers Presented at the Conference on Small Area Statistics, American Statistical Association,* Pittsburgh, Pa., August 23, 1968; Census Tract Papers, Series GE-40, No. 5, Washington, D. C.: Government Printing Office, 1969, pp. 9–25.

[19] A. H. Schmidt and W. Z. Zafft, "Programs of the Harvard University Laboratory for Computer Graphics and Spatial Analysis," in John C. Davis and Michael J. McCullagh, eds., *Display and Analysis of Spatial Data,* New York: Wiley, 1975, pp. 231–243; Laboratory for Computer Graphics and Spatial Analysis, *Lab-Log,* Cambridge: Harvard University Press, 1977, pp. 6–22.

[20] Proximal maps depict zones created from data values assigned to particular points. The area from each point to an imaginary line equidistant between each pair of adjacent points is shaded with the respective value (Figure 11–2).

[21] For a recent discussion of the accuracy, reliability, legibility, and other features of SYMAP-produced maps, see Elri Liebenberg, "Symap: Its Uses and Abuses," *The Cartographic Journal,* **13** (1) (June 1976), 26–36.

[22] Peucker points out that a distinction should be made between two types of maps: intermediate and final ones. Intermediate maps serve as an aid for further analysis during a research project, whereas final maps are part of the result of the project. Intermediate maps that may play an important role in a recursive research cycle do not have to be of high quality, but they do have to be produced quickly and relatively cheaply; see Thomas K. Peucker, *Computer Cartography,* Washington, D. C.: Association of American Geographers, Resource Paper No. 17, 1972, p. 61. Also in this connection, see J. T. Coppock, "Maps by Line Printer," in Davis and McCullagh, *Display and Analysis of Spatial Data* (op. cit.), pp. 137–154.

also an excellent demonstration of the efficiency and economy of computer-produced charts, especially when the production is on a mass scale. Figure 11–4 is one of more than 140 spot maps in a single report representing various kinds of data based on the 1969 Census of Agriculture.[23]

The dots on these maps were located within subareas of the nation's 3076 counties. The dot-mapping system was developed by Wendell K. Beckwith under the direction of Joel Morrison at the Cartographic Laboratory of the University of Wisconsin—Madison. The basic system utilizes several computer-mapping packages developed at the laboratory. The data required for the dot-

mapping system consist of individual totals of the data items, the land area of each county, and a center of the county shown as a pair of longitude and latitude coordinates. These data items were then processed through a computer program that calculates the average density of dots for each unit in respect to the land area of the county and the absolute number of dots that apply to that county. The density value is then screened by a 16-level land-use

[23] United States Bureau of the Census, *Graphic Summary of the 1969 Census of Agriculture*, Special Reports, Vol. V, Part 15, Washington, D. C.: Government Printing Office, 1973.

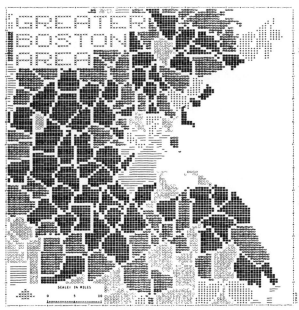
Conformant Map

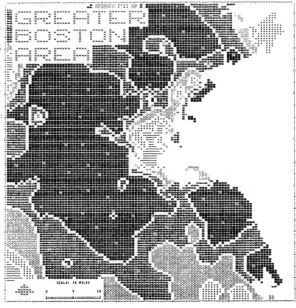
Contour Map

Proximal Map

Figure 11–2. Examples of three of the five basic types of maps that can be created by SYMAP (Synagraphic Mapping System). (From Laboratory for Computer Graphics and Spatial Analysis, Harvard University, Lab-Log, Cambridge, January 1977, p. 7.)

filter to further position the dots with regard to the agricultural subareas of the county. A numeric check was maintained on the number of dots that should fall in an area and the number of dots actually placed in that area.[24]

This system has been redesigned by Frederick R. Broome of the Geography Division of the Census Bureau for the preparation of dot maps in the series of individual state reports for the 1974 Census of Agriculture. The new system operates more quickly and is able to use more accurate land-use classifications as filters to control the placement of

dots. The output is produced directly on 10-in. film ready for reproduction.

Three-dimensional Map with Column Charts Superimposed

Figure 11–5 is an illustration of a computer-generated three-dimensional map with 14 pairs of grouped columns drawn in oblique projection. The program known as CENVUE was originally developed by W. R. Tobler of the University of Michigan and made operational on the CDC 6400/CYBER computer system by Carl Youngman of the University of Washington. It was further

---

[24] Ibid., p. 14.   Most of this descriptive summary was quoted verbatim.

Figure 11–3. A choropleth map produced by CALFORM Program on an IBM 370 computer and pen plotter. (From Laboratory for Computer Graphics and Spatial Analysis, Harvard University, Girl Scout Membership in Eastern Massachusetts: A Demographic Analysis, 1973.)

PERCENTAGE OF GIRLS, 7-8 YEARS OLD WHO ARE BROWNIES

GIRL SCOUTS OF THE USA MEMBERSHIP

STUDY: EASTERN MASSACHUSETTS REGION: 1972

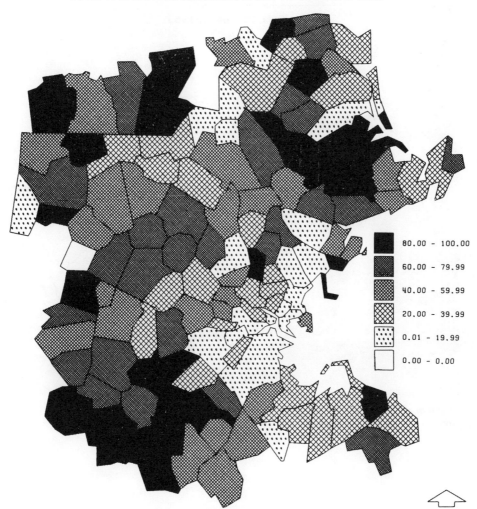

```
80.00 - 100.00
60.00 - 79.99
40.00 - 59.99
20.00 - 39.99
0.01 - 19.99
0.00 - 0.00
```

modified by Tomoki Noguchi of the University of Washington.[25]

The CENVUE(s) program is designed to draw automatically a three-dimensional map using a large digital computer and plotter. It can be used for various purposes in plotting statistical data in geographical space.

For example, Figure 11–5 portrays the mode of travel to work by automobile (driver only) or bus for 14 community areas in the city of Seattle. Although there are detectable differentials in mode of travel to work from one area to another, the overwhelming importance of the automobile with only the driver is clearly revealed.

Map with Two-dimensional Segmented Symbols

Figure 11–6 further exemplifies the versatility of the computer in creating almost any kind of graphic form. From a pragmatic point of view, an important concern in producing a map of this kind is whether the use of a computer can be justified in terms of time and cost. In the case of Figure 11–6,

however, this chart was largely an experimental by-product in developing the PCPMP program (proportional circle-pie mapping program). Perhaps from a purely cost-effective point of view, it might be less expensive to draw a relatively simple map of this kind by conventional manual techniques.

Map Portraying Three-dimensional Surface

The three-dimensional map of Iowa showing the distribution of population in 1970 (Figure 11–7) was generated by the SYMVU mapping program re-

[25] Tomoki Noguchi, *Producing Three-Dimensional Computer-Drawn Graphics of Geographic Data: A User's Manual for the Cenvue(s) Program,* Working Paper No. 42, Urban Transportation Program, Seattle: University of Washington (February 1976); Tomoki Noguchi and Jerry Schneider, *Data Display Techniques for Transportation Analysis and Planning: An Investigation of Three Computer Produced Graphics,* Seattle: Department of Civil Engineering and Urban Planning, University of Washington, June 1976.

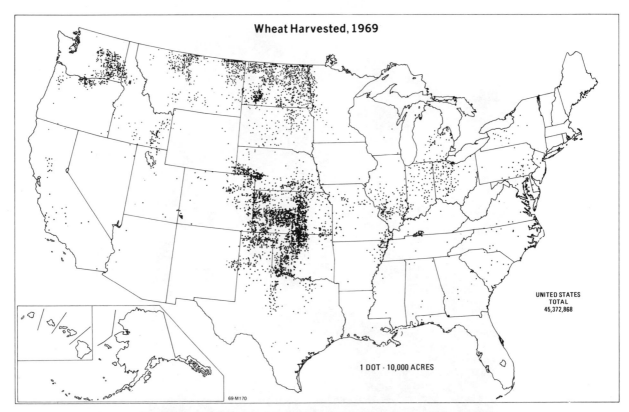

Wheat Harvested, 1969

UNITED STATES
TOTAL
45,372,868

1 DOT - 10,000 ACRES

69-M170

Figure 11–4. Spot or dot map made by electronic computer. (From U.S. Bureau of the Census, Graphic Summary of the 1969 Census of Agriculture, Special Reports, V, Part 15, Washington: Government Printing Office, 1973, p. 117.)

ferred to earlier. The SYMVU program was developed by the Harvard University Laboratory for Computer Graphics and Spatial Analysis. It uses a line plotter to represent gridded spatial data as a three-dimensional surface.[26]

---

[26] In this connection, see the discussion on isopleth mapping in Chapter 8.

[27] United States Bureau of the Census, *Federal-State Cooperative Program for Population Estimates,* Current Population Reports, Series P-26, No. 76–49, July 1977.

Choropleth Map with Continuous Intervals

Recently the U.S. Bureau of the Census[27] has developed a computer generated choropleth map in which the crosshatching patterns are continuous rather than discrete. In the conventional choropleth map the crosshatching patterns are divided into separate and mutually exclusive divisions in which each specific interval is represented by a distinct

MODE OF TRAVEL TO WORK BY COMMUNITY AREA, AUTO (DRIVER ONLY) OR BUS

CITY OF SEATTLE, WASHINGTON, 1970

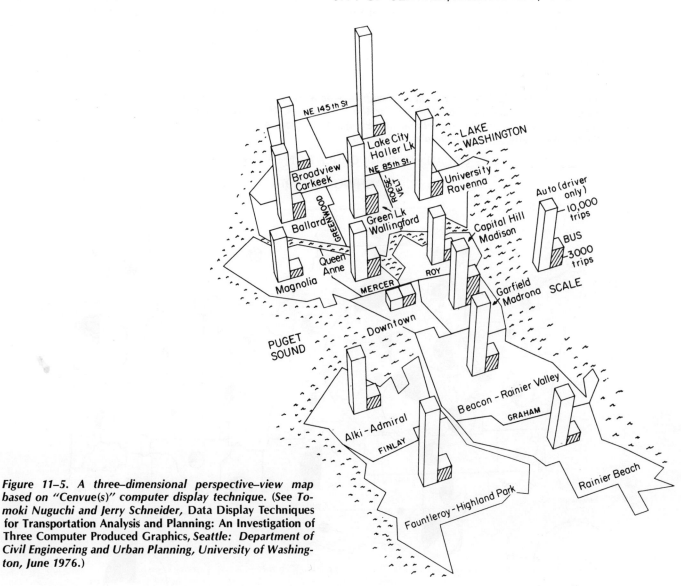

Figure 11–5. A three–dimensional perspective–view map based on "Cenvue(s)" computer display technique. (See Tomoki Nuguchi and Jerry Schneider, Data Display Techniques for Transportation Analysis and Planning: An Investigation of Three Computer Produced Graphics, Seattle: Department of Civil Engineering and Urban Planning, University of Washington, June 1976.)

pattern. Figure 11–8 is unlike the conventional choropleth map in that the density of the cross-hatching is directly proportional to the values of the data and there are no breaks representing specifically defined class intervals. In other words, the density of shading (amount of blackness) is directly correlated with the values portrayed. Certainly, such a hatching scheme is very logical, but whether such a gradation is superior to the conventional discrete hatching system can be answered only by further study and experimentation. We do know that according to empirical findings of psychology, psychophysics and optics the amount of blackness in a series of objects and the intensity of sensation produced upon the eye, are not a linear relationship. For example, a pattern with a ratio of 50% black to white does not necessarily produce a sensory impression halfway between that produced by solid black and that produced by white. The overall quality of Figure 11–8 is impressive and in

̄terms of drafting standards is far superior to the average computer-generated choropleth map.

COMPUTER-GENERATED STATISTICAL CHARTS

One of the more important recent (1976) contributions to computer-generated graphics has been the innovative operational techniques developed by the United States Bureau of the Census in connection with the construction of hundreds of charts for *Status* (*STAT*istics, *U*nited *S*tates), a monthly periodical produced as a collaborative effort by various agencies of the federal government. After extensive experimentation, including the publication of prototype issues and other materials, the first edition of *Status* was released in July 1976. As a consequence of insufficient funds its publication was suspended after the October issue. *Status* was

Figure 11–6. Map of State of Washington with two–dimensional segmented symbols portraying urban and rural populations for the 39 counties. [From George Cook, Population Map Prepared by Proportional Circle Mapping Program, Academic Computer Center, Newsletter, 11, (10), October 1976, p. 1.]

URBAN - RURAL POPULATION BY COUNTIES

WASHINGTON: 1970

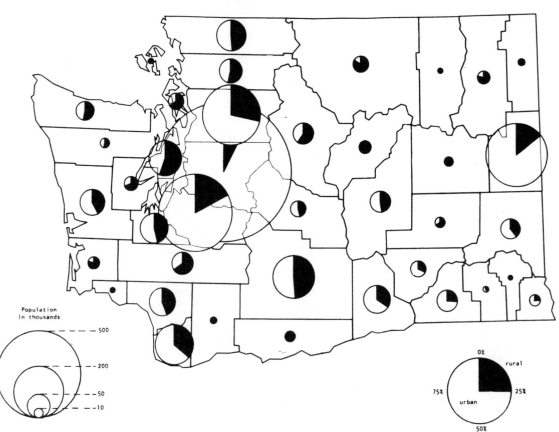

projected as a monthly chart book of social and economic trends for both the general public and for decision makers in business, government, and education. From a technical point of view, significant features of this new computer-generated system of graphics are as follows: (1) simplified general-purpose plotting programs, (2) speed of production, and (3) high technical and esthetic quality of charts.

---

[28] Most of this descriptive summary was extracted directly from a paper by Vincent P. Barabba, "Automatic Statistical Graphics: A Tool for Communication," American Statistical Association, *Proceedings of the Social Statistics Section, 1976,* Part I, pp. 82–88. Mr. Barabba is former Director of the U.S. Bureau of the Census.

More specifically, the essential features of this system are as follows:[28] With respect to the hardware, the central processor is a UNIVAC 1110 computer. A graphics terminal, consisting of a CRT, keyboard, and screen is a unit in which instructions are fed to the computer by an operator. The operator is able to see on the screen what is actually being constructed from information fed to the computer. If the resulting chart previewed on the screen (Tektronix display scope) is not satisfactory, further or modified instructions can be issued to the computer. When the chart produced on the screen is deemed satisfactory, a copy of the chart in final form can be produced by the computer and its auxiliary equipment. Also, as a further check before the

POPULATION DISTRIBUTION
STATE OF IOWA: 1970

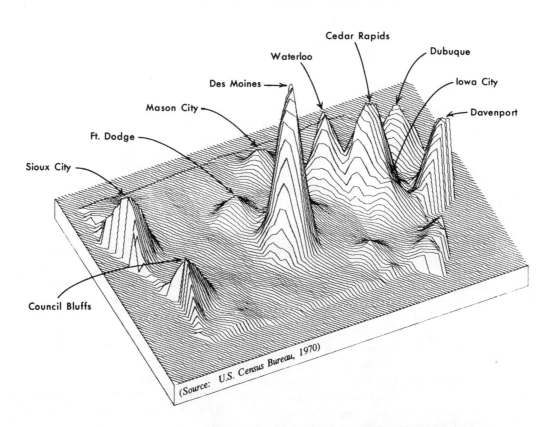

Figure 11–7. Map portraying distribution of population in Iowa shown as a three–dimensional surface. The SYMVU program was used in the preparation of this map. (From Philip Franklin, Atlas of Primary Medical and Dental Manpower in Iowa, Iowa City: Institute of Urban and Regional Research, University of Iowa, 1976, Report No. 8, p. 1. Map prepared under the direction of Dr. Gerard Rushton of the University of Iowa.)

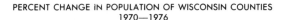

PERCENT CHANGE IN POPULATION OF WISCONSIN COUNTIES
1970—1976

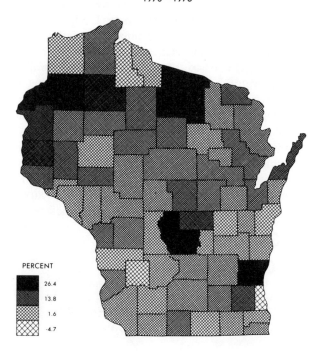

PERCENT

26.4
13.8
1.6
-4.7

Figure 11–8. Computer–generated choropleth map with continuous patterns of crosshatching. (From U.S. Bureau of Census, Current Population Reports, Federal-State Cooperative Program for Population Estmates, Series P–26, No. 76–49 July 1977, p. 7.)

final finished draft of the chart is completed, a small preliminary proof print of the chart may be obtained in seconds from a copying machine linked to the graphics terminal (CRT). After the instructions are received by the computer from the graphics terminal, two other important pieces of computer-driven hardware actually produce the hard copy. They are the Xynetics flatbed plotter and the computer-output system, Information International Incorporated, FR-80 COM unit (computer output on microfilm). The flatbed plotter actually draws the charts from instructions received from the computer. The flatbed plotter is basically a table on which drawing paper, mylar or other material is held in place by vacuum and above which a gantry of pens is mounted. The pens can be soft-tipped. ball-point, or liquid ink and may be of different colors. The charts printed in *Status* are colored, but the actual color processing must be done by subsequent printing techniques. In the future, however, the Census Bureau plans to develop a system that would provide full color capability. Color components that will have to be added to the present hardware already have been developed by companies outside the Census Bureau.

One of the outstanding features of the automated statistical graphics system of the Census Bureau is the simplified software that has been developed. These programs can be used effectively by anyone even if not particularly well versed in computer techniques. Most of the instructions are in English. At this time three general purpose plotting programs have been developed for: (1) pie charts, (2) bar and column charts, and (3) arithmetic time-series charts. For example, the pie-chart program encompasses the following types of pie charts and related elements and characteristics: (1) pie charts containing up to 20 sectors, (2) labels, percentages, and numbers associated with each sector, (3) spatial separation of sectors, and (4) additional text and lettering. Any number of charts may be placed on a single page, and any size of page up to 40 in. by 30 in. may be used.

Figures 11–9, 11–10, and 11–11 are illustrations of charts produced by the Census Bureau computer graphic system during the past several months. Figure 11–9 is a pie chart with nine separate slices or sectors. The entire chart, including the lettering, arrows, and crosshatching, was drawn on the flatbed plotter. With the exception of the three subtitles, the two column charts and the single bar chart in Figure 11–10 were produced by computer. In Figure 11–11 the four arithmetic line charts, except for the subtitles, curve labels, and the de-

Percent Distribution of Employment by Industry Division

United States -- 1973

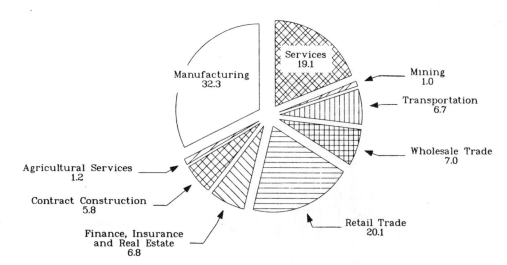

Figure 11–9. An illustration of a pie chart generated by a computer. (From J. A. Johnson, Piechart: A General Purpose Plotting Program, U.S. Bureau of the Census, November 1976, p. 50.)

tailed tabulation in the lower left-hand corner, were made by computer.

ADDITIONAL ILLUSTRATIONS OF STATISTICAL CHARTS

Figures 11–12 and 11–13 are illustrations of statistical charts processed on an IBM 370/168 and printed on a 13-in. drum plotter.[29] Figure 11–12 is a multiple-surface or stratum chart portraying trends in inventory and loan quantities of cotton from 1954 to 1975. The ordinal axis indicates bales of cotton in millions and the abscissal scale, semiannual calibrations from June 1954 to June 1975. The lower stratum represents the amount of inventory cotton and the upper stratum, the amount of loan cotton. The rulings, hatching patterns, and lettering were made by a pen on a drum plotter.

Figure 11–13 was made with the same hardware as Figure 11–12. However, Figure 11–13 is noticeably more complicated since it represents two basic graphic forms—a combination of a subdivided-

column chart and an arithmetic line chart. It will be observed that Figure 11–13 has two scales, the one on the left expressed in billions of bushels for the series of columns and the one on the right, in dollars per bushel for the two curves. Both of these charts are very readable and conform to the mechanical requirements of acceptable statistical charts. However, they do lack certain esthetic qualities, particularly the lettering and hatching patterns. Also, the curves in Figure 11–13 should be heavier and more forceful. As indicated previously, these limitations are attributable to the hardware used in the preparation of these charts.

Figure 11–14 portrays two arithmetic line charts and one column chart from the January 1975 *Monthly Chart Book* of the Federal Reserve System. The publication comprises 87 pages of charts, most of the pages with two or three charts and a few pages with up to as many as five to eight charts. These charts were made on the Gerber Scientific Instrument Company automatic drafting/digitizing hardware.

MICROGRAPHICS

A very significant development in automated cartography and graphics in recent years has been

---

[29] Information in letter dated May 17, 1977 by Edward J. Mathews, Chief, Data Operations Branch, Data Systems Division, Agricultural Stabilization and Conservation Service, U.S. Department of Agriculture.

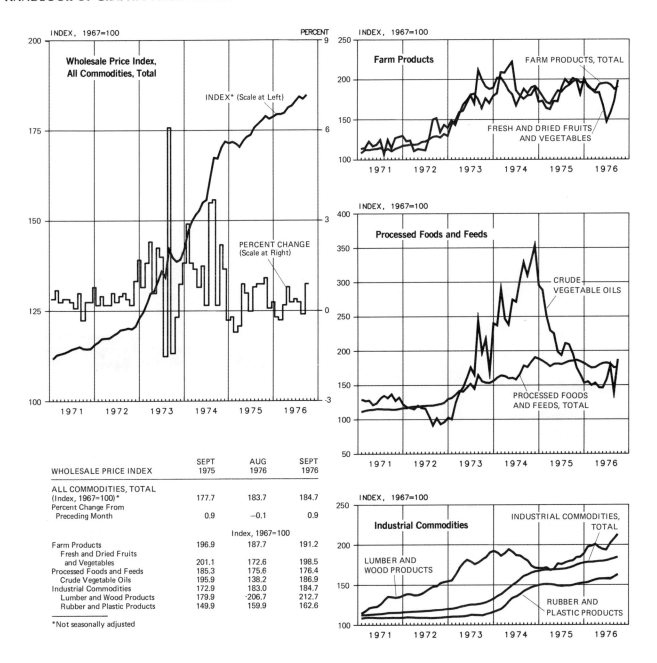

WHOLESALE PRICE INDEX	SEPT 1975	AUG 1976	SEPT 1976
ALL COMMODITIES, TOTAL (Index, 1967=100)*	177.7	183.7	184.7
Percent Change From Preceding Month	0.9	−0.1	0.9
		Index, 1967=100	
Farm Products	196.9	187.7	191.2
Fresh and Dried Fruits and Vegetables	201.1	172.6	198.5
Processed Foods and Feeds	185.3	175.6	176.4
Crude Vegetable Oils	195.9	138.2	186.9
Industrial Commodities	172.9	183.0	184.7
Lumber and Wood Products	179.9	·206.7	212.7
Rubber and Plastic Products	149.9	159.9	162.6

*Not seasonally adjusted

SOURCE BUREAU OF LABOR STATISTICS

Figure 11–10. Computer–generated bar and column charts. (From U.S. Bureau of the Census, unpublished material originally prepared for Status. Status, *a monthly chartbook of social and economic trends was suspended because of lack of funds after the fourth and final pilot issue in October, 1976.)*

"micrographics," using a high-precision COM unit to produce graphics and maps. The quality of the charts achieved by micrographics is superior to those produced by any other existing technique. Since the staff of the U.S. Bureau of the Census has been responsible for most of the developmental work in this area, this discussion is focused on their experience and procedures.[30]

The system is a blend of conventional techniques and a COM automatic drafting operation.

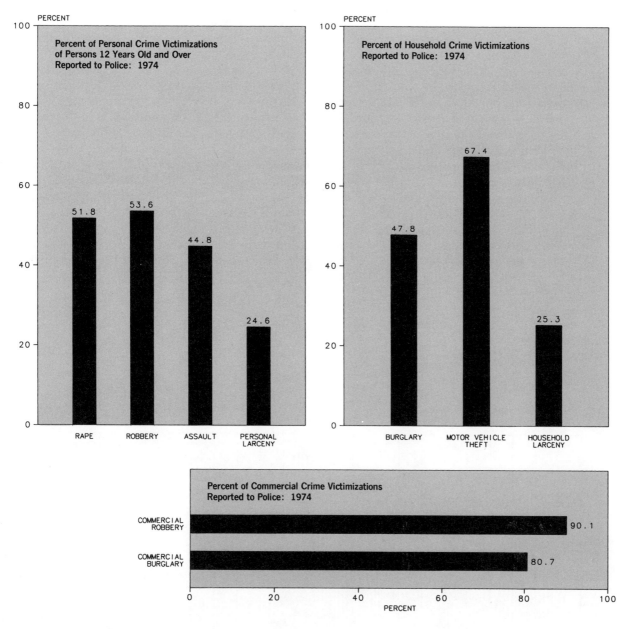

Figure 11–11. Series of arithmetic line charts produced by electronic computer. (From U.S. Bureau of the Census, unpublished material originally prepared for Status. Status, a monthly chartbook of social and economic trends was suspended because of lack of funds after the fourth and final pilot issue in October, 1976.)

---

[30] The following materials on "micrographics" represent direct quotations from Richard H. Schweitzer, *Mapping Urban America with Automated Cartography*, U.S. Bureau of the Census, Washington, D. C.: Government Printing Office, 1973; Richard H. Schweitzer, "Computer Mapping with Micrographics," in *Geographic Base (DIME) File System: A Forward Look*, Conference Proceedings, Boston, April 16–17, 1974, Washington, D. C.: Government Printing Office, 1974, pp. 113–121; Frederick R. Broome, "Micrographics: A New Approach to Cartography at the Census Bureau," in *Geographic Base (DIME) System–A Local Program*, Conference Proceedings, Columbus, November 18–19, 1974, Washington, D. C.: Government Printing Office, 1975, pp. 28–39; Richard H. Schweitzer, Jr., "Micrographics: A New Approach to Automated Cartography and Graphics," *Proceedings of 22nd International Technical Communication Conference*, Anaheim, California, 1975, pp. 305–316.

Figure 11–15 summarizes the major aspects and steps of this system. As indicated previously, every computer-mapping technique requires a machine-readable file of descriptive information about each area to be mapped. Also, for example, in constructing a choropleth map the interior surface area and/or perimeter must be described in very specific terms before the computer can correctly and uniformly assign the desired symbols to them. Individual areas or polygons can be described in one of two ways: (1) in terms of the individual boundary-line segments required to enclose the polygon or (2) by individual strips required to cover or "paint" the surface of the polygon. In the micrographics system the latter method is used. This is accomplished by a program called SCAN.

As the COM unit reacts to the sets of plotting instructions, each area is rapidly "painted" on the CRT and the film. For example, the computer (UNIVAC 1108) takes 2.8 min to create a SCAN file for the nation's 3076 counties that is comprised of more than 180,000 vectors. This operation is done only once each time the same area is to be mapped at the same scale, and the SCAN file is stored for later use. The last computer operation before the production of a plot tape is the merging of the classed data with the intermediate file produced by the SCAN program. The file of areas is sorted by class intervals so that all the areas for the first class intervals are grouped together and so on for as many classes as have been defined. Each set of areas that have been grouped by class intervals is plotted on a

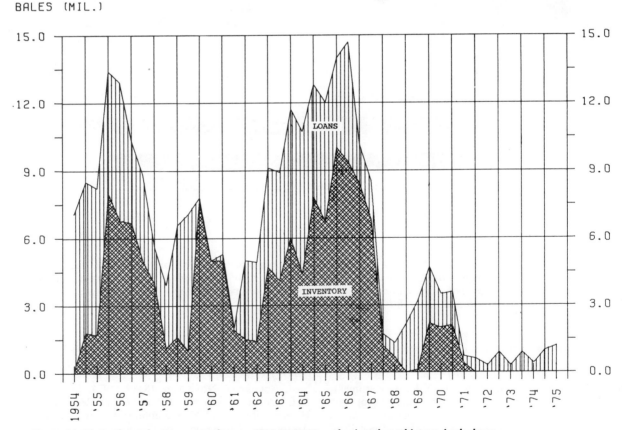

Figure 11–12. Surface chart processed on an IBM 370/168 and printed on thirteen-inch drum plotter. (From United States Department of Agriculture, Agricultural Stabilization and Conservation Service, Commodity Credit Corporation Charts, Washington: 1976, p. 50.)

separate frame of microfilm. The resulting output tape is a properly formatted tape containing the required commands so that the COM unit can plot on each map one class interval per frame with descriptive titles and class identification. Because of the technique of sweeping across each line so that the entire polygon is covered, the film is completely exposed where the electron beam was instructed to draw and is left unexposed in the remainder of the image. After the tape is plotted, the film is processed as full reversal negatives in an automatic film-processing unit. This produces a black negative with clear windows where the selected areas or polygons were located on the film image. The negatives (35 mm) are taken to a standard photographic laboratory for the processing required to produce the desired maps. All the remaining steps utilize only conventional film-processing procedures to enlarge the film images and produce screened publication negatives ready for printing. Briefly, this approach to automated cartography has simply automated the tedious, time-consuming activities required to produce window negatives and has left the other time-tested techniques unchanged.[31]

---

[31] Many of the Census Bureau maps produced by means of the micrographic system are colored. A detailed discussion of the various kinds of maps and atlases that have been published is discussed in the following paper: Morton A. Meyer, Frederick R. Broome, and Richard H. Schweitzer, ''Color Statistical Mapping by the U.S. Bureau of the Census,'' *The American Cartographer*, **2** (2) (October 1975), 101–117.

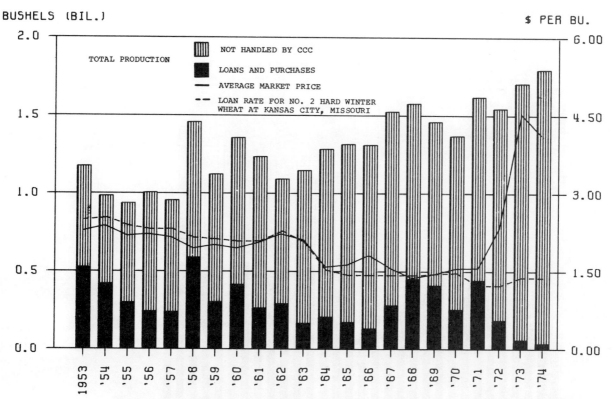

Figure 11–13. Combination subdivided column and rectilinear coordinate line chart processed on an IBM 370/168 and printed on thirteen inch drum plotter. (From United States Department of Agriculture, Agricultural Stabilization and Conservation Service, Commodity Credit Corporation Charts, Washington: 1976, p. 104.)

LONG-TERM INTEREST RATES

MONTHLY AVERAGES

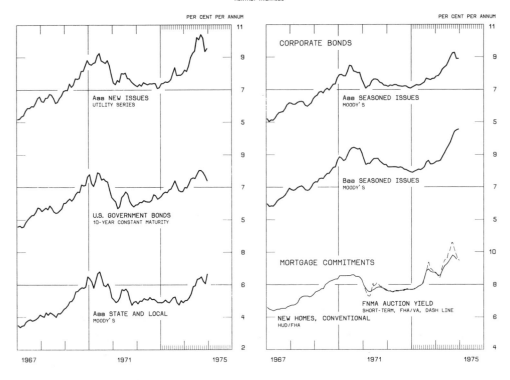

PER CENT PER ANNUM

Aaa NEW ISSUES
UTILITY SERIES

U.S. GOVERNMENT BONDS
10-YEAR CONSTANT MATURITY

Aaa STATE AND LOCAL
MOODY'S

1967   1971   1975

PER CENT PER ANNUM

CORPORATE BONDS

Aaa SEASONED ISSUES
MOODY'S

Baa SEASONED ISSUES
MOODY'S

MORTGAGE COMMITMENTS

FNMA AUCTION YIELD
SHORT-TERM, FHA/VA, DASH LINE

NEW HOMES, CONVENTIONAL
HUD/FHA

1967   1971   1975

LONG-TERM BORROWING

NET FUNDS RAISED BY PRIVATE DOMESTIC NONFINANCIAL SECTORS

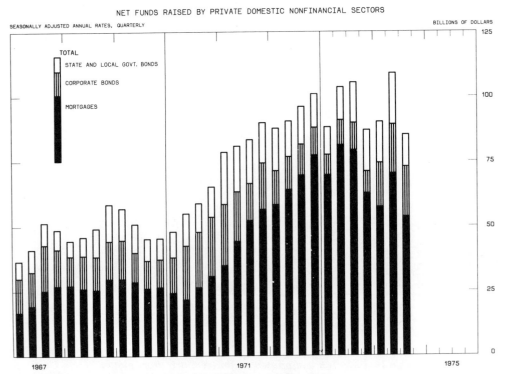

SEASONALLY ADJUSTED ANNUAL RATES, QUARTERLY

BILLIONS OF DOLLARS

TOTAL
STATE AND LOCAL GOVT. BONDS

CORPORATE BONDS

MORTGAGES

1967   1971   1975

Figure 11–14. Illustration of charts prepared on Gerber photo-plotting system. (From Board of Governors Federal Reserve System, Federal Reserve Monthly Chart Book, **Washington: January 1975, p. 30 and p. 73.)**

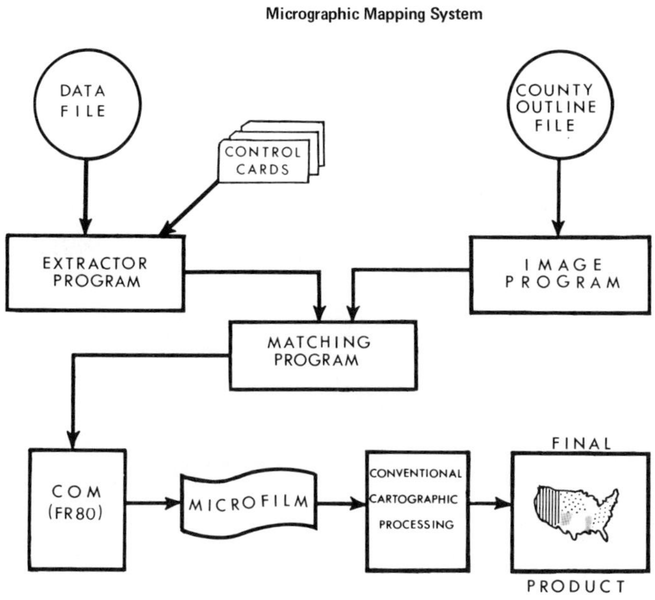

Micrographic Mapping System

Figure 11–15. Flow chart portraying major steps in micrographic mapping system. (From Richard H. Schweitzer, Jr., "Micrographics: A New Approach to Automated Cartography and Graphics," Proceedings of the 22nd Technical Communication Conference, 1975, pp. 305–316, and Frederick R. Broome, "Micrographics: A New Approach to Cartography at the Census Bureau," in Geographic Base (DIME) System—A Local Program, *Conference Proceedings, Columbus, November 1974, Washington: Government Printing Office, 1974, pp. 28–39.)*

GENIGRAPHICS

"Genigraphics" is an electronic computer-based system developed by the General Electric Company for the primary purpose of producing graphic illustrations in full color in the form of slides. It also can produce other kinds of hard copy. The capabilities of the Genigraphic system are represented by a number of standard formats that include matrix charts, bar, column, and line graphs, and area charts as well as combinations of the standard formats and a variety of other graphic elements. It can create, manipulate, store, transmit, and record artwork in digital form. The primary components consist of the artist console, graphics processor, film recorder, operating programs, and associated graphics library. The artist console is the focal point of the system. It consists of an image processor, a color-TV working medium, an alphanumeric keyboard, and artist creation and manipulation controls. The graphics processor is a high-performance, general-purpose computer consisting of a central processor, a disk-storage unit, a dual magnetic tape storage unit, and a keyboard printer. Although the purchase price of the Genigraphics system is relatively high, it is possible to have special work performed on a service basis at relatively reasonable cost.

NAME INDEX

SUBJECT INDEX